A NEW JUVENILE JUSTICE SYSTEM

FAMILIES, LAW, AND SOCIETY SERIES
General Editor: Nancy E. Dowd

A New Juvenile Justice System

Total Reform for a Broken System

Edited by Nancy E. Dowd

With a Foreword by Charles J. Ogletree, Jr.

NEW YORK UNIVERSITY PRESS

New York and London

NEW YORK UNIVERSITY PRESS
New York and London
www.nyupress.org

References to Internet websites (URLs) were accurate at the time of writing. Neither the author nor New York University Press is responsible for URLs that may have expired or changed since the manuscript was prepared.

Library of Congress Cataloging-in-Publication Data
A new juvenile justice system : total reform for a broken system / edited by Nancy E. Dowd ; with a foreword by Charles J. Ogletree, Jr.
pages cm — (Families, law, and society series)
Includes bibliographical references and index.
ISBN 978-1-4798-9880-0 (cl : alk. paper)
1. Juvenile justice, Administration of—United States. I. Dowd, Nancy E., 1949– editor.
II. Series: Families, law, and society series.
KF9779.N49 2015
364.360973—dc23 2014045476

New York University Press books are printed on acid-free paper, and their binding materials are chosen for strength and durability. We strive to use environmentally responsible suppliers and materials to the greatest extent possible in publishing our books.

Manufactured in the United States of America

10 9 8 7 6 5 4 3 2 1

Also available as an ebook

To James Bell—who inspires us all

CONTENTS

    State Is the Parent   296
    Robin Rosenberg and Christina L. Spudeas

17. Breaking the School-to-Prison Pipeline: New Models for
    School Discipline and Community Accountable Schools   301
    Kaitlin Banner

18. No More Closed Doors: Ending the Educational
    Exclusion of Formerly Incarcerated Youth   311
    David Domenici and Renagh O'Leary

19. Collateral Consequences of Juvenile Court: Boulders
    on the Road to Good Outcomes   333
    Sue Burrell

    About the Contributors   349

    Index   353

FOREWORD

CHARLES J. OGLETREE, JR.

Professor Nancy E. Dowd has compiled a wonderful and important book on reforming the juvenile justice system. Professor Dowd is no stranger to this area. In her scholarship, teaching, and speeches she has given around the country, she has discussed the rights of juveniles in the justice system. This book offers a new and compelling perspective on juvenile justice reform and why we should support the rights of children.

As we think about how slowly we have revised the system for children, it is important to look back at the history of the treatment of juveniles in the juvenile justice system. In the 1960s the U.S. Supreme Court, in the case of *In re Gault*,[1] made clear that juveniles should be treated differently but that this separate system required careful scrutiny. In the opinion written by Justice Fortas, the Court cautioned,

> The highest motives and most enlightened impulses led to a peculiar system for juveniles, unknown to our law in any comparable context. The constitutional and theoretical basis for this peculiar system is—to say the least—debatable. And in practice . . . the results have not been entirely satisfactory. Juvenile court history has again demonstrated that unbridled discretion, however benevolently motivated, is frequently a poor substitute for principle and procedure. In 1937, Dean Pound wrote: "The powers of the Star Chamber were a trifle in comparison with those of our juvenile court. . . ." The absence of substantive standards has not necessarily meant that children receive careful, compassionate, individualized treatment. The absence of procedural rules based on constitutional principle has not always produced fair, efficient, and effective procedures. Departures from established principles of due process have frequently resulted not in enlightened procedure, but in arbitrariness.[2]

As this book makes clear, the juvenile justice system has been a disappointing one. Yet the Court has shown some tendencies toward treating juveniles with more justice in the twenty-first century. In the case of *Roper v. Simmons* (2005),[3] the Supreme Court decided that juveniles who are younger than 18 should not be executed. In a 5–4 decision, Justice Kennedy, writing for the majority, concluded that there was much room and much to be done to address the issues of juvenile justice. Justice Kennedy recited the history and treatment of juveniles and made it clear that what states were doing was inappropriate. In concluding that the juveniles should not be subject to the death penalty, the majority opinion highlighted three reasons:

> Three general differences between juveniles under 18 and adults demonstrate that juvenile offenders cannot with reliability be classified among the worst offenders. First, as every parent knows, and as the scientific and sociological studies respondent and his *amici* cite tend to confirm, "a lack of maturity and an underdeveloped sense of responsibility are found in youth more often than in adults and are more understandable among the young. These qualities often result in impetuous and ill-considered actions and decisions." . . . ("Even the normal 16-year-old customarily lacks the maturity of an adult"). It has been noted that "adolescents are overrepresented statistically in virtually every category of reckless behavior." . . . In recognition of the comparative immaturity and irresponsibility of juveniles, almost every State prohibits those under 18 years of age from voting, serving on juries or marrying without parental consent. . . . The second area of difference is that juveniles are more vulnerable or susceptible to negative influences and outside pressures, including peer pressure. . . . ("[Y]outh is more than a chronological fact. It is a time and condition of life when a person may be most susceptible to influence and to psychological damage"). This is explained in part by the prevailing circumstance that juveniles have less control, or less experience with control, over their own environment. . . . ("As legal minors, [juveniles] lack the freedom that adults have to extricate themselves from a criminogenic setting"). The third broad difference is that the character of a juvenile is not as well formed as that of an adult. The personality traits of juveniles are more transitory, less fixed.[4]

This book comes at a time when the Court is continuing to evolve in its jurisprudence about juveniles. In 2010 and 2012, the Supreme Court decided two cases that concluded that it was also unconstitutional to sentence juveniles to life in prison without the possibility of parole, because of their lack of development or lack of maturity, as well as their potential for rehabilitation. These decisions echo Justice Kennedy's reasoning in in *Roper v. Simmons*. Even when the offense involved was murder, a case that generated a close 5–4 decision, the Court concluded that sentencing a juvenile to life without the possibility of parole was cruel and unusual and violated his or her constitutional rights.

This book is a compelling one that offers much to its readers about how children should be treated in the twenty-first century. It offers a new vision of a system of juvenile justice that goes beyond revisions in punishments to infusing a new system with interdisciplinary insights about children and devoting such a system to the goal of helping every child to be a successful adult and citizen. Those who have written chapters include academics, practitioners, and activists engaged in the effort to support youth, who imagine in this volume a different, more productive juvenile justice system consistent with our core values.

The book makes a powerful case for why juveniles should and must be treated differently and why they have been unfairly punished in our existing system. This is a must-read book for all parents, academics, activists, and children to understand why our children must learn to grow and appreciate the differences in our society before they are treated like adults and why we need to create a system that gives all children that opportunity.

NOTES

1 387 U.S. 1 (1967).
2 *Id.* at 17–19, quoting Dean Pound, foreword to *Social Treatment in Probation and Delinquency*, by Pauline V. Young (New York: McGraw-Hill, 1937), xvii.
3 543 U.S. 551 (2005).
4 *Id.* at 569–570 (internal citations omitted).

ACKNOWLEDGMENTS

This extraordinary collection envisioning an entirely new juvenile justice system emerged as a result of a collective commitment to move beyond critique and reform to imagine the kind of system that would support and assist youth in becoming adults connected and committed to their communities and able to achieve their dreams to the full extent of their talents. This project began at the second juvenile justice workshop organized by the Center on Children and Families (CCF) at the University of Florida Levin College of Law in the spring of 2013. Shani Mahiri King, the codirector of CCF, was instrumental in envisioning the workshop and this volume and was tireless in organizing, promoting, and engaging in the conference. His contribution was priceless. Other faculty who contributed enormously to planning the workshop include Meshon Rawls, Stacey Steinberg, Whitney Untiedt, Ken Nunn, Katheryn Russell Brown, Teresa Drake, and Jason Nance. Debbie Kelley, the program assistant for CCF, provided extraordinary support and comprehensive planning. Anju Katuvettoor Davidson, assistant director of the Center for the Study of Race and Race Relations, provided invaluable support, as did Jessica Budnitz of the Harvard Law School Child Advocacy Project.

Critical research assistance and preparation of the manuscript for this volume has been provided by Stephanie Galligan, who ensured that these diverse contributions were melded into a single manuscript.

Former Dean Robert Jerry strongly supported CCF's Juvenile Justice Project, of which this book was a part, and was extraordinarily dedicated to the goal of this volume. In addition, funding for this project was made possible due to the resources of the David Levin Chair in Family Law.

James Bell not only challenged us with his plenary, but his method and process of making workshops be productive and critical, and include crosscutting voices, was the model for the foundational meeting that generated this volume and the volume itself. He continues to be a tireless advocate for kids and an inspiration for us all.

Finally, I offer my gratitude to my colleagues, friends, and family, who have provided support, critique, and encouragement to me throughout this project and continue to inspire me to do all I can to make things better.

Nancy E. Dowd

Introduction

Re-visioning Youth Justice

NANCY E. DOWD

What did you do as a kid, and as a teenager? Who were you as a teenager?[1]

Maybe you had a perfect childhood, in a perfect family, in a supportive community. More likely, there were ups and downs along the way, and if you were lucky, your parents and your community helped and supported you as you grew up. If you had learning disabilities, someone noticed and resources were brought to bear to help you. If you were distressed when your parents divorced, acted out in class and got in fights with classmates, teachers and counselors figured out what was going on and got you into therapy, or a coach took you under her wing. If you were the different one, the oddball, who did not really fit in, you nevertheless were protected from bullying and appreciated for your uniqueness. Maybe everything was not always perfect, but you knew that your family and your community had your back and that things could be worked out and problems solved. Ideally, you developed your talents and your dreams. But that is not the case for everyone.

Did you ever get into trouble? Get kicked out of school? Get arrested? Charged? Locked up? If any of this happened, did it have a permanent impact on your life?

If you did something that could have gotten you into trouble, you are part of the vast majority of people who engaged in behavior at some point while growing up that violates the law. When you are a teenager, all the usual criminal laws apply, and in addition, there are laws that only apply to you because you are a teenager. At the same time, the normal adolescent developmental pathway involves risk taking, poor judgment, peer influence, and other factors that create a perfect storm for engaging in misbehavior. If you were a teenager who got in trouble, the conse-

1

quences often could get you into more trouble. Probation conditions include curfews, not missing school or misbehaving at school, not hanging out with particular friends, and being respectful to teachers and parents. The chances are great that a teenager will not be perfect at complying with these conditions. Probation violations may trigger even more serious consequences even if the original offense was nothing serious.

So what happened to you? Likely that depends. You simply may never have been caught. And if you were, if you come from a family with resources, you have a pretty good shot even in the worst circumstances of escaping relatively unscathed—avoiding arrest, not being charged or incarcerated, not having a record, or only having a record that did not pose a major hurdle for you to continue your education or get a job. If you are white and if you are female, you would likely have been treated differently by those who work in the juvenile justice system. But if you are a person of color, if you are a male, and if you come from a low-income family, or if all three of these factors converge, then you may have experienced different and more severe consequences—consequences that may have had a significant impact throughout your life. Your race, gender, and class factors make it much more likely that you will be caught. You might have come into contact with police and the juvenile justice system not only on the streets but also possibly at school. If you did not already know, you soon found out that the juvenile justice system did not help; it hurt. It did not give you a second chance but instead marked you in a way that made everything that followed more challenging. Instead of putting you on the right track, it started you down a difficult path in which your past mistakes affected all of your future choices.

Our goal for all youth should be support, opportunity, and success. Their well-being is our well-being. The welfare of all is essential to who we are as a society, as a nation. Yet we have a juvenile justice system that in large part is a failure. It disserves youth, increases criminal conduct and threats to public safety, functions in a racially and ethnically biased way, and harms the youth that come within its doors. The services that are available to children in the juvenile justice system are not commensurate with the risks and the needs posed by each individual child. Furthermore, the fact that this system most heavily burdens disenfranchised and historically subordinated communities threatens to reinforce structures of subordination along enduring divides of race, class, gender, sexuality, and nationality. The existing system does not serve society, and it does not serve the youth who come into contact with the system. The parents of youth with resources quickly realize this and mobilize resources to get their children, who may have significant needs, out of the system as quickly as possible. Low-income parents and high-risk kids, and disproportionately kids of color or kids with mental health needs, are not so lucky.[2]

Many have criticized and critiqued the current system—including judges, prosecutors, public defenders, defense lawyers, advocates for youth, teachers, and scholars. Judged solely on its outcomes (with pockets of exceptions), it is a failed system. The critique and analysis of the old is critical to building a different system. But critique can also be a quagmire where it seems impossible to imagine a different framework, and reform is cabined into tinkering with a bankrupt structure. Devotion to critique and amassing more data about the problems do not necessarily show us a way forward and may perversely act as a roadblock to moving beyond this failed system.

This volume is focused on re-visioning the system. Collectively this project represents an effort to envision a system of support for young people that works to ensure their development as engaged, productive citizens and that simultaneously serves the community's legitimate goals of public safety by reducing crime, particularly serious crimes. The insights and challenges of the authors come from a diverse group that includes academics, advocates, policy drafters, and workers in the trenches, from the statewide director of the juvenile justice system to the public defender in a major metropolitan area.[3]

Grounded in practice, empirical data, and multidisciplinary knowledge, the contributors suggest both macro-level principles and micro-level programs and policies. Identifying strategies, programs, reforms, and principles to improve outcomes for kids, they by no means cover every aspect of a re-visioned juvenile justice system, but its outlines and operating principles are clear.

Armed with that vision, the authors suggest immediate, concrete steps to achieve a reoriented juvenile justice system that aims to serve and support youth, to enhance their opportunity for success as adults, and to encourage their connection to the community. It would be a system that evaluates needs, solves problems, demands accountability from youth, and serves public safety. It would be a system that would be held accountable to achieve well-being for youth, to act fairly and equitably, to improve public safety, and to serve and partner with the communities within which it functions. There is no doubt that kids must be held responsible for their conflict with the community's norms and laws. The goal of a reframed system must be public safety as well as youth well-being. Those goals are in harmony, not in opposition.

The task to which the authors in this volume set themselves in re-visioning the system revolves around three core ideas: (1) to ask how the ideals of equality, freedom, liberty, and self-determination can transform the juvenile justice system; (2) to improve the odds that children who have been labeled as "delinquent" can make successful transitions to adulthood; and (3) to contribute to reforms focused on locking up fewer youth, relying more on proven, family-focused and community-based interventions, and creating opportunities for positive youth development.[4]

What would a re-visioned system look like? In brief, it would be the systemic, institutional manifestation of what happened to those of you who, as kids, needed support, rehabilitation, and guidance to take re-sponsibility and reorient from bad decisions and bad behavior. Systemi-cally, it would ensure such support for all kids. Essential resources would be provided without differentiation driven by biases or stereotypes, recognizing differences among youth. All youth would benefit because their support structure would be strengthened, and necessary services would be available. The key systems of education, mental health, health care, and child welfare would be the primary component parts of a re-framed youth justice system aimed at preventive interventions and early diversion, evaluation, and problem solving tied to the particular needs of each child. Actions and behavior in school, on the streets, or at home would trigger an assessment of needs linked to these systems as well as programs, policies, and practices designed to rehabilitate youth. Such a system would not demand less of youth; rather, it would demand more. But it would also give more, support more, when youth were identi-fied with underlying needs, and when youth would take responsibility for behavior and engage in restitution or other appropriate means to be accountable for harms caused. It would also redirect the bulk of youth currently in the existing system to more appropriate and successful family- and community-centered programs to serve their underlying needs.

Systems would act collaboratively. They would be particularly attentive to youth patterns that signal heightened needs, and systemic failure to meet those needs or exacerbation of harm. For example, kids crossing over from foster care to law breaking and juvenile justice involvement, or, the framing of misbehavior in school as law breaking necessitating suspension, expulsion, or police/judicial action, would be treated as evidence of unmet needs and of systemic failure requiring immediate action to reverse those outcomes. Where misconduct is not tied to an underlying issue, such as mental health issues, substance abuse, or family dysfunction or rejection, but to typical adolescent behavior, the pipelines and trajectories would lead to opportunities for a second chance and lifetime success.

Detention and incarceration, which produce serious harm and little good, would not be the hallmark of this system. Rather, within this re-visioned system, detention and incarceration would be a last resort, an outcome dictated by either the seriousness of the youth's conduct, the youth's inability or unwillingness to rehabilitate, or the failure of other options to ensure public safety and a positive outcome. This rejection of incarceration would bring us into harmony with the practices of the rest of the world, which bases rejection of incarceration not on cultural differences from the U.S. or unrealistic and unsupported assumptions about youth but rather on the hard empirical evidence that incarceration is extremely costly, diverts scarce resources, and increases recidivism rather than enhancing public safety.

To be sure, there are related, broad issues beyond the scope of the juvenile justice system that need to be addressed as well. At the top of the list are systemic racism and poverty. But at the very least, the system of juvenile justice should be held to function without reflecting or exacerbating class privilege, racial and ethnic disparities, or other subordination based on other identity characteristics, including gender and sexual orientation. Every child deserves that guarantee of opportunity; our systems cannot justifiably function any other way if we are true to our most fundamental principles.

A juvenile justice system dedicated to children's well-being and public safety would be accountable for achieving those goals by means that respect the humanity of all youth and contribute to the humanity of us all. This volume is divided into five parts that flesh out this new vision.

***

James Bell sets the agenda in Part I for all that follows in "Child Well-Being: Toward a Fair and Equitable Public Safety Strategy for the New Century." As Bell powerfully argues, the current system has utterly failed youth and society, and the ills of that system rest on children and communities of color. The failure of the system to help kids is demonstrated by the persistence of recidivism without making the community more secure. As Bell demonstrates, this failure is inextricably tied to our "incarceration addiction," as incarceration is singularly unsuccessful as a tool to achieve child well-being or community safety. It is also linked to the use of the juvenile justice system to solve youth issues for which it is poorly designed and ineffective, including mental health and substance abuse issues.

Just as significantly, the pervasiveness of racial and ethnic disparities condemns the system as indefensible based on our principles of equality and justice. Race is the elephant in the room in the juvenile justice system, an inescapable demonstration of structural inequality and institutional racism. Bell links our current system to its historical origins in blatant racial differentiation that excluded black children as undeserving of public concern for child well-being.

Bell sketches out the principles and form of a new youth justice system grounded in a core principle: the cure for the ills of humanity is more humanity. Humanity means dedication to child well-being. Consistent with that core principle, Bell argues we should (1) eliminate incarceration as a permissible outcome for virtually all youth and recommit to rehabilitation of youth with a system characterized by diversion programs and targeted resolution of the underlying issues causing youth to violate the law; (2) aggressively develop community-based and family-based solutions aimed to support youth development and designed to address youth issues and problems; and (3) support and demand better outcomes from those systems that can help youth, including education, mental health, and health care. The juvenile justice system that Bell envisions is characterized by practices and outcomes that are restorative, are equitable, and increase child well-being.

The chapters that follow reflect, elaborate, and expand on Bell's vision. Focusing on some of the core components of Bell's agenda begins in Part II, with Bart Lubow's exploration of the task of breaking our incarceration addiction. In "A Silent Sea Change: The Deinstitutionalization Trend in Juvenile Justice," Lubow chronicles the recent downward trend in incarceration in the juvenile justice system. Significantly, Lubow points out, deinstitutionalization has not changed at all the stark pattern of racial and ethnic disparity in the juvenile justice population. As Lubow also makes clear, while the reduction is dramatic, the U.S. rate of institutionalization remains grossly out of proportion to the rate of other nations. The American pattern is not explained by anything other than underlying assumptions and failed practices, not by higher rates of crime or more difficult youth behavior. As he concludes, our goal should be to aggressively reduce the use of incarceration not only because no other country has found the practice useful, not only because research demonstrates its ineffectiveness, but because our kids deserve better. Incarceration is an option that perversely forecloses effective responses to the problems of children and youth while simultaneously damaging them and limiting their opportunities.

Tim Decker literally challenges us to consider "Starting from a Different Place: The Missouri Model." Decker provides a comprehensive picture of what the juvenile justice system can be, using the example of reforms in the Missouri juvenile justice system. He emphasizes the critical role of leadership, culture, and values. Decker reminds us that the vision of a different system is not unrealistic, impossible, or impractical. According to him, however, it cannot be done simply by a top-down mandate of programs without a deep, meaningful commitment at the human level to real, local change and reorientation.

Although the juvenile justice system was founded with the core principle of rehabilitation, it is now mired, Decker argues, in punishment. System change requires nothing less than system transformation. Decker identifies culture as the critical component. Beliefs and assumptions drive "what we do around here," and so it is the culture that has to change. For Decker, the key to that cultural change is for policy makers to answer the question, "What if your child was the next one in the door?" His goal is not simply to identify policies, practices, and programs that would work. Rather, more fundamentally, he challenges us to make all children our children.

Decker articulates core components of culture change and its manifestations in the Missouri system. Families and communities are critical partners, and the orientation of the system is localized and responsive rather than hierarchical and frightening. The power of Decker's chapter is its rich theoretical perspective linked to the practical, pragmatic application statewide to a single system that has become a national model.

Peter Leone highlights education as the "third rail" of needed reform, in the sense of both no longer funneling disciplinary problems into the juvenile justice system and, more broadly, providing meaningful education that assures youth real opportunity as adults. In "Doing Things Differently: Education as a Vehicle for Youth Transformation and Finland as a Model for Juvenile Justice Reform," Leone argues that academic insufficiency is just as significant as disciplinary criminalization as failures of the existing educational system. Reorienting this integral part of a youth support system is consistent with a different system of juvenile justice. Leone's approach is proactive, targeted at known risk factors and support for success.

What Leone adds is a specific concrete example of a seismic national shift in thinking and goals that led to a re-visioned juvenile justice system that functions in this dramatically different way. He outlines the transformation of the Finnish system from a harsh Soviet model to a system geared to provide support and reorientation for youth. Leone unpacks the constituent parts of this reframed system, including the dynamic that brought it about. As he points out, the reformed system is grounded on the perspective that delinquent conduct or youth misbehavior is a *social* problem. His example reminds us, just as Decker's does at a state level, of what is possible and the critical importance of literally how we think about youth.

Integral to a re-visioned system as set forth by Bell, Decker, and Leone is the removal from the juvenile justice system of populations of youth who belong elsewhere because they have problems that are not dealt with by the core function of the juvenile justice system as that system is presently constituted. Simply removing youth from the juvenile justice system is not enough; rather, services are essential in a setting of support and care. One of the largest component groups of youths who fit this profile is those who have mental health issues.

David Katner focuses on this group in the last chapter in this section, "Delinquency, Due Process, and Mental Health: Presuming Youth Incompetency." Katner details the number of youth who have mental health issues and exposes the inadequacy of current systems to provide them with help. Mental health issues constitute the other elephant in the room of the existing system: like racial disparities, mental health disparities significantly skew the system. Both issues mirror the toxic environments and systemic subordination by race and class that affect youth. Fundamentally wrongheaded is the location of mental health issues in the existing juvenile justice system. Misbehavior due to mental health issues requires treatment, not confinement. Katner argues that the extent of mental health issues and their link to misbehavior that triggers contact with the current juvenile justice system should, consistent with due process, mean that youth are assumed not competent when they become entangled with the juvenile justice system. He suggests this approach as a way to divert youth to support and help for mental health issues.

Katner's vision of the place of mental health with respect to youth is proactive services, rehabilitative services providing high-quality care, and intervention either through diversion to a well-functioning mental health system or the incorporation of such a system within a reimagined juvenile justice system.

The next part of the volume shifts to exploring essential perspectives and thinking about juvenile justice. In Part III, the authors remind us, just as Decker and Leone pointed out, how important are our thinking and assumptions, our values, and what we use as guiding principles. Mark Fondacaro provides a critical perspective on the emerging developmental orientation of juvenile justice in "Why Should We Treat Juvenile Offenders Differently than Adults? It's Not Because the Pie Isn't Fully Baked!" Fondacaro reminds us that we should remain skeptical and open to revision of principles that we might collectively embrace for a new juvenile justice system. While recent U.S. Supreme Court cases have begun to build on a perspective that justifies treating youth differently because of their developmental differences, making them less culpable and more amenable to rehabilitation, Fondacaro challenges us to consider what more recent research is telling us. According to Fondacaro, that research tells us that *adults* also are not developmentally unchanging, and therefore that research challenges the increasingly punitive orientation of the adult criminal justice system. He cautions, therefore, that we not separate the two systems in a way that preserves untenable assumptions based on myth rather than current scientific realities. This is particularly critical while the ability to transfer and charge youth as adults remains part of the system applied to juveniles.

Fondacaro challenges some of the most basic assumptions about mental state and criminal responsibility that are foundational to a retribution model. He argues instead for a forward-looking model to prevent recidivism, using collaborative interdisciplinary teams and knowledge to achieve the best individualized results.

Richard Redding focuses on the disconnect between evidence-based policies and practices and the failure to utilize them, in "Lost in Translation No More: Marketing Evidence-Based Policies for Reducing Juvenile Crime." At the outset, Bell reminded us that it is our values, assumptions, and beliefs that have confounded change; Decker and Leone also focus on the key role of culture to accomplish change. Redding pushes more deeply into our attachment to punishment and skepticism about rehabilitation. These responses persist even in the face of contrary evidence that shows that punishment, particularly incarceration, correlates with recidivism and engaging in more serious criminal acts, not deterrence.

Redding outlines a way to market evidence-based policies by using evidence-based persuasion techniques. He suggests using these principles to create a narrative that emphasizes reducing crime, increasing public safety, and increasing cost effectiveness, along with the rightful place of punishment.

The last two chapters in this part remind us that issues of gender and sexuality are critical to re-visioning as well and, just as with race, cut across all aspects of a new juvenile justice system. In "Building on Advocacy for Girls and LGBT Youth: A Foundation for Liberatory Laws, Policies, and Services for All Youth in the Juvenile Justice System," Barbara Fedders examines two critiques of the existing system, by advocates for girls and for LGBT youth, which have focused on the claim that the juvenile justice system was created for boys and thus not only renders these groups invisible but also is biased against them and does them unique harm. The outcome of both critiques has been to call for gender-responsive programming intended specifically for girls and LGBT youth. Fedders questions the underlying assumptions of these solutions and whether a more universal approach would be better. In addition, she calls for a critique of the juvenile justice system's assumptions about boys, the acknowledged focus of the system. Challenging whether the system serves boys and young men is essential to ensuring that any re-visioned system keeps in mind the gender and sexual orientation, as well as intersectional identities, of all youth and questions the implicit goals of such as system in relation to societal gender norms.

What emerges from this analysis is a fascinating challenge to the categories themselves as essentialist, rendering invisible the importance of intersectional identity. Fedders also reminds us that class is as important a difference in outcomes for youth, whatever other identities they embrace, as class generally impacts outcomes for any youth problem or misbehavior that brings them into contact with the juvenile justice system.

Shannan Wilber focuses in a different way on LGBT youth, calling for a more radical reform agenda that aims to keep these youth out of the system entirely, by calling attention to why they end up there in the first place, in "Invest Upstream to Promote the Well-Being of LGBT Youth: Addressing Root Causes of Juvenile System Involvement." Much like those who want to dismantle the school-to-prison pipeline, Wilber wants to dismantle the pipeline from schools, and an equally important one from families, that drives the disproportionate presence of LGBT kids in the juvenile justice system. Even more significantly, she aims to tackle structural inequality and lack of support and instead provide the resources and support for all youths to be able to freely express who they are without the challenges of bias and worse.

Part IV focuses on critical actors in system change. Each of these chapters resonates with the developmental insights explored by Mark Fondacaro and others in this volume, calling for the full infusion of what we know of adolescents in a reformed system. The chapters in this part call for prosecutors, public defenders, police, judges, and legislators all to become critically competent in this knowledge and to incorporate its insights for the benefit of youth and the community.

One of the hallmarks of the juvenile justice system is discretion and the potential to use that discretion to keep kids out of the system, to get them services when they need it from robust helping systems, to divert them when they engage in misbehavior to programs and services that will put them back on track. One critical component of discretion is exercising this power in a fair and just way. In "Correcting Racial Disparities in the Juvenile Justice System: Refining Prosecutorial Discretion," Kristin Henning focuses on the pervasive racial disparities in the existing juvenile justice system and the role of prosecutors as key actors to eliminate this scourge from the justice system and to support good outcomes for all children.

Henning sets out the most recent data that adds to the enormous compilation of scholarship on the presence of racial and ethnic bias in the current juvenile justice system. This developmental data shows that the developmental arc does not vary by race or class. Perceptions and stereotypes render the same conduct differently by the youth's race or ethnicity. The dismantling of racial bias at a social/cultural level is demanding and complex. But Henning argues that concrete, achievable steps can be taken by prosecutors that will have a significant impact on this issue, and she particularly focuses on the charging phase. She sets out specific guidelines and calls for the tracking of decision making by race and neighborhood in order to assure that youth of color have the maximum opportunity for positive outcomes. She critically examines the National District Attorneys' Association National Prosecution Standards and suggests revisions to incorporate multidisciplinary developmental research on adolescents to inform charging decisions and maximize the rehabilitative potential for youth. Second, she calls for the close monitoring of decision making to change the prosecutorial culture about bias. Third, she reminds us that for most youths, age is the factor that most affects a change in behavior: they develop, grow, and behave differently as they become more mature. Interventions focused on fostering that process require, as she puts it, knowing what works, and knowing what does not, and using those criteria to inform dispositions. She also calls for strong community involvement and partnership, again echoing a core component of Bell's agenda that we confront our negative stereotypes about the communities of youth of color and utilize their strengths instead of assuming weakness. Broad-based prosecutorial conceptions of their role would mean a broad community-based partnership that would target structural inadequacies that are toxic to youth and contribute to misbehavior.

Equally important for youth as fair prosecutors are strong advocates should they have to navigate the juvenile justice system. Clearly this is the case with the existing system, but the role of advocates for youth would be just as critical in a re-visioned juvenile justice system. Carlos Martinez, in "Helping Adolescents Succeed: Assuring a Meaningful Right to Counsel," provides a view from the trenches in this essay arguing for a robust, well-supported, highly trained public defender as critical to youth achieving an outcome that can lead to their eventual successful rehabilitation.

The need for strong representation is critical both currently and in a re-visioned system. It is particularly important at present because the potential consequences are so drastic, affecting youths' futures in substantial and life-changing ways. Equally as significant, inadequate, poorly trained, overburdened public defenders are another point of systemic, structural bias that contributes to pervasive racial bias in the juvenile justice system. The support of low-income youth and kids of color who we know are the targets of bias requires strong advocacy.

Martinez exposes in great detail how structural bias works to create a perfect storm of underrepresentation that is nevertheless cloaked as "adequate" and therefore constitutional. Because the consequences are so severe and the biases are so significant and pervasive, the role of the public defender is critical. Martinez's model of robust, effective advocacy based on well-trained lawyers with reasonable caseloads within the existing juvenile justice system equally serves as the model for a re-visioned system because the same robust advocacy would be a critical component to ensure the healthy functioning of a system with a different culture, policies, practices, and partners. In Bell's broad agenda, as well as those of Decker, Henning, and Lubow, the public defender plays a critical but quite different role, to ensure that collaborating systems are available to youth and that appropriate diversion occurs; to partner with police to that end; and to provide support and assist in decision making to exhaust alternatives to incarceration or to foster the best outcomes for the limited number of youth for whom incarceration is appropriate. In the transition away from our addiction to incarceration, the public defender clearly would play a critical strategic role.

A particular decision that implicates not only prosecutors but also judges and legislators is the decision to transfer youth from the juvenile court system to the adult criminal justice system. The widespread process of transfer has been much critiqued, yet it persists because of the persuasiveness of assumptions about public safety and the necessity of punishment, despite the data indicating that transfer not only does not serve those goals but actually leads to counterproductive results. Richard Mora and Mary Christianakis, in "Fit to Be T(r)ied: Ending Juvenile Transfers and Reforming the Juvenile Justice System," bring us the voices of youth they work with, reminding us what the existing system tells them—of their failure, worthlessness, and bleak prospects. Under their re-visioned system, transfer would end, as it is glaringly inconsistent with developmental research and the underlying core value of rehabilitation. A new system would be reinvigorated with a vision of services and meaningful demands of youth to achieve successful outcomes as adults.

Finally, Lisa Thurau and Sia Henry focus on police—in the particular instance of questioning youth and whether *Miranda* warnings should be given but, more generally, examining police questioning, custody, and interaction in the context of adolescent development. In "Applying *J.D.B. v. North Carolina*: Toward Ending Legal Fictions and Adopting a Model for Police Questioning of Youth," they present a case study of appellate decisions since the U.S. Supreme Court decided *J.D.B.*, in which the Court held that police must take the age of youth into account when determining if *Miranda* warnings are required. They find significant differentiation and underutilization of this opinion. As they point out, a stronger implementation of *J.D.B.* would encourage erring on the side of youths' lack of developmental maturity and treating youth fairly but also not taking advantage of their developmental immaturity. They point to the ready availability of standards that incorporate developmental research into questioning of youth, under the standards of the International Association of Chiefs of Police and the Commission on the Accreditation of Law Enforcement Agencies.

In Part V, the authors further explore the critical component of Bell's agenda that a re-visioned juvenile justice system would include well-functioning systems of support for youth whether or not they had come into contact with the police but nevertheless were exhibiting behaviors needing assessment, attention, support, and services. Those systems function both separately and in collaboration with any juvenile justice system but particularly if the juvenile justice system is reconceptualized as one focused on child well-being.

Wendy Bach, in "What If Your Child Were the Next One in the Door? Reimagining the Social Safety Net for Children, Families, and Communities," asks us to focus on the needs of the youth and families who currently dominate the juvenile justice population, low-income families and youth of color. Picking up on the question raised by Tim Decker— "What if your child was the next one in the door?"—Bach reminds us that that question assumes a middle- or upper-class child, whose parent would seek services and programs, such as counseling or substance abuse treatment, as needed for his or her child. The parent would try to determine whether what was going on with his or her child was youthful indiscretion or a manifestation of other issues that need to be addressed. Bach calls for providing that same level of available services and support for low-income families and children, to enable proactive intervention or diversion, if a child came into the juvenile justice system and needed services and rehabilitation. Class, like race and gender, is a critical thread to examine throughout the system.

Bach also reminds us that poverty policy has an impact on youth, by creating risk in their lives that is not experienced by kids and families with more resources. Rather than devise programs for at-risk kids, she calls for taking on the risks themselves and compares that approach to the substantial costs of instead dealing with predictable consequences. Bach calls for implementing a supportive state for poor youth to maximize their life outcomes in the same way that families with resources do for their kids. Just as critical in her view is an underlying assumption of the value of these families and treatment of them and their communities with respect and dignity, instead of monitoring, intrusiveness, and negativity.

Elizabeth Frankel reminds us that another segment of youth experience the criminalization and exacerbation of their situation by virtue of the interaction between the juvenile justice system and the immigration system, and therefore a re-visioned system must disentangle this malfunction and approach the situation of immigrant youth with appreciation for the circumstances of their status. In "Immigrant Children: Treating Children as Children, Regardless of Their Legal Status," she details how immigrant youth in the juvenile justice system are frequently reported to the immigration system, so that their problems are compounded. Involvement in the immigration system may complicate and exacerbate their disposition in the juvenile justice system, and they fail to get counseling and advocacy to deal with the issues they face in the immigration system. Frankel calls for a juvenile justice system that sees immigration status as another issue that needs services and support in order to achieve the best possible outcome for youth, including their independent right to legal status based on the their dependency (because their parents brought them into the country or because they came for valid reasons and can qualify for a visa). Consistent with the goal of less incarceration, this would reduce or eliminate the incarceration of these youth in both systems.

Another intersecting system, child welfare and foster care, is similarly important to the functioning of a re-visioned juvenile justice system, as outlined by Robin Rosenberg and Christina Spudeas in "Crossover Youth: Youth Should Benefit When the State Is the Parent." Youth in foster care and juvenile justice systems frequently become a crossover statistic, moving from one system to the other. Rosenberg and Spudeas argue that this outcome, and the policies that fail to address it, fundamentally misapprehend what the role of the state should be for a child removed from his or her family and placed in foster care. When the state stands as the parent, they argue, the child should benefit from an improvement in his or her situation, not further deterioration or failure to deal with the circumstances that brought removal, circumstances that may have consequences for the positive development of the child. The state should do what good parents do: intervene and provide support and resources aimed at rehabilitation and dealing with underlying problems, and not permitting misbehavior to have long-term serious consequences. Rosenberg and Spudeas focus on providing better support and training to caregivers, alternatives to calling police, and ensuring that all understand that services must be trauma-informed for this population of youth who have suffered abuse and neglect, in order to prevent crossover and to provide robust support for kids if they do become involved with the juvenile justice system.

The final chapters focus on education. In "Breaking the School-to-Prison Pipeline: New Models for School Discipline and Community Accountable Schools," Kaitlin Banner reminds us that the juvenile justice system would look quite different if it was not receiving youth into the system from schools. Much like the foster youth focused on by Rosenberg and Spudeas, and David Katner's earlier chapter on kids with mental health issues, kids who misbehave in school need interventions to solve their problems, not suspension, expulsion, and/or referral to the juvenile justice system. Not only does that require that when schools confront misbehavior, they *not* refer kids to the juvenile justice system, but it also means that school discipline must function differently. Reform requires not only in-school change but also that systems of support for youth be strongly funded and well functioning so that misbehavior tied to underlying issues can be addressed rather than trigger a punitive response that fails to provide needed services for learning disabilities, mental health issues, substance abuse, and so on. Banner identifies models for what schools should do and therefore what this restructuring would look like.

Equally as important is dealing with the educational needs of those youth who do enter the deep end of the current juvenile justice system and planning for the transitional needs of youth as they return to their communities. In "No More Closed Doors: Ending the Educational Exclusion of Formerly Incarcerated Youth," David Domenici and Renagh O'Leary identify a different piece of the interrelation between juvenile justice and education, the issue of how formerly incarcerated youth complete their education, a critical goal for achieving competency and opportunity as an adult. Lack of educational opportunity for many system-involved youth is also related to the poor quality of schools they attended before they ended up in trouble. Incarcerated youth are often subject to minimal educational resources when imprisoned, exacerbating their low achievement levels. Domenici and O'Leary focus on the third piece of the education issue, educational exclusion. When youth exit prisons and detention centers, frequently their high school refuses to readmit them and sends them instead to an even more poorly resourced alternative school or an adult GED course structured for adults, not youth.

Domenici and O'Leary sketch a vision of educational inclusion that not only allows youth back into their public comprehensive high schools but also addresses their educational issues in a way that will accomplish the goal of high school graduation and opportunity for further education. As they point out, education is the "third rail" of juvenile justice reform, essential to prevent kids from being unnecessarily involved in the juvenile justice system, essential to the opportunity of all kids, and even more essential for system-involved kids who respond positively to rehabilitation and then must be welcomed back into school and community.

Finally, Sue Burrell broadens the lens, in "Collateral Consequences of Juvenile Court: Boulders on the Road to Good Outcomes," to consider whether juvenile justice involvement should have lifelong consequences. Currently the consequences of system involvement, as noted earlier by Martinez, can have a permanent impact on youth. Burrell tells us why and argues that this makes no sense because it undermines rehabilitated youth in ways that are punitive and retributive rather than focused on child well-being.

Burrell reminds us, as Bach does, that it does not happen this way for children of parents with resources, who minimize such outcomes by early intervention and support to prevent the triggers of arrest, charging, prosecution, or incarceration from generating a lifetime mark on the record of a young person. But for those (some with means but mostly those without) for whom that does not occur, collateral consequences affect education, employment, licensing for various professions, joining the military, adjusting their immigration status, or obtaining a driver's license. The failure to seal records combined with the technology of the Internet makes obtaining this information easy and the misuse of the information common. Burrell's pragmatic solutions would limit or eliminate these consequences by, for example, restoring the practice of closing juvenile records. And as she reminds us, we need to recall who disproportionately is burdened when we do not do so and how that builds on other structural inequalities that render our commitment to equality for all ephemeral.

This volume is rich with ideas, experience, and knowledge. Most importantly, it is rich with passion, a passion for kids and for justice. This rich diversity of voice, experience, and focus, deliberately chosen, demonstrates that dialogue, sharing, learning, and growth are essential to making a new system a reality and moves in small, conscious steps in that direction.

NOTES

1 These questions were inspired by similar ones asked by Sue Burrell at the workshop that generated this volume (Sue Burrell, chap. 19 in this volume).

2 See, generally, Nancy E. Dowd, ed., *Justice for Kids: Keeping Kids Out of the Juvenile Justice System* (New York: NYU Press, 2011).

3 See "About the Contributors" section.

4 The genesis of this volume was a conference organized by the Center on Children and Families at the University of Florida Fredric G. Levin College of Law in April 2013. Most, although not all, of the authors were part of a group of approximately 60 academics, policy makers, advocates, and workers in the juvenile justice system who brought their deep knowledge, skills, and determination to the task of engaging in intense debate and discussion on envisioning a new juvenile justice system grounded in these core principles.

PART I

Setting the Agenda

1

Child Well-Being

*Toward a Fair and Equitable Public Safety Strategy
for the New Century*

JAMES BELL

Introduction

At the beginning of the twenty-first century, the social and economic
indicators for children in neighborhoods of intense poverty were bleak,
and public policy was seemingly bereft of innovative ideas. Policies such
as "zero tolerance," "stop and frisk," and gang injunctions reflected worn
and tired approaches to youthful misbehaviors by pathologizing neighborhoods and criminalizing normal adolescent behavior under the guise
of protecting public safety. During this same period, while income and
health disparities grew, graduation rates declined and incarceration rates
increased for young people of color.

Advocates, organizers, philanthropists,[1] and others resisted these
hostile headwinds with bold analyses of structural racism's impact on
youth justice. Research and scholarship revealed that low-income communities were forced into a set of choices that inevitably led to poor
outcomes.[2] Approaches and solutions to structural impediments were
created, were diligently vetted, and slowly formed a counternarra-
tive that highlighted the inherent values, cultural stability, and vitality
of people in these neighborhoods. Sound ideas existed to transform
neighborhoods.

A new vision requires civil society to see itself as a champion of
human potential whose mission is to shape minds, touch souls, and
motivate bodies. Václav Havel told us that hope is not optimism over
pessimism but an orientation of the spirit.[3] We must use humanity, restoration, and equity as an orientation of the spirit to change the conversation toward child well-being, allowing us to achieve equity and
excellence as the preferred strategy for true public safety.

A major structural impediment to this vision is the existing juvenile justice system. This is a system that has failed youth and failed society. We incarcerate more youth and adults than any other country in the world. Our incarceration addiction is expensive, with costs increasing four times from 1988 to 2008, to $47.3 billion.[4] Our youth incarceration rate is just as high as that for adults and is even more dramatically higher than the rate in any other country in the world.[5] The juvenile justice system has failed to achieve greater public safety; to the contrary, the system's overreliance on incarceration generates greater recidivism, as well as the likelihood of more serious criminal activity and adult criminal justice involvement. The system does not rehabilitate most kids. This failure is disproportionately placed on youth of color, who are disproportionately represented at every phase of the juvenile justice system and are most likely to experience the most severe outcomes. The juvenile justice system, therefore, fails both youth and society. It particularly burdens youth of color, undermining our core principles of justice and equality.

It is a fundamental principle of our democracy that justice be administered fairly and equitably. The notion that skin color, income, residence, gender, or identity can heighten or determine deprivation of liberty violates the underpinnings of our system of jurisprudence. Indeed, constitutional and federal law demands that race and ethnicity receive additional scrutiny to determine if significant differences in treatment are discriminatory.

This chapter examines disparities by race and ethnicity in the juvenile justice system and deconstructs the drivers of disparities in order to craft more appropriate and just responses for children, families, and communities of color. A system that serves youth of color is a system that would serve all children, a system delinked from a history and tradition of systemic oppression and instead centered around child well-being.

Because our existing failed system has its roots in the historical treatment of youth of color in the U.S. youth justice system, that history is the subject of section 1, demonstrating that current disparities in treatment draw from this historical legacy. Section 2 provides an overview of current thinking about racial and ethnic disparities and the role federal policy has played in defining this issue. For 25 years, we have engaged in "adoration of the question" of racial and ethnic disparities, studying and gathering data, without gaining much ground. Section 3 fleshes out a new vision for juvenile justice, consistent with the research of scholars and activists, that is grounded in child well-being for all children. This vision requires well-functioning systems of mental health, health care, and education, as well as a juvenile justice system structured to serve children's needs and to support rehabilitation. In this re-visioned system, we would break our incarceration addiction and permit the use of incarceration only in limited circumstances as a last, uncommon resort.

I. Disparate Treatment Then and Now

Our existing juvenile justice system, laced with racial and ethnic disparity, is a logical link in a long history of race-conscious policies dictating that the detention of youth of color would be different than that of White youth coming into contact with the penal system for the same categories of offense. Especially in the nineteenth century, the exclusion of Black youth from White juvenile facilities created in that century often resulted in the placement of Black youth in adult prisons. Black children were also incarcerated younger than White children, had fewer opportunities for advancement upon discharge, and suffered a disproportionately higher death rate.

The overrepresentation of youth of color in the early penal system served as a convenient solution for labor needs in the post–Civil War South. A significant reason for opening the Baltimore House of Reformation for Black Children in Maryland, for example, was articulated as "the need for agricultural labor through [the] state, as well as the great want of competent house servants."[6] The demand for cheap labor after the Civil War was quickly satisfied through widespread arrests of Blacks for minor violations under Jim Crow laws to fuel "convict leasing," which has been described by Pulitzer Prize–winning historian David Oshinsky as a system "worse than slavery."[7] This practice continued through the twentieth century.

During the same period, Native American tribes not yet displaced by federal policies were attempting to maintain restorative justice practices such as family meetings and talking circles.[8] But in 1885, Congress passed the Major Crimes Act, essentially obliterating centuries-old restorative justice approaches to youth misbehavior and replacing them with a punitive model that persists today on and around Indian reservations.[9]

The problems that many youth advocates confront today were present even in the earliest days of the juvenile court. Just before the turn of the twentieth century, Jane Addams and other child advocates established the first juvenile court in Chicago. From its inception, Black children represented a greater percentage of the court caseload than their overall population and were substantially underrepresented in the agencies and services contracted to assist youth. These practices were first documented four decades after the establishment of the juvenile court by researcher Mary Huff Diggs. In her review of 53 juvenile courts, Diggs reported, "It is found that Negro children are represented in a much larger proportion of the delinquency cases than they are in the general population. . . . An appreciably larger percent of the Negro children came in contact with the courts at an earlier age than was true with the white children."[10] Diggs also observed, "Cases of Negro boys were less frequently dismissed than were white boys. Besides, they were committed to an institution or referred to an agency or individual much more frequently than were white boys."[11]

It is important to recount this history to fully understand the entrenchment of racial and ethnic disparities in today's youth justice system. In its early history, the inequitable treatment of youth of color in the youth justice system was the result of intentional and blatant race-based policies. Today, our policies are allegedly race neutral but remain steeped in the same legacy of structural racism.

II. Racial and Ethnic Disparities

A. From DMC to RED

1. RACE, ETHNICITY, AND SHIFTING DEMOGRAPHICS

Racial and ethnic disparities represent one of the most intransigent and disturbing issues facing youth justice in the United States. While constituting approximately 38% of the population eligible for detention, youth of color represent almost 70% of juveniles in secure confinement, a huge increase over the past decade.[12] This startling overrepresentation and increase in the degree of overrepresentation occurred while arrest rates for serious and violent crimes declined by 45%.[13]

Traditionally, the discussion of overrepresentation of young people of color in the youth justice system has been mainly devoted to Black and White youth. It is critical that the analysis include Latinos, Asians, Pacific Islanders, and Native Americans to accurately represent the patterns in the system. Rather than refer to these patterns as disproportionate minority representation (DMC), it is more accurate to identify them as racial and ethnic disparities (RED) to capture the broader reality of the patterns within the juvenile justice system, particularly as demographically we are moving to a majority-minority demographic.

According to the most recent data, African American youth are treated more harshly at all stages of the juvenile justice system, resulting in a cumulative disadvantage. While only 16% of the African American youth population is of sufficient age for detention, they represent 28% of juvenile arrests, 37% of detained youth, and 58% of youth admitted to state adult prison.[14]

Similar disparities exist for Latino youth, although the number of cases contained in local and national data sets is a significant undercount. The National Center on Juvenile Justice analyzed 2005 data from the National Juvenile Court Data Archive and was able to provide limited data on Latino youth, because only 13 of 42 jurisdictions consistently reported ethnicity data.[15] Nevertheless, the data accounted for approximately 63% of the nation's Latino youth population. The data revealed that Latino youth represented 29% of the juvenile population (ages 0–17), 27% of delinquency cases, and 56% of the cases that were petitioned; and of those cases that were petitioned, 78% were adjudicated delinquent.[16] A refined analysis of the data to expose contact points where disparity emerges found that Latino youth as compared to White youth were 4% more likely to be petitioned, 16% more likely to be adjudicated delinquent, 28% more likely to be detained, 41% more likely to receive an out-of-home placement, and 43% more likely to be waived to the adult system.[17]

As of the 2000 census, Latinos are the largest minority group in the U.S.[18] Latinos, 52 million strong as of July 2012, are, in addition, the fastest growing group of Americans.[19] Between 2005 and 2050, the Latino population is projected to triple, while the White population is projected to grow just 4%.[20] According to U.S. Census Bureau projections, by 2050, one in three Americans will be Latino.[21]

As a group, the Latino population in the U.S. is a young population. In 2009, Latinos under the age of 18 accounted for a third of the Latino U.S. population, as compared to one-quarter of the population as a whole.[22] In 2012, the median age of Latinos in the United States was 27, compared to 37 years old for the overall U.S. population.[23] Latino youth are projected to account for 35% of the youth population in the United States by 2050.[24]

In certain jurisdictions, Asians constitute the population overrepresented in the juvenile justice system, while in others, it is Pacific Islanders or Native Americans. Native American youth in areas in which they are concentrated, for example, continue to suffer the fallout of centuries-long displacement and occupation. They have less access to services and are granted disproportionately harsher sanctions including secure confinement and transfers to the adult criminal system.[25] It is critical to the equitable operation of the juvenile justice system to identify and engage with ethnic populations of color to dissipate or prevent disproportionality in the system.

2. THE MYTH OF RACE-NEUTRAL DECISION MAKING

There are several decision points within the youth justice system at which the overrepresentation of youth of color is commonly measured. These include cite and release, arrest, diversion after arrest, referral to a detention facility, and admission to detention. At each key decision point, juvenile justice professionals exercise judgments about how young people and their families should be handled. Monitoring of these decision points pursuant to federal policy reveals that youth of color are funneled deeper into the system for behaviors similar to their White counterparts when controlling for the offenses.[26]

For example, data reveal that White youth are more likely to be diverted from formal processing than are youth of color. Additionally, more youth of color are referred and admitted to detention than are their White counterparts for similar behavior.[27]

A recent survey showed that 32 of 44 states found evidence of ethnic or racial differences in youth justice system decision making that were unaccounted for by differential criminal activity.[28] A recent review of studies on disproportionality found that the effects of race and ethnicity on youth justice decision making do not reflect overt bias but rather reflect a subtle, indirect impact that accumulates over the youth justice decision-making landscape.[29]

Overrepresentation of youth of color is rampant at all levels of youth justice systems across the country. Forward movement in the field is obstructed by the constant and misdirected citation of extrajudicial factors such as poverty and lack of a father in the home as significant determinants of law violations.

Defaulting to these social determinants as rationales for disparate treatment of youth of color in the justice system does a disservice to us all. It allows decision makers an escape route for race effects and establishes the elimination of racism and poverty as the only solution for equitable treatment—two things we have been unable to eliminate in human history. Instead we should be examining the policies and practices of justice professionals to determine their efficacy, equity, and impact on youth of color.

B. The Role of Federal Policy

The modern history of identifying and analyzing disparities has largely been defined by the Juvenile Justice Delinquency and Prevention Act (JJDPA).[30] Through the JJDPA and research and publications funded by the Office of Juvenile Justice and Delinquency Prevention (OJJDP), the federal government has played a central role in defining the scope, reasons, and responses to race and ethnic disparities in the U.S. juvenile justice system.[31] Federal attention to this issue has evolved over the years, from the initial focus on confinement (disproportionate minority confinement, DMC) to the current process of assessing disparities at each phase of the system, or contact (disproportionate minority contact, DMC).

The JJDPA was designed to influence state juvenile justice policy by providing monetary incentives for compliance with federal mandates. Toward that end, it dictated two core requirements that states had to meet to receive funding: (1) remove offenders from pretrial lockup and (2) deinstitutionalize status offenders. In 1988, Congress amended the JJDPA to add a third requirement: (3) that each state address the issue of disproportionate minority confinement in secure facilities.[32]

In 2002, Congress amended the JJDPA once again, directing states to address disproportionate contact of youth of color within the youth justice system, not just their confinement in secure detention.[33] This change from confinement to contact acknowledged that disparities exist at other stages of the youth justice system and broadened the required inquiry to all decision points, while arguably taking the focus off confinement—the most oppressive locus of disparities. While recognizing the presence of racial and ethnic disparities at all stages of the youth justice process, the focus should be on the disparate treatment of youth of color.

Despite federal attention to race and ethnic disparities since the late 1980s,[34] the problem persists, raising real questions about the effectiveness of federal leadership. OJJDPs oversight of state compliance with the DMC mandate has been inconsistent, with few states penalized for failures to comply and with states that did document disproportionality failing to develop and implement remedial plans.[35]

While the fact and extent of racial and ethnic disparities in the youth justice system are well established, there continues to be discussion about the cause. Two theories have been proposed over the years: differential offending and differential treatment.[36]

Differential offending considers racial and ethnic disparities in the youth justice system the result of different patterns and rates of offending among youth by race and ethnicity.[37] These different offense patterns are posited in the type, seriousness, and frequency of offense and have even been explained in sociological terms as an expression of "oppositional culture."[38] In contrast, differential treatment explains that disparities result from differences in the treatment of White youth and youth of color at each of the discretionary decision points within the juvenile justice system.

Differential treatment, the view advanced by OJJDP,[39] is consistent with the way disparities increase as juveniles move deeper into the juvenile justice system. Research shows that racial differences become larger as juveniles move from arrest to detention, formal processing, out of home placement, and waiver into the adult system, experiencing the cumulative effect of justice system decisions.[40]

Today, debate over which theory explains disparities is less important than the undisputed facts that youth of color are present at each stage of the justice system in numbers disproportionate to their presence in the population, and these disparities increase as youth move further along the youth justice process.[41] Differential offending alone cannot explain the nature and extent of racial and ethnic disparities that are well documented in the youth justice system.[42]

Researchers have found that youth of color are more likely than their White counterparts to be arrested and referred by police for formal processing,[43] to be securely detained,[44] and to receive harsher dispositions. Rates of out-of-home placement in secure facilities for youth of color adjudicated for drug offenses are a case in point. An analysis of 2003 data found that 73% of adjudicated drug-offense cases involved a White youth, while White youth constituted 58% of drug-offense cases resulting in out-of-home placement and 75% of cases resulting in formal probation.[45]

In contrast, 25% of drug-offense cases involved an African American youth, but African American youth constituted 40% of adjudicated drug-offense cases resulting in out-of-home placement and 22% of drug-offense cases resulting in formal probation. Additionally, 24% of adjudicated cases received a disposition of out-of-home placement, while 62% resulted in a court disposition of probation, which allows youths to return to their community rather than remain in a secure facility.[46]

In all offense categories, White youth were underrepresented among those receiving out-of-home placements, and the reverse was true for Black youth. In 2003, Black youth represented 25% of the youth adjudicated delinquent for drug offenses but 40% of those taken out of their homes and communities. In contrast, White youth represented 73% of youth adjudicated delinquent for drug offenses, while 58% of their drug cases resulted in out-of-home placement, with 75% of the cases resulting in formal probation.[47]

An important qualitative study demonstrating structural racism involved the perceptions of court officials (i.e., probation) of similarly situated White and Black youth, suggesting that officials' race-based biases are a factor contributing to disparities. The study's examination of court records found that court officials had different perceptions and explanations for the motivations of Black and White youth in court. Court officials were more likely to explain delinquent behavior by Black youth by internal factors, such as having a lack of meaningful life goals or needing to be held accountable, while similar behavior of White youth was explained in relation to external factors such as having a difficult family life. Thus, the Black youth were perceived more negatively than were the White youth.[48]

The history of disparities in the juvenile justice system illustrates a progression of policies and practices resulting in embedded racial and ethnic inequities. Indeed, the trend in the U.S. has been to criminalize the very nature of adolescence.

Heretofore the youth justice system has practiced the "justice" quotient with an overreliance on incarceration as the primary instrument of social control. This reliance on the tools and technologies of incapacitation leaves little room for the "youth" part of the equation. There is much we are learning about the adolescent brain and youthful behavior that argues against the traditional "lock 'em up" ethos that has been so pervasive and unsuccessful.

III. A New Vision: Child Well-Being

A. The Need for Strongly Funded, Well-Performing Mental Health, Health, and Educational Systems to Provide for and Protect Low-Risk, High-Needs Youth

The youth justice system has become the default warehouse for low-risk, high-needs youth whose needs should be served by other public systems. The unmet needs of poor youth of color are a significant driver of their entry into the youth justice system.

Juvenile justice research is replete with evidence of the connection between low-risk youth involved in the youth justice system and unmet social needs. Research has clearly documented the school-to-prison pipeline, and increasingly practitioners and academics understand the connection between posttraumatic stress disorder and detention.[49] Up to 70% of youth in the youth justice system have a mental health disorder, while more than 20% have a serious mental illness.[50]

A groundbreaking study by the American Psychological Association in 2007 found that youth of color were often given diagnoses that led to confinement.[51] The disparity in judgment of mental disorders between minority and nonminority youth by clinicians was noteworthy. Controlling for context and clinicians' characteristics, clinicians were less likely to judge a disorder present in youth who were Black or Latino than those who were White. One possibility considered for this disparity was that when clinicians were faced with antisocial behavior, they may have judged White youths as having a mental disorder (and directed them to treatment) but judged minority youths to have behavioral issues (and directed them to the justice system).[52]

While improving the capacity of the youth justice system to deliver mental health services may seem like the obvious solution, it is not the appropriate venue to deliver such services to young people.[53] After all, it is not often that people with sufficient financial and other resources suggest having their child placed in a locked cell in order to receive counseling.

In 2011, I interviewed youth-serving professionals on a variety of topics regarding nonjudicial drivers into the youth justice system. Dr. David Arredondo[54] is intimately familiar with the provision of mental health services in the youth justice system in Santa Clara County, California. He works closely with the specialized Juvenile Mental Health Court and observes the juvenile detention facilities that have become an unfortunate referral source for too many young people with behavioral health issues.

Dr. Arredondo noted that youth detention facilities are ineffective and sometimes inhumane in their typical responses to the needs of children with behavioral health problems. He believes that placing youth in secure confinement does not reduce harm but in fact may have the opposite effect. He avers that congregate living environments are almost always harmful to young people with behavioral health issues because of the negative peer influences and the lack of staff skills and interest to intervene appropriately.

While there is a clear need to use detention for a very small number of dangerous youth, Dr. Antoinette Kavanaugh,[55] a consulting therapist for the Cook County Juvenile Court, recommends family-based community alternatives to detention as a better approach for youth with behavioral health problems. She also has observed in her practice that youth of color with behavioral health issues are referred to the youth justice system for behaviors while their White counterparts are not.

A typical example of how the existing system fails to help kids, an example raised by both of these experts, involves a youth whose parents are not getting along at home, who comes to school and is teased by other students before class. Frustrated, the young man kicks the garbage can sitting near the door, which bounces near the teacher. This conduct creates an important decision point wherein youth of color are too often

sent to the youth justice system when the teacher calls the "school resource officers" to implement zero-tolerance policies, while White youth
are diverted toward nonjudicial evaluative services. Once the young person is in detention, his or her problems are exacerbated, and the youth
can easily be propelled deeper into the system.

Similarly, practitioners working in long-term youth incarceration facilities observe that psychotropic medications are used early and often.
They see firsthand young people with behavioral health problems that
are turbocharged into the deep end of the system, and the use of psychotropic medications is primarily for controlling behavior rather than
addressing symptoms.

Secure confinement facilities were built to be correctional in nature
and in order to reduce harm; special behavioral units are increasingly
being utilized throughout the country to accommodate these young
people. Long-term confinement is not appropriate for these young people, who need school-based and community service responses.

A related issue is the state of behavioral health practices in the larger
community that drive young people of color into the youth justice system. It is not unusual for young people of color, especially those living
in communities of concentrated poverty, to experience depression or to
self-medicate with alcohol or drugs. For these youth, rarely are there options in their communities for evaluation and treatment. There is agreement among all the experts whom I interviewed that access to crisis
intervention and school-based and community behavioral health services are practically nonexistent. Moreover, what few services exist are
often not culturally or linguistically appropriate. Importantly, there is insufficient infrastructure in the health, education, and behavioral health
sectors to counteract the "tough on crime" rhetoric that has criminalized
adolescence and driven youth of color into the justice system in unconscionable numbers.

Similarly, the youth justice system is not equipped to respond to the
needs of low-risk youth who present with substance abuse issues. In
2006, nearly 10% of youth ages 12–17 reported being actively engaged
in drug usage.[56] Research shows that there is a direct connection between youth who end up in trouble with the law and the abuse of drugs
and alcohol. These youth are disproportionately from low-income communities and communities of color. Overusing detention is inherently

harmful and will not solve the problem, much less accelerate youth recovery.

Differential treatment also exists in the physical health realm. Health-related issues that impact juvenile justice system involvement include trauma or, as John Rich describes it, adversity.[57] Dr. Nadine Burke, M.D., M.P.H., medical director of the Bay View Child Health Center in San Francisco, posits that the clinical effects of childhood trauma need to be given more attention as a serious medical epidemic and significant contributor to overincarceration of youth of color. Each child exposed to trauma has a different susceptibility to the effects of that trauma, as illustrated in the work of Victor Carrion,[58] director of the Early Life Stress Program at Stanford University. Children range in their resilience to trauma; however, there is a certain point at which even the most resilient child will suffer effects. The earlier example of the child kicking the garbage can is not atypical. It is as likely as not that the young person exhibiting this type of behavior or some type of "willful defiance" will be sent to the youth justice system, since classroom teachers have total discretion in their response to disruption. Zero-tolerance policies do not lend themselves to a trauma-informed approach.

According to the work of Sandra Bloom,[59] teachers and administrators want to suppress aggressive behavior rather than address its causes. Schools in neighborhoods of concentrated poverty, in particular, have been turned into a culture of escalated violence with cameras, cops, and metal detectors. Everything about that environment does nothing to calm the trauma that youth of color predominantly experience. In order to establish a trauma-informed sanctuary with a set of principles and protocols, educators must become sophisticated in understanding what trauma does to the body, to young people, and to the teachers themselves.

Societal norms, policies, and practices, therefore, play a more significant role in referrals to the youth justice than does differential offending. In order to positively engage these drivers of disparities related to mental health, school policies, trauma, and lack of basic community services, we will have to take a different approach.

B. Child Well-Being as the Preferred Community Safety Strategy for Youth Accountability and Rehabilitation and Community Support and Safety

Deeply embedded beliefs continue to inform our jurisprudential system today. Those beliefs are filled with dialectics that are clearly difficult to overcome. For example, there are the beliefs that the state should have limited power over individuals, coexisting simultaneously with the belief that retribution and punishment must be meted out to maintain social control. "Spare the rod and spoil the child" is just one of the many legacies that still persist. Our jurisprudence as created and maintained by society's elites has lurched in fits and starts between mercy and revenge.

Throughout history, voices have risen to intercede against and mitigate the forces of retribution, but the alchemy of punishment and incarceration has been too powerful to overcome. John Augustus, considered the "father of probation," was one of the first. A shoemaker by trade, he believed that the object of the law was to "reform criminals, prevent crime and not punish maliciously, or from a spirit of revenge."[60] He pushed his way into the criminal courts in the 1840s and convinced judges to allow him to watch over children by procuring employment for them or securing their attendance at school.

Today, the "tough on crime" mantra and its related legislative agenda have led to unprecedented levels of mass incarceration in the United States. It is no coincidence that this retributive approach to "public safety" has resulted in a greater impact on youth of color. Between 1971 and 1990, the expenditures for incarceration for all populations in the United States have increased a whopping 313%. As costs increase, practitioners in the justice community have noted the increase in young people coming to their doors from schools and with behavioral health issues. Indeed, while legislators have lavished billions of dollars on incarceration, other child-serving agencies have been gutted. These facts were made clear in a recently released report by the National Sheriffs Association and the Treatment Advocacy Center, which documented that there are more mentally ill people in jails and prisons than in hospitals.[61]

Indeed, we need an aspirational, visionary, and forward-looking concept of public safety that responds to behavioral transgressions in ways that are restorative, are equitable, and increase public well-being yet is mindful that some young people are so damaged that they must be separated from society. If one were to unpack the container of ideas that drives our existing system, one would find an ideology of custody and control rather than interventions and services. Thus, the mandates and apparatus of custody, control, and deprivation form the backbone of youth justice practices. This includes the frequent use of incarceration as a primary instrument of social control. It is this default justice system reflex that reduces its ability to reduce harm. Indeed, for those of us who want positive outcomes rather than increasing harm, this is a fundamental difference in approach.

Proponents of the use of secure confinement as the first response to adolescent transgressions see incarceration not as harmful but rather as most appropriate for young people considered threats to public safety. While the use of incarceration has deep historical roots, its current misuse is made easier because its utility is imposed mostly on young people of color.

For too long, the youth justice field has been wedded to practices that are steeped in historical mores that ignore current information about adolescent development and societal norms regarding weapons, sex, gender, technology, health, and family structure, among other things. Regardless of the complexities and needs of youth and families, this system has hardly changed its available options since the mid-nineteenth century.

Any analysis of our current overreliance on all forms of secure confinement—be it jails, detention, camps, or long-term secure placements—without examining the structural violence that lies at its core leaves much to be desired. The use and acceptance of structural violence as a key component of social control is risky, dangerous, and harmful to civil society and must be resisted. Indeed, there are structural imperatives that have a huge gravitational pull that has well-meaning professionals eagerly embracing this deficit-based view of communities of color by adopting an ethos that accepts incarceration as an unfortunate but necessary byproduct of getting youth of color services. Often, officials are correct in their assessment that a youth is in need of various services, but the practice of using need as a justification for secure confinement is problematic because it fails to objectively assess the actual risk to public safety and/or flight posed by the youth in question.

Furthermore, the practice sends the subjective message to every incarcerated youth that *your* life, *your* time, and *your* circumstances are less important than those of a youth with means. This notion is supported by policies that unnecessarily remove youth from their schools, homes, and communities. As discussed earlier, simply because a young person has several needs (educational, emotional, psychological, etc.) does not mean that he or she poses any significant risk to the community or is in need of secure confinement.

I propose a different vision and approach. We must move to break the addiction to using incarceration, and as with any addiction, we must take small but strategic steps away from the jailhouse door and toward child well-being, equity, and excellence.

First, we must implement legislative barriers to the use of incarceration as a first resort. That means entire cohorts of minor offenses that currently fill the calendars of the halls of justice would be directed away. Data reveal that the overwhelming numbers of offenses handled by the courts are nonviolent property offenses. Therefore, I am proposing responses wherein approximately 60% of referrals to the criminal justice system would be handled informally or through case managers located in the community. Services to law violators and their families would be provided by a combination of social workers and safety officers. These safety officers would be community members with a broad range of training.

The burden for using locked facilities would shift. Case managers would have to make a clear showing about how using incarceration is beneficial to the victim and to the community. Justice professionals would be rewarded for improving life outcomes rather than complying with increasingly irrelevant conditions of probation. Instead of measuring contacts with probation, we would measure assistance in gaining employment, educational attainment, literacy, reduced family disruption, and violence reduction.

For those cases that are more serious, we would strengthen community mediation and arbitration. In almost all cases except sexual assault, child molestation, or domestic violence involving great bodily injury, a hearing process would be created that involves professionals, community members, the perpetrator, and the victim to try to resolve the matter with restorative principles that require accountability without destroying human dignity. Incarceration would be a last resort, and then it would be handled in community settings.

It is only after restorative methods have been tried and failed that a petition for court processes could be sought. The court processes would vary significantly from our current practice. Hearings would be before a combination of judicial officers and community members. The focus would be to make decisions about appropriate services to determine which community service provider is most appropriate, based on its ability to rehabilitate the child. Due process protections are not eliminated, but at the same time, the goal is to get to disposition and services more quickly.

This approach allows for deprivation of liberty but envisions an approach that is grounded in successful community-based programs that serve youth and maintain safety with secure detention only as a last resort. Such programs have been proven to be successful in providing linkages and access to services that meet the needs of youth of color, thereby giving them opportunities to be productive and to thrive in our communities.

Conclusion

As the numbers of youth of color and the resources needed to confine them increase at astronomical rates, it is time to reexamine how we as a society respond to young people in trouble with the law. There is no need for us to be addicted to a system that is structurally incapable of meeting the needs of youth and families. Let us imagine and construct a new system of justice for youth that is equitable, effective, restorative, and age appropriate by implementing an innovative approach to accountability and reform.

NOTES

1   Philanthropic organizations include the Annie E. Casey Foundation, Atlantic Philanthropies, the John D. and Catherine T. MacArthur Foundation, the Robert Wood Johnson Foundation, and the California Endowment.

2   Angela Blackwell, Stewart Kwoh, and Manuel Pastor, *Uncommon Common Ground: Race and America's Future* (New York: Norton, 2010).

3   Václav Havel, *Disturbing the Peace: A Conversation with Karel Hvizdala*, translated by Paul Wilson (New York: Random House, 1990).

4 John Smith, Kris Warner, and Sarika Gupta, *The High Budgetary Cost of Incarceration* (Washington, DC: Center for Economic and Policy Research [CEPR], June 2010), http://www.cepr.net/documents/publications/incarceration-2010-06.pdf.

5 Neal Hazel, *Cross National Comparisons of Youth Justice* (London: London Youth Justice Board, 2008), cited in Richard A. Mendel, *No Place for Kids: The Case for Reducing Juvenile Incarceration* (Baltimore: Annie E. Casey Foundation, 2011), http://www.aecf.org/m/resourcedoc/aecf-NoPlaceForKidsFullReport-2011.pdf.

6 Geoff K. Ward, *The Black Child-Savers: Racial Democracy and Juvenile Justice* (Chicago: University of Chicago Press, 2012), 74.

7 David M. Oshinsky, *Worse than Slavery: Parchman Farm and the Ordeal of Jim Crow* (New York: Free Press, 1996).

8 John Popuart, John Redhourse, Melanie Peterson-Hickey, and Mary Martin, *Searching for Justice: American Indian Perspectives on Disparities in Minnesota Criminal Justice System* (St. Paul, MN: American Indian Policy Center, 2005), http://www.crimeandjustice.org/researchReports/American%20Indian%20Perspectives%20on%20Disparities%20in%20the%20Minnesota%20Criminal%20Justice%20System.pdf.

9 The Major Crimes Act, 17 U.S.C. § 1153 (1885).

10 Mary Huff Diggs, "The Problems and Needs of Negro Youth as Revealed by Delinquency and Crime Statistics," *Journal of Negro Education* 9, no. 3 (1940): 313.

11 *Id.* at 316.

12 Richard A. Mendel, *Two Decades of JDAI: A Progress Report; From Demonstration Project to National Standard* (Baltimore: Annie E. Casey Foundation, 2009), http://www.aecf.org/m/resourcedoc/aecf-TwoDecadesofJDAIfromDemotoNatl-2009.pdf.

13 Barry C. Feld, *Bad Kids: Race and the Transformation of the Juvenile Court* (New York: Oxford University Press, 1999), cited in Douglas W. Nelson, *A Road Map for Juvenile Justice Reform* (Baltimore: Annie E. Casey Foundation, 2008), http://datacenter.kidscount.org/db_08pdf/2008_essay.pdf.

14 National Council on Crime and Delinquency, *And Justice for Some: Differential Treatment of Youth of Color in the Justice System* (Oakland, CA: National Council on Crime and Delinquency, January 2007), http://www.nccdglobal.org/sites/default/files/publication_pdf/justice-for-some.pdf.

15 Neelum Arya, Francisco Villarruel, Cassandra Villanueva, and Ian Augarten, *America's Invisible Children: Latino Youth and the Failure of Justice*, Race and Ethnicity Series 3 (Models for Change policy brief, 2009), http://www.modelsforchange.net/publications/213.

16 *Id.*

17 Francisco A. Villarruel and Nancy E. Walker, with Pamela Minifee, Omara Rivera-Vázquez, Susan Peterson, and Kristen Perry, *¿Dónde Está la Justicia? A Call to Action on Behalf of Latino and Latina Youth in the U.S. Justice System* (East Lansing: Building Blocks for Youth, Michigan State University Institute for

Children, Youth, and Families, 2003), http://www.opensocietyfoundations.org/
sites/default/files/donde_esta.pdf.

18 Lloyd Vries, "Hispanics Now Largest US Minority," CBS News Online, January 21,
2003 (reporting announcement of Census Bureau, on the basis of 2000 census),
http://www.cbsnews.com/news/hispanics-now-largest-us-minority/.

19 U.S. Census Bureau, "Facts for Features: Hispanic Heritage Month 2013: Sept.
15–Oct. 15," news release, July 30, 2013, http://www.census.gov/newsroom/releases/
archives/facts_for_features_special_editions/cb13-ff19.html (Hispanic population is
17% of total population); Jeffrey S. Passel, D'Vera Cohn, and Mark Hugo Lopez,
"Hispanics Account for More than Half of Nation's Growth in the Past Decade"
(Pew Research, Hispanic Trends Project, March 24, 2011), http://www.pewhispanic.
org/2011/03/24/hispanics-account-for-more-than-half-of-nations-growth-in-past-
decade/ ("The 2010 Census counted 50.5 million Hispanics in the United States,
making up 16.3% of the total population. The nation's Latino population, which was
35.3 million in 2000, grew 43% over the decade. The Hispanic population also
accounted for most of the nation's growth—56%—from 2000 to 2010.").

20 Jeffrey S. Passel and D'Vera Cohn, "U.S. Population Projections: 2005–2050" (Pew
Research, Hispanic Trends Project, February 11, 2008), http://www.pewhispanic.
org/2008/02/11/us-population-projections-2005-2050/.

21 U.S. Census Bureau, "An Older and More Diverse Nation by Midcentury," news
release, August 14, 2008, http://www.census.gov/newsroom/releases/archives/
population/cb08-123.html ("Minorities, now roughly one-third of the U.S.
population, are expected to become the majority in 2042, with the nation
projected to be 54 percent minority in 2050. By 2023, minorities will comprise
more than half of all children. The Hispanic population is projected to nearly
triple, from 46.7 million to 132.8 million during the 2008–2050 period. Its share of
the nation's total population is projected to double, from 15 percent to 30 percent.
Thus, nearly one in three U.S. residents would be Hispanic. In 2050, the nation's
population of children is expected to be 62 percent minority, up from 44 percent
today. Thirty-nine percent are projected to be Hispanic (up from 22 percent in
2008), and 38 percent are projected to be single-race, non-Hispanic white (down
from 56 percent in 2008).").

22 National Council of La Raza, "20 FAQs about Hispanics: Twenty of the Most
Frequently Asked Questions about Hispanics in the U.S.," http://www.nclr.org/
index.php/about_us/faqs/most_frequently_asked_questions_about_hispan-
ics_in_the_us/#sthash.dbtWvc6v.dpuf (accessed December 29, 2013).

23 U.S. Census Bureau, "Median Age by Race and Hispanic Origin: 2012 and 2060,"
December 14, 2012, http://www.census.gov/newsroom/cspan/pop_proj/20121214_
cspan_popproj_12.pdf. The projections according to this data are that by 2050 the
median age will be 41 overall and 34 for Latinos.

24 Passel and Cohn, *supra* note 20.

25 Christopher Hartney and Linh Vuong, *Created Equal: Racial and Ethnic
Disparities in the U.S. Criminal Justice System* (Oakland, CA: National Council on

Crime and Delinquency, March 2009), http://www.nccdglobal.org/sites/default/
files/publication_pdf/created-equal.pdf.

26 Smith, Warner, and Gupta, *supra* note 4.

27 Hazel, *supra* note 5.

28 Darnell F. Hawkins and Kimberly Kempf-Leonard, eds., *Our Children, Their
Children: Confronting Racial and Ethnic Differences in American Juvenile Justice*
(Chicago: University of Chicago Press, 2005).

29 National Council on Crime and Delinquency, *supra* note 14.

30 Juvenile Justice and Delinquency Prevention Act of 1974 (JJDPA), 42 U.S.C. § 5601
et seq. (1974).

31 Hawkins and Kempf-Leonard, *supra* note 28.

32 JJDPA, 42 U.S.C. § 5661(a)(1)(B)(viii).

33 JJDPA, 42 U.S.C. § 5633(a)(22).

34 Michael J. Leiber, "Disproportionate Minority Confinement (DMC) of Youth:
An Analysis of State and Federal Efforts to Address the Issue," *Crime and
Delinquency* 48, no. 1 (2002): 3–45, http://www.sagepub.com/stohrstudy/
articles/10/Leiber.pdf.

35 Perry L. Moriearty, "Combating the Color-Coded Confinement of Kids: An Equal
Protection Remedy," *New York University Review of Law and Social Change* 32
(2008): 285–343.

36 Donna M. Bishop, "The Role of Race and Ethnicity in Juvenile Justice Processing,"
in Hawkins and Kempf-Leonard, *supra* note 28, at 23–82; Alex R. Piquero,
"Disproportionate Minority Contact," *Future of Children* 18, no. 2 (2008): 59–79.

37 *See* Piquero, *supra* note 36.

38 Elijah Anderson, *Code of the Street: Decency, Violence, and the Moral Life of the
Inner City* (New York: Norton, 1999).

39 Paul E. Tracy, "Race, Ethnicity, and Juvenile Justice: Is There Bias in Post-arrest
Decision Making?," in Hawkins and Kempf-Leonard, *supra* note 28, at 300–348.

40 See *supra* note 14.

41 *Id.*

42 *Id.*

43 *Id.*

44 Eleanor Hinton Hoytt, Vincent Schiraldi, Brenda V. Smith, and Jason Ziedenberg,
*Pathways to Juvenile Detention Reform: Reducing Racial Disparities in Juvenile
Detention* (Baltimore: Annie E. Casey Foundation, 2002).

45 Richard M. Lerner, Michael D. Wiatrowski, Megan Kiely Mueller, Christopher M.
Napolitano, Kristina L. Schmid, and Anita Pritchard, "A Vision for the American
Juvenile Justice System," in *Juvenile Justice: Advancing Research, Policy, and
Practice*, edited by Francine T. Sherman and Francine H. Jacobs, 92–108
(Hoboken, NJ: Wiley, 2011).

46 National Council on Crime and Delinquency, *supra* note 14.

47 Barry Krisberg, *Juvenile Justice: Redeeming Our Children* (Thousand Oaks, CA:
Sage, 2005).

48 George S. Bridges and Sara Steen, "Racial Disparities in Official Assessments of Juvenile Offenders: Attributional Stereotypes as Mediating Mechanisms," *American Society Review* 63 (1998): 554.

49 John Rich, Theodore Corbin, Sandra Bloom, Linda Rich, Solomon Evans, and Ann Wilson, *Healing the Hurt: Trauma-Informed Approaches to the Health of Men and Boys of Color* (Philadelphia: Drexel University School of Public Health: Center for Nonviolence and Social Justice; Drexel University College of Medicine: Department of Emergency Medicine, 2009).

50 Jennie L. Shufelt and Joseph J. Cocozza, *Youth with Mental Health Disorders in the Juvenile Justice System: Results from a Multi-state Prevalence Study*, Research and Program Brief (Delmar, NY: National Center for Mental Health and Juvenile Justice, June 2006), http://www.ncmhjj.com/wp-content/uploads/2013/07/2006_Youth-with-Mental-Health-Disorders-in-the-Juvenile-Justice-System1.pdf.

51 Kathleen J. Pottick, Stuart A. Kirk, Derek K. Hsieh, and Xin Tian, "Judging Mental Disorder: Effects of Client, Clinician, and Contextual Differences," *Journal of Consulting and Clinical Psychology* 75, no. 1 (2007): 1–8.

52 *Id.*

53 Thomas Grisso, "Adolescent Offenders with Mental Disorders," *Future of Children* 18, no. 2 (2008): 143–164, http://futureofchildren.org/futureofchildren/publications/docs/18_02_07.pdf.

54 David Arredondo, M.D., is a diplomate of the Board of the American Academy of Psychiatry and Neurology and the founding director of the Children's Program for troubled youth (childrensprogram.wordpress.com).

55 Antoinette Kavanaugh, Ph.D., is a forensic clinical psychologist.

56 Substance Abuse and Mental Health Services Administration, *Results from the 2011 National Survey on Drug Use and Health: Summary of National Findings*, NSDUH Series H-44, HHS Publication No. (SMA) 12-4713 (Rockville, MD: Substance Abuse and Mental Health Services Administration, 2012), http://www.samhsa.gov/data/nsduh/2k11results/nsduhresults2011.htm.

57 See Moriearty, *supra* note 35.

58 Victor Carrion is a child and adolescent psychiatrist at Stanford's Lucile Packard Children's Hospital (http://med.stanford.edu/profiles/Victor_Carrion/).

59 Dr. Sandra L. Bloom is a board-certified psychiatrist and graduate of Temple University School of Medicine. More information and a list of her selected publications can be found at http://publichealth.drexel.edu/Faculty/Faculty-Member/5034/facultyid--99/#research.

60 John Augustus, *A Report of the Labors of John Augustus, for the Last Ten Years, in Aid of the Unfortunate* (Boston: Wright and Hasty, 1939), 17.

61 E. Fuller Torrey, Aaron D. Kennard, Don Eslinger, Richard Lamb, and James Pavale, *More Mentally Ill Persons Are in Jails and Prisons than Hospitals: A Survey of the States* (Arlington, VA: Treatment Advocacy Center and National Sheriffs' Association, May 2010), http://www.treatmentadvocacycenter.org/storage/documents/final_jails_v_hospitals_study.pdf.

PART II

Core Components

2

A Silent Sea Change

The Deinstitutionalization Trend in Juvenile Justice

BART LUBOW

American reliance on confinement for youth charged with or convicted of delinquent acts is a critical characteristic of our juvenile
justice system. It is also wildly out of sync with the practices of other
nations. Though cross-country comparisons are somewhat difficult,
given the idiosyncrasies or inadequacies of the varied databases, a
rough approximation published in 2008 revealed that the U.S. juvenile
incarceration rate was anywhere from 5 to 35 times greater than other
economically developed, democratic countries[1] (see figure 2.1). In that
analysis, the U.S. rate stood at 336 per 100,000 youth incarcerated,
whereas the next highest rate was 69 per 100,000 in South Africa.
Data from Japan, Finland, and Sweden revealed that those countries
incarcerated virtually no minors. These different rates of incarceration were not explained by crime statistics: U.S. juvenile violent-crime
rates were only marginally higher than in many of these other nations.
And while the overall U.S. rate of confinement, as discussed in this
chapter, has decreased substantially since that analysis, these reductions still leave the U.S. the world's leader in youth confinement. This
chapter documents this significant downward trend in incarceration
and the factors that have led to this change in the U.S. pattern, while
reminding us that we remain far from an ideal system in which confinement would be used sparingly, consistent with the practices of
other nations and our knowledge of youth and delinquency.

Recent Trends

Approximately every two years, the U.S. Census Bureau conducts a survey of juvenile residential facilities across the United States, the data

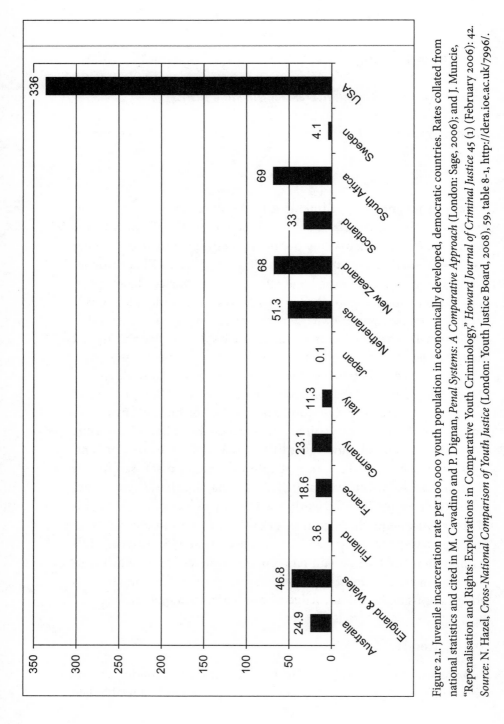

Figure 2.1. Juvenile incarceration rate per 100,000 youth population in economically developed, democratic countries. Rates collated from national statistics and cited in M. Cavadino and P. Dignan, *Penal Systems: A Comparative Approach* (London: Sage, 2006); and J. Muncie, "Repenalisation and Rights: Explorations in Comparative Youth Criminology," *Howard Journal of Criminal Justice* 45 (1) (February 2006): 42. *Source:* N. Hazel, *Cross-National Comparison of Youth Justice* (London: Youth Justice Board, 2008), 59, table 8-1, http://dera.ioe.ac.uk/7996/.

from which is published by the Office of Juvenile Justice and Delinquency Prevention.[2] Known as the Census of Juveniles in Residential Placement (CJRP), the survey is a one-day count of young people who have been assigned a bed in a residential facility as a result of delinquency charges pending or adjudicated in a juvenile court. Facilities surveyed include both long-term, postdispositional institutions (often referred to as training schools or youth corrections facilities), as well as short-term facilities such as local detention centers or temporary shelters. Approximately 62 percent of the youth identified through CJRP in 2011 were committed to long-term institutions,[3] where lengths of stay typically exceed 90 days. The survey instrument and methodology were revised in 1997, so rates for the period prior to these revisions are not entirely comparable. However, for purposes of illustrating aggregate trends, the older data certainly suffice.

Figure 2.2 presents overall rates of youth confinement for the period 1975–2011. Beginning in 1975, reliance on confinement steadily increased, from a low of 241 per 100,000 youth to a high of 381 in 1995, when a total of 107,637 youth were held in these varied facilities on the survey's snapshot date. Juvenile confinement rates increased by approximately 4.5 percent annually during the most rapid phase of this growth, from 1979 to 1987. Beginning in 1997, however, these rates began what at first was a very gradual decline, decreasing at an annual rate of 2.3 percent between 1997 and 2006. By then, the overall rate of confinement had decreased to 289 youth per 100,000, a 23 percent decrease from its high point. Subsequently, the annual rate of deinstitutionalization more than tripled, resulting in a juvenile confinement rate of 196 per 100,000 youth in 2011. Overall, juvenile confinement rates are down 49 percent since 1995 (45 percent since 1997, when the survey instrument was changed). According to the 2011 CJRP, 61,423 youth were confined on the day of the survey snapshot, a decrease of more than 46,000 since 1999. The juvenile commitment rate (those locked up as a result of a court-ordered sanction, excluding youth confined pending court or awaiting placement) dropped an astounding 14 percent between 2010 and 2011.[4]

This juvenile confinement trend, noteworthy in a nation that increased its adult incarceration rate by approximately 500 percent over the past four decades, has occurred in virtually all states. As figure 2.3 shows, 47 states reduced youth confinement between 1997 and 2011,

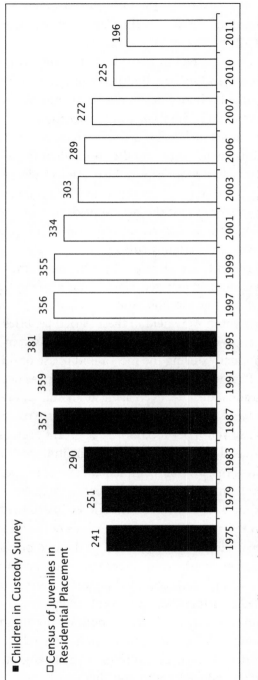

Figure 2.2. Overall rates of confinement, 1975–2011. *Sources:* For Children in Custody rates: B. Smith, "Children in Custody: 20-Year Trends in Juvenile Detention, Correctional, and Shelter Facilities," *Crime & Delinquency* 44 (4) (October 1998): 526, http://cad.sagepub.com/content/44/4/526.abstract; for Census of Juveniles in Residential Placement rates: Melissa Sickmund, T. J. Sladky, Wei Kang, and Charles Puzzanchera, "Easy Access to the Census of Juveniles in Residential Placement (EZACJRP)," Office of Juvenile Justice and Delinquency Prevention, http://www.ojjdp.gov/ojstatbb/ezacjrp/ (accessed December 1, 2013).

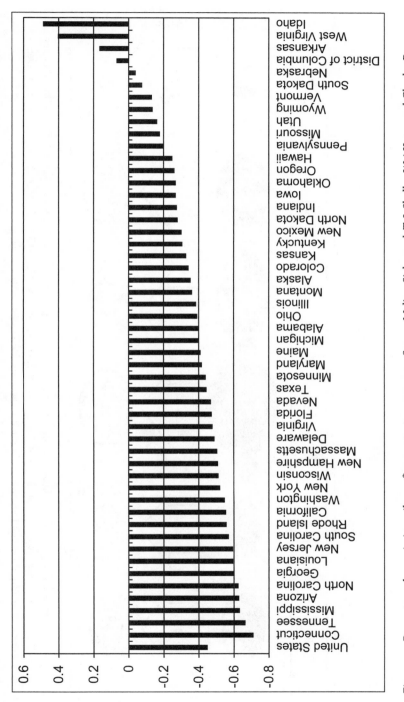

Figure 2.3. Percentage change in juvenile confinement rate, 1997–2011. *Source:* Melissa Sickmund, T. J. Sladky, Wei Kang, and Charles Puzzanchera, "Easy Access to the Census of Juveniles in Residential Placement (EZACJRP)," Office of Juvenile Justice and Delinquency Prevention, http://www.ojjdp.gov/ojstatbb/ezacjrp/ (accessed December 1, 2013).

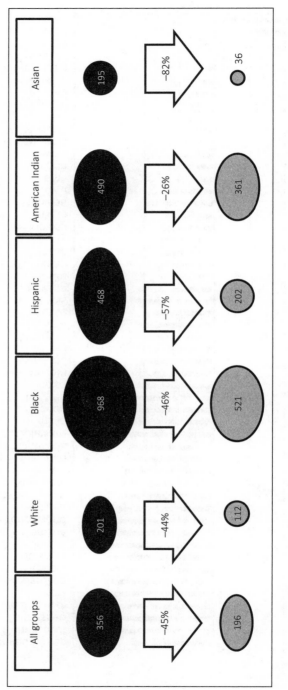

Figure 2.4. Percentage change in juvenile confinement rate, by race/ethnicity, 1997–2011. *Source:* Melissa Sickmund, T. J. Sladky, Wei Kang, and Charles Puzzanchera, "Easy Access to the Census of Juveniles in Residential Placement (EZACJRP)," Office of Juvenile Justice and Delinquency Prevention, http://www.ojjdp.gov/ojstatbb/ezacjrp/ (accessed December 1, 2013).

including 16 where the decreases exceeded 50 percent, a genuine sea change in correctional population trends.

In addition to high rates of confinement, another signature characteristic of American juvenile justice is the differential rates of confinement across racial and ethnic subpopulations, which raises the question of whether the recent deinstitutionalization trend applies equally across all subgroups. Figure 2.4 disaggregates the recent trend by race/ethnicity, revealing that with the notable exception of Native American youth (whose confinement rate has fallen just 26 percent), all subpopulations experienced decreases in rates of confinement of at least 44 percent. These data also reveal, however, that the extreme disparities in rates of confinement for youth of color persist. African American youth, for example, experienced a 46 percent decrease in their rate of confinement between 1997 and 2011 but are still confined at a rate approximately 4.7 times greater than their white peers and 2.7 times greater than all youth.

A Critique of Juvenile Confinement

The large reductions in confinement rates, especially over the past five years, are unusual, even historic, and they enjoy widespread support from both juvenile justice practitioners and reform advocates. Why? Aside from the obvious discomfort generated by the contradiction between the United States' proclaimed commitment to liberty and freedom, on the one hand, and its reputation for locking up far more children than similar countries do on the other, a broad and deep critique of juvenile confinement in the U.S. has also been forcefully articulated and widely embraced.

Perhaps the most extensive and influential recent critique of American youth corrections is Richard Mendel's monograph *No Place for Kids: The Case for Reducing Juvenile Incarceration*.[5] This analysis begins by noting that, over the past 40 years, 80 percent of the states have operated juvenile institutions whose conditions were so violent, restrictive, and bereft of basic services that either a federal court intervened or a major scandal erupted.[6] Mendel further notes that these patterns of abusive conditions are not simply relics of the past, transgressions that more modern administrators have learned to avoid. The majority of these patterns of persistent maltreatment were revealed only since

2000. This means either that administrators have not learned from past problems or—more likely—that environments such as these are toxic by nature.

Kids in juvenile confinement facilities are frequently subjected to physical abuse and excessive use of force by staff. According to the Associated Press, for example, 13,000 claims of abuse were reported from 2004 through 2007.[7] In 2010, the federal government released a report on sexual abuse that found that 12 percent of youth (one out of eight) in juvenile facilities had been victimized during the prior year by staff or other youth.[8] A more recent analysis[9] reduced this estimate of institutional sexual abuse to one in ten confined youth, hardly a cause for celebration. Far too frequently, confined youth are also physically or chemically (e.g., mace) restrained and isolated in their cells for lengthy periods.

Public sympathy for youth subject to these abusive conditions tends to be undermined by the perception that youth confined because of juvenile court actions pose uncontrollable public safety risks. But only about 11 percent of juvenile detention admissions, and a similar percentage of youth committed into residential facilities by juvenile courts, are for the FBI's "violent index offenses." In many states, as many as half of the kids in confinement are youth committed for misdemeanors. Youth are more likely to be in these places for property offenses, violations of court orders, and low-level drug charges than they are for acts of interpersonal violence.[10] These data strongly suggest that the system's reliance on confinement is, as Mendel reports, unnecessary.

Juvenile confinement is even more questionable as a social policy priority when long-term outcomes are examined. Multiple recidivism studies reveal that youth discharged from corrections facilities are rarely rehabilitated or deterred from future criminal behavior.[11] For example, in states that measure recidivism three years after discharge, about three-quarters of formerly confined youth are rearrested for a new offense. Many studies indicate that incarceration is no more effective than probation or alternative sanctions when it comes to reducing future criminality; others suggest that correctional placements exacerbate criminality. Incarceration is especially ineffective for less serious offenders, whose risk of future criminal behavior may increase as a consequence of confinement in these facilities.

Besides being abusive, unnecessary, and ineffective, youth confinement is extraordinarily expensive to operate. According to the American Correctional Association, it costs, on average, $88,000 per year to incarcerate a single youth in a juvenile correctional facility. By comparison, a four-year public university costs less than $8,000 per year.[12] The high cost of confinement has important consequences: it distorts juvenile justice budgets so that the lion's share of public dollars is devoted to a relatively small percentage of the overall court caseload. Investments in delinquency prevention or early intervention programs, therefore, are effectively precluded because so many dollars are required to support the system's "deep end." This phenomenon is especially disturbing because we have learned so much over the past couple of decades about what works to combat juvenile crime. "Evidence-based programs," for example, have been rigorously tested and repeatedly shown to produce better long-term results than juvenile confinement does,[13] yet investments in these programs remain limited because public dollars continue to go predominantly for confinement.

What Is Going On?

Despite the fact that reductions in youth confinement have been nearly universal across the states, the national trend is essentially the sum of many varied parts rather than the consequence of a clearly articulated or widely embraced policy shift. This is understandable, given state and local responsibility for juvenile justice operations and the federal government's traditionally passive perspective about these systems' use of confinement. Though the various deinstitutionalization experiences indicate that these reductions in confinement share some common stimuli and strategies, the stories have been idiosyncratic, varying significantly from one state to the next.[14]

A number of states have moved to reduce confinement as a result of litigation over unconstitutional conditions of confinement or repulsion over scandals in youth corrections facilities. Texas, for example, responded to a 2006 sexual abuse scandal by enacting legislation limiting the types of offenses for which youth could be committed (while also appropriating funds to localities for local programming and supervision of the youth who could no longer be placed in state facilities). In California, revelations regarding conditions in the facilities moved the state legislature to limit committable offenses to the most serious violent crimes and, again, to provide state funding for local programs and services.

In other jurisdictions, fiscal concerns have been the primary stimulus for reductions in confinement. New York City, for example, made substantial investments in evidence-based programming several years ago to minimize the city's spending on state commitments, to achieve better youth outcomes, and to enhance public safety. When deep reductions in commitments did not produce the dollar savings anticipated (because the state charged ever-higher per diems as the population was reduced), Mayor Michael Bloomberg successfully championed a new "Close to Home" bill that authorizes New York City to operate its own continuum of services for most adjudicated youth and allocates a portion of the state's previous share of costs for the city's kids to help finance these new facilities and programs. Georgia recently enacted substantial modifications of its juvenile code, including limiting the types of offenses for which youth could be committed and modifying mandatory minimum provisions for certain offenses, in part to turn the curve regarding projected future costs of youth corrections. State officials anticipate that the recent legislative changes should save more than $85 million over the next five years by reducing youth correctional facility populations.

In yet other states, reductions in youth corrections populations appear to reflect more thoughtful and effective use of administrative discretion, primarily in the form of reductions in lengths of stay for committed youth. In Indiana, for example, juvenile corrections officials, heeding research showing that the impact of length of stay on future recidivism is minimal,[15] utilized their discharge authority to place youth in the least restrictive, community-based environments (on the basis of their individual needs and risk levels), thereby downsizing their overall incarcerated youth population.

Perhaps the strongest example of how greater administrative dexterity has contributed to reduced confinement is the collective experience of local sites participating in the Juvenile Detention Alternatives Initiative (JDAI). Though JDAI is primarily focused on safely reducing the population of youth confined in local detention facilities, its more than 200 sites report reductions in state commitments by the same percentage as they have reduced reliance on local detention (43 percent), powerfully demonstrating the influence that pretrial status has on dispositions.[16] The 112 JDAI sites that shared recent data on state commitments reported that they sent 5,254 fewer youth to state youth corrections facilities in 2011 than they did in the year preceding their participation in the detention reform initiative. These changes cannot be attributed purely to state-level policy shifts or crime trends: a recent JDAI evaluation found that JDAI counties reduced their commitments at rates considerably greater than nonparticipating counties in the same state.[17]

Other commentators, however, have cautioned against making exaggerated claims about how policy and practice reforms have reduced reliance on confinement, primarily pointing out that these reductions coincide with a unique period of decreases in juvenile crime.[18] There is no question that juvenile crime has decreased dramatically since approximately 1995, the same period during which juvenile confinement decreased. But as others have noted, this pattern has been the exception rather than the rule.[19]

Over the past four decades, since Richard Nixon declared a "war on crime," the relationship between crime and confinement has hardly been clear. Certainly, adult corrections populations do not show the same pattern as juvenile corrections: adult crime is also down considerably over the past 15 years, but adult corrections populations have only just begun to show very slight reductions. Claims that juvenile incarceration goes up and down as a function of the havoc kids are causing, therefore, attribute far more rationality to the system than it deserves. For example, this explanation does not clarify why local detention populations increased for several years after juvenile crime started to drop.[20] Similarly, the crime-drop hypothesis does not explain why adjacent counties or states often have radically different appetites for confinement despite similar crime patterns. And if crime trends are the primary driver of juvenile detention and incarceration, why is it that those patterns change so frequently when a new judge takes the bench, a new prosecutor is elected, or a particularly ugly crime is in the headlines? No significant analysis, moreover, has examined an obvious alternative hypothesis to explain the crime-confinement correlation: that juvenile crime is down, at least in part, because juvenile confinement is used less frequently.

Perhaps the biggest influence that juvenile crime reductions have on juvenile confinement is the ideological space that they provide to policy makers and practitioners. When crime is not the public's number-one concern, creative leaders and administrators can experiment with new policies, practices, and programs in ways not possible when pressure to be "tough on crime" is highest. Significant innovation is possible in this less polarized context, and initiatives such as JDAI can gain traction and spread. The emergence of Right on Crime, a conservative group advocating both juvenile and adult corrections reforms, is but one strong indication that the playing field has changed.[21]

In all likelihood, the deep reductions in juvenile confinement are a function of complex interactions among many factors: reduced juvenile crime rates, innovations in policy and practice, repulsion over abuse in facilities, and serious worries about the fiscal health of state and county governments. The absence of a conclusive analysis of "what is going on" should not, however, cloud the main point: juvenile confinement is way down, perhaps an early and unexpected harbinger that the era of mass incarceration may be ending.

Conclusion

The deep reductions in the juvenile justice system's reliance on confinement in recent years are a unique phenomenon in American correctional history, one obviously worthy of much deeper study and explanation than is possible in this brief chapter. As scholars and practitioners consider this important phenomenon, at least three key challenges need to be kept in mind.

First, despite the magnitude of the decreases described here, no one should imagine that the youth corrections system has now been "right sized." A careful examination of the CJRP data reveals, for example, that even after this extensive culling of the population of confined delinquents, only one quarter of youth in custody on a given day are locked up for a violent index offense, while nearly 40 percent are incarcerated for rather minor offenses (including technical probation violations and various misdemeanors; see figure 2.5). Put another way, a strong argument can still be made that we are confining many youth unnecessarily or inappropriately.

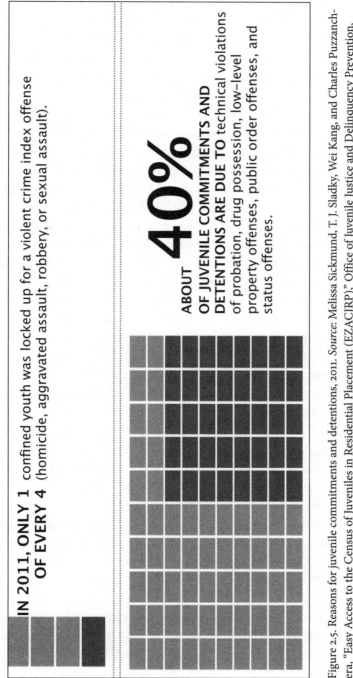

Figure 2.5. Reasons for juvenile commitments and detentions, 2011. *Source:* Melissa Sickmund, T. J. Sladky, Wei Kang, and Charles Puzzanchera, "Easy Access to the Census of Juveniles in Residential Placement (EZACJRP)," Office of Juvenile Justice and Delinquency Prevention, http://www.ojjdp.gov/ojstatbb/ezacjrp/ (accessed December 1, 2013).

Second, but intimately related to the continued presence of many relatively minor offenders in juvenile justice institutions, these systems are only at the early stages of reform. Few jurisdictions are anywhere near the finish line in introducing and perfecting all or most of the various policies, practices, and programs that, in proper alignment, should ensure that these reductions are deepened and sustained over the long term. Experience in various reform endeavors—JDAI being a notable example—indicates that significant initial progress in improving system outcomes is often attained simply by calling attention to problems (e.g., unnecessary detention), which inspires system personnel to reconsider and change the standards previously relied on in daily decision making. However, new attitudes alone are unlikely to yield lasting progress. Rather, concrete system improvements, such as objective screening tools to guide admissions decisions or weekly detention reviews to minimize lengths of stay, are required to embed those "reconsidered standards" in formal practices. In so doing, a permanent system infrastructure is constructed that can sustain often-fragile reform ambitions and ensure they survive leadership transitions and predictable challenges (such as an inevitable uptick in juvenile crime). What major policy and practice reforms are put in place, how broadly and how well they are implemented, and whether they are subjects of continuous improvement efforts are questions whose answers will determine whether reduced reliance on confinement will be sustained and deepened.

Finally, practitioners and policy makers must recognize that reductions in confinement provide a unique opportunity to refocus system reform efforts from "doing less harm" to "doing some good." This opportunity is likely to be missed, however, if it is not taken up intentionally and aggressively. As startling and heartening as the recent reductions in confinement are, they derive primarily from a growing recognition of the limited benefits of institutional confinement and its huge downsides regarding public safety, youth development, and cost to taxpayers. The factors that conspire to produce the United States' unique youth incarceration rate—broad system overreach; ineffective probation services; inadequate defense representation; structural racism and implicit bias; minimal family focus or engagement; and incomplete, inaccurate, and untimely data—all await important transformations if juvenile justice systems are to effectively focus their resources on improving youth well-being, including significant behavioral change that reduces recidivism.

Viewed from this perspective, the marked trend away from juvenile confinement is most properly seen as a critical first step and a call for further action, not a cause for contented satisfaction. But it is also a powerful signal that real system change could—I would argue should—begin with a genuine commitment to radically reduce confinement to no more than a fraction of its current use. One can only wonder what marvelous innovations we might see if the safety net of confinement were removed and juvenile justice practitioners were forced to respond to youthful offending much as they respond to their own children's transgressions.

NOTES

1 Neal Hazel, *Cross-National Comparison of Youth Justice* (London: Youth Justice Board, 2008).

2 Melissa Sickmund, T. J. Sladky, Wei Kang, and Charles Puzzanchera, "Easy Access to the Census of Juveniles in Residential Placement (EZACJRP)," Office of Juvenile Justice and Delinquency Prevention, http://www.ojjdp.gov/ojstatbb/ezacjrp/ (accessed December 1, 2013).

3 Sickmund et al. *supra* note 2. Longer-term residential facilities include those that the CJRP classifies as "long-term secure," "group homes," "ranch/wilderness camps," and "boot camps." On the date of the 2011 census, 57 percent of youth in these facilities had already been there for more than 90 days. In contrast, among those in shorter-term facilities ("detention centers," "shelters," and "reception/diagnostic centers"), only 14 percent had been there that long, and 53 percent had been there for 20 days or less.

4 Pew Charitable Trust, Public Safety Performance Project, "Latest Data Show Juvenile Confinement Continues Rapid Decline," August 28, 2013, http://archive.today/If258.

5 Richard A. Mendel, *No Place for Kids: The Case for Reducing Juvenile Incarceration* (Baltimore: Annie E. Casey Foundation, 2011), http://www.aecf.org/m/resourcedoc/aecf-NoPlaceForKidsFullReport-2011.pdf.

6 Ibid. at 5–9.

7 Holbrook Mohr, "AP: 13K Claims of Abuse in Juvenile Detention Since '04," *USA Today*, March 2, 2008.

8 Allen J. Beck, Paige M. Harrison, and Paul Guerino, *Sexual Victimization in Juvenile Facilities Reported by Youth, 2008–09* (Washington, DC: Bureau of Justice Statistics, January 2010).

9 Allen J. Beck, Marcus Berzofsky, Rachel Caspar, and Christopher Krebs, *Sexual Victimization in Prisons and Jails Reported by Inmates, 2011–12* (Washington, DC:

Bureau of Justice Statistics, May 2013), http://www.bjs.gov/content/pub/pdf/svpjri1112.pdf.

10 Mendel, *supra* note 6, at 13–15.

11 Ibid. at 9–12.

12 Ibid. at 19.

13 Ibid. at 16–19.

14 See, for instance, Sarah Breyer and Marc Levin, *The Comeback States: Reducing Youth Incarceration in the United States* (Washington, DC: National Juvenile Justice Network & Texas Public Policy Foundation, 2013); and Spike Bradford, *Common Ground: Lessons Learned from Five States That Reduced Juvenile Incarceration by More than Half* (Washington, DC: Justice Policy Institute, 2013).

15 Kristin Parsons Winokur, Alisa Smith, Stephanie R. Bontrager, and Julia L. Blankenship, "Juvenile Recidivism and Length of Stay," *Journal of Criminal Justice* 36, no. 2 (2008): 126–137; Thomas A. Loughran, Edward P. Mulvey, Carol A. Schubert, Jeffrey Fagan, Alex R. Piquero, and Sandra H. Losoya, "Estimating a Dose-Response Relationship between Length of Stay and Future Recidivism in Serious Juvenile Offenders," *Criminology* 47, no. 3 (2009): 699–740.

16 Annie E. Casey Foundation, *Juvenile Detention Alternatives Initiative: 2012 Annual Results Report* (Baltimore: Annie E. Case Foundation, 2013), http://www.aecf.org/m/resourcedoc/AECF-JDAI2012AnnualResultsReport-2013.pdf.

17 Chief Justice Earl Warren Institute of Law and Social Policy, *JDAI Sites and States: An Evaluation of the Juvenile Detention Alternatives Initiative: JDAI Sites Compared to Home State Totals* (Berkeley: Chief Justice Earl Warren Institute of Law and Social Policy, University of California–Berkeley School of Law, November 2012), https://www.law.berkeley.edu/files/JDAI_Rep_1_FINAL.pdf.

18 Jeffrey Butts, "Are We Too Quick to Claim Credit for Falling Juvenile Incarceration Rates?," Juvenile Justice Information Exchange, March 7, 2013, http://jjie.org/are-we-too-quick-to-claim-credit-for-falling-juvenile-incarceration-rates/.

19 Nate Balis and Tom Woods, "Reform Matters: A Reply to Jeffrey Butts," Juvenile Justice Information Exchange, March 17, 2013, http://jjie.org/reform-matters-a-reply-to-jeffrey-butts/.

20 Richard A. Mendel, "Juvenile Justice at a Crossroads," *AdvoCasey* (Annie E. Casey Foundation) 5, no. 1 (2003): 19–20.

21 Right on Crime is a project of the Center for Effective Justice at the Texas Public Policy Foundation, in partnership with the Justice Fellowship.

3

Starting from a Different Place

The Missouri Model

TIM DECKER

You lie awake in your metal bunk bed in a large, unfurnished, barracks-style room. You look around the unit and see 48 other inmates in their prison-issued orange jumpsuits, one part of a large secure facility serving 350. Multiple rules are posted on the wall, but few are actually followed. There are bars on the windows, and all the furniture is either steel or plastic and is bolted down to the concrete floor. Graffiti covers walls and furniture. You can't help but wonder how your life got out of hand so quickly. You haven't seen your family for months. They live 150 miles away.

You gently rub the bruised area around your eye and wonder when your rival will return from the special management unit, known by the inmates as either "isolation" or "lockdown." He has spent several days there, 23 hours a day in an individual cell with little or no access to school or activities. He has to be even angrier. The uniformed guards are across the way with extensive training in behavior management and control and with quick access to handcuffs, shackles, and mace just in case something starts. You cannot remember their names, but it really does not matter because everyone calls them "officer" or "sir." They call each other by names often heard in the military, such as sergeant and lieutenant. You've learned to follow their commands, just do your time until you are eligible for parole.

Does any of this sound familiar? The images are reflective of what the general public typically associates with traditional adult correctional facilities or prisons. The unfortunate reality is that this may also describe the experience of many youths in the juvenile correctional system, more generally described as the juvenile justice system.

The architects of a separate system of justice for youthful offenders embraced rehabilitation rather than punishment as its central mission. The juvenile justice system was intended to promote accountability, to prevent reoffending, and to treat youth fairly—each of which is best served by a rehabilitative orientation.[1] There have been important reforms in areas such as detention utilization, judicial processes, validated risk assessment, and alternatives to incarceration. Nevertheless, there are over 79,000 young people in residential placement[2] who are caught in an inescapable web of ineffective and harmful confinement programs. For these young people, the evolution of the juvenile system has not changed their experience in a significant way. This chapter is devoted to assisting policy makers, system leaders, families, and communities to fundamentally change the experience for young people and families, creating meaningful benefits for their communities as well.

The juvenile justice system was intended to provide a fundamentally different response to adolescent behavior than that of the adult correctional system. Medical research, practitioners' experience, developmental science, and repeated legal decisions have affirmed that adolescents are fundamentally different from adults. The lingering problem is that the juvenile justice system never fully separated from the adult system. It is a bad marriage that never ends. In many cases, the agencies still live in the same house (e.g., adult corrections agency) or have separated but taken with them tremendous baggage in the form of distorted assumptions, habits, or punitive and ill-informed practices. For example, youth corrections programs typically require young people to wear prison-style uniforms. What is the developmental value of an orange jumpsuit or one of any color? Some people may rationalize it as a security measure or a way of making sure no one has nicer clothes or that no one wears gang attire. Does anyone really believe this is the reason? Or is it really about submission, conformity, and control? This is clearly a demeaning and dehumanizing intervention that has no proven developmental value for the young person and likely decreases public safety in the long run. When this practice is combined with staff members wearing law-enforcement-style uniforms, systems are on the pathway to traditional adult corrections.

These practices persist because of beliefs, including stereotypes about the young people, their families, and their neighborhoods; entrenched organizational cultures; and a lack of organized political, professional, and public will for the courageous work of system transformation. To better understand what is involved, we have to look below the surface. Systems are like icebergs. The organizational structure and practices on the surface are kept afloat by the foundational issues under the surface. Implementing authentic system and culture change involves attending to what lies below the surface.

Culture is most broadly described as "how we do business around here." It is often rooted in expressed or unexpressed beliefs and assumptions. Think for a moment about what you might say to a friend or colleague about what it is really like to work for your organization or, better yet, how young people, families, and communities might experience your organization. This provides some hints about the culture of the organization, regardless of the espoused vision, mission, philosophy, or strategic plan.

As long as young people in the system are viewed as criminals or inmates, families as noncaring, and certain neighborhoods as hopeless, leaders may knowingly or unknowingly tolerate and accept unsafe conditions, punitive and oppressive approaches, and intolerable failure rates. We may even accept the costs of incarceration and other coercive or punitive measures because of perceptions that they enhance control and increase public safety, even though there is substantial evidence to the contrary.

The good news is that there is a better way. Take just a minute to imagine a different experience:

> It is morning and time to get up for breakfast, do chores, and get ready for school and the day's rigorous schedule. You step onto the floor of your group's home-like dormitory and move to your personal closet to pick out clothes for the day. There are just ten other young people in your group. The staff members wear normal clothes and are addressed by their first names. You call a "circle" to get the group's attention so you can talk about some feelings that kept you awake in the middle of the night. The group quickly assembles and is seated in the group's living room to listen and provide support. You suspect that your feelings are somehow connected to childhood experiences and concerns about your family. The group offers time in the daily group meeting that evening and assures you they will be there anytime you need to talk. You know they will support you

in a way that makes it possible to achieve the goals set by you and your family. The group is a safe place, and you know the staff care, almost as if you were their own child. Then you are off to school, where you will stay with your group while participating in challenging lessons and receiving individualized help. You never realized how intelligent you were. You now plan to go to college after receiving your diploma. You will work with your service coordinator, who has been working with you throughout, as you lead your own transition process with extensive involvement from your family and community. You reflect for a moment and remember that you're one of the lucky ones—you live in Missouri or one of the other jurisdictions implementing Missouri-style reforms.

The question for policy makers seeking to reform juvenile justice is a fundamental one—if your child were the next one to enter the system, which reality would you choose? It is a choice between a traditional correctional approach and a therapeutic and developmental approach grounded in adolescent developmental science. It is a choice between coercion, punishment, and harm, on one hand, and safety, growth, healing, and opportunity, on the other.

The very assumptions on which many youth correctional programs are based are counter to research and experience related to the cognitive, behavioral, and emotional development of adolescents. For that reason, the juvenile justice system needs to establish a firewall between itself and the adult correctional system, carefully filtering what gets through to make sure it is not a developmentally inappropriate, punitive, or harmful virus that will infect the system and render it ineffective. This is a constant struggle for even the best of systems. We must begin by being disciplined about language and referring to the system as "youth in custody" as opposed to "youth corrections."

Taking the next steps requires visionary leadership; organizational culture change; effective strategies, structures, and practices; deliberate constituency building to sustain the change; and a focus on continuous improvement and results. It also requires tackling many of the myths that preserve the current system, create entrenched resistance to change, and undermine progress. The following sections tackle these important issues and provide a framework for change using what has been implemented in the Missouri juvenile justice system. It is a vision for nationwide change grounded in an existing blueprint that works for young people and society.

I. Leadership and Culture Change

The single most important achievement of Missouri's Division of Youth Services (DYS) is the development of a system and culture that will endure, achieving exemplary results for years to come. The Missouri approach is more than a program model. While structural changes such as least restrictive environments, small programs close to home, and family-like groups have been vehicles for change, the organizational culture has clearly fueled the change. The culture is like a healthy tree that has roots that run deep and wide. You can see it in the faces of young people.

A common myth expressed by visitors to DYS programs is that somehow the young people in Missouri must be different. They are respectful, friendly, hopeful, articulate, and resourceful. They do not look like inmates. Those observers who have trouble reconciling the difference may point to one or two statistics or stereotypes about young people as a way of saying that the approach will not work in their jurisdiction. My colleagues and I at DYS often respond by noting that over 66% of the young people in the system are felony offenders, 65% are 16 or older, 34% have an educational disability, 49% have documented mental health conditions, and even more have experienced substance use or abuse. There is another myth that "all the tough ones are transferred into the adult system." This is simply not supported by the facts. During calendar year 2012, there were 55 young people certified (waived) to adult courts in Missouri, and several were returned to our dual-jurisdiction program. In Missouri, there are no direct waiver provisions or prosecutorial discretion for juveniles. All cases in which certification is considered are decided by a family court judge. Missouri's Adult Correctional Unit for young people under age 17 is often without any residents. Many states have far more young people waived to adult court than Missouri does.

At the end of the day, we are all serving a very challenging population. These youths are involved in problematic and harmful behavior in their families, schools, or communities, and that needs to stop. The question is how to go about helping them.

There is an old expression that says that "whatever you focus on grows," and that is certainly true in this instance. We are hopeful about the potential of our young people, and others should be too. Those who have trouble accepting this optimism would be better served by addressing the system's built-in contempt for young people and belief systems and stereotypes that sell them short and limit their potential.

Changing systems involves much more than practice changes. Sometimes to change your destination, you have to "start from a different place." The process of moving forward and improving conditions and results involves a simple-to-understand and difficult-to-implement formula:

Culture Change × Proven Practices × Quality = Results

This different place is grounded in a set of beliefs and philosophical frameworks. Attending to organizational culture involves moving beyond assumptions and creating shared beliefs about the young people and families, the nature of the work and purpose of the organization, and the people who need to be involved in the process.

A common approach to poor outcomes and inadequate or harmful practices in traditional juvenile corrections is to implement program improvement processes grounded in adult correctional theory, as well as to adopt new program models or practices that may address some symptoms while ignoring other factors leading to healthy adolescent development. The limitation of this approach is that it often amounts to a simple "rebooting" of the existing system. As with a home computer or laptop, when you reboot the system, you end up back at the same place. The system may simply become better at implementing an outdated program. The youth-in-custody system needs more than a simple rebooting. It needs culture change and an operating platform that is trauma informed, developmental, and therapeutic.

Missouri DYS closed its largest two training schools in 1981 and 1983 after working throughout the 1970s to establish an array of group homes and small community-based treatment facilities that paralleled similar reform efforts in Massachusetts led by youth services director Jerome Miller. While these were important steps in Missouri's new direction, what followed was the development of fundamentally different core beliefs that were to guide and sustain system changes for years to come. Imagine for a moment a system whose foundation is rooted in the following belief statements:

Safety and structure are the foundation of treatment. Meeting basic needs and providing physical and emotional safety is the foundation of treatment. Young people need to know that people care enough about them to expect them to succeed. This is demonstrated by our ability to provide safety and structure.

Each person is special and unique. Through the process of individualized services and supports, young people recognize the value and strengths of self and others and are challenged and inspired to reach their full potential.

People can change. Even though change is often difficult and naturally leads to resistance and fear, people more readily embrace change when included in the process. Young people need to be guided and supported to try new behaviors, practice those behaviors, succeed, and learn from their mistakes as they internalize positive changes.

People desire to do well and succeed. All young people need approval, acceptance, and the opportunity to contribute. Programs and services must be structured in a manner that builds on these universal needs.

Emotions are not to be judged. Feelings are not right or wrong. Personal disclosure and reconciliation of life experiences are important for healing and personal growth. As a part of the treatment process, young people explore behaviors, thoughts, and emotions.

All behavior has a purpose and is often a symptom of unmet needs. Challenging behavior is often symptomatic of core issues or patterns. Services are designed to help address these needs and assist young people in investigating and understanding their history, their behavior, and healthy alternatives and facilitating internalized change.

People do the best they can with the resources available to them. Young people often have limited resources, and a lack of knowledge and awareness of behavioral and emotional options. In the situations they have experienced, their behavior may have seemed logical and understandable.

The family is vital to the treatment process. Families want the best for their children. Family expertise and participation is essential in the treatment process and has the potential to impact the entire family in a positive way.

True understanding is built on genuine empathy and care. Respect and appreciation for the inherent worth and dignity of self and others forms the foundation of safety, trust, and openness necessary for change to occur. Demonstrating respect and appreciation for the worth of young people and families is essential.

We are more alike than different. Everyone has fears, insecurities, and basic needs including safety, attention, and belonging. Normalizing and attending to these needs assists young people in meeting their needs in positive and productive ways.

Change does not occur in isolation. Young people need others. Treatment is structured to assist young people in experiencing success through helping others and being helped. Accessing community resources enables young people to develop healthy supportive relationships with peers, adults, family, and their neighborhoods and communities.

We are a combination of our past and present. Young people have learned through a wide variety of experiences. Self-discovery and linking past and present experiences creates knowledge, skills, and emotional capacity to succeed in the home and community.

Respect and embrace diversity. Services, supports, and interactions demonstrate respect for and build on the values, preferences, beliefs, culture, and identity of the young person, their family, and their community. Diversity in expression, opinion, and preference is embraced.

A productive and consistent belief system leads to a more ambitious vision and a fundamentally different philosophical approach. If we view young people as a product of their past experiences, as a work in progress, and as a potential resource to others, we are compelled to weave together a safe and humane system that supports personal development and change, and to continuously work to make it better.

On the basis of these belief statements, a very ambitious vision evolved in the Missouri system: "Every young person served by Missouri DYS will become a productive citizen and lead a fulfilling life." While preventing reoffending is central to the vision, achieving it involves preparing young people with the skills, experiences, and supports for a productive and fulfilling life. Jurisdictions interested in transformative culture change could begin with a deliberate set of beliefs and a compelling vision that leaders, staff, partners, and young people and families can relate to and get excited about.

Moving from a traditional correctional approach to treatment, rehabilitative, and developmental approaches involves profound philosophical and structural differences. The differences are illustrated in the strategic priorities of the organization, the structure, and the language, as illustrated in table 3.1.

Table 3.1

Traditional/correctional	Rehabilitative/developmental
• External controls	• Systemic approach—safety building blocks
• Overuse of lockup, large geographically isolated programs	• Continuum of services, small programs close to home
• Punishment and coercion	• Rehabilitation and growth
• Positional power, autocratic, devalued relationships	• Healthy hierarchy, boundaries, relationships
• Inmates, residents, prisoners	• Young people
• Majors, lieutenants, sergeants	• Leaders, managers, directors
• Correctional officers, security workers, parole officers	• Youth workers, counselors, service coordinators
• Family/community as problem	• Family/community as partners
• Regimentation and rules	• Positive structure and order
• Custodial supervision	• Engaged interaction
• Focus on survival needs	• Deliberate group process and social-emotional competence
• Behavioral compliance and fear	• Internalized change and self-motivation

Traditional correctional approaches grounded in punishment and control cause further harm and negatively impact results. They are often based in fear and shame, creating a survival mentality for staff and young people. Feelings are typically ignored, and the vulnerability that is so important to an internalized change process is viewed as a weakness. The potentially harmful impact of institutions cannot be effectively dealt with in isolation.

Supporting authentic culture change and moving away from traditional adult correctional approaches provides the opportunity to create a system driven by a fundamentally different philosophy. The following sections explore basic principles and a recommended framework for reform of the youth-in-custody system.

II. Basic Principles

Least Restrictive Environment

The least restrictive environment, and one close to home, should be provided to all young people. The movement of a young person from home to a more restrictive setting should only be considered after a diligent, inclusive, and thorough decision-making process, balanced by objective risk assessment and administrative checks and balances.

Geographically isolated training schools, youth prisons, and boot camps isolate and institutionalize young people. These archaic and ineffective approaches have no place in the future landscape of juvenile justice. Combined over the past four decades, 57 lawsuits in 33 states plus the District of Columbia and Puerto Rico have resulted in a court-sanctioned remedy in response to alleged abuse or otherwise unconstitutional conditions in juvenile facilities.[3] These actions have often been in response to unsafe conditions, excessive use of isolation or restraint, or lack of basic services in areas such as health, mental health, and education. Large institutions utilizing traditional adult correctional approaches with young people is a recipe for further harm, failure, and increased risks to the general public.

Humane Environment

A key priority of youth-in-custody programs must be to maintain public safety while creating physical and emotional safety for the young people. There is a powerful myth that undermines change and better results for youth in custody. The myth is that law-enforcement-style uniforms for staff, prison-like jumpsuits, bars covering everything in sight, handcuffs, shackles, and other coercive forms of control increase safety for staff and young people. Nothing could be further from the truth.

While it may seem counterintuitive, small programs with a more natural, home-like environment and a therapeutic focus are far safer than are those that operate on a more traditional correctional platform with extensive hardware, security staff, and practices such as mechanical restraints and isolation.

Comparing youth-in-custody programs serving similar youth, staff in programs with a correctional approach are 13 times more likely and youth in these programs are 4.5 times more likely to be assaulted with injury than are those in programs utilizing a therapeutic approach.[4] When you broaden the lens to include sexual victimization, the rates grow exponentially as the size of the facility grows; ranging from 1.3% for facilities with 1–9 youths to 10.2% for facilities with over 100 youths. In addition, when compared to states across the country, 5 of the 14 sites determined to have a low rate of sexual victimization were in Missouri.[5] Humane environments also have important implications for public safety. Programs with a control philosophy actually increase recidivism rates, while those with a therapeutic philosophy reduce them.[6]

As Missouri DYS moved forward facilitating a humane, rehabilitative, and developmental culture in the organization and programs, core practices and tools were developed to support leadership and staff in building and maintaining safe programs.

Many aspects of traditional institutional and correctional practices in juvenile justice include punitive and coercive approaches that devalue young people and create fertile ground for safety issues and maltreatment. Security is very important; however, many staff in custody programs mistake security for safety. Even with the best security tools and high-tech equipment, young people are still not protected from harm, and public safety may be compromised. Safety and security are enhanced by creating a humane culture of care. This ultimately keeps young people safe—not hardware, fences, or cameras.

One of the ways staff understand the basics of an environment free from harm is the Missouri DYS *safety building blocks*. While Missouri has traditionally operated very safe programs, this process has allowed the system to eliminate the use of isolation or separation and mechanical restraints at all levels of residential care. During the last full reporting period (July 2012–June 2013), these interventions were *never* used across 32 residential programs serving an average daily population of over 740 young people.

The safety building blocks focus on five areas: basic expectations, basic needs, engaged supervision, clear boundaries and communication, and unconditional positive regard. Organizations that tap into the inherent dignity of all within the system will experience a workforce that does not tolerate hurtful behaviors. From day one, young people are to be treated with respect and dignity regardless of their situation.

The safety building blocks create safety in a natural and humane manner. When young people have clear and reasonable expectations, they can be held accountable without being judged, berated, or abused. Operating with unconditional positive regard for young people and families provides the opportunity to see beyond problematic behavior and address the core issues that brought them into the system.

Many young people in the youth-in-custody system have not consistently had their basic needs met for food, clothing, and shelter due to abuse, neglect, poverty, and other factors. If programs do not assist young people in meeting basics needs in healthy ways, it can lead to bartering, hoarding, misuse of power by youth and staff, and a harmful environment. Teaching young people self-care and providing an opportunity for them to belong to a group in a positive way builds self-image and relationship skills, enhancing their ability to navigate potentially detrimental situations.

Abusive behavior thrives on isolation and chaos. DYS experienced a decrease in all critical incidents when staff-to-student ratios were increased to 1:6 and a policy of engaged, eyes-on awareness supervision was implemented. In all programs, staff are required to see all youth at all times, except during hygiene, and even then, staff are strategically placed and aware. Staff members are expected to be involved in all group activities, not just to stand by or patrol the sidelines.

Young people require highly structured daily programming designed to meet their treatment and educational needs. By keeping youth productively engaged and structuring the involvement of staff members, opportunities for unproductive or harmful interactions are decreased.

Trauma-informed conditions and physical and emotional safety create the opportunity for young people's self-expression and discovery, healing, empathy, conscious choice, natural logical consequences, hope, accountability, and corrective experiences.

Group Treatment Approach

Group counseling has the greatest potential to reduce rates of reoffending.[7] A group approach should be the primary method for providing treatment services because it offers the opportunity for peer support, experiential learning, and development of social-emotional competency.

Missouri closed its large training schools in 1981 and 1983 in favor of a continuum of small programs located around the state. The continuum begins with community-based programs, which are operated by the courts and effectively divert three out of every four youthful offenders who commit an offense that may otherwise lead to commitment to custody. For those not successfully diverted, DYS operates a continuum of 32 small residential treatment programs and ten-day treatment centers, the largest single program having 50 beds.

Small programs are important; however, they are just part of the story. Young people are not separated by offenses but rather are assigned to the least restrictive environment on the basis of objective risk and needs assessment, as well as input from the court and the young person's family. Of Missouri's 710 allocated residential beds, only 190 are maintained as hardware-secure environments, with an external fence but absolutely no individual cells. Young people wear regular clothes, and regardless of the level of care, programs are furnished as home-like environments with regular furniture, drapes, decorative walls, and even pets.

Regardless of the size of the program, all young people are assigned to a small group of 10–12, with stable and consistent staff teams. Relationships matter and are a primary change agent. Bill Milliken, founder of a national organization for at-risk youth, is credited with regularly reminding people that "it's relationships, not programs, that change children."[8] The effectiveness of programs is directly impacted by the quality of relationships and the extent to which they support young people in establishing healthy and productive relationships.

Front-line staff members do not see their role as a security guard providing "custodial supervision" until a clinician arrives to provide counseling or pharmacological therapy. They are with the young people more than anyone else and are primary facilitators of the change process. Young people in custody settings need far more services than a twice-a-week therapy session. Effective residential care provides opportunity for an intensive 24/7 treatment process with qualified staff and a supportive peer-group process.

Young people need the developmental opportunity provided by a small group. Being a productive and contributing member of society involves successfully navigating and receiving support from groups— whether a family, a work team, a school environment, or a community setting. Young people in groups have the opportunity to give and receive support through strong reciprocal relationships with group members. They experience trust and reassurance as they tackle core issues, are provided opportunities for leadership, and develop social-emotional competence.

Dr. Daniel Goleman, best-selling author of books on emotional intelligence and social intelligence, describes the Missouri DYS youth experience this way:

> Half a dozen times a day the members form into a circle to check in with each other to say how they feel. . . . They meet for activities that are designed to enhance camaraderie and cooperation, foster empathy and accurate perceptions of each other, and build communication skills and trust. All of that constructs a secure base and provides them with the social abilities they so desperately need.[9]

Goleman is describing the "circle-up" process and group-building activities that are part of the fabric of daily life in a Missouri DYS treatment facility. In addition to 60- to 90-minute daily group meetings that include family genograms and other self-exploration opportunities, young people and staff are able to call a circle at any point during the day. Once they do, everyone stops what he or she is doing and comes to the circle. Circles are used to share feelings, to ask for help or support from the group, to make group decisions, to better understand expectations, to set boundaries, and to work through conflicts in a healthy and productive way. These trauma-informed and developmentally appropriate opportunities are created by the small-group process and the significant training and development of front-line staff.

Developmental Approach

Individual treatment planning is essential to the identification and delivery of services and supports for young people and families. It is based on their strengths, needs, core issues, best practice strategies, and developmental supports and opportunities. A young person's release from residential care and eventual discharge from aftercare in the community is optimally connected in some way to his or her progress in reducing risk and increasing protective factors. Every young person is different, and it is difficult to fit individuals into a "program box." We must make the program fit the young person and family, not the other way around.

This goal requires a combination of objective assessment instruments and deliberate processes that engage the young person, family, and community. This goes far beyond aftercare or parole conditions that force compliance and provide a mechanism for violating the young person's community status and pulling him or her deeper into the custody system. The "Pathways to Desistance" study has shown that young people who receive community supervision and are involved in community-based services are more likely to attend school, to go to work, and to avoid further offending.[10]

Through a partnership with the Full Frame Initiative,[11] Missouri is placing increased emphasis on conditions of well-being typically associated with healthy young people, families, and communities. We often ask ourselves the question of "what will be there for the young person and family once we are out the picture." We cannot simply be a quality service provider that leaves young people unprepared to navigate the transition to adulthood.

Breaking intergenerational cycles of poverty, violence, and trauma requires simultaneously supporting progress in five domains—at the individual, family, and community levels.[12] The five domains provide a universal framework for planning and action that is transformative and aligned with our core beliefs and vision:

Social connections: a sufficient number and diversity of relationships that allow every person to give and receive information, emotional support, and material aid; to create a sense of belonging and value; and to foster growth.

Safety: the ability of a person to be his or her authentic self and not to be at heightened risk of physical or emotional harm. For the youth-in-custody system, this involves preventing harm to the community, as well as to the young person.

Stability: the ability to expect one's situation and status to be fundamentally the same from one day to the next, so that there is adequate predictability and small obstacles do not set off cascading problems. This relates closely to familiar concepts such as resiliency, permanency, and certainty.

Mastery: feeling in control of one's fate and decisions and experiencing some correlation between efforts and outcomes. This may involve developing and accessing skills and knowledge and building confidence.

Meaningful access to relevant mainstream resources: the ability to meet needs in ways that are not onerous and are not degrading or dangerous. Ultimately, young people and families can develop the capacity to be their own case manager.

While these concepts may seem like a stretch for youth-in-custody systems, a vision for the future should certainly include ambitious transition frameworks that are grounded in proven risk-reduction strategies, child and family well-being, and positive youth development.

Continuity of Services and Relationships

Given the importance of relationships and the multisystemic nature of the work, planning and coordination of services is of utmost importance. Young people in the system have experienced little predictability or stability from those who are working on their behalf. They have been frequently handed off between agencies and case workers. It is not uncommon for a young person to have a probation officer or institutional case manager but then be handed off during reentry to a parole officer who does not even know the young person or his or her family. This is wasteful and ineffective.

In Missouri, a single service coordinator works with the young person and family throughout the entire process. This includes implementing risk, asset, and needs assessment within days of court commitment, coordinating a team approach to treatment planning, building relationships and strengthening the family while the young person is in residential care, and coordinating transition back to the community. The service coordinator serves as the primary advocate for the young person and family and plans for transition (reentry) beginning on day one.

Comprehensive and Integrated Approach to Treatment and Education

Organizational culture and structural changes provide a foundation for system reform and must be combined with effective practice models. As the evidence-based practice movement evolves, it is important to note that research regarding youth-in-custody settings is limited, and often facilities lack any consistent therapeutic model. We certainly know a great deal about what does not work, as well as having experience with practices that are clearly promising.

Punitive practices are unquestionably the most common and least effective. These practices are based on the belief that behavior change will occur as a result of punishing the young person's misbehavior. Interventions have only an arbitrary connection to the behavior and are not logical, natural, or therapeutic. The approach implies superiority and control in the adult and inferiority in the young person. At best, the intervention coerces superficial submission. Long-term, sustained punitive approaches have an oppressive quality that increases tension, anger, hostility, resentment, and the occurrence of acting-out behaviors.

A close cousin of the punitive approach is the wide array of behavior modification programs. This usually involves rewards or punishments to reduce or eliminate problematic behavior, often involving a point system or behavioral checklist. Behavioral modification can be a tool for reinforcing positive behaviors; however, the approach is counterproductive to sustainable change. It may lead to getting stuck on symptoms, chasing behaviors, and not focusing on core issues and skills necessary to prevent reoffending. The focus is on external reward, instead of internalized change. Young people and staff can spend enormous amounts of time and energy counting points, missing opportunities for personal growth. There is also a tendency for the point system to devolve into a punitive system of behavioral control, instead of behavior change.

Punitive approaches also create a self-reinforcing negative control loop. When punitive approaches are used, an "us against them" mental-

ity develops, hostility grows, and acting out increases. This cycle fur-
thers negative perceptions and lowers expectations for the young people,
creating a rationale for further restrictions and punitive measures. Often
the important activities such as the ability to attend school, to learn social skills, and to visit with family members are the first things to go.
These interventions promote hopelessness and ultimately lead staff to
conclude that humane, therapeutic, and developmental approaches will
not work for the "type of youth" they serve.

Cognitive approaches are an important part of the mix because they
focus on recognizing unhelpful or destructive patterns of thinking and
modifying them with more realistic or helpful ones, thereby impacting
behavior. The challenge is that these approaches often ignore the emotional or systemic aspects of behavior. While our thoughts can cause us
to feel or behave in a certain way, they are certainly not the only factor
impacting our feelings or decisions. Trauma-impacted young people
and adults may feel a certain way and not even know why, because their
emotions are connected to past experiences.

The trauma-informed care movement has appropriately challenged
systems to better understand the impact of trauma and to take a
systemic approach to program planning, beginning with concept of
"do no harm." Young people in custody settings are often retrauma-
tized by many aspects of their system experience. The movement to
therapeutic environments and developmental approaches is an important step in the right direction, along with ensuring physical and
emotional safety. Once safety is ensured, many young people will
need trauma-specific treatment as part of their array of services and
supports.

The youth-in-custody system ideally focuses on preventing young
people from progressing to the doorstep of residential care and then
providing a comprehensive response for those who do. This focus is
consistent with research on increasing effectiveness of juvenile justice
programs through focusing the most effective and costly programs on
high-risk young people, accessing multiple coordinated services, ensuring a therapeutic philosophy, involving families, and providing a sufficient amount of service.[13]

Missouri encourages a "Fully Integrated Treatment Approach" focused on creating the following program characteristics:

1. Individualized treatment planning based on asset, risk, and needs assessment
2. Youth and family development including healthy peer-to-peer and adult-child relationships, self-awareness and insight, skill development, resolution of core issues, behavioral change, family and community connections, and natural support networks
3. Individualized and integrated educational approach through a "therapeutic one-room schoolhouse"
4. Predictable daily group meetings providing sacred time, emotional safety, trauma work, self-acceptance, and accountability
5. Ongoing treatment activities and trauma-informed group "circles" to build group cohesion, to resolve conflicts, and to build social-emotional competence
6. Regular engagement with family and community providing opportunities to strengthen social connections, to build empathy, and to support prosocial activities
7. Leadership and youth development opportunities within both the group and the community

As the comprehensiveness of the approach grows, the impact is magnified. This is where another common myth emerges—the belief that therapeutic programs are "soft on crime." Just because a program is not oppressive or harmful does not mean it is not difficult. The Fully Integrated Treatment Approach is far more rigorous than just doing time, and it achieves exemplary results.

Two-thirds of the young people discharged from Missouri DYS remained "law-abiding" after three years. This performance has remained consistent over the past five years, ranging from 66% to 68%. Missouri defines "law-abiding" as young people who did not recidivate to DYS or become involved in the adult correctional system through either parole or incarceration. Perhaps even more striking is that only 8.3% are reincarcerated within three years.[14] These measures are even more impressive given that the time period does not begin until after all residential and aftercare services are complete. In contrast, many systems measure for shorter time periods and often while aftercare or probation services remain in place, reinforcing short-term compliance rather than long-term outcomes.

Education in youth-in-custody settings must be guided by three Rs. While the traditional understanding of "three Rs" as reading, writing, and arithmetic is important, three Rs in custody settings means responsibility, resources, and results. Young people are often disenfranchised from traditional education settings, requiring a thoughtful and innovative response to their educational needs.

Responsibility involves a "do what it takes" philosophy anchored by an understanding that all young people are capable of learning and succeeding in a career of their choosing. This involves individual learning plans for all students and nontraditional learning strategies.

Youth-in-custody systems need to align education with other strategies. Missouri DYS found it necessary to establish itself as an accredited school district. Relying on public education settings or local school districts to provide education programming in youth-in-custody settings usually makes it very difficult to integrate treatment and education.

Resources involves creating policies that ensure educational resources follow the student, providing custody settings with access to state, local, and federal funding streams associated with daily school attendance, Title I, and special education. This provides quality teachers, access to appropriate learning materials and technology, support for special needs, and professional development to continually increase the quality of education.

Results involves prioritizing education completion, data-driven decisions, identifying individual learning styles and educational needs, finding what works, and being adamant about the importance of educational success.

Implementing the three Rs in Missouri has led to the establishment of an education approach in which 43% of 16- to 21-year-olds earn a GED or high school diploma, compared to 15% nationally, and 99% of students improve in math and reading, compared to 73% nationally.[15] The approach involves the treatment group remaining together for school, a teacher and youth specialist working side by side to help the student, a supportive group culture, and a variety of instructional strategies and pathways to completion.

Family Voice, Choice, and Engagement

Young people and family members who have a long-term relationship with them have a unique stake in the process and its outcomes. The likelihood of successful outcomes and family involvement is increased when the process reflects family members' priorities and perspectives.

Youth-in-custody systems must address underlying assumptions that undermine productive partnerships with families and develop robust structures and training designed to increase family partnerships. The "families as experts" approach acknowledges that professionals do not know or have the same long-standing commitment to a young person as a caring and supportive family member does. As explored earlier, systems should strive for continuity in the staff working with families so that a genuine partnership can develop. Visiting at a time and place that is comfortable for the family is important, as are flexible visitation policies and transportation to create regular and meaningful family contact.

Staff should be trained in family systems and provided the skills necessary to support the family hierarchy and to communicate with families in a deliberate and respectful manner. Families should be offered family counseling and other proven family-strengthening interventions, as well as access to wraparound services that will stabilize the family situation and improve chances of success. In Missouri DYS, both parents and students earn GEDs and participate in annual graduation ceremonies. Family members also serve on local advisory boards and participate as partners in the system-improvement process.

Community Engagement

Communities are important partners for youth-in-custody systems. A two-way value-added relationship with the community provides the opportunity for reciprocal relationships with young people and provides broader support to families through natural helping networks. Community members have the opportunity to develop accurate perceptions of the young people and to view them as a resource in the community, and they provide meaningful support and opportunities for positive youth development. The transition of young people is enhanced by these meaningful relationships, supports, and opportunities.

Missouri maintains a Statewide Advisory Board and Community Liaison Councils at all program sites. These groups play a pivotal role in connecting policy makers and communities with young people in a positive way and providing natural support networks for young people as they leave the system. Community Liaison Councils keep communities informed and build local support for the programs. Members participate in fundraising for college scholarships and other forms of support, lead youth development classes for young people, and act as compassionate mentors for young people who are disconnected from community.

Responsive, Localized, and Collaborative

Collaboration across systems and the development of collaborative leadership skills within communities are the most effective ways to magnify the impact of public resources. Systems are generally more responsive and collaborative when young people are close to home and when decision making is decentralized and focused on building ownership and accountability from leaders, staff, families, and communities. Local knowledge and relationships lead to increased access to resources and strengthening of communities through local problem solving.

Conclusion

Reforming youth-in-custody systems involves visionary leaders, culture change, and proven practice frameworks. It will take a systemic perspective, beyond what best practice models provide. Young people, families, and communities need to be the central focus, and we need to build on strengths. It will involve quality practitioners who are engaged and valued, strong partnerships, and increased accountability. Most of all, it will take "hard heads and soft hearts,"[16] combining determination to find what works and enough compassion to remember why it matters.

NOTES

1 National Research Council, *Reforming Juvenile Justice: A Developmental Approach*, Committee on Assessing Juvenile Justice Reform, Richard J. Bonnie, Robert L. Johnson, Betty M. Chemers, and Julie A. Schuck, eds., Committee on Law and Justice, Division of Behavioral and Social Sciences and Education (Washington, DC: National Academies Press, 2013).

2 Office of Juvenile Justice and Delinquency Prevention (OJJDP), *Juveniles in Residential Treatment, 2010*, Juvenile Offenders and Victims: National Report Series Bulletin (Washington, DC: U.S. Census Bureau, June 2013).

3 Richard A. Mendel, *No Place for Kids: The Case for Reducing Juvenile Incarceration* (Baltimore: Annie E. Casey Foundation, 2011), http://www.aecf.org/m/resourcedoc/aecf-NoPlaceForKidsFullReport-2011.pdf.

4 Richard A. Mendel, *The Missouri Model: Reinventing the Practice of Rehabilitating Youthful Offenders* (Baltimore: Annie E. Casey Foundation, 2010).

5 Bureau of Justice Statistics, *Sexual Victimization in Juvenile Facilities Reported by Youth, 2012* (Washington, DC: U.S. Department of Justice, 2013).

6 Mark W. Lipsey, James C. Howell, Marion R. Kelly, Gabrielle Chapman, and Darin Carver, *Improving the Effectiveness of Juvenile Justice Programs* (Washington, DC: Center for Juvenile Justice Reform, 2010).

7 Ibid.

8 Communities in Schools, "About Us," http://www.communitiesinschools.org/about/.

9 Daniel Goleman, *Social Intelligence: The New Science of Human Relationships* (New York: Bantam Dell, 2006), 285–287.

10 He Len Chung, Carol A. Schubert, and Edward P. Mulvey, "An Empirical Portrait of Community Reentry among Serious Juvenile Offenders in Two Metropolitan Cities," *Criminal Justice and Behavior* 34 (2007): 1402–1426.

11 Katya Fels Smyth, *The Full Frame Initiative: The Five Domains of Wellbeing* (Greenfield, MA: Full Frame Initiative, 2013).

12 Ibid.

13 Lipsey et al., *supra* note 6.

14 Missouri Department of Social Services, *Division of Youth Services, Annual Report, Fiscal Year 2013* (Jefferson City: Missouri Department of Social Services, 2013).

15 Liann Seiter and Dorothy Seidel, *Students in Title I, Part D, Neglect Programs* (Washington, DC: National Evaluation and Technical Assistance Center for Children and Youth Who Are Neglected, Delinquent, or At-Risk [NDTAC], 2013).

16 Julie Boatright-Wilson, Harvard Kennedy School, Ash Center for Democratic Governance and Innovation, comment about DYS staff during 2008 "Innovations in American Government" site visit.

4

Doing Things Differently

Education as a Vehicle for Youth Transformation and Finland as a Model for Juvenile Justice Reform

PETER E. LEONE

Introduction

Compared to the rest of the industrialized world, justice policies and practices in the United States are abysmal. While some variability exists in juvenile justice practices and policies across the states, the District of Columbia, and Puerto Rico, in general our system of juvenile justice is punitive, ineffective, and expensive.[1] The devolution of the United States from being a world leader in juvenile justice policy and practice to its current status as a nation that locks up a disproportionate number of its youth engaged in delinquent behavior, especially minority youth and youth with disabling conditions, did not happen overnight. The past 40 years have seen a steady degradation of both juvenile and criminal justice policies in the U.S.

This chapter begins with a brief examination of the state of juvenile justice in the U.S., including the cost and ineffectiveness of current practices. I then review the nexus between school failure, suspension, and juvenile justice involvement, arguing that school failure and suspension increase youths' vulnerability to delinquency. Education, to the contrary, is critical to rehabilitation and crime prevention. Finally, I explore Finland's experience in transforming its system of juvenile and criminal justice since the 1960s from one that resembled the Soviet and now Russian systems to one that resembles its Nordic neighbor states.

I make two broad and basic assertions about juvenile justice reform. First, education, a vehicle for youth transformation and empowerment, has been largely neglected for youth most vulnerable to juvenile justice system involvement. Too often these youth are marginalized by schools through frequent suspension that disconnects youth from school and leads to dropout. For those youth who become involved in the juvenile justice system, the education services they receive while incarcerated are substantially inferior to those available to other youth. Second, although juvenile justice reform presents considerable challenges to current ways of thinking about and responding to crime and delinquency, Finland provides an excellent example of system transformation. During the past half century, the Finns have transformed their juvenile and criminal justice system from a punitive, expensive, and ineffective one to one that produces better outcomes at less cost without sacrificing public safety.[2]

The Failure of Current Juvenile Justice Practices in the U.S.

With a juvenile incarceration rate of over 300 per 100,000 youth, the U.S. leads the world in the rate at which we detain and imprison our youth.[3] One of the most recent reports on the status of juvenile justice practices, the Annie E. Casey Foundation's report *No Place for Children*, chronicles much of what is wrong with the current system.[4] Among other things, our system of juvenile justice with its heavy reliance on incarceration does not contribute to public safety, is expensive and ineffective, and exposes youth to violence and conditions that increase the likelihood of youth persisting in delinquent and criminal behavior.[5] Further, the system has a disparate impact on youth of color and youth with disabling conditions.[6] In recent years, the rate of juvenile incarceration has declined in many states[7] but continues to be much higher than in the rest of the world.

The association between juvenile crime, arrests, and incarceration rates is decidedly mixed. For example, data show that in California lower rates of juvenile incarceration coincided with lower juvenile crime rates.[8] In contrast, in Texas from the mid-1990s to 2006, increasing rates of juvenile incarceration were also accompanied by lower crime rates.[9] In spite of policies that discourage or prohibit confinement of youth for status offenses, this practice continues to contribute to the rate of juvenile incarceration.[10]

Estimates of the cost of juvenile incarceration vary widely. The American Correctional Association estimates that, on average, it costs states

$240.99 per day or about $88,000 a year for every youth in a juvenile correctional facility.[11] In New York, the Office of Child and Family Services (OCFS) estimated that it cost up to $266,000 annually to incarcerate one juvenile in a state institution in New York.[12] The Virginia Department of Juvenile Justice reported that its expenditures for incarcerated youth for fiscal year 2012 were more than $85,000 per youth.[13] Missouri has estimated that it spends between $65,000 and $84,000 per youth for a year of incarceration, depending on the security level of the youth.[14]

High rates of rearrest and reoffending suggest that juvenile incarceration is largely ineffective in decreasing subsequent delinquent behavior.[15] The Missouri Division of Youth Services (DYS) reported that three years following youths' release from custody, approximately one-third of them return to DYS or adult prison.[16] Illinois estimated that approximately 60% of a sample of youth released from Illinois Department of Juvenile Justice facilities were rearrested during the first year after their release, and cumulatively more than 80% of youth were arrested within three years of their release.[17] Thomas Loughran and his colleagues conducted a longitudinal analysis of juvenile incarceration and subsequent arrest in two large metropolitan areas and found no effect of incarceration on subsequent juvenile arrests.[18]

There is substantial evidence that youth experience neglect and, in some cases, harm while incarcerated in juvenile prisons. The U.S. Department of Justice (DOJ), operating under the Civil Rights of Institutional Persons Act (CRIPA), has investigated scores of juvenile correctional facilities over the past twenty years. Its finding letters, often prelude to a settlement agreement with state or local government operators of these facilities, document instances of abuse and neglect of youth by staff. The DOJ investigations have found excessive use of force, sexual abuse, inadequate programming, and cruel and demeaning disciplinary practices.[19] The Youth Law Center, the Juvenile Law Center, the Children's Law Center, the American Civil Liberties Union, and other public-interest law firms have also filed suit over abuse and neglect in juvenile corrections.[20] In addition to being ineffective, costly, and harmful to youth, the current system of juvenile justice in the United States locks up a disproportionate number of minority youth and youth with disabling conditions.[21]

Many of the current ineffective, expensive, and harmful juvenile justice practices have been driven by an underinformed public, political expediency, and the media. A nationwide poll commissioned by the Center for Children's Law and Policy showed that the public overwhelmingly endorsed providing youth involved in delinquent behavior with opportunities to develop new skills and to make successful transitions to adulthood.[22] While education programs in secure facilities frequently fail to adequately serve youth, the public schools in many communities serving low-income and minority youth often contribute to the subsequent problems experienced by incarcerated children and adolescents.[23]

School Failure, Suspension, and Delinquency

For many youth, failure and suspension from school often precede juvenile justice system involvement. Children who struggle academically and socially in school are at great risk for retention in grade and school exclusions. High-stakes testing and accountability have created conditions in many public schools in which "low performers" and "bad actors" are at risk for exclusion in part because their performance on standardized measures does not reflect well on the quality of the school. Researchers have examined issues associated with school suspensions and have found that numerous school factors such as poverty, minority representation, low teacher expectations, and school mobility are linked to high rates of suspension.[24] These findings suggest that schools serving the most vulnerable children respond the most negatively to student needs. Christine Christle and her colleagues found that schools with high rates of suspension relied primarily on exclusionary practices to maintain school safety.[25] In contrast, they found that schools with low rates of suspension used school-wide behavioral intervention programs to promote appropriate behavior. Consistent with these findings, Michael Krezmien found that high student mobility, high percentage of African American enrollment, poor teacher quality, poverty, and poor student performance on high-stakes assessments were all related to the risk of suspension and the risk of disproportionate suspension of minority students and students with disabilities.[26] Together, these findings indicate that schools with the greatest number of problems respond the most punitively to school misbehavior, contributing to the school-to-prison pipeline.

Daniel Losen, Tia Martinez, and Jon Gillespie analyzed school suspensions during the 2009–2010 school year in nearly 500 school districts in California.[27] They found gross disproportionality in rates of suspensions, with African American, Latino, and American Indian youth as well as students with disabling conditions suspended at much higher rates than their peers. In the ten California school districts with the highest rates of suspension, nearly one in four youth were suspended for infractions that were often discretionary, such as disrespect, defiance, and dress-code violations. More recently, Losen and Martinez analyzed suspensions in more than 26,000 middle and high schools in the U.S. during the 2009–2010 school year.[28] Similar to their findings from analysis of California school suspensions published earlier, they found African American and Latino students at higher risk for suspension than other students in the same schools. Further, when they compared analysis of data from the 1972–1973 school year, they found the rate of increase in the use of suspensions for Black students 11 times higher than the rate of increase for White students during this same period. Losen and Martinez also reported that within school districts, wide variation in suspension practices existed, as did an intersection among race, gender, and disability status.[29] For example, during the 2009–2010 school year, more than one-third of Black, male students with disabilities were suspended.

Tony Fabello and his colleagues studied school exclusion and related outcomes for three seventh-grade cohorts—nearly one million secondary school students—in Texas over a six-year period.[30] They found that nearly 60% of all youth were suspended during middle or high school, with African American students and those with disabilities disproportionately removed from school. Of those youth receiving school disciplinary sanctions, the median number of suspensions was four. While White, Hispanic, and African American students were suspended from school at similar rates for mandatory violations of the school code, the vast majority of suspensions were for discretionary acts; similar to findings of other studies,[31] these data showed gross disproportionality by race and disability status in the rate at which students were suspended.[32]

School suspensions have been driven in part by the "zero tolerance" rhetoric for school disciplinary infractions. In theory, this approach suggested an equitable, if intolerant, response to serious violations of the school code. However, the evidence indicates that zero tolerance has not been applied in an evenhanded manner and that most behavioral infractions resulting in suspension are for offenses such as insubordination and disrespect. The process of frequent suspensions, subsequent dropout, and juvenile justice system involvement has been referred to as the "school-to-prison pipeline,"[33] and the "schoolhouse to jailhouse track."[34] While establishing causal relationships between school misconduct and subsequent juvenile justice system involvement is difficult, some evidence suggests that schools have increasingly referred students directly to the police or to courts in recent years,[35] effectively criminalizing school misbehavior. Many youth entering juvenile detention facilities have a history of school failure, suspensions, and special education identification.[36]

While many youth suspended and/or expelled have not been served well by the public schools, once incarcerated, youth often receive inadequate education services and do not have the opportunity to complete their education or to develop career and technical skills while in custody. The quality of education programs in juvenile corrections in many states is substantially inferior to what children experience in the public schools. Class actions have been initiated on behalf of incarcerated youth in more than 20 states during the past 25 years for violations of education rights, particularly for youth with disabilities.[37] Local and state-operated juvenile prisons have frequently failed to meet state and federal regulations with regard to curriculum, teacher qualifications, instructional practices, and discipline.

In summary, many youth involved in the juvenile justice system have been served poorly when in the public schools. Minority youth and students with disabilities have been disproportionately suspended and have higher rates of school dropout than other youth. When these youth become involved in the justice system, they continue to receive inferior education services. The failure of public school systems to serve youth well is one part of the problem; another critical component is the juvenile justice system. The next section begins with a discussion of efforts to reform this system.

Juvenile Justice Reform in the United States

During the past 20 years, a number of juvenile justice system reforms have been launched in an effort to transform the current system. Models for Change, funded by the MacArthur Foundation, is a multistate initiative designed to transform juvenile justice through the development of innovative program practices in areas such as aftercare, mental health, and community-based alternatives to incarceration.[38] Through research, analysis, and dissemination, Models for Change has demonstrated the potential for system change in juvenile justice policy and practice.

Another juvenile justice system reform effort, launched by the Annie E. Casey Foundation, is the Juvenile Detention Alternative Initiative, or JDAI. Initiated more than 20 years ago, JDAI has developed and documented policies and practices to create a more effective and efficient juvenile justice system. JDAI sites across the United States have improved outcomes for youth using improved screening tools, data-based decision making, and collaborations among agencies serving youth and their communities. In doing so, JDAI sites have demonstrated effective alternatives to incarceration.[39]

Another systemic change project is the Center for Juvenile Justice Reform (CJJR) at Georgetown University.[40] CJJR, with the support of several foundations, has attempted to promote systemic change in juvenile justice through intensive training of leaders in both the public and private sectors. Participants in CJJR certificate programs create projects designed to improve services and outcomes for youth in their home communities.

Several juvenile justice reform efforts target specific groups of youth, certain practices, and juvenile justice system legislation. Reclaiming Futures, supported by the Robert Wood Johnson Foundation, targets substance abuse among youth involved in the juvenile justice system.[41] Another initiative, the Campaign for Youth Justice, is focused on ending the practice of trying youth in the adult criminal justice system.[42] A more recent systems-change initiative, the National Campaign to Reform State Juvenile Justice Systems, targets state and local reform efforts designed to align legislation and policies with evidence-based practices. This effort, jointly funded by a number of foundations, attempts to reduce the number of youth in custody and to save taxpayer resources and maintain public safety in the process.[43]

Transforming Juvenile Justice: Education Reform and Lessons from Finland

The myriad of juvenile justice reform efforts in the U.S. have played an important role in highlighting inequities, inefficiencies, and failures of the current system. Arguably, recent reductions in the rates at which juveniles are incarcerated in many states are associated with these juvenile justice reforms and the dissemination of information about evidence-based practices.[44] However, long-term sustainable juvenile justice reform requires fundamental changes in the ways in which schools serve their most vulnerable children as well as changes in our beliefs and attitudes about juvenile delinquents.

Many children in the United States do not receive the quality education services to which they are entitled. Across the U.S. and within states, there are great inequities in resources available to schools and school districts associated with state funding formulas for education.[45] Data from the National Center for Education Statistics show that schools with the fewest low-income students and the lowest percentage of minority students receive substantially more general-education revenues than do schools with higher poverty and percentage of minority youth.[46] State supreme courts have ruled funding formulas in nearly 20 states unconstitutional.[47] While student academic performance is affected by a number of factors, inequitable funding for schools drains teaching talent and resources from high-poverty and high-minority student districts. Differences in levels of support affect the quality and continuity of the teacher corps within schools and school districts and have an impact on student achievement. The academic performance of Black, Latino, and other minority youth consistently trails that of White youth.[48]

The relationships among education achievement, literacy, and delinquent and criminal behavior are complex. However, there is consistent evidence that higher rates of education attainment are associated with lower rates of criminal behavior.[49] Among other things, higher levels of education and higher skill levels may provide economic opportunities not available to those who have fewer skills and lower levels of education. Presumably, higher levels of education can raise wages, may make criminal behavior less desirable, and may alter the social networks of individuals.[50] Systemic education reform that addresses inequality in support for schools in low-income communities is an essential part of ensuring that more youth complete school and have skills that enable them to pursue advanced training and/or postsecondary education. Related to the need to reform systems of funding schools across the states is the need to ensure that schools do not disproportionately exclude minority students and youth with disabilities and contribute to low levels of academic achievement.[51] As data from the *Breaking Schools' Rules* report on Texas's schools documented so well, high rates of suspension are associated with juvenile justice system involvement and have consequences for youth and their communities.[52] School suspension and expulsion have been linked to juvenile justice system involvement, though specific pathways vary.[53]

It is beyond the focus of this chapter to describe in detail the systemic changes needed in the education system that would address, in part, the challenge of juvenile justice reform. However, evidence suggests that improved school outcomes for youth most vulnerable to juvenile justice involvement—members of ethnic and racial minority groups, low-income students, and youth with disabilities—are an important part of the process. Schools have the potential to change youths' trajectories toward delinquent behavior in spite of considerable challenges.[54]

Beyond the considerable work under way that is required to change schools from being complicit in the "school-to-prison pipeline," juvenile justice reform requires rethinking ways in which we respond as a nation to delinquent behavior. A number of chapters in this volume address ways in which the courts, advocates, and juvenile justice agencies can respond to delinquent behavior in ways that are more equitable and produce better outcomes. Beyond transforming features of our current system, a complementary and long-term approach to juvenile justice reform involves examining the success experienced by Finland in transforming its juvenile and criminal justice system.

The Finnish Transformation

More than 60 years ago, Finland's criminal justice system in some respects resembled the current system in the United States. Nearly 100 years of Russian rule and influence had shaped Finnish penal practices. In the 1940s and '50s, the Finnish rate of incarceration was more than 200 per 100,000, four times the rate of many other European countries and comparable to countries under Soviet influence.[55] In the 1960s, the Finns developed an awareness that their juvenile and criminal justice policies and rates of incarceration were out of step with the other Nordic countries.[56] Political leaders interested in shedding comparisons to Russia began to systematically transform their justice system. Over the next few decades, the Finnish government introduced an unprecedented number of acts and amendments that promoted community-based sanctions and reduced the prison population.[57] By 2000, the rate of incarceration was approximately 50 per 100,000, about one-quarter of the rate just after the end of World War II. Tapio Lappi-Seppälä attributes Finland's success to "macro-level structural factors and ideological changes in penal theory, as well as legal reforms and changing practices of sentencing and prison enforcement."[58]

While much of the available literature on the changes in the Finnish justice system addresses adults charged with criminal offenses, some information about the system's response to juveniles is available. While the age of criminal responsibility is 15 in Finland, youthful offenders between the ages of 15 and 17 are tried as minors and can fall under the jurisdiction of both the child welfare and the juvenile justice systems.[59] Youths under age 15 involved in delinquent or criminal activities are referred to social services. Both the child welfare and juvenile justice systems experienced major transformations during the 1960s through the 1980s. Policies and statutes that emerged from system reform focused on the best interests of the child coupled with family support. Large institutional residential settings—reflective of an emphasis on custody and control—were replaced by small community-based settings.[60]

Juveniles and young adults in Finland are rarely sentenced to prison and never receive a life sentence; 18- to 21-year-olds make up less than

2% of the prison population, and those sentenced to prison are eligible for parole after serving one-third of their sentence.[61] The most common punishment meted out by the courts is a fine; social skills instruction, employment support, and twice-weekly meetings with supervisors are frequent sanctions. Mediation, introduced in Finland in 1983, is a voluntary option for all parties and is most frequently used with youthful offenders.[62] For the few youth sentenced to prison or a residential placement, the average sentence is four months.[63]

The dramatic changes in the Finnish juvenile justice system were rooted in two principles: (a) public agencies should act in the best interest of the child, and (b) family-centered approaches are the preferred means of responding to delinquency.[64] Underlying the changes in the Finnish juvenile justice system is a belief that crime and delinquent behavior are social problems. "The whole theoretical criminal justice framework and conceptualization of the aims and means of criminal policy underwent a dramatic change, as the social sciences and planning strategies merged with the criminal justice policy analysis."[65] Dramatic declines in incarceration rates between 1950 and 2000 in Finland were not accompanied by comparable increases in crime rates.[66]

While the transformation of Finland's system of juvenile and criminal justice has been dramatic, the obvious question—"Would it work in the States?"—has to be asked. Differences between the comprehensive child welfare system in Finland and current services in the U.S. complicate comparisons between the two countries.[67] The juvenile justice system in the U.S. represents different challenges than those faced by the Finns when contemplating system reform during the past 60 years. Beyond cultural, political, and demographic differences between the two nations, there are elements of the changes in Finland that could assist us in reforming the system in the United States. One important part of the process that occurred in Finland has already begun to occur in the United States. During the past several years, there has been public debate across the political spectrum about the high cost of our ineffective juvenile justice system.[68] In response, a number of states have taken steps to revise statutes and regulations and to create prevention programs as well as alternative sanctions for youth in the juvenile justice system.[69] Rates of juvenile incarceration have fallen in recent years as states have adopted more evidence-based and community-based practices to respond to juvenile crime.

With regard to schools, a growing awareness of the nexus between school failure, school exclusion, and risk for involvement in delinquent behavior has led to a national effort to draw attention to the problems created by school suspensions and the importance of creating policies and programs to respond to behavior problems in the schools. For example, the Council of State Governments' School Discipline Consensus Project is working with advocates, families, professionals, and policy makers to craft documents that can guide alternatives to suspension.[70] "Doing things differently" begins with public discussion about the relationship between education and delinquent behavior and continues with dissemination of information about transformation of juvenile justice systems. Finland provides one example of a system that transformed itself from an expensive, punitive, and inefficient system to one with relatively low rates of juvenile incarceration and improved outcomes for youth.

A Final Note

People concerned about high rates of juvenile incarceration and ineffective and damaging outcomes for youth need to create and sustain the conversation about juvenile justice reform. Transforming the quality of education services and support for youth enmeshed in the justice system is an important element of system reform; some have called for the transformation of the juvenile system into an educational system.[71] Public discussion that suggests that our Soviet-style system of juvenile justice is in dire need of reform is part of the process. Politicians in the U.S. drive juvenile and criminal justice policy. In other countries, particularly in western Europe, social scientists and professionals shape juvenile and criminal justice policy and practice. Finland provides a good example of how one nation—albeit a much smaller one than the U.S.—transformed its juvenile and criminal justice system to one that is more equitable and effective. High-quality education programs for the most vulnerable youth are an essential part of reform. If Finland can transform its system of juvenile justice, why can't we?

NOTES

1 Richard A. Mendel, *No Place for Kids: The Case for Reducing Juvenile Incarceration* (Baltimore: Annie E. Casey Foundation, 2011), http://www.aecf.org/m/ resourcedoc/aecf-NoPlaceForKidsFullReport-2011.pdf.

2. Matti Joutsen, Raimo Lahti, and Pasi Poölöönen, *Criminal Justice Systems in Europe and North America: Finland* (Helsinki, Finland: HEUNI, European Institute for Crime Prevention and Control, affiliated with the United Nations, 2001).

3 Mendel, *supra* note 1.

4 Ibid.

5 Ibid.

6 James Bell, chap. 1 in this volume; David R. Katner, chap. 5 in this volume.

7 Pew Charitable Trusts, Public Safety Performance Project, "Latest Data Show Juvenile Confinement Continues Rapid Decline," August 28, 2013, http://archive. today/If258; Spike Bradford, *Common Ground: Lessons Learned from Five States That Have Reduced Juvenile Confinement by More than Half* (Washington, DC: Justice Policy Institute, 2013), http://www.justicepolicy.org/uploads/justicepolicy/ documents/jpicommonground.pdf; Bart Lubow, chap. 2 in this volume.

8 Criminal Justice Statistics Center, California Department of Justice, *Crime in California 2009* (Sacramento: California Department of Justice, 2009), http:// ag.ca.gov/cjsc/publications/candd/cd09/preface.pdf; Mike Males and Daniel Macallair, *The California Miracle: Drastically Reduced Youth Incarceration, Drastically Reduced Youth Crime* (San Francisco: Center on Juvenile and Criminal Justice, July 2010), http://www.cjcj.org/uploads/cjcj/documents/The_California_ Miracle.pdf.

9 Mike Males, Christina Stahlkapf, and Daniel Macallair, *Crime Rates and Youth Incarceration in Texas and California Compared: Public Safety or Public Waste?* (San Francisco: Center on Juvenile and Criminal Justice, June 2007), http://www. cjcj.org/uploads/cjcj/documents/Crime_Rates_and_Youth_Incarceration_in_ Texas_and_California_Compared.pdf.

10 Patricia J. Arthur and Regina Waugh, "Status Offenses and the Juvenile Justice and Delinquency Prevention Act: The Exception That Swallowed the Rule," *Seattle Journal for Social Justice* 7, no. 2 (2009): 555–576, http://digitalcommons. law.seattleu.edu/sjsj/vol7/iss2/10.

11 American Correctional Association, *American Correctional Association 2008 Directory: Adult and Juvenile Correctional Departments, Institutions, Agencies, and Probation and Parole Authorities* (Alexandria, VA: American Correctional Association, 2008).

12 New York State Juvenile Justice Advisory Group, *Tough on Crime: Promoting Public Safety by Doing What Works* (New York: New York State Juvenile Justice Advisory Group, 2010).

13 Virginia Department of Juvenile Justice, *Data Resource Guide, FY2012* (Richmond: Virginia Department of Juvenile Justice, 2012), http://www.djj.virginia.gov/pdf/

AboutDJJ/DRG/Expenditures_and_Staffing.pdf; Alan Vanneman, Linda
Hamilton, Janet Baldwin Anderson, and Taslima Rahman, *Achievement Gaps:
How Black and White Students in Public Schools Perform in Mathematics and
Reading on the National Assessment of Educational Progress*, NCES 2009-455
(Washington, DC: National Center for Education Statistics, Institute of Education
Sciences, U.S. Department of Education, 2009).

14 Missouri Department of Social Services, *Division of Youth Services Annual Report
Fiscal Year 2012* (Jefferson City: Missouri Department of Social Services, 2012),
http://dss.mo.gov/re/pdf/dys/youth-services-annual-report-fy12.pdf.

15 Thomas A. Loughran, Edward P. Mulvey, Carol A. Schubert, Jeffrey Fagan, Alex
R. Piquero, and Sandra H. Losoya, "Estimating a Dose-Response Relationship
between Length of Stay and Future Recidivism in Serious Juvenile Offenders,"
Criminology 47, no. 3 (2009): 699–740.

16 Missouri Department of Social Services, *supra* note 14.

17 Jordan Boulger, Lindsay Bostwick, and Mark Powers, *Juvenile Recidivism:
Exploring Re-arrest and Re-incarceration of Incarcerated Youth in Illinois* (Chicago:
Illinois Criminal Justice Information Authority, 2012).

18 Loughran et al., *supra* note 15.

19 U.S. Department of Justice, "CRIPA Investigation of Oakley and Columbia
Training Schools in Raymond and Columbia, Mississippi," CRIPA findings letter,
June 19, 2003, http://www.justice.gov/crt/about/spl/documents/oak_colu_miss_
findinglet.pdf; U.S. Department of Justice, "Investigation of the Marion Juvenile
Correctional Facility, Marion, Ohio," CRIPA findings letter, May 9, 2007, http://
www.justice.gov/crt/about/spl/documents/marion_findlet_5-9-07.pdf; U.S.
Department of Justice, "Investigation of the Indianapolis Juvenile Correctional
Facility, Indianapolis, Indiana," CRIPA findings letter, January 29, 2010, http://
www.justice.gov/crt/about/spl/documents/Indianapolis_findlet_01-29-10.pdf.

20 E.g., *Johnson v. Upchurch*, U.S. District Court, District of Arizona, No. Civ. 86-195
TUC RMB, Consent Decree, 1993; *Christina A. v. Bloomberg*, U.S. District Court,
District of South Dakota, Southern Division, Civ. 00-4036, Settlement
Agreement, 2000.

21 Howard N. Snyder and Melissa Sickmund, *Juvenile Offenders and Victims: 2006
National Report* (Washington, DC: U.S. Department of Justice, Office of Juvenile
Justice and Delinquency Prevention, 2006), http://www.ojjdp.gov/ojstatbb/
nr2006/downloads/NR2006.pdf; Mary M. Quinn, Robert B. Rutherford, Peter E.
Leone, David M. Osher, and Jeffrey M. Poirier, "Youth with Disabilities in Juvenile
Corrections: A National Survey," *Exceptional Children* 71 (2005): 339–345; Daniel
P. Mears and Laudan Y. Aron, *Addressing the Needs of Youth with Disabilities in
the Juvenile Justice System: The Current State of Knowledge* (Washington, DC:
Urban Institute, November 2003), http://www.urban.org/UploadedPDF/410885_
youth_with_disabilities.pdf; Michael P. Krezmien, Candace A. Mulcahy, and Peter
E. Leone, "Detained and Committed Youth: Examining Differences in
Achievement, Mental Health Needs, and Special Education Status," *Education and*

Treatment of Children 31, no. 4 (2008): 445–464; Kristin Henning, chap. 10 in this volume.

22 Center for Children's Law and Policy, *Potential for Change: Public Attitudes and Policy Preferences for Juvenile Justice Systems Reform Executive Summary* (Washington, DC: Center for Children's Law and Policy, 2007), http://www.macfound.org/media/article_pdfs/CCLPPOLLINGFINAL.PDF.

23 David Domenici and Renagh O'Leary, chap. 18 in this volume.

24 Christine A. Christle, C. Michael Nelson, and Kristine Jolivette, "School Characteristics Related to the Use of Suspension," *Education and Treatment of Children* 27, no. 4 (2004): 509–526; Michael P. Krezmien, "Understanding Disproportionate Suspensions of Minority Students and Students with Disabilities: A Multilevel Approach" (Ph.D. diss., University of Maryland, 2007), http://hdl.handle.net/1903/6664; Russell J. Skiba, Reece L. Peterson, and Tara Williams, "Office Referrals and Suspension: Disciplinary Intervention in Middle Schools," *Education & Treatment of Children* 20, no. 3 (1997): 295–315.

25 Christle, Nelson, and Jolivette, *supra* note 24.

26 Krezmien, *supra* note 24.

27 Daniel J. Losen, Tia Martinez, and Jon Gillespie, *Suspended Education in California* (Los Angeles: Civil Rights Project, UCLA, April 2012), http://civilrightsproject.ucla.edu/resources/projects/center-for-civil-rights-remedies/school-to-prison-folder/summary-reports/suspended-education-in-california/SuspendedEd-final3.pdf.

28 Daniel J. Losen and Tia Elena Martinez, *Out of School and Off Track: The Overuse of Suspensions in American Middle and High Schools* (Los Angeles: Civil Rights Project, UCLA, 2013), http://civilrightsproject.ucla.edu/resources/projects/center-for-civil-rights-remedies/school-to-prison-folder/federal-reports/out-of-school-and-off-track-the-overuse-of-suspensions-in-american-middle-and-high-schools/OutofSchool-OffTrack_UCLA_4-8.pdf.

29 Ibid.

30 Tony Fabello, Michael D. Thompson, Martha Plotkin, Dottie Carmichael, Miner P. Marchbanks III, and Eric A. Booth, *Breaking Schools' Rules: A Statewide Study of How School Discipline Relates to Students' Success and Juvenile Justice Involvement* (New York: Council of State Governments Justice Center / Public Policy Research Institute, July 2011), http://knowledgecenter.csg.org/drupal/system/files/Breaking_School_Rules.pdf.

31 Losen and Martinez, *supra* note 28; Losen, Martinez, and Gillespie, *supra* note 27; Michael P. Krezmien, Peter E. Leone, and Georgianna M. Achilles, "Suspension, Race, and Disability: Analysis of State-Wide Practices and Reporting," *Journal of Emotional and Behavioral Disorders* 14 (2006): 217–226; Skiba, Peterson, and Williams, *supra* note 24.

32 Fabello et al., *supra* note 30.

33 American Civil Liberties Union, *What Is the School-to-Prison Pipeline?* (New York: American Civil Liberties Union, June 2008), https://www.aclu.org/racial-justice/what-school-prison-pipeline.

34 Advancement Project, "Ending the Schoolhouse to Jailhouse Track," http://www.advancementproject.org/issues/stopping-the-school-to-prison-pipeline (accessed December 1, 2013).

35 Michael P. Krezmien, Peter E. Leone, Mark S. Zablocki, and Craig S. Wells, "Juvenile Court Referrals and the Public Schools: Nature and Extent of the Practice in Five States," *Journal of Contemporary Criminal Justice* 26 (2010): 273–293.

36 Krezmien, Mulcahy, and Leone, *supra* note 21.

37 Peter E. Leone and Sheri Meisel, "Improving Education Services for Students in Detention and Confinement Facilities," *Children's Legal Rights Journal* 17, no. 1 (1997): 2–12.

38 Models for Change, "Reform Areas," http://www.modelsforchange.net/reform-areas/index.html (accessed December 1, 2013).

39 Annie E. Casey Foundation, "Juvenile Justice," http://www.aecf.org/work/juvenile-justice/ (accessed November 24, 2013).

40 Center for Juvenile Justice Reform, home page, http://cjjr.georgetown.edu/.

41 Reclaiming Futures, home page, http://www.reclaimingfutures.org/.

42 Campaign for Youth Justice, home page, http://www.campaignforyouthjustice.org/.

43 National Campaign to Reform State Juvenile Justice Systems, *National Campaign to Reform State Juvenile Justice Systems* (September 2013), http://www.publicinterestprojects.org/wp-content/uploads/2013/09/Campaign-History.pdf.

44 Bradford, *supra* note 7.

45 Bruce D. Baker and Sean P. Corcoran, *The Stealth Inequities of School Funding: How State and Local School Finance Systems Perpetuate Inequitable Student Spending* (Washington, DC: Center for American Progress, 2012).

46 Thomas B. Parrish and Christine S. Hikido, *Inequalities in Public School District Revenues*, National Center for Education Statistics, U.S. Department of Education, NCES 98-210 (Washington, DC: U.S. Department of Education, 1998).

47 James E. Ryan, "Schools, Race, and Money," *Yale Law Journal* 109, no. 2 (1999): 249–316.

48 Susan Aud, Mary Ann Fox, and Angelina KewalRamani, *Status and Trends in the Education of Racial and Ethnic Groups*, National Center for Education Statistics, U.S. Department of Education, NCES 2010-015 (Washington, DC: U.S. Government Printing Office, 2010); Vanneman et al., *supra* note 13.

49 Lois M. Davis, Robert Bozick, Jennifer L. Steele, Jessica Saunders, and Jeremy N. V. Miles, *Evaluating the Effectiveness of Correctional Education: A Meta-analysis of Programs That Provide Education to Incarcerated Adults* (Santa Monica, CA: Rand, 2013), http://www.rand.org/pubs/research_reports/RR266.html; Lance

Lochner and Enrico Moretti, "The Effect of Education on Crime: Evidence from Prison Inmates, Arrests, and Self-Reports," *American Economic Review* 94 (2004): 155–189; Lance Lochner, "Education Policy and Crime," in *Controlling Crime: Strategies and Tradeoffs*, edited by Philip J. Cook, Jens Ludwig, and Justin McCrary (Chicago: University of Chicago Press, 2011), 465–520; Lance Lochner, "Nonproduction Benefits of Education: Crime, Health, and Good Citizenship," in *Handbook of the Economics of Education*, edited by Eric A. Hanushek, Stephen Machin, and Ludger Woessmann, vol. 4, 183–282 (Amsterdam: Elsevier Science, 2011).

50 Lochner, "Nonproduction Benefits of Education," *supra* note 49.

51 Anne Gregory, Russell J. Skiba, and Pedro A. Noguera, "The Achievement Gap and Discipline Gap: Two Sides of the Same Coin," *Educational Researcher* 39 (2010): 59–68.

52 Fabello et al., *supra* note 30.

53 Rolf Loeber, Kate Keenan, and Quanwu Zhang, "Boys' Experimentation and Persistence in Developmental Pathways toward Serious Delinquency," *Journal of Child and Family Studies* 6, no. 3 (1997): 321–357.

54 Maisha T. Winn and Nadia Behizadeh, "The Right to Be Literate: Literacy, Education, and the School-to-Prison Pipeline," *Review of Research in Education* 35 (2011): 147–173.

55 Tapio Lappi-Seppälä, "Reducing the Prison Population: Long-Term Experiences from Finland," in *Crime Policy in Europe: Good Practices and Promising Examples*, edited by Council of Europe Publishing, 139–158 (Strasbourg, France: Council of Europe, 2004); Tapio Lappi-Seppälä, "Penal Policy in Scandinavia," *Crime and Justice* 36, no. 1 (2007): 217–295.

56 Nils Christie, *Crime Control as Industry*, 3rd ed. (New York: Routledge, 2000).

57 Lappi-Seppälä, "Reducing the Prison Population," *supra* note 55; Lappi-Seppälä, "Penal Policy," *supra* note 55.

58 Lappi-Seppälä, "Reducing the Prison Population," *supra* note 55, at 140.

59 Tapio Lappi-Seppälä, "Finland: A Model of Tolerance?," in *Comparative Youth Justice*, edited by John Muncie and Barry Goldson, 177–195 (London: Sage, 2006).

60 Ibid.

61 Markku Heiskanen and Anna Vuorelainen, "Finland," in *Crime and Punishment around the World*, vol. 4, *Europe*, edited by Marcelo Aebi and Véronique Jaquier, 103–114 (Santa Barbara, CA: ABC-CLIO, 2010).

62 Lappi-Seppälä, "Penal Policy," *supra* note 55.

63 Heiskanen and Vuorelainen, *supra* note 61.

64 Lappi-Seppälä, "Finland," *supra* note 59; Lappi-Seppälä, "Penal Policy," *supra* note 55.

65 Lappi-Seppälä, "Penal Policy," *supra* note 55, at 230–231.

66 Lappi-Seppälä, "Finland," *supra* note 59.

67 Sirpa Utriainen, "Child Welfare Services in Finland," *Child Welfare* 68, no. 2 (1984): 129–140.

68 Douglas N. Evans, *Pioneers of Youth Justice Reform: Achieving System Change Using Resolution, Reinvestment, and Realignment Strategies* (New York: Research and Evaluation Center, John Jay College of Criminal Justice, City University of New York, 2012).

69 Bradford, *supra* note 7.

70 Council of State Governments, School Discipline Consensus Project, home page, http://csgjusticecenter.org/youth/projects/school-discipline-consensus-project/.

71 Steve Suits, Katherine Dunn, and Nasheed Sabree, *Just Learning: The Imperative to Transform Juvenile Justice Systems into Effective Educational Systems* (Atlanta: Southern Education Foundation, 2014), http://www.southerneducation.org/getattachment/b80f7aad-405d-4eed-a966-8d7a4a12f5be/Just-Learning-Executive-Summary.aspx.

5

Delinquency, Due Process, and Mental Health

Presuming Youth Incompetency

DAVID R. KATNER

Juveniles with unmet mental health needs are at much higher risk for involvement with the juvenile justice system, and often the very behavior causing them to be arrested and charged is a manifestation of the mental health disorders from which they suffer.[1] Nevertheless, juveniles with mental health problems continue to fill detention facilities at a disproportionate rate, often without having ever been diagnosed or treated.[2]

The demographics of delinquency cases expose unmet mental health needs in such large and compelling numbers that due process mandates the incorporation of mental health services in the juvenile justice system. This chapter proposes elimination of the current legal presumption that juveniles are competent to stand trial. It suggests that competency be affirmatively established and, in the absence of competency, that juvenile cases be transferred to diversionary programs with mental health services as the focus of interventions. The systemic goal of incorporating due process must include provision of much-needed mental health services to reduce recidivism among young offenders.

Of all children in the juvenile justice system, 65% to 70% meet criteria for diagnosable mental health problems in the American Psychiatric Association's *Diagnostic and Statistical Manual of Mental Disorders*, fifth edition (*DSM-5*). The majority of these children suffer comorbid disorders, yet they are not diagnosed until they become involved in juvenile justice. This chapter reviews the frequency of these diagnoses within this population, then proposes neutralizing or reversing the legal presumption dating back hundreds of years that all who appear in criminal courts are presumed competent, at least as that presumption is currently applied to cases involving children. The juvenile court competency presumption is based on the adult criminal court presumption. The legal presumption, however, predates current knowledge about adolescent behaviors, developmental immaturity, and mental illness in this population. By eliminating a presumption of competency, juvenile justice can devote its limited resources to screening, evaluating, and treating the many forms of disorders and illnesses that are so prevalent among the adolescents charged with delinquency and criminal misconduct. This refocus of community resources is designed to reduce or eliminate recidivist behavior.

I. Frequency of Mental Health Problems in the Juvenile Justice Population

Thinking of the city of New Orleans and its delinquency cases as a microcosm may help to conceptualize the sheer magnitude of mental health issues in the delinquency system. Following the flooding and near destruction of the city of New Orleans after Hurricane Katrina in 2005, the juvenile justice system presented many challenges for the judiciary and the members of the bar but most especially for children and their families involved in the system. Initially, massive numbers of children were appearing in court cases and presenting with symptoms of posttraumatic stress disorder (PTSD) and other diagnosable conditions. While this may have been a natural occurrence in a community suffering such widespread devastation, the large numbers of children with diagnosable mental health issues did not diminish even years after the deadly storm. The large numbers of PTSD juvenile cases following Katrina were quickly supplanted by large numbers of juveniles diagnosed with attention deficit hyperactivity disorder (ADHD), depression, substance use disorder, bipolar disorder, and schizophrenia. In fact, the diagnosed conditions and comorbid disorders of many children appearing in the New Orleans juvenile court system appeared to have no connection with the aftermath of the hurricane whatsoever.

Data collected from juveniles in detention nationwide mirror the rate of diagnosable mental health problems of New Orleans youth years after the Katrina flood. Many recent studies have shed light on the high

frequency rate of juvenile offenders suffering mental health problems.[3]
Researchers have concluded that

> the majority of youth involved with the juvenile justice system have men-
> tal health disorders. . . . Studies consistently document that anywhere
> from 65% to 70% of youth in the juvenile justice system meet criteria for a
> diagnosable mental health disorder. Further, recent estimates suggest that
> approximately 25% of youth experienced disorders so severe that their
> ability to function is significantly impaired. In a recent multi-state men-
> tal health prevalence study conducted by the National Center for Mental
> Health and Juvenile Justice on youth in three different types of juvenile
> justice settings, over 70% of youth were found to meet criteria for at least
> one mental health disorder. Disruptive disorders were most common, fol-
> lowed by substance use disorders, anxiety disorders and mood disorders.
> The majority of youth had multiple diagnoses.[4]

About two-thirds of incarcerated youth demonstrate at least one diagnosable psychiatric disorder, and comorbidity is identified in over half
of this population.[5] There are parallels with the mental health profile of
adult offenders.[6] In many instances, the population of adult offenders in
need of mental health services outnumbers the total population of adults
in mental health facilities in the same communities, and presumably this
also occurs in the juvenile justice system.[7]

Despite the high rate of diagnosable juvenile mental health problems,
many juveniles are not identified as needing mental health services until
they become involved in the juvenile or adult criminal court system. A
number of contributing factors help to explain this phenomenon:

> Typically, children and adolescents with disruptive problems do not seek
> help for their problems. Most often parents obtain mental health service
> for their children voluntarily but some parents may not always see the
> need for such a service. Additionally, treatment may be very expensive,
> even for those who have health insurance. Health insurers may not cover
> child disruptive disorders. Or they may require a diagnosis, which leaves
> out children in the early stages of development who have sub-threshold
> numbers of symptoms. Also, logistic problems such as transport and
> childcare for other children may make it very difficult to comply with

a treatment regime. Thus, knowledge of the problem, willingness to do something about it, and ability to take action all need to be present for treatment to be possible.[8]

By documenting the large and constant percentage of juveniles in detention facilities who meet diagnostic criteria for mental illness, we know how widespread our concerns should be for youth. Moreover, whether one relies on anecdotal accounts of reducing juvenile recidivism through the provision of mental health services or empirical studies demonstrating reductions in recidivist behaviors following mental health services,[9] the positive impact of providing mental health services to adolescents in the juvenile justice system is easy to document.

However, there is currently an amazing lack of resource response to address these mental health issues.[10] Specialized mental health courts of limited jurisdiction offer resources and treatment modalities for juveniles and a knowledge base for the professionals involved in such courts in a way not found in more traditional delinquency and adult criminal court systems.[11] While some jurisdictions have experimented with such specialized courts, widespread adoption of such courts of limited jurisdiction has yet to occur.

II. Reimagining Juvenile Competency

The extent of mental health issues among youth involved in the existing juvenile justice system should trigger due process concerns about the constitutionality of the current framework of the system. Due process as applied to juvenile proceedings has continued to change and evolve over time. The process of delinquency hearings prior to Gerald Gault's hearing in Arizona in the 1960s would not satisfy today's notion of due process of law. Similarly, our knowledge of the mental health conditions of juveniles and adolescents involved in delinquency systems has evolved and changed over time. Assumptions that served us well as recently as 30 years ago would today be rejected. As court systems have increased their sensitivity and awareness of the unique aspects of adolescence and the behaviors associated with adolescence, the time has come for reconsidering a long-embraced legal assumption that all people in criminal cases are competent to assist counsel and to proceed to trial.

If we recognize that an identifiable, significant segment of the population is in need of mental health services, then a major component of the juvenile justice system must encompass the provision of mental health services designed to reduce initial offenses and recidivist criminal activities. While at one point in our history, ensuring that juveniles had access to counsel and that their right to confrontation would be protected was enough, today with our knowledge about the severe mental health problems the majority of the adolescents in court systems demonstrate, we can no longer turn a blind eye and allege that the due process rights of these children are respected. In order to adequately protect the due process rights afforded juveniles, we must unravel the legal assumption that they are competent when they arrive in court.

A. Competency

Dating back to the fourteenth century, common law courts have declined to allow prosecutions of criminal defendants found to be "incompetent."[12] Much of the juvenile legal system's application of the doctrine of competency to stand trial is based on the application of criminal law with respect to adult defendants. The U.S. Supreme Court's decision in *Dusky v. United States*[13] requires a criminal defendant to have sufficient present ability to consult with his or her lawyer with a reasonable degree of rational as well as factual understanding of the proceedings against him or her in order to be deemed competent to stand trial. Many juvenile disorders such as ADHD or anxiety disorders that might have a major impact on an adolescent's competency to stand trial would rarely be raised in connection with adult offenders, and consequently, the case law that has evolved in adult criminal cases should be expected to overlook conditions that are more relevant in cases involving juveniles.[14]

Currently, challenging a juvenile's competency to stand trial suspends the process of juvenile justice until and unless the juvenile's competency can be established or, in some cases, until competency can be restored. This is a mechanism that provides assessment of juvenile mental health needs, but it often results in simply delaying the justice process rather than achieving meaningful diversion or any long-lasting resolution of the pending legal case in the juvenile justice system. If the mental evaluations conducted to determine competency reveal diagnosable mental illness, courts need to address the unmet mental health problems of the juveniles appearing before them. This assumes that the juveniles have not been identified as suffering mental illness through their school systems or by their families. However, even if adolescents have been identified as suffering mental illness, many jurisdictions lack the financial resources to order or provide adequate mental health services for them.

The current concept of competency for delinquency cases reflects a working legal presumption that all juveniles are competent to stand trial.[15] If, to the contrary, we were to recognize that the vast majority of juveniles in detention facilities suffer from diagnosable mental health problems, then we have good reason to rethink the underlying assumption that all juveniles are presumed competent to stand trial. By altering this one legal presumption and thus eliminating any presumptions about the ability of juveniles to assist counsel to prepare for their adjudication hearings, we can wipe the slate clean and begin the juvenile justice process with no preconceived generalizations. This fundamental change to juvenile delinquency cases would open the door to the recognition of unmet mental health needs requiring the highest priority in the system. Mental illness in and of itself does not compel a finding of lack of competency; but that is not the argument that is being made here. Although many juveniles may well be assessed as competent to stand trial and may not present with any unmet mental health issues, many more juveniles may have mental health issues and should be expected to be found not competent and in need of mental health services. This approach to juvenile justice is intended to fundamentally change the objectives and functioning of the delinquency system.

Under the system whereby legal presumptions of competency are eliminated, the juvenile in consultation with counsel would have the right to assert that he or she is competent to stand trial. However, states would be free to determine whether either the state's attorney or the court should challenge the juvenile's competency and thus trigger the need to schedule a competency evaluation and hearing. Under this proposal, either the juvenile, defense counsel, or the court itself might raise the issue of the child's competency. Nevertheless, there would no longer be a legal presumption that the child is competent to stand trial or to go forward with an adjudication hearing.

If the child—or his or her counsel—does not stipulate to competency, then the state would be required to establish competency before the adjudication hearing could be scheduled. If there is a finding that the juvenile is not competent to stand trial, then the court would be required to provide adequate services either to "restore" competency or to divert the child's case to a mental-health-based process. This would be accomplished within the framework of existing diversion procedures and processes that typically involve prosecutorial discretion or court-ordered diversion, and therefore I am not proposing a change to this component of juvenile justice. In some instances, such as a case in which a child tests with a very low IQ and is determined to be mentally retarded, competency restoration may not be a viable option.[16] Mental retardation alone may not be dispositive of a child's competency to stand trial, but mild to moderate mental retardation might result in a clinical finding that the juvenile is not competent. Because this is an irreversible organic condition, it is unlikely that any state-provided competency services will cause the juvenile to "regain" competency and for the adjudication hearing to be rescheduled. Thus, such cases cause state systems to consider whether state mental health services serve any identifiable purpose in connection with the delinquency petition. Nevertheless, the total number of cases involving juveniles diagnosable with mental retardation does not appear to be the major source of court decisions that juveniles lack competency to stand trial.

The current state "competency restoration" programs involving classroom education, whereby juveniles are trained to identify the roles of the various attorneys and actors in delinquency adjudications, may have limited applications in many delinquency cases. Such processes fail to focus on the *ability* of the juvenile to assist in the preparation of a defense. Often, there is a lack of communication between the competency-restoring program and the juvenile's counsel; thus, there may be no basis for concluding that the juvenile following classroom training has been "restored" to competency. There is much room for improvement in the area of competency-restoration services for juveniles in delinquency systems.

Nevertheless, competency challenges may help the court system identify with some specificity the mental health needs of the juveniles appearing in delinquency cases. In some jurisdictions, a juvenile's competency may be challenged by defense counsel, the prosecution, or even the court itself. Such legal procedures may raise ethical concerns whereby the various roles of the attorneys become confused, and may perhaps lead to inappropriate communications between the accused juvenile and the judge or the prosecution.

In many instances in which juveniles are found to lack competency to stand trial, the unmet mental health needs of such juveniles can be addressed by court procedure, and then these juveniles can be referred for treatment. It is the process of identifying mental health problems and then the subsequent treatment of the mental health problems that should be incorporated into the model of juvenile justice.

Currently, the national movement that advances accountability for juvenile offenders often overlooks the most significant issue present in the majority of juvenile justice cases: unmet mental health, behavioral, and mood disorders, along with substance use problems. If these conditions are treated as mere corollaries to the juvenile justice process, then there is no reason to assume that current levels of recidivism should alter over time. One group of researchers concluded,

> Punitive responses to juvenile crime (e.g., the incarceration of juvenile offenders in correctional facilities) are far more expensive than less harsh alternatives (e.g., providing juvenile offenders rehabilitative services in community settings). Furthermore, there is little evidence that these more punitive policies are more effective in deterring future criminal activity, and some evidence that overly punitive responses, such as the incarceration of juvenile offenders in adult facilities, actually may increase juvenile offending.[17]

However, if the reduction of recidivism among youthful offenders is identified as a major societal goal in the juvenile justice system, then restructuring the system would make sense.

B. Developmental Immaturity: An Additional Competency Factor

The MacArthur Competency Study focused on the application of the legal definition of competency to stand trial as it has developed for adults in criminal proceedings and sought to apply the same factors to juveniles, but it took into account the impact of developmental immaturity, which is identifiable in the majority of adolescents.[18] The findings of this study were significant. If one were to neutralize the effects of mental illness on adolescent competency and focus exclusively on adolescent developmental immaturity, the study concluded that a massive number of juveniles would likely still be declared not competent to stand trial. The MacArthur Study concluded that

> juveniles aged 15 and younger are significantly more likely than older adolescents and young adults to be impaired in ways that compromise their ability to serve as competent defendants in a criminal proceeding. . . . Approximately one third of 11- to 13-year-olds, and approximately one fifth of 14- to 15-year-olds are as impaired in capacities relevant to adjudicative competence as are seriously mentally ill adults who would likely be considered incompetent to stand trial. (356)

Thus, recognition of the extraordinarily high rate of juvenile mental illness should not be the only factor that influences the proposed reform of the juvenile justice system. Even if adolescents are assessed and diagnosed properly, and if they are given access to effective mental health treatment and appropriate medications, any systemic change must consider the consequences of developmental immaturity on the juveniles' ability to assist counsel in the preparation of their defense.

Delaying the handling of juvenile adjudication hearings until the court is able to conclude that the accused juvenile is sufficiently mature to be able to properly assist counsel in a trial setting would take into consideration the eventual process of adolescent maturation. However, such a delay poses serious procedural problems for prosecutors and defense counsel alike. The loss of potential witnesses over the passage of time, the destruction of evidence or complications from the chain of custody of forensic evidence, and the uncertainty of witness testimony resulting from the delay in the commencement of legal proceedings must be considered. Thus, a legal doctrine must evolve to make possible the delay when it is found to be necessitated by the child's lack of competency.

The U.S. Supreme Court has repeatedly acknowledged the inherent limitations of adolescents and children caught up in the legal system. The Court declared, "The law has historically reflected the same assumption that children characteristically lack the capacity to exercise mature judgment and possess only an incomplete ability to understand the world around them. . . . Indeed, even where a 'reasonable person' standard otherwise applies, the common law has reflected the reality that children are not adults."[19]

Competency evaluations must take into consideration mental illness, mental retardation, and developmental immaturity, but systemic reform must contemplate all of these factors if reduction of the rate of recidivism becomes one of the most important goals of the juvenile justice system. By altering systemic goals to focus on providing much-needed mental health services and treatment to the majority of juveniles in delinquency systems, communities can expect to reduce prison expenditures and to break the chain of juveniles transitioning from delinquency behaviors into adult criminal misconduct.

III. Systemic Issues and System Change

A. Unmet Needs and Reduced Available Mental Health Services

Although identification and diagnosis of mental illness and mental retardation is the first step in the treatment process, availability of mental health services in many communities has decreased dramatically over the years. Additionally, over the most recent decades, more and more persons suffering mental illness have had their treatments and mental services shift away from once-functional psychiatric hospitals and clinics to jails, prisons, and juvenile detention centers.[20] One group of researchers looking at the interconnection between criminal justice systems and mental health systems concluded,

> Just as public mental hospitals once served as the institutions of last resort for the care and confinement of mentally ill persons, jails have become the last secure environment in most communities for the control of mentally ill persons when they are unmanageable and noncompliant. The U.S. Justice Department has reported that nearly 284,000 people with mental illnesses were in jail or prison on any given day—about 16 percent of the incarcerated population and more than four times the resident census in state mental hospitals.[21]

The number of available state hospital beds throughout the U.S. has decreased from 339 per 100,000 people at the highest point in 1955 to just 22 beds per 100,000 by the year 2000.[22] Much of the deinstitutionalization began in the early 1970s when patients were released from state hospitals to nursing homes or other community settings, thus releasing the states from funding 100% of their daily costs.[23] The passage of the Medicare and Medicaid amendments to the Social Security Act in the late 1960s opened the door for states to pass on the costs of mental health services to the federal government.[24] By the 1990s, states provided fewer and fewer mental health services for their populations, and this included the reduction of public-funded mental health services for adolescents.

> During the 1990s, state after state experienced the collapse of public mental health services for children and adolescents and the closing of many—in some states, all—of their residential facilities for seriously disturbed youths. The juvenile justice system soon became the primary referral for youths with mental disorders. In California, the *Los Angeles Times* (November 21, 2000) reported that "absent adequate mental health services, the cop has become the clinician . . . the jail has become a crisis center," and quoted the chief of correctional services of the Los Angeles County Sheriff's Department as acknowledging that the Los Angeles County Jail was now the largest de facto mental health facility in the nation.[25]

Since the year 2000, the number of available inpatient state psychiatric hospital beds has declined even further. The National Association of State Mental Health Program Directors (NASMHPD) reports that the number of state psychiatric beds decreased by 14% between 2005 and 2010, from a total of 50,509 to a total of 43,318, with an additional 1,249 beds scheduled to be eliminated. This would be a 17% reduction in available beds since the year 2005.[26] These reductions place the current number of state psychiatric beds per capita at the same level as in the year 1850, or 14 beds per 100,000 persons in the general population.[27]

The effect of these reductions in mental health services and hospital beds has reached a crisis point.[28] Today, there are three times as many people with serious mental illness in jails and prisons than in hospitals.[29]

The majority of detention facilities lack the necessary trained personnel, the resources, or the expertise to properly handle—let alone to treat— these incarcerated individuals with mental illness.

Currently, states transfer the most serious juvenile offenders into the adult criminal system. Legal transfer legislation is often based on an assumption that transferring juveniles into adult criminal systems results in an overall reduction in the amount of crime within a community. These legal transfer provisions do not in any way diminish the unmet mental health needs of the juvenile population.

Prevalence rates of psychiatric disorders found in youths transferred to *adult* criminal courts are not significantly different from rates of psychiatric disorders found in youths appearing in *juvenile* courts.[30] The proposed alternative approach (eliminating the legal presumption of competency to stand trial) to juvenile justice would reverse this recent procedure of transferring ever-larger numbers of juveniles into adult systems. The justification for this policy reversal would be to provide actual rehabilitative services focused on the unmet mental health needs of the population. This is the key to refocusing limited tax dollars on building a system designed to reduce recidivism and to provide meaningful intervention services to a population that benefits little from increasing reliance on detention and incarceration.[31] Unless these youthful offenders are going to be locked up in prison systems indefinitely, they will one day be released back into society. When they are returned to their home communities, they return without the benefit of having been assessed, treated, or medicated for mental health problems or substance abuse problems, which do not simply disappear on their own with the passage of time.

B. Proposals for Systemic Change

In 2006, the *Blueprint for Change: A Comprehensive Model for the Identification and Treatment of Youth with Mental Health Needs in Contact with the Juvenile Justice System* was developed by the National Center for Mental Health and Juvenile Justice in connection with the Council of Juvenile Correctional Administrators.[32] In addition to the proposals outlined in the *Blueprint for Change*, the following proposals are offered to help shift the focus of current delinquency procedures.

1. REVERSING THE PRESUMPTION OF COMPETENCY OF JUVENILES TO STAND TRIAL

As argued earlier in this chapter, given the vast amount of data painting a picture of the majority of juveniles in delinquency systems as demonstrating *DSM-5* diagnostic criteria, the current legal presumption that all juveniles brought into the court system should be presumed to be competent must be reconsidered. The presumption should either be neutral, and assessment should be required to determine affirmatively that the juvenile meets legal competency requirements; or the presumption should be reversed altogether, and adolescents should be assumed not to be competent to stand trial unless and until affirmatively shown otherwise. The general legal presumption with respect to the competency of adult offenders is consistent with the adult system's goal of holding offenders accountable for their misconduct. The dynamics involved in the juvenile population are significantly different. The vast majority of juvenile offenders do not engage in recidivist misconduct following their initial involvement with juvenile court. There is a significant minority of juvenile recidivist offenders, however, who are thought to be responsible for a disproportionate amount of all crime committed in most communities. This segment of the juvenile population should be identified, but even this group of offenders should not be legally presumed to be competent to stand trial.

Reversal of the competency presumption would help alter the mechanism of juvenile delinquency so as to focus on the adolescent's mental health needs and the connection they have with the charged misconduct. Adolescents are often charged with delinquent behaviors that are consistent with their diagnosed disorders according to the *DSM-5*. Rather than continuing to assume that a separate system for juveniles is needed, yet failing year after year to provide sufficient resources in the juvenile justice system, the reversal of the competency presumption would significantly alter the focus of juvenile court proceedings. This would compel courts to take more seriously the magnitude of mental health problems demonstrated by the adolescent population.

Rather than devoting time and energy toward conducting adjudication hearings and proving pending charges, the state's efforts would convert to identifying the disorders that can be diagnosed and then seeking out treatment modalities with proven success to assist in altering delinquent behavior and, more importantly, to help decrease or eliminate recidivist misconduct by juvenile offenders. This effort is designed to reduce overall community expenditures devoted to handling juvenile crime, to help reduce recidivist misconduct and spare the community the consequences of future crime, and to help break the cycle of juveniles graduating from crime during their adolescence into crime during their adulthood.

2. UNIVERSAL SCREENING FOR MENTAL HEALTH PROBLEMS

One of the more recent studies of the connection between mental health services and recidivism concluded first and foremost that mental health screening and assessment, including comprehensive, universal, and scientifically sound procedures, must be employed.[33] The high frequency rate of psychiatric disorders, along with comorbid psychiatric disorders, identified among youths in both the juvenile and adult justice system suggests that universal screenings and evaluations should be the norm and not the exception. Because legal professionals lack training in recognizing mental health issues, resources must be developed to train the lawyers involved in mental health proceedings. In addition, to proactively identify mental health issues, screening should be considered in other systems for youth, particularly the education system.

3. GREATER UTILIZATION OF DIVERSION PROGRAMS

As many jurisdictions have been expanding the role of diversionary programs in their communities, whereby the office of the prosecutor withholds delinquency charges in the event that an accused juvenile successfully completes a diversionary program, the discretionary provision of diversion should be placed in the control of the court, rather than left to the discretion of the district attorney or prosecutor. This would allow for the judge to exercise discretion when determining which juveniles should be given access to services rather than immediately going forward with litigation. The default of the current diversionary practice procedure usually results in most cases being prosecuted, with diversion being made available in exceptional cases. If the rates of mental health problems are as high as the literature concludes, then the default procedure should be to divert the vast majority of cases initially and then to rely on adjudication as a means of resolving only the minority of cases.

The justification for this reversal of legal process is the statistical data that support the extraordinarily high rates of mental illness, mental retardation, conduct disorders, substance use disorders, and developmental immaturity that define the population found in juvenile court proceedings and those adolescents who are eligible for transfer into adult criminal court systems. Relying more frequently on diversion programs allows the state to reserve the right to resort to filing a delinquency petition in the event that the juvenile is noncompliant with the diversion program's requirements, such as participation in multisystemic therapy (MST) programs, mentoring in juvenile justice, intensive parole,[34] compliance with prescribed medications, participation in other therapeutic programs, successful participation and attendance in school, or compliance with family rules.

4. APPLYING DUE PROCESS PRINCIPLES TO PROVIDE MENTAL HEALTH SERVICES TO JUVENILES

In the alternative to expanding the role of diversionary programs, we should consider the conversion of all juvenile delinquency cases to a mental-health-based system in which the incoming juvenile is assessed and diagnosed, and mental health services are the first response to the juvenile's entry into the system. If the overwhelming majority of juveniles petitioned as delinquent can be diagnosed as developmentally immature, mentally retarded, mentally ill, substance dependent, or manifesting comorbid disorders, then these issues should be given the highest priority, rather than attempting to define the juvenile's accountability for misconduct.[35] While accountability is a worthwhile component of any system of justice, the dynamics of this population are substantially different from those of the adult population, and there is an opportunity to work toward preventing any future misconduct, an opportunity that is dependent on the system's recognition of the nature of the mental illness, developmental immaturity, and behavioral factors that contribute greatly toward future delinquent behavior. Juveniles who satisfy competency standards would proceed forward in the more traditional juvenile justice system, while those found not to be competent would be diverted[36] out of more traditional delinquency proceedings and screened, diagnosed, and provided with treatment or medication in order to specifically address and reduce the likelihood of recidivist behaviors.[37] Juveniles' compliance with recommended treatment modalities and medications would continue their placement in the diversionary mental health track. Comprehension, voluntariness of participation, and adjudicative competency continue to remain as legal issues that require assessment of the juvenile participants. Noncompliance with court-ordered treatment and medication regimens could expose the juvenile and/or the parents or caregivers to enforcement hearings, sanctions, or contempt rulings.

The overall impact of these suggested systemic changes should result in a decrease in the number of incarcerated juveniles and an increase in the number of juveniles diagnosed with mental health issues requiring treatment and medication specifically targeted at their conditions. This should give rise to a significant reduction in juvenile recidivist misconduct. Although many jurisdictions offer some form of diversionary services currently, this approach would increase the total number of juveniles who might benefit from treatment of their mental conditions and increase the availability of diversion to entry-level offenders. The overwhelming data substantiating the extraordinarily high rate of mental health problems in this population justify the shifting presumption of competency along with the adoption of the systemic goal of reducing juvenile recidivism.

By refocusing the juvenile justice system on preventing recidivism and addressing unmet mental health needs, we can better serve the needs of communities while applying a specific goal other than retribution, which calls for no specific services, no assessments, and no mental health services for adolescents.[38] Of course, in order for such intervention services to be effective, they must be adequately funded and have some indicia of reliability. If the overall result of the reversal of the presumption of competency, combined with the screening of juvenile mental health needs, diverts greater numbers of juveniles out of traditional juvenile justice systems, then the monies otherwise dedicated to nonspecific probation services or incarceration could be better utilized in the provision of therapeutic and mental health services.

The estimated cost of $240 per day for the institutionalization of a juvenile—which does not include any costs associated with mental health services or medications—would go a long way toward paying for professional services that we now consider successful alternatives[39] to simple incarceration with no preparation for the adolescents' return to their home communities. It is far more expensive to incarcerate a juvenile for a year than to fund a year of rehabilitative services.[40] This is not to suggest that the cost to taxpayers for the creation of more widespread mental health courts would be de minimis.[41] Rather, these intervention systems provide a more fiscally sound and effective alternative to status quo models of incarceration:

> Bruce Winick, considered one of the pioneers of the therapeutic jurisprudence movement, acknowledges that some alternatives, like assertive community treatment and police diversion programs, may indeed be better interventions than utilizing mental health courts. However, Winick favors the use of mental health courts over the criminalization of persons with mental illnesses, realizing that the mental health system has a tendency to drop its problems on the courthouse doorsteps. Haimowitz does not see mental health courts as the only answer but agrees that they can be part of the solution. Lurgio et al. contend that the implementation of an integrated, specialized mental health court is a step toward establishing "a unified, accountable, case management system for maintaining the mentally ill in the community."[42]

Retribution as a systemic goal does not benefit the delinquent juveniles; nor does it benefit the victims of the offenses, and it certainly does not benefit the community in any meaningful way. If we are able to properly identify juveniles with treatable mental health problems, then the system should focus all of its resources on providing the appropriate treatment modalities. If the delinquency system maintains the status quo approach of holding juveniles accountable first and foremost, and of transferring more juveniles into adult criminal systems, then the lessons learned from other disciplines about developmental immaturity, mental health problems, and mood disorders will continue to fall on deaf ears. The data available on astronomical rates of juveniles with serious mental disorders currently serving time in detention facilities and adult jails are compelling. With the inability of states to adequately finance juvenile mental health services, the burdens of handling this population have continued to shift to delinquency and adult criminal systems. This shifting process has resulted in fewer available mental health services overall for juveniles. The question we must address is whether anyone seriously believes that by providing little or no mental health services to juveniles we should expect any significant improvement in the working of the delinquency system. The clear answer is no. We are the beneficiaries today of a wide array of multidisciplinary studies and research focusing on the dynamics of juvenile involvement in delinquency, the treatment modalities that have succeeded and failed, and the experiences of those jurisdictions that have created courts of limited jurisdiction focusing on substance abuse and mental health issues.

The unique American system of justice captured the world's attention as the first juvenile courts came into existence and responded to the many unmet needs of the country's most vulnerable community members. Today, we have an opportunity to regain the world's attention and to transform the juvenile justice system into what its original advocates sought to create: a separate system for children and adolescents designed to meet their needs and to help prevent future misconduct. By eliminating the legal presumption of competency to stand trial and requiring assessments and evaluations of the juveniles entering delinquency systems, we can focus community mental health resources in a manner designed to reduce or eliminate recidivist misconduct and hopefully to break the link between juvenile and adult criminal misconduct.

NOTES

1 Justice Policy Institute, *The Costs of Confinement: Why Good Juvenile Justice Policies Make Good Fiscal Sense* (Washington, DC: Justice Policy Institute, May 2009), 17 ("While researchers estimate that upwards of two-thirds of young people in detention centers could meet the criteria for having a mental disorder, a little more than a third need ongoing clinical care—a figure twice the rate of the general adolescent population."), *citing* Thomas Grisso, *Double Jeopardy: Adolescent Offenders with Mental Disorders* (Chicago: University of Chicago Press, 2004).

2 "For example, in a multi-site study with almost 10,000 youths in a range of juvenile justice settings, almost 65% of incarcerated juveniles and 60% of detained juveniles met criteria for one or another disorder." Machteld Hoeve, Larkin S. McReynolds, Gail Wasserman, "Service Referral for Juvenile Justice Youths: Associations with Psychiatric Disorder and Recidivism," *Administration and Policy in Mental Health Services Research* 41 (2014): 379.

3 Hans Steiner, Ivan Garcia, and Zakee Matthews, "Posttraumatic Stress Disorder in Incarcerated Juvenile Delinquents," *Journal of the American Academy of Child and Adolescent Psychiatry* 36, no. 3 (1997): 357–365.

4 Kathleen Skowyra and Joseph J. Cocozza, *A Blueprint for Change: Improving the System Response to Youth with Mental Health Needs Involved with the Juvenile Justice System*, Research and Program Brief (Delmar, NY: National Center for Mental Health and Juvenile Justice, June 2006), http://www.ncmhjj.com/wp-content/uploads/2013/07/2006_A-Blueprint-for-Change.pdf.

5 Hoeve, McReynolds, and Wasserman, *supra* note 2.

6 *See* Robert Constantine, Ross Andel, John Petrila, Marion Becker, John Robst, Gregory Teague, Timothy Boaz, and Andrew Howe, "Characteristics and Experiences of Adults with a Serious Mental Illness Who Were Involved in the Criminal Justice System," *Psychiatric Services* 61 (2010): 451–457.

7 E. Fuller Torrey, Aaron D. Kennard, Don Eslinger, Richard Lamb, and James Pavle, *More Mentally Ill Persons Are in Jails and Prisons than Hospitals: A Survey of the States* (Alexandria and Arlington, VA: National Sheriffs Association / Treatment Advocacy Center, May 2010), http://www.treatmentadvocacycenter.org/storage/documents/final_jails_v_hospitals_study.pdf.

8 Magda Stouthamer-Loeber and Rolf Loeber, "Lost Opportunities for Intervention: Undetected Markers for the Development of Serious Juvenile Delinquency," *Criminal Behaviour and Mental Health* 12 (2002): 72.

9 Paul Lichtenstein, Linda Hallder, Johan Zetterqvist, Arvid Sjölander, Eva Serlachius, Seena Fazel, Niklas Längström, and Henrik Larsson, "Medication for Attention Deficit-Hyperactivity Disorder and Criminality," *New England Journal of Medicine* 367 (2012): 2013: "All analyses suggested that there were reductions of 17 to 46% in criminality rates during treatment [with ADHD medications] periods."

10 One study concluded,

Despite high mental health need, service access among justice-involved youths is generally low. For example, among juvenile detainees, only 40% of those with substance use disorder and only 34% of those with anxiety, mood, or disruptive behavior disorders had received earlier treatment in their communities. As further documentation of their unmet service need, in one study of incarcerated youths, only 6% received a referral to mental health services. In another, among youths in various juvenile justice settings referred to juvenile courts, the court's decision included a mental health referral for only 2% of female and 4.5% of male youths.

Hoeve, McReynolds, and Wasserman, *supra* note 2, at 379 (internal citations omitted).

11 Justice Policy Institute, *supra* note 1, at 4.

12 Norman G. Poythress, Richard J. Bonnie, John Monahan, Randy Otto, and Steven K. Hoge, *Adjudicative Competence: The MacArthur Studies* (New York: Kluwer Academic / Plenum, 2002), 39.

13 362 U.S. 402 (1960).

14 As Thomas Grisso notes, "Many mood, anxiety, and attention deficit disorders create cognitive and emotional impairments in youths that are the equivalent of

those seen in more serious disorders of adulthood . . . especially when they add to already deficient abilities associated with 'normal' immaturity of adolescents." Grisso, *supra* note 1, at 176.

15 In *Medina v. California*, 505 U.S. 437, 112 S. Ct. 2572, 120 L. Ed. 2d 353 (1992), the Supreme Court upheld a state law that placed the burden of proof as to competency to stand trial on the defendant, and ruled that due process had not been violated because the law was not fundamentally unfair.

16 This is not to suggest that children with mental retardation may never be found to be competent, such as in cases of borderline mental retardation. The Supreme Court's perspective on defendants with mental retardation is somewhat curious. In *Atkins v. Virginia*, 536 U.S. 304 (2002), the Court ruled,

> Because of their impairments, [the mentally retarded] have diminished capacities to understand and process information, to communicate, to abstract from mistakes and learn from experience, to engage in logical reasoning, to control impulses, and to understand the reaction of others. . . . *Their deficiencies do not warrant an exemption from criminal sanctions, but they do diminish their personal culpability.*

> *Id.* at 318 (emphasis supplied).

17 Daniel S. Nagin, Alex R. Piquero, Elizabeth S. Scott, and Laurence Steinberg, "Public Preferences for Rehabilitation versus Incarceration of Juvenile Offenders: Evidence from a Contingent Valuation Survey," *Criminology & Public Policy* 5 (2006): 629 (internal citations omitted).

18 Thomas Grisso, Lawrence Steinberg, Jennifer Woolard, Elizabeth Cuffman, Elizabeth Scott, Sandra Graham, Fran Lexcen, N. Dickon Repucci, and Robert Schwartz, "Juveniles' Competence to Stand Trial: A Comparison of Adolescents' and Adults' Capacities as Trial Defendants," *Law and Human Behavior* 27 (August 2003): 333–363 (hereafter cited in the text as MacArthur Study).

19 *J.D.B. v. North Carolina*, 131 S. Ct. 2394, 2397, 564 U.S. ___, No. 09-11121 (slip op., 2011).

20 H. Richard Lamb and Linda E. Weinberger, "The Shift of Psychiatric Inpatient Care from Hospitals to Jails and Prisons," *Journal of the American Academy of Psychiatry & Law* 33, no. 4 (2005): 529–534.

21 Marisa Elena Domino, Edward C. Norton, Joseph P. Morrisey, and Neil Thakur, "Cost Shifting to Jails after a Change to Managed Mental Health Care," *Health Services* 39, no. 5 (2004): 1379 (internal citation omitted).

22 Lamb and Weinberger, *supra* note 20.

23 *See* Domino et al., *supra* note 21, at 1381.

24 *Id.*

25 Grisso, *supra* note 1, at 5 (internal citations omitted).

26 Risdon N. Slate, Jacqueline K. Buffington-Vollum, and W. Wesley Johnson, *The Criminalization of Mental Illness: Crisis and Opportunity for the Justice System*, 2nd ed. (Durham, NC: Carolina Academic Press, 2013), 125.

27 *Id.*

28 Marc Lacey, Kevin Sack, and A. G. Sulzberger, "States' Budget Crises Cut Deeply into Financing for Mental Health Programs," *New York Times*, January 20, 2011, http://www.nytimes.com/2011/01/21/us/21mental.html.

29 Torrey et al., *supra* note 7.

30 Jason J. Washburn, Linda A. Teplin, Laurie S. Voss, Clarissa D. Simon, Karen M. Abram, and Gary M. McClelland, "Psychiatric Disorders among Detained Youths: A Comparison of Youths Processed in Juvenile Court and Adult Criminal Court," *Psychiatric Services* 59, no. 9 (2008): 965–973: "Among youths processed in adult criminal court, 68% had at least one psychiatric disorder and 43% had two or more types of disorders. Prevalence rates and the number of comorbid types of disorders were not significantly different between youths . . . in adult criminal courts and those . . . in juvenile court" (965).

31 In 2009, the average cost of state-funded, postadjudication residential facilities for juveniles was $240.99 per day per juvenile, with roughly 93,000 juveniles held in detention facilities across the country. Justice Policy Institute, *supra* note 1, *citing* American Correctional Association, *2008 Directory: Adult and Juvenile Correctional Departments, Institutions, Agencies, and Probation and Parole Authorities* (Alexandria, VA: American Correctional Association, 2008).

32 *See* Skowyra and Cocozza, *supra* note 4, at 2.

33 Larkin S. McReynolds, Craig S. Schwalbe, and Gail A. Wasserman, "The Contribution of Psychiatric Disorder to Juvenile Recidivism," *Criminal Justice & Behavior* 37 (2010): 214: "Overall, the findings of this study support the universal screening for mental health problems for all youths entering the juvenile justice system."

34 It should be noted that the three most expensive rehabilitation programs are multisystemic therapy (estimated at $5,681 annually in 2003, according to the Washington State Institute for Public Policy), mentoring in the juvenile justice system (estimated at $6,471 in 2003), and intensive parole (estimated at $5,992 annually in 2003). Nagin et al. *supra* note 17, at 640.

35 This proposal does not represent a radical departure from existing court procedures, as approximately 170 mental health courts currently operate across the country (in comparison to nearly 2,500 drug courts), but current practices have not been thoroughly studied for overall effectiveness. *See* Nancy Wolff, Nicole Fabrikant, and Steven Belenko, "Mental Health Courts and Their Selection Processes: Modeling Variation for Consistency," *Law & Human Behavior* 35, no. 5 (October 2011): 402–412.

36 *Id.*

37 "Among patients with ADHD, we found an inverse association between pharmacologic treatment for ADHD and the risk of criminality" (involving the study of 16,087 men and 9569 women with ADHD from 2006 through 2009). Lichtenstein et al., *supra* note 9, at 2014.

38 One researcher concluded that "most people are unaware of the significant numbers of mentally ill youth involved with the juvenile justice system. Much of

society views juvenile offenders as 'bad kids in need of punishment.' In truth, there are large numbers of juvenile offenders who are 'ill kids in need of treatment.'" Lisa Melanie Boesky, *Juvenile Offenders with Mental Health Disorders: Who Are They and What Do We Want with Them?* (Alexandria, VA: American Correctional Association, 2002), 3.

39 Steve Aos, *Washington State's Family Integrated Transitions Program for Juvenile Offenders: Outcome Evaluation and Benefit-Cost Analysis* (Olympia: Washington State Institute for Public Policy, December 2004).

40 Nagin et al., *supra* note 17, at 643.

41 "The initial outlay of resources and personnel costs of a mental health court may be higher than the current total expenditures for incarceration of persons with mental illnesses. Initially guaranteeing treatment services and access to antipsychotic medications may be more expensive than merely putting persons in jail and having them mentally decompensate. . . . However, the long range objective must be to prevent people from recycling through the system." Risdon N. Slate, Jacqueline K. Buffington-Vollum, and W. Wesley Johnson, *The Criminalization of Mental Illness: Crisis and Opportunity for the Justice System*, 2nd ed. (Durham, NC: Carolina Academic Press, 2013), 408.

42 *Id.* (internal citations omitted).

PART III

Essential Perspectives

6

Why Should We Treat Juvenile Offenders Differently than Adults?

It's Not Because the Pie Isn't Fully Baked!

MARK R. FONDACARO

There is a wide degree of consensus among behavioral scientists, child advocates, policy makers, and the general public that we should treat juveniles who commit crimes differently than we treat adult offenders—at least some juveniles. This consensus begins to break down a bit when we focus on older or so-called mature adolescents, especially those who engage in very serious offenses. However, even in the latter context, the U.S. Supreme Court has indicated that some mitigation is appropriate.[1]

In fact, in a relatively recent string of cases, the Supreme Court has held that offenders under the age of 18 were not only ineligible for the death penalty, in *Roper*,[2] but ineligible for life without parole for non-capital crimes, in *Graham*,[3] and ineligible for life without parole for capital crimes when no individualized assessment is provided, in *Miller*.[4] In all three cases, the Court justified its decisions on the grounds that in comparison to adults who commit similar offenses, juveniles are less culpable and therefore deserving of less punishment, embracing a diminished culpability model of juvenile justice.

In this chapter, I provide a brief overview of the diminished culpability model, acknowledging some of the practical gains this model has helped to achieve in the area of juvenile justice reform. I then point out some of the potential scientific, legal, and social costs associated with uncritical advocacy of this approach. Finally, I discuss alternative justifications for treating juveniles differently than adult offenders. My conclusion is that we should indeed treat juvenile offenders differently than we currently treat adult offenders—but that this differential treatment should not be because they are less mature or malleable (which many of them may be) but because the emerging lesson from empirical research is that we should not be treating *adult* offenders the way we do in the adult criminal justice system.

I. Developmental Differences and the Diminished Culpability Model of Juvenile Justice

In an effort to reverse the trend toward harsh punishment of juvenile offenders, child advocates and developmental researchers have joined forces and have made the case, drawing on behavioral and neuroscience research, that juveniles should be treated less harshly than adult offenders because they are less culpable.[5] Proponents of the diminished culpability model of juvenile justice argue that juvenile offenders are deserving of less punishment because they are developmentally different from adults: less mature, more susceptible to outside influences, and less crystallized in the development of their personal identity and character than are adults who commit comparable crimes. Juveniles are a work in progress, on their way toward full development but not yet "fully baked" autonomous adults. When they reach adulthood and are presumed fully baked, then traditional principles of criminal responsibility and punishment are fully justified.

II. Gains, Challenges, and Costs Associated with the Diminished Culpability Model

The diminished culpability model is anchored in both developmental differences research and a retributive model of criminal justice.[6] This model reflects the dominant academic view among juvenile justice scholars, dovetails with general public conceptions of youth crime, and has been adopted by the U.S. Supreme Court. Overall, the embrace of this view has led to important human rights gains for juveniles facing the death penalty and sentences of life without the possibility of parole. This is truly a giant step forward in the evolving standards of decency embedded in the fundamental principles of the U.S. Constitution. However, there also are potential long-term costs associated with the uncritical embrace of the diminished culpability model. Chief among the concerns is that the diminished culpability model is anchored in a retributive model of criminal justice that relies on assumptions about human behavior that are increasingly being challenged by rapid advances in behavioral, neuroscience, and intervention research.[7] Overall, the present marriage of the existing body of developmental differences research with traditional retributive models of criminal responsibility and punishment runs the risks of (1) embracing empirically discredited assumptions about human behavior; (2) conflating folk psychology and commonsense beliefs with empirically based scientific understandings of human behavior; (3) abandoning many older, so-called mature adolescents to the adult criminal justice system; (4) failing to identify and address adult offenders whose psychosocial and neurobiological functioning and development may be indistinguishable from that of adolescent offenders; and (5) placing too much weight on judgments of past mental state as the basis for legal responsibility. A comprehensive review of the literature relevant to these concerns is well beyond the scope of this chapter. However, I will identify and highlight some of the most important findings.[8]

First, on the issue of *scientific skepticism about the assumptions underlying retribution as a justification for punishment,* Joshua Greene and Jonathan Cohen in their seminal analysis, "For the Law, Neuroscience Changes Nothing and Everything," conclude that scientific advances will and should result in "a shift away from punishment aimed at retribution in favour of a more progressive, consequentialist approach to the criminal law."[9] Their conclusions rest on a growing body of research that challenges the following empirically unsubstantiated assumptions about human behavior that are fundamental to retributive justifications for punishment:

- We can reliably and accurately judge someone's past mental state.[10]
- Conscious will is the primary author of human behavior.[11]
- Cognitions or thoughts (mens rea) concurrently actuate human behavior (actus reus).[12]
- Human behavior is largely guided by conscious, rational deliberation rather than unconscious processes.[13]

Retributive justice assumes a rational actor who consciously decides whether to obey the law and therefore engages in criminal behavior actuated by conscious thought. This actor's degree of culpability is based on his or her mental state, or mens rea, at the time of the offense—a past state of mind that the law presumes can be determined reliably and accurately by a jury or the judge. The body of research noted earlier calls these underlying assumptions about human behavior into question and therefore challenges the very foundation of retributive justice.

Second, *limitations on the developmental differences research call into question the validity of the conclusion that juveniles are different from adults in a legally material way.* With respect to juveniles, the body of developmental differences research summarized in the research literature and presented to the Supreme Court in *Roper, Graham,* and *Miller* focused on the issue of whether juveniles who break the law should be punished in the same manner and to the same extent as adults who commit comparable offenses.[14] The Supreme Court adopted the view expressed in this body of research that juvenile offenders deserve less punishment than adult offenders because their culpability is mitigated by diminished decision making, greater susceptibility to coercive influences, and character development that is a work in progress—that is, that their personal identity is not yet fully crystallized.[15] You might expect that most, if not all, of the research relied on would be based on comparisons of juvenile offenders with adult offenders. Unfortunately, that was not typically the case. In addition, proponents of this view pivot from focusing on juvenile and adult offenders who have committed comparable crimes to "typical" adolescents and adults—suggesting that the former are less culpable because "their criminal conduct is driven by transitory influences that are constitutive of this developmental stage."[16] This conceptual framework is rooted in principles of normative adolescent and adult development. However, *criminal behaviors committed by both juveniles and adults are sometimes the product not of normative development but of abnormal adolescent and adult development influenced by a range of social stressors and biological and psychological vulnerabilities.*

Even within the field of normative human development, developmental psychologists commonly take a life-course perspective, in which psychosocial development is conceptualized as a dynamic and multifaceted process, subject to ongoing change and contextual influences, rather than viewing development as a fixed and unchanging end state reached at the age of 18 or even 25 and beyond. Overall, when the best of the available research findings on developmental differences on issues of maturity, susceptibility to coercive influences, and identity development are combined, there is no clear scientific basis for drawing the dividing line between juveniles and adults at the age of 18. In fact, if the empirical evidence is to serve as a guide, the line would probably be drawn well into the third decade of life, if at all. Moreover, with respect to cognitive functioning, developmental psychologists would acknowledge that the typical nine-year-old child exceeds the legal threshold for being able to form the intent to commit a crime.

On the other hand, clinical and community psychologists focus on the psychological, social, and biological factors that contribute to the development of problem behavior, including aggressive and criminal behavior, and also draw on empirical research demonstrating the extent to which various interventions at the psychological, biological, and social levels of analysis can bring about behavioral change for both adolescents and adults. The multiple and interacting factors that can influence the development, treatment, and prevention of criminal behavior for both adolescents and adults are regarded as much more complex than merely poor individual decision making caused by one's level of developmental maturity.

On the issue of susceptibility to peer influence, although the Supreme Court relied largely on speculation for the *Roper* decision, more recent evidence suggests that on average, normal adolescents are more susceptible to peer influences than are normal adults. However, again this says nothing about how either normal or delinquent youth compare to the typical adult offender in terms of susceptibility to peer influences. Moreover, although the developmental researchers and the Supreme Court treat susceptibility to peer influence as an internal, dispositional characteristic of the adolescent, it is entirely possible that adults are less susceptible to peer influences because peers are less common features of their social context but that they are more susceptible to the outside influences of family members or significant others. More to the point, *it is possible that adult offenders are just as susceptible to negative peer influences as are typical adolescents or adolescents who commit crimes;*

studies that include adult offenders as a comparison group are needed to address this issue empirically.

On the issue of less crystallization of character for adolescents, the Supreme Court adopted *a view of character and character development that reflects an overly simplified model of personal identity development.* The model adopted provides a caricature of personal identity as a fixed internal attribute of the individual that is in a state of flux during adolescence and then crystallizes and becomes unified and stable in adulthood. More modern, ecologically oriented theory and research suggests that identity development is an ongoing process that changes across the life span rather than a fixed end state and that people have varied and multifaceted identities, both personal and social.[17]

Related to this issue is the view of the Supreme Court that juveniles deserve less punishment because they are more responsive to treatment. Although this makes intuitive sense and is consistent with folk-psychology conceptions of adolescent malleability, scientific evidence is not available to support this conclusion because *we have not tried to do the kinds of multisystemic interventions with adults that might have demonstrated effects on their prospects for change.* Recall that a few decades ago, behavioral scientists, clinicians, and the legal community were all in agreement that "nothing works" with juvenile offenders and that they could not be rehabilitated. Now, with "state of the art" multisystemic interventions, we can reduce recidivism rates among serious juvenile offenders from around 70 percent to 20 percent.[18] A shift in how we think about and respond to criminal behavior in adults would be necessary before we could evaluate their relative ability to respond to evidence-based interventions.

In sum, although the diminished culpability model has been widely embraced by the Supreme Court, policy makers, and the legal academic community, recent interdisciplinary scholarship has begun to question the scientific and legal basis and moral legitimacy of the diminished culpability model.[19] Although, as noted, there are clear and important gains associated with the Supreme Court's embrace of this view, there are also potential long-term costs, not only to juveniles and adults accused and convicted of serious crimes but to the credibility of science and the legitimacy of the criminal law. This will be especially true to the extent that the gradual but steady accumulation of empirical evidence suggests that our retributive justifications for adult punishment do not stand up to scientific scrutiny and the ongoing and inevitable advances in the behavioral and biological sciences. Adolescent immaturity is just one example of the growing number of diminished capacities that undermine the legitimacy of retributive justifications for punishment.[20]

III. Alternative Justifications for Treating Juveniles Differently than Adults

If the legal fictional homunculus at the core of retributive models of criminal responsibility continues to shrink in response to inevitable advances in the behavioral and biological sciences, the moral and legal basis for retribution as the primary justification for punishment of criminal behavior will be undermined as well. Although gallant efforts are being waged by advocates for the status quo to slim down the nature, scope, and depth of mens rea required to justify retributive sanctions,[21] these efforts are likely to have difficulty over time preventing legal reforms informed both by accumulating empirical research about biopsychosocial influences on human behavior and by principled legal analysis. With increasing empirical challenges to assumptions needed to legitimize retributive punishment, there is likely to be a policy shift toward more consequentialist justifications for legal sanctions, empirically established limiting principles of government intervention, and empirically based rules to guide criminal law and procedure aimed at crime prevention and recidivism reduction rather than indeterminate, deontological notions of just deserts.

A potential shift toward a more consequentialist approach to both juvenile and adult criminal justice begs the question of what such a system might look like. As Christopher Slobogin and I have argued elsewhere, there is more procedural flexibility with the juvenile justice system because due process in that system is grounded primarily in the due process clause of the Fourteenth Amendment and principles of fundamental fairness rather than the explicit text of the Fifth and Sixth Amendments.[22] These procedural differences between the juvenile and adult system are most pronounced at the adjudicatory or culpability phase of the process. Once legal responsibility is established, however, any required procedural distinctions between the juvenile and adult system are substantially, if not completely, diminished. This allows for broad flexibility in both systems to adopt the fairest and most effective procedures for implementing a fully consequentialist regime for responding to criminal behavior.

In the juvenile realm, a consequentialist, risk- and resource-management model of juvenile justice would be guided by the following principles. First, it would be forward-looking, aimed at recidivism reduction, rather than backward-looking and aimed at retributive punishment. Second, the system would draw on legal expertise and judicial authority to determine legal culpability and to provide graduated responses and incentives to encourage offenders' compliance with dispositional requirements. The limiting principle guiding intervention would be the least restrictive intervention capable of promoting compliance and reducing recidivism risk to a low level on the basis of actuarial risk-assessment measures. The interaction and relationship between the judicial authority and juvenile offender would be guided by principles of procedural justice to enhance compliance. Moreover, the maintenance of a role for a judicial officer with authority to sanction noncompliance would serve to enhance public acceptance of a more consequentialist approach to juvenile justice. Third, the judicial authority would be complemented with an interdisciplinary group of professionals with expertise in human development, clinical and community intervention, education, mental and physical health, program evaluation, and organizational management. Decision making at the individual, program, system, and policy levels would be evidence based and draw on the expertise of this interdisciplinary risk- and resource-management team. Finally, the system would be ecologically self-aware and establish relations with other relevant youth-socializing institutions such as schools; the health care, mental health, and child welfare systems; and the adult criminal justice system.

Overall, the eventual adoption of a more consequentialist, risk- and resource-management model of juvenile justice would mean that we were clearly treating juvenile offenders differently than we currently treat adult offenders—not because the personal identities of juveniles are not fully baked but because the legal system is folding all of the available and emerging scientific ingredients into its recipe for a truly just system for juvenile offenders. Over time, this recipe may even be perfected to provide a more fair and effective system of criminal justice for adults as well.

Acknowledgments

The research for this chapter was completed while the author was on sabbatical as a visiting professor at Duke University's Center for Child and Family Policy. The views and analysis presented in this chapter are drawn from and expanded on in "Rethinking the Scientific and Legal Implications of Developmental Differences Research in Juvenile Justice," *New Criminal Law Review* 17 (2014): 407–441.

NOTES

1   *Roper v. Simmons*, 543 U.S. 551 (2005).

2   *Id.*

3   *Graham v. Florida*,130 S. Ct. 2011 (2010).

4   *Miller v. Alabama*, 132 S. Ct. 2455 (2012).

5   Laurence Steinberg and Elizabeth Scott, "Less Guilty by Reason of Adolescence: Developmental Immaturity, Diminished Responsibility, and the Juvenile Death Penalty," *American Psychologist* 58, no. 12 (2003): 1009–1118.

6   *See generally* Elizabeth Scott and Laurence Steinberg, "Social Welfare and Fairness in Juvenile Crime Regulation," *Louisiana Law Review* 71 (2010): 35–97.

7   *See generally* Emad H. Atiq, "How Folk Beliefs about Free Will Influence Sentencing: A New Target for the Neuro-Determinist Critics of Criminal Law," *New Criminal Law Review* 16, no. 3 (2013): 449–493.

8   *See generally* Mark R. Fondacaro, "The Injustice of Retribution: Toward a Multi-systemic Risk Management Model of Juvenile Justice," *Journal of Law & Policy* 20 (2011): 145–165.

9   Joshua Greene and Jonathan Cohen, "For the Law, Neuroscience Changes Everything and Nothing," *Philosophical Transactions of the Royal Society B* 359 (2004): 1775.

10 Laurence J. Severance, Jane Goodman, and Elizabeth Loftus, "Inferring the Criminal Mind: Toward a Bridge between Legal Doctrine and Psychological Understanding," *Journal of Criminal Justice* 20 (1992): 107–120.

11 Daniel M. Wegner and Thalia Wheatley, "Apparent Mental Causation: Sources of the Experience of Will," *American Psychologist* 54 (1999): 480–492.

12 Roy F. Baumeister, E. J. Masicampo, and Kathleen D. Vohs, "Do Conscious Thoughts Cause Behavior?," *Annual Review of Psychology* 62 (2011): 331–361.

13 John A. Bargh and Tanya L. Chartrand, "The Unbearable Automaticity of Being," *American Psychologist* 54, no. 7 (1999): 462–479.

14 Steinberg and Scott, *supra* note 5, at 1009.

15 *Id.*
16 *Id.* at 1011.
17 *See generally* Urie Bronfenbrenner, *The Ecology of Human Development: Experiments by Nature and Design* (Cambridge: Harvard University Press, 1979); John E. Schulenberg, Arnold J. Sameroff, and Dante Cicchetti, "The Transition to Adulthood as a Critical Juncture in the Course of Psychopathology and Mental Health," *Development and Psychopathology* 16 (2004): 799–806.
18 Charles M. Borduin, Barton J. Mann, Lynn T. Cone, Scott W. Henggeler, Bethany R. Fucci, David M. Blaske, and Robert A. Williams, "Multisystemic Treatment of Serious Juvenile Offenders: Long-Term Prevention of Criminality and Violence," *Journal of Consulting and Clinical Psychology* 63, no. 4 (1995): 569–578.
19 *See* Christopher Slobogin and Mark R. Fondacaro, *Juveniles at Risk: A Plea for Preventative Justice* (New York: Oxford University Press, 2011).
20 Michael S. Gazzaniga, *Who's in Charge? Free Will and the Science of the Brain* (New York: HarperCollins, 2011).
21 Nita A. Farahany, "A Neurological Foundation for Freedom," *Stanford Technology Law Review* 2012 (2011): 4; Stephen J. Morse, "Determinism and the Death of Folk Psychology: Two Challenges to Responsibility from Neuroscience," *Minnesota Journal of Law, Science & Technology* 9 (2008): 1–36.
22 Slobogin and Fondacaro, *supra* note 19, at 97–101.

7

Lost in Translation No More

Marketing Evidence-Based Policies for Reducing
Juvenile Crime

RICHARD E. REDDING

Across the political spectrum, all share the goal of reducing juvenile crime. "Evidence-based" (i.e., empirically demonstrated to be effective in rigorous scientific studies) juvenile offender programs are consistent with the increasing demand from policy makers, funders, and consumers for evidence-based practices in many arenas, including medicine, education, and social services.[1] Yet the demand for such practices often does not translate to juvenile justice, with rehabilitative programs being perceived as too ineffective, costly, and lenient because they fail to satisfy society's retributive need to punish offenders.[2]

Even though effective evidence-based programs have been available for 20 years,[3] they still "are not funded well and are not penetrating the marketplace of social services for youth."[4] The public, policy makers, prosecutors, and judges will support and utilize evidence-based programs when apparent conflicts between the demand for evidence-based programs, concerns about program effectiveness and costs, and the felt need for punishment are reconciled. This can be accomplished if we use evidence-based persuasion strategies to effectively communicate the compatibility of these three goals.

Three Objections to Evidence-Based Programs: Punishment Is Necessary, Punishment Works, and Rehabilitation Is Ineffective

I have spoken to community groups, testified before state legislatures on juvenile justice legislation, and provided expert testimony in juvenile homicide cases. I make the case that trying and sentencing juveniles as adults (commonly known as "transfer" or "waiver" to the criminal court) has counterrehabilitative effects, exacerbates recidivism, and does not deter would-be offenders[5] and that evidence-based rehabilitation programs are more effective. One response I hear reveals what Franklin Zimring calls "the punitive necessity of waiver," when juvenile crime is serious enough that it requires, for punishment's sake, a sentence exceeding that which can be meted out by the juvenile courts.[6] Judges, for instance, usually will concede that the prosecutor's case for transfer failed on deterrence or rehabilitation grounds but say that their decision to transfer the youth was based on the seriousness or heinousness of his or her offense, which deserved a tough sentence.

Consider a case involving two 14-year-old African American boys, one of whom urged the other to join him in stealing money from his 78-year-old great grandmother, whom they struck multiple times with a hatchet. One understands why the juvenile court judge, though persuaded that transferring the case to criminal court would improve neither long-term deterrence nor the prospects of rehabilitation, felt that this premeditated brutal murder necessitated transfer, despite the youths' reduced maturity and culpability given their tender age.[7] With respect to their race and concerted criminal acts, this case is prototypical of the juvenile offender cases adjudicated in our criminal courts. African American youth are vastly overrepresented, accounting for 46% of the juvenile cases transferred to criminal court and 57% of juveniles incarcerated in state prisons.[8] And juvenile crime usually has a strong social component,[9] often involving peer pressure and the adolescent desire to impress and be liked by peers,[10] with unsupervised or unoccupied youth running together with the wrong crowd. Yet in other ways, this case is not representative of the juvenile cases transferred to criminal court, which commonly involve older juveniles whose offenses are not terribly violent, if violent at all.[11] How the public, legislators, prosecutors, and judges react to these cases, in which the punitive necessity of transfer is less compelling, is instructive about the assumptions underlying their support for punitive policies.

First, the public often responds that punishment is necessary, even in cases lacking any utilitarian reason for punishment. Studies show that people express a desire to punish even when they cannot identify any practical purpose it would serve and even when punishment clearly is unnecessary to prevent reoffending (e.g., when the defendant has become paralyzed). They consider recidivism prevention less relevant to sentencing, except for cases in which the offender's criminal intent to harm was relatively low.[12] Thus, people are driven by retributive concerns: that is, what is the offender's just deserts? Retribution, which is punishment for the moral sake of punishment rather than for utilitarian reasons (to deter or rehabilitate), has a long tradition in moral philosophy and is the foundation of virtually all systems of criminal justice. Punishment is seen as necessary to right the scales of justice, to exact the moral debt that offenders owe to their victims and society, and to affirm the personhood and dignity of victims and offenders alike (rather than treating the latter as automatons lacking free will).[13] Retribution carries with it a moral condemnation; as one early American law professor wrote in 1883, "it is morally right to hate criminals."[14] For these reasons, unlike rehabilitation programs, punishment regimes are not held to account for reducing recidivism or deterring crime.[15]

Second, the public thinks that punishment works, and it often questions studies showing that punishment-oriented policies fail to prevent juvenile crime and have counterrehabilitative effects on offenders.[16] The public is unpersuaded by the counterintuitive nature of the studies' findings and seize on their limitations (e.g., the inability to identify and control for all possible selection effects in studies comparing recidivism outcomes in transferred versus nontransferred youths), while pointing out that declining juvenile crime rates must be due to "get tough" responses to juvenile offenders. Indeed, people may eschew research because everyone thinks he or she is an expert on crime control,[17] with an intuitive sense of what works, and people's intuition tells them that the way to prevent crime is to punish offenders. This is especially true for conservatives; among juvenile court judges, there is a correlation between political conservatism, support for punishment-oriented juvenile justice policies, and the belief that transfer is an effective deterrent.[18] In addition, sometimes people suspect that studies were corrupted by liberal, results-driven social scientists overly sympathetic to offenders.[19] And in individual cases, prosecutors argue that they exercise their discretion appropriately and seek transfer or tough sentences only in the worst cases warranting it, even though research indicates otherwise[20] and despite what we know about the biases that creep into such discretionary judgments.[21]

Third, in opinion surveys, the public expresses a willingness to pay for crime prevention and offender rehabilitation programs, but only if such programs are effective,[22] and that is the rub. Much of the public, skeptical of the possibility of true reform, believes that rehabilitation programs are ineffective, reflecting the myth that offenders are "bad apples" who cannot be rehabilitated.[23] In any case, the public's willingness to pay for evidence-based programs has not translated into politicians campaigning or voting for such expenditures, which they fear will paint them as "soft on crime"—the political death knell. But as a leading criminologist says, "I have found very few policy makers unwilling to at least listen to the empirical research when you frame it within the context of public protection."[24]

Evidence-Based: What the Research Says about Punishment and Rehabilitation

Fortunately, science belies the widely held assumptions that harsh punishment is an effective deterrent and that rehabilitation programs are ineffective or fail the cost-benefit test. Research shows that adjudicating juveniles in criminal courts and imposing adult sentences produces counterrehabilitative and nondeterrent effects, as documented in two recent comprehensive reports promulgated by the Centers for Disease Control and Prevention[25] and the U.S. Department of Justice.[26] Thanks to substantial scientific advances in understanding the causes and correlates of juvenile crime, we have developed effective methods for identifying those youth at high risk for offending, preventing juvenile crime through programs targeted at these high-risk youth, and rehabilitating even serious, violent, and chronic juvenile offenders,[27] as demonstrated by meta-analyses (the statistical pooling of results across studies) of 548 treatment outcome studies with juvenile delinquents.[28] Effective programs typically are comprehensive family- and community-based treatments that identify and address the multiple risk factors (at the school, neighborhood, family, and child levels) contributing to a child's delinquency,[29] as well as the child's unique characteristics that may affect his or her response to treatment, and tailor the treatment regimen accordingly.[30] This type of matching of services to each child's risk and needs profile produces substantial reductions in recidivism (down to 25% recidivism) as compared to services that do not match in this way (down to only 75%).[31] Programs also must be of sufficient duration (about six months or longer) to produce lasting effects, have well-trained service providers who are held accountable for outcomes, and be monitored to ensure quality and that they faithfully adhere to the treatment model.[32]

One of the most effective treatments is multisystemic therapy (MST), which is an intensive, multimodal, family-based treatment that intervenes with the child's family, school, and peer networks, focusing on improving parental discipline and supervision, improving family relations, providing social and problem-solving skills training for the child, decreasing the youth's association with delinquent peers, improving school performance, and increasing the youth's involvement in prosocial activities.[33] MST has been found in rigorous evaluation studies to reduce recidivism even among chronic juvenile offenders, which is typically very high, down to 22%,[34] and has also demonstrated impressive recidivism reductions with juvenile sex offenders, drug-abusing juvenile offenders, and violent juvenile offenders.[35] Most evidence-based interventions, however, produce more modest outcomes, reducing recidivism by 10%–30%,[36] but as discussed later, even these outcomes achieve huge cost savings. Since the majority of crime is committed by a small percentage of habitual offenders who become the "career criminals"—a phenomenon known in criminology as the 7% problem[37]—the most cost-effective programs will be targeted at this group of juveniles,[38] which modern risk-assessment technology permits us to do.[39] Consider that a recent program employing this approach with high-risk youth in Chicago produced a 46% reduction in shootings by youth, a 32% reduction in youth homicides, a reduction in the juvenile detention center population from 1,500 to 275, and a $297 million cost savings over four years.[40]

Indeed, what about the costs of rehabilitation programs compared to the benefits they produce in saving money and reducing crime? Spending on crime control, jails, and prisons now accounts for about 30% of state budgets, with the cost of housing just one juvenile inmate being as high as $200,000 per year in some states.[41] Yet economic analyses suggest that "the benefits to society in terms of crime reduction are unlikely to outweigh the explicit monetary costs of housing and maintaining an additional inmate," with a benefit-cost ratio "substantially less than one."[42] The costs of long sentences usually outweigh any crime-control benefits, though relatively short sentences may reduce recidivism.[43] Because preventing a high-risk or early offending youth from becoming a career criminal saves close to $2 million,[44] programs "need only produce a modest level of crime reduction to fully pay back the costs and produce a dividend for government and crime victims."[45] For example, an intervention that costs $7,000 per youth (roughly the average cost of the most effective intensive programs) would save money even when it diverts only one out of every 250 youths from a life of crime.[46] But evidence-based programs do far better than that. Large-scale studies comparing the cost of treatment or prevention against the benefits of reduced recidivism and crime prevention (e.g., measuring recidivism among treatment versus control groups of offending or at-risk youth) show that the most effective programs have a $10 to $25 return on investment for every dollar spent; even the least effective programs produce a $2 return for every dollar spent.[47] For example, it is estimated that effective prevention programs can reduce crime in California by 22%, resulting in 220,000 fewer crimes every year.[48] And such economic analyses underestimate the total cost savings because they do not capture the costs of police investigation and court adjudication, public-safety efforts, social service, health care and insurance, costs to offenders' families, and the intangible costs to victims and communities, such as fear of crime and diminished quality of life.[49]

Using Evidence-Based Persuasion Tactics: Communicating Research Findings in the Language of Policy Makers

Given the clear scientific evidence and the costs to society as well as to offenders of overly punitive responses to juvenile crime, we have the responsibility to persuade the public and policy makers that available evidence-based preventive and rehabilitative programs are effective, worth the cost, and compatible with reasoned and measured punishment and that more punitive responses are not worth the cost. And when lawyers litigate cases in the juvenile or criminal courts, they need to persuade prosecutors and judges that the best way to prevent the juvenile from reoffending is through the use of proven rehabilitative programs, in most cases, under juvenile court jurisdiction that imposes measured but not counterrehabilitative punishment. Judges knowledgeable about the ineffectiveness of transfer as a deterrent are less likely to transfer juvenile offenders than are judges who think otherwise,[50] and judges' dispositional decisions are influenced by their knowledge of the effectiveness and availability of dispositional options.[51] Thus, educating judges about the ineffectiveness of transfer and the effectiveness of evidence-based rehabilitation programs should impact their decisions, as demonstrated by educational programs in Florida that dramatically reduced the number of cases transferred.[52] The focus should be on how rehabilitative programs can prevent reoffending, which will resonate with all judges, rather than on the difficult life circumstances that may have led the offender to crime, which may not resonate with retribution-oriented judges.[53]

To convince policy makers and the public, we must use evidence-based persuasion tactics. Research in social psychology, linguistics, and communication studies has identified a large number of factors affecting persuasion, but six sets of principles are especially relevant here. First, people typically reject arguments that conflict too much with their moral and political worldviews while having a bias toward evidence that supports their beliefs.[54] Judgments on moral issues such as how society should respond to offenders are driven by five overarching considerations: harm/care, fairness/reciprocity, loyalty, authority/respect, and purity/sanctity.[55] Conservatives are guided by all five concerns but most particularly loyalty, respect, and sanctity, whereas liberals are usually guided mainly by concerns for fairness and caring.

Second, people's receptivity to policy arguments can change dramatically as a function of how the arguments are "framed" or characterized. Framing can be tailored to the target audience, with different frames being effective with different audiences.[56] For example, when the problem of income inequality is described as the rich making more than the poor instead of the poor making less than the rich, support for redistributive tax policies increases,[57] describing a charge as a "carbon offset" rather than a "tax" increases support for it among Republicans but has no effect on Democrats' support,[58] and framing environmental problems as ones of impurity (rather than Earth saving) enhances support for proenvironmental policies among conservatives.[59]

Third, people prefer simple over complex ways of thinking about policy.[60] Thus, familiar simplistic stereotypes (e.g., juvenile offenders as "superpredators" or "morally defective")[61] and commonsensical myths (e.g., juvenile offenders are rational actors who calculate the likelihood of arrest and punishment)[62] are more attractive than complex counternarratives rehearsing the scientific evidence.[63]

Fourth, stories and narratives that personalize an issue, triggering an emotional response, will be more persuasive than dry facts,[64] and fear-invoking narratives are especially powerful.[65] Because people strive to avoid losses more than they seek to achieve gains,[66] negative information usually has a greater impact than positive information.[67] For example, public health campaigns emphasizing the negative consequences of engaging in a particular activity are often more effective than those emphasizing the benefits of not doing so.[68]

Fifth, people defer to expert opinion and will often change their opinion as a result of information provided by experts unless they doubt the experts' credibility,[69] which they likely will if they perceive a conflict between their worldview and that of the expert (such as conservative policy makers vis-à-vis liberal social scientists). Sixth, there often is a "false consensus effect" whereby people sense that more people share the perceived majority view than is actually the case,[70] yet the more frequently an argument is repeated, the more likely it is to be accepted.[71]

Applying these six persuasion principles, one can readily see why the "rehabilitation does not work with juvenile offenders who must be punished" narrative has been so effective, particularly among conservative audiences. It frames the issue with respect to simplistic, familiar stereotypes about juvenile offenders and casts the problem as the moral issues of offenders not respecting authority and violating the sanctity of the code of civilized behavior, and the necessity of punishment to vindicate the victims and prevent further harm to the community. High-profile cases of violent juvenile crime generate fear in the public, triggering an emotional response that relies on these stereotypes and moral heuristics. And people perceive that others in the community share their views— one often hears talk that the justice system coddles criminals and does not punish sufficiently or effectively. The public rarely hears from experts about the effectiveness of rehabilitation, and when it does, it often dismisses them as "bleeding-heart liberals" or "ivory tower" academics who do not understand the real world.

Reframing the Narrative: It's about Economics (and Smaller Government!)

> Today's criminal justice system is big government on steroids, and the responsibility for taming its excesses falls to those committed to smaller government: conservatives. We fight against big government, excess spending, unaccountability, and bureaucracy in nearly every other segment of spending.
> Grover Norquist, president of Americans for Tax Reform[72]

> Conservatives are known for being tough on crime, but we must also be tough on criminal justice spending. That means demanding more cost-effective approaches that enhance public safety.
> William J. Bennett, former secretary of education and director of the Office of Drug Control Policy[73]

The argument for rehabilitation often succeeds with liberal policy makers. What we must do is reframe the narrative so that the argument will also succeed with conservative policy makers and the general public. We need a simple narrative that activates their moral concerns, that is consistent with their beliefs and experiences, and that provides new data and information (on cost-effectiveness) that they can accept into their worldview, conveyed by people they trust. We must frame the issue as one of reducing crime and ensuring public safety but, even more than that, of economic accountability that saves the taxpayers money (money that could be spent on other law enforcement efforts, such as more police officers and community policing), and we must do so while affirming the rightful place for punishment. We must convey this message frequently, using conservatives among the messengers whenever possible, and in a context conveying that many others in the community share this same view.

Indeed, according to a U.S. Justice Department study, policy makers overestimate public support for punitive criminal justice policies and underestimate support for rehabilitation.[74] Consider Right on Crime, a conservative organization in Texas (having the support of Jeb Bush, Newt Gingrich, Grover Norquist, Ed Meese, Bill Bennett, John DiI-ulio,[75] and Michael Reagan) that "makes the conservative case for re-form: fighting crime, prioritizing victims, and protecting taxpayers."[76] Right on Crime notes that "liberal ideas . . . failed to effectively monitor many criminal justice programs to determine whether they were truly providing taxpayers with the results commensurate with their cost.[77] . . . The question underlying every tax dollar that is spent on fighting crime ought to be: Is this making the public safer?"[78] Framing the problem as one of huge costs to the state of Texas of incarcerating so many offenders and cost savings of alternative approaches, the organization promotes "evidence-based practices" instead:

> Cost-effective interventions that leverage the strengths of families and communities to reform troubled youths are critical to a successful juve-nile justice system. . . . Funds should only be spent on programs that are supported by evidence. . . . [We should] ensure that youth who would be most successful in non-residential programs are not placed in costly residential settings. . . . In Texas, for example, incarceration in a state juvenile facility costs approximately $270 per day while diversion or su-pervision programs range from $7 to $73 per day. . . . Research has found unnecessary incarceration may actually make lower-risk youths more likely to re-offend.[79] . . . While the growth of incarceration took many dangerous offenders off the streets, research suggested that it reached a point of diminishing returns, as recidivism rates increased. . . . In most states, prisons came to absorb more than 85 percent of the corrections budget.[80] . . . State and federal spending on corrections has grown 400% over the past 20 years, . . . and 1 in 8 full-time state government employees works in corrections. . . . How is it "conservative" to spend vast amounts of taxpayer money on a strategy without asking whether it is providing taxpayers with the best public safety return on their investment?[81]

Note how this conservative organization frames the issue, particularly in the last sentence. Although public safety is strongly emphasized,[82] that goal is stated within the larger frame of saving taxpayers money and reducing the size of government, which are moral imperatives for conservatives. There is good reason why Right on Crime frames the issue this way. Conservatives tend to be skeptical that rehabilitation works (and they do not want to hear psychologists and sociologists framing offenders as victims of society who offended because of their difficult life circumstances), even when you show them empirical evidence of effectiveness. It is an easier sell when that evidence is framed within an economic context as well as a context of making juvenile justice centered in local communities and families rather than "big government" state prisons and detention facilities. We need to shift the financial incentives away from incarceration toward community-based programs, and we should encourage the public and policy makers to demand accountability for costs and outcomes from the juvenile justice system.[83] If we do so, the evidence-based practices will win the day. As one astute politician explained to me, "the right does not believe in psychology, but it sure believes in economics."

At the same time, we should be mindful that the converse is also true: psychology does not believe in the right, and that is a problem if we wish to persuade conservatives. It is important that liberal social scientists acknowledge the proper place for punishment within rehabilitation, while communicating that incarceration is the most costly and least effective punishment available. Cost-effective punishments are community- and family-based, such as house arrest and electronic monitoring, restitution, group homes, parental discipline (e.g., removal of privileges and behavioral contracting), and short-term detention. We should encourage the public to demand accountability from punishments in terms of cost-effectiveness and achieving identifiable goals (e.g., utilitarian goals, serving the needs of crime victims, promoting public confidence in the justice system).[84] As Judge Michael Marcus explains, "affording 'just deserts' a blanket exemption from accountability for achieving any social purpose is our single most significant barrier to responsible [policy]."[85]

But the future for positive juvenile justice reform appears bright. In the past decade, almost half the states have changed their juvenile codes to decrease their reliance on adjudicating and sentencing juveniles as adults while instead encouraging greater use of nonincarcerative rehabilitative options, including in relatively conservative states such as Georgia, Idaho, Missouri, Texas, and Utah[86] and with support from conservative lawmakers. Legislative changes in Colorado, for instance, were supported by the Republican house majority whip and passed with a healthy bipartisan legislative majority, and Ohio Republican governor John Kasich supported reform legislation in his state, saying, "what we know is if we can successfully apply community treatment, we have much better outcomes than when we lock people up."[87] We must make the public and policy makers aware of these trends, since an evidence-based persuasion principle is that people will tend to follow the crowd, yet they often misestimate what the crowd believes. Given the pervasiveness of negative stereotypes and myths about juvenile offenders and the possibility for reform, advocates need to counter these misconceptions with information about the changes that states are making and why they are making these changes—to reduce taxpayer costs by preventing crime and reoffending. That is an argument that resonates with conservatives and liberals alike.

NOTES

1 R. E. Redding, "Evidence-based sentencing: The science of sentencing policy and practice," *Chapman Journal of Criminal Justice* 1 (2009): 1–19.

2 K. A. Dodge, "Framing public policy and prevention of chronic violence in American youths," *American Psychologist* 63 (2008): 573–590; E. J. Latessa, "The challenge of change: Correctional programs and evidence-based practices," *Criminology & Public Policy* 3 (2004): 547–560; R. E. Redding, *Juvenile transfer laws: An effective deterrent to delinquency?*, Juvenile Justice Bulletin, NCJ-220595 (Washington, DC: U.S. Department of Justice, Office of Juvenile Justice and Delinquency Prevention, 2008).

3 S. W. Henggeler, "Treatment of violent juvenile offenders—We have the knowledge: Comment on Gorman-Smith et al.," *Journal of Family Psychology* 10 (1996): 137–141.

4 Dodge, *supra* note 2, at 574.

5 Redding, *supra* note 2.

6 F. Zimring, "The punitive necessity of waiver," in J. Fagan and F. Zimring (eds.), *The changing borders of juvenile justice: Transfer of adolescents to the criminal court* (pp. 207–224) (Chicago: University of Chicago Press, 2000), 207.

7 M. R. Fondacaro and L. G. Fasig, "Judging juvenile responsibility: A social ecological perspective," in N. E. Dowd, D. G. Singer, and R. F. Wilson (eds.), *Handbook of children, culture, and violence* (pp. 355–374) (Thousand Oaks, CA: Sage, 2006).

8 R. E. Redding and B. Arrigo, "Multicultural perspectives on delinquency among African-American youths: Etiology and intervention," in *Comprehensive handbook of multicultural school psychology* (pp. 710–743) (Hoboken, NJ: Wiley, 2005).

9 F. Zimring, *American youth violence* (New York: Oxford University Press, 1998).

10 C. S. Fried and N. D. Reppucci, "Criminal decision making: The development of adolescent judgment, criminal responsibility and culpability," *Law and Human Behavior* 25 (2001): 45–61.

11 R. E. Redding, "Juveniles transferred to criminal court: Legal reform proposals based on social science research," *Utah Law Review* 1997:709–763; Redding, *supra* note 2.

12 E. Aharoni and A. J. Fridlund, "Punishment without reason: Isolating retribution in lay punishment of criminal offenders," *Psychology, Public Policy & Law* 18 (2012): 599–625.

13 J. Dressler, *Cases and materials on criminal law*, 6th ed. (St. Paul, MN: Thomson West, 2012).

14 Ibid., 80, quoting J. F. Stephen, *A history of the criminal law of England* (London: Macmillan, 1883).

15 M. H. Marcus, "Conversations on evidence-based sentencing," *Chapman Journal of Criminal Justice* 1 (2009): 61–127.

16 For reviews, see Centers for Disease Control and Prevention, *Effects on violence of laws and policies facilitating the transfer of youth from the juvenile to the adult justice system* (Atlanta: Centers for Disease Control and Prevention, 2007); R. E. Redding, "Adult punishment for juvenile offenders: Does it reduce crime?," in N. E. Dowd, D. G. Singer, and R. F. Wilson (eds.), *Handbook of children, culture, and violence* (pp. 375–394) (Thousand Oaks, CA: Sage, 2006).

17 Latessa, *supra* note 2.

18 R. E. Redding and K. B. Hensl, "Knowledgeable judges make a difference: Judicial beliefs affect juvenile court transfer decisions," *Juvenile & Family Court Journal* 62 (2011): 15–24.

19 Redding, *supra* note 16.

20 Children's Action Alliance, *Improving public safety by keeping youth out of the adult criminal justice system* (Phoenix, AZ: Children's Action Alliance, 2010); Redding, *supra* note 11; Redding, *supra* note 2.

21 Redding, *supra* note 11; D. Kahnemann, *Thinking, fast and slow* (New York: Macmillan, 2011).

22 E.g., M. A. Cohen, R. Rust, S. Steen, and S. Tidd, "Willingness-to-pay for crime control programs," *Criminology* 42 (2004): 86–106.

23 See Dodge, *supra* note 2.

24 Latessa, *supra* note 2, at 549.

25 Centers for Disease Control, *supra* note 16.

26 Redding, *supra* note 2.

27 M. W. Lipsey, "The primary factors that characterize effective interventions with juvenile offenders: A meta-analytic overview," *Victims & Offenders* 4 (2009): 124–147; R. Loeber and D. P. Farrington (eds.), *Serious and violent juvenile offenders: Risk factors and successful interventions* (Thousand Oaks, CA: Sage, 1998); R. E. Redding, "Youth violence through the lens of normal and pathological

development," *Contemporary Psychology* 48 (2003): 759–764; Redding, *supra* note 1; R. E. Redding, N. E. Goldstein, and K. Heilbrun, "Juvenile delinquency: Past and present," In K. Heilbrun, N. E. Goldstein, and R. E. Redding (eds.), *Juvenile delinquency: Assessment, prevention, and intervention* (pp. 1–18) (New York: Oxford University Press, 2005).

28 M. W. Lipsey, "Can interventions rehabilitate serious delinquents?," *Annals of the American Academy of Political & Social Science* 564 (1999): 142–166; Lipsey, *supra* note 27.

29 While the relative importance of the delinquency risk factors varies somewhat according to the child's age, living circumstances, and type of delinquency (minor, violent, or chronic), research has identified the typical significant risk factors that are amenable to intervention and treatment. These include intraindividual factors (substance abuse, mental health problems, poor social problem-solving skills), family factors (inadequate parental supervision, ineffective discipline), school factors (truancy, poor academic achievement, unaddressed learning disabilities), peer factors (association with delinquent peers, gang membership), and community factors (exposure to neighborhood violence and drug dealing). See S. W. Henggeler, P. Cunningham, S. K. Schoenwald, C. M. Borduin, and M. D. Rowland, *Multisystemic treatment of antisocial behavior in children and adolescents*, 2nd ed. (New York: Guilford, 2009).

30 D. A. Andrews and J. Bonta, *The psychology of criminal conduct*, 5th ed. (Newark, NJ: LexisNexis, 2010).

31 T. A. Viera, T. A. Skilling, and M. Peterson-Badali, "Matching court-ordered services to treatment needs," *Criminal Justice & Behavior* 36 (2009): 385–401.

32 S. W. Henggeler, G. B. Melton, M. J. Brondino, D. G. Scherer, and J. D. Hanley, "Multisystemic treatment with violent and chronic juvenile offenders and their families: The role of treatment fidelity in successful dissemination," *Journal of Consulting & Clinical Psychology* 65 (1997): 821–833; Henggeler et al., *supra* note 29; Lipsey, *supra* note 27.

33 Henggeler et al., *supra* note 29.

34 C. M. Borduin, B. J. Mann, L. T. Cone, S. W. Henggeler, B. R. Fucci, D. M. Blaske, and R. A. Williams, "Multisystemic treatment of serious juvenile offenders: Long-term prevention of criminality and violence," *Journal of Consulting & Clinical Psychology* 63 (1995): 569–578.

35 See Henggeler et al., *supra* note 29.

36 See Lipsey, *supra* note 28; Lipsey, *supra* note 27.

37 See A. Blumstein and J. Cohen, "Characterizing criminal careers," *Science* 237 (1987): 985–991.

38 See Dodge, *supra* note 2; R. J. Zagar, W. M. Grove, and K. G. Busch, "Delinquency best treatments: How to divert youths from violence while saving lives and detention costs," *Behavioral Sciences & the Law* 31 (2013): 381–296.

39 See Andrews and Bonta, *supra* note 30; Redding, *supra* note 1.

40   Zagar et al., *supra* note 38.

41   Ibid.

42   R. Johnson and S. Raphael, "How much crime reduction does the marginal prisoner buy?," *Journal of Law & Economics* 55 (2012): 302.

43   D. S. Abrams, "The imprisoner's dilemma: A cost-benefit approach to incarceration," *Iowa Law Review* 98 (2013): 905–969.

44   M. A. Cohen, "The monetary value of saving a high-risk youth," *Journal of Quantitative Criminology* 14 (1998): 5–33.

45   B. C. Welsh, R. Loeber, B. R. Stevens, M. Stouthamer-Loeber, M. A. Cohen, and D. P. Farrington, "Costs of juvenile crime in urban areas: A longitudinal perspective," *Youth Violence & Juvenile Justice* 6 (2008): 19.

46   See Dodge, *supra* note 2.

47   See Zagar et al., *supra* note 38.

48   Ibid.

49   See R. Johnson and S. Raphael, "How much crime reduction does the marginal prisoner buy?," *Journal of Law & Economics* 55 (2012): 275–310; Welsh et al., *supra* note 45; R. G. Wright, "Criminal law and sentencing: What goes with free will?," *Drexel Law Review* 5 (2013): 1–48.

50   Redding and Hensl, *supra* note 18.

51   E. P. Mulvey and N. D. Reppucci, "The context of clinical judgment: The effect of resource availability on judgments of amenability to treatment in juvenile offenders," *American Journal of Community Psychology* 16 (1988): 525–545.

52   See D. M. Bishop, "Injustice and irrationality in contemporary youth policy," *Criminology & Public Policy* 3 (2004): 633–644; C. A. Mason and S. Chang, *Rearrest rates among youth incarcerated in adult court* (Miami: Miami-Dade County Public Defender's Office, 2001).

53   See R. E. Redding and D. C. Murrie, "Judicial decision making about forensic mental health evidence," in A. M. Goldstein (ed.), *Forensic psychology: Emerging topics and expanding roles* (pp. 683–707) (Hoboken, NJ: Wiley, 2007).

54   S. Lewandowsky, U. K. H. Ecker, C. M. Seifert, N. Schwarz, and J. Cook, "Misinformation and its correction: Continued influence and successful debiasing," *Psychological Science in the Public Interest* 13 (2012): 106–131.

55   J. Graham, J. Haidt, and B. A. Nosek, "Liberals and conservatives rely on different sets of moral foundations," *Journal of Personality & Social Psychology* 96 (2009): 1029–1046.

56   See G. Lakoff, H. Dean, and D. Hazen, *Don't think of an elephant! Know your values and frame the debate* (New York: Chelsea Green, 2011); A. R. Pratkanis, "Social influence analysis: An index of tactics," in A. R. Pratkanis (ed.), *The science of social influence: Advances and future progress* (pp. 17–82) (New York: Psychology Press, 2007); A. Tversky and D. Kahnemann, "The framing of decisions and the psychology of choice," *Science* 211 (1981): 453–458.

57   R. M. Chow and J. Galak, "The effect of inequality frames on support for redistributive tax policies," *Psychological Science* 23 (2012): 1467–1469.

58 D. J. Hardisty, E. J. Johnson, and E. U. Weber, "A dirty word or a dirty world? Attribute framing, political affiliation, and query theory," *Psychological Science* 21 (2010): 86–92.

59 M. Feinberg and R. Willer, "The moral roots of environmental attitudes," *Psychological Science* 23 (2012): 1–7.

60 D. Heath and C. Heath, *Made to stick: Why some ideas survive and others die* (New York: Random House, 2007); Kahnemann, *supra* note 21.

61 Dodge, *supra* note 2.

62 For a study refuting this myth, see R. E. Redding and E. J. Fuller, "What do juvenile offenders know about being tried as adults? Implications for deterrence," *Juvenile & Family Court Journal* 55, no. 3 (2004): 35–44.

63 Lewandowsky et al., *supra* note 54.

64 Heath and Heath, *supra* note 60; Pratkanis, *supra* note 56.

65 Pratkanis, *supra* note 56.

66 Pratkanis, *supra* note 56; Tversky and Kahnemann, *supra* note 56.

67 Pratkanis, *supra* note 56.

68 K. B. Wright, L. Sparks, and H. D. O'Hair, *Health care communication in the 21st century* (New York: Wiley-Blackwell, 2012).

69 See L. Alison, L. Almond, P. Christiansen, S. Waring, N. Power, and G. Villejoubert, "When do we believe experts? The power of the unorthodox view," *Behavioral Sciences & the Law* 30 (2012): 729–748; Pratkanis, *supra* note 56.

70 Lewandowsky et al., *supra* note 54.

71 Pratkanis, *supra* note 56.

72 Quoted in Right on Crime, "What Conservatives Are Saying," http://www.rightoncrime.com/the-conservative-case-for-reform/what-conservatives-are-saying/ (accessed June 1, 2014).

73 Ibid.

74 U.S. Department of Justice, National Institution of Corrections, *Promoting public safety using effective interventions* (Washington, DC: U.S. Department of Justice, National Institution of Corrections, 2001).

75 John DiIulio, a professor of political science at the University of Pennsylvania and former director of the Office of Faith-Based and Community Initiatives under President George W. Bush, popularized the stereotype of "superpredator" juvenile offenders. "America is now home to thickening ranks of juvenile 'superpredators'—radically impulsive, brutally remorseless youngsters, including ever more preteenage boys, who murder, assault, rape, rob, burglarize, deal deadly drugs, join gun-toting gangs and create serious communal disorders." J. DiIulio, W. J. Bennett, and J. P. Walters, *Body count* (New York: Simon and Schuster, 1996). He later recanted his "young superpredators" theory and began promoting rehabilitation as an alternative to incarceration. See Elizabeth Becker, "As Ex-Theorist on Young 'Superpredators,' Bush Aide Has Regrets, *New York Times*, February 9, 2001, http://www.nytimes.com/2001/02/09/us/as-ex-theorist-on-young-superpredators-bush-aide-has-regrets.html.

76 Right on Crime, home page, http://www.rightoncrime.com/.

77 Right on Crime, "The Conservative Case for Reform," http://www.rightoncrime.com/the-conservative-case-for-reform/ (accessed June 1, 2014).

78 Right on Crime, "Protect Communities," http://www.rightoncrime.com/the-conservative-case-for-reform/protect-communities/ (accessed June 1, 2014).

79 Right on Crime, "Priority Issues: Juvenile Justice," http://www.rightoncrime.com/priority-issues/juvenile-justice/ (accessed June 1, 2014).

80 Right on Crime, "What's Gone Wrong," http://www.rightoncrime.com/the-criminal-justice-challenge/whats-gone-wrong/ (accessed June 1, 2014).

81 Right on Crime, "Cost to the Taxpayer," http://www.rightoncrime.com/the-criminal-justice-challenge/cost-to-the-taxpayer/ (emphasis added; accessed June 1, 2014).

82 The Campaign for Youth Justice, a leading advocacy organization for juvenile justice reform, notes that "research on recidivism showing that youth are more likely to re-offend when prosecuted in adult criminal court has proved invaluable. Policymakers are most interested in the impact on public safety when they consider policy reforms on juvenile justice." Campaign for Youth Justice, *State trends: Legislative victories from 2011–2013* (Washington, DC: Campaign for Youth Justice, 2013), 9. It notes also the importance of relying on state experts and state-specific research and of getting buy-in on reform efforts from key stakeholders.

83 G. Prisco, "When the cure makes you ill: Seven core principles to change the course of juvenile justice," *New York Law School Law Review* 56 (2011–2012): 1433–1473.

84 Marcus, *supra* note 15.

85 Ibid. at 72.

86 See Campaign for Youth Justice, *supra* note 82.

87 Ibid.

8

Building on Advocacy for Girls and LGBT Youth

A Foundation for Liberatory Laws, Policies, and Services for All Youth in the Juvenile Justice System

BARBARA FEDDERS

Since the 1980s, juvenile justice reform advocates have argued that girls in the system have unique needs and experiences[1] and that system actors have engaged in biased treatment against girls.[2] More recently, advocates for lesbian, gay, bisexual, and transgender (LGBT) youth have made similar arguments.[3] Over time, both groups of advocates have succeeded in raising awareness about these populations, creating and promulgating "best practice" guidelines for working with these youth[4] and changing laws, policies, and practices for treatment of girls and LGBT youth in the juvenile justice system.[5] As with all other young people in the system, there is still far to go in creating a scheme that is both fair and effective at nurturing youth development. Measured by the increase in scholarship and advocacy on the topic, however, considerable progress has been made with respect to girls and LGBT youth.

In this chapter, I unpack the specific arguments made by these advocates with a twofold aim: to consider (1) whether girls and LGBT youth constitute coherent and distinct groups that warrant separate consideration for treatment by system actors, or whether their needs might be better served by more universal strategies; and (2) whether and how advocates' arguments might be applied to the experiences and treatment of the heterosexual, gender-conforming boys who continue to constitute the majority of youth in the system. Thinking carefully about gender and sexuality is an essential component of any re-visioning, innovation, and reform of the juvenile justice system. I conclude that an enriched advocacy strategy would include a more intersectional analysis that recognizes the multiple sites of oppression for girls and LGBT youth.[6] I conclude further that the focus on gender by advocates for girls and LGBT youth must extend to include boys.[7] Advocates must recognize the ways in which gender norms shape all youth and affect both their pathways into the system and their treatment by system actors once they are there.

I. Advocacy for Girls and for LGBT Youth

A. Girls

Over the past twenty years, the population of girls in the juvenile justice system has increased significantly. In 1992, approximately 300,000 girls were prosecuted in juvenile court on delinquency charges, which made girls 20 percent of the total delinquency court population. By 2008, the number of girls sent to juvenile court had increased by 45 percent to 440,057, making them nearly 30 percent of total referrals. In 2010, the number of girls referred dropped to 381,488, but since the number of boys also declined, girls' referrals remained close to 30 percent of the total.[8]

In step with the rise in the population of girls in the system, advocacy on behalf of girls has also increased. Beginning in the late 1980s and picking up momentum throughout the next decade, scholars, lawyers, and lay activists began to make the case that girls in the system share certain relevant experiences that make them different from boys in the system and thus worthy of separate consideration and treatment with respect to research, policies, and programs.[9] Moreover, they argued, girls suffered from neglect and inattention because they constituted a relatively small, though rising, share of the delinquency population that rendered them an afterthought in juvenile justice policy making.[10]

Advocates for girls pointed to the following characteristics shared by girls in the system: higher rates of trauma than boys, notably sexual assault and sexual abuse, and exposure to domestic violence;[11] a primarily internalized response to that trauma in the form of depression, self-mutilation, and substance use;[12] and a higher incidence of mental health disorders and unidentified learning disabilities as compared with boys.[13] They also noted data tending to show that girls' delinquency was less chronic and less serious than that of boys.[14] They emphasized the central role played by running away in girls' delinquency involvement;

both boys and girls run away from home, but studies indicate that 75 percent of runaways are female; and these girls are disproportionately likely to become involved in the system as a result.[15] Girls are more likely than boys to be referred to the system for status offenses[16] and are disproportionately arrested for home-based violence, primarily assault and aggravated assault.[17]

Advocates emphasized the role played by family difficulties in girls' offending: while boys in the system similarly come from families with high levels of conflict and stress, the impact of such problems is greater on girls.[18] Surveys of girls have revealed that girls in the system "search for adults to act as proxy family members who would provide safety and 'someone to talk to,' on a continuing basis";[19] specifically, they seek counseling for abuse, sex and sexuality education, and childbirth and parenting.[20]

Advocates also identified a tendency on the part of juvenile court actors—judges, probation officers, prosecutors, and even defense counsel—to seek to detain girls for minor offenses and technical violations of probation in circumstances in which they would not detain boys.[21] Advocates attributed the disproportionately high use of secure confinement to an effort to protect girls from harm, including sexual victimization; a fear of girls who are sexually active and a desire to protect them from themselves; and an intolerance of girls who diverge too sharply from gender norms by being outwardly uncooperative and noncompliant.[22]

On the basis of these differences, advocates for girls have promoted "gender-responsive" programming that they argue will address girls' unique needs. Federal funds are available for such programming.[23] One example is a girls-only program in Boston, Massachusetts, created to address the quickly growing population of girls committed to that state's Department of Youth Services.[24] The program was designed to encourage girls to connect with a "strengths-based" local community group that would access job training and placement, as well as "empowerment groups," among other services. Another example is "Girls Court," a post-adjudication court for girls in Hawai'i.[25] The court is staffed entirely by women; the all-female space is essential to the court's founders' vision of "honor[ing] the female experience" by "creat[ing] an environment where girls receive services while feeling physically and emotionally safe."[26] The program is small; during each session, it serves a cohort of eight girls.[27] Created in 2004, the Girls Court "seeks to recognize the fundamental differences between male and female juvenile offenders as well as their different pathways to delinquency and, in doing so, act efficiently, creatively, and innovatively to stem the quickly rising tide of female delinquency."[28] The court seeks to provide life-skills training, alternative education and vocational training, mental health treatment, domestic violence prevention, medical services, health education, teen pregnancy prevention, substance abuse treatment, mentoring, and family strengthening through court-based programs and community partners. The girls attend open court every four weeks; in these sessions, they are both praised and held accountable for their actions. They must attend "Girls Group," in which they discuss issues related to reproductive health, domestic violence, sexual exploitation, and substance abuse. Further, the girls participate in esteem-building and relationship-strengthening activities, including community service projects and various forms of creative expression, such as art therapy.[29]

B. LGBT Youth

Advocates for LGBT youth in the juvenile justice system have begun to draw attention to the seemingly disproportionate presence of these youth in the system, as well as biased treatment they must endure. Though LGBT youth represent just 5 to 7 percent of the United States' overall youth population, they compose 13 to 15 percent of those currently in the juvenile justice system.[30] Approximately 300,000 gay and transgender youth are arrested and/or detained each year. Approximately 13 percent of youth in detention facilities are LGBT.[31]

Advocates have noted that this overrepresentation has multiple causes. For one, LGBT youth are disproportionately arrested, charged, and adjudicated for sex offenses such as "crimes against nature" laws[32] and age-of-consent laws in cases that the system typically overlooks when heterosexual youth are involved.[33] Research suggests, nonetheless, that the largest contributing factors to the pathways of LGBT youth into the system are family conflict and school problems.[34]

Family is too often the mechanism that initiates a young person's path toward the child welfare and juvenile justice systems. A parent or guardian may disapprove of a youth's gender-nonconforming clothes, same-sex girlfriend or boyfriend, or questioning of his or her gender identity. Such family discord can lead to a parent or guardian petitioning a juvenile court to initiate an "ungovernability" or "incorrigibility" status-offense action against a child.[35] Family discord may also involve physical abuse. One study found that over 30 percent of gay men and lesbians reported suffering physical violence from a family member as a result of disclosure or discovery of their sexual orientation.[36] Young people hurt in this way may be removed by child protective services and placed in foster care.

Advocates have also discussed the ways in which disclosure or revelation of sexual orientation can lead to homelessness. One study found that 26 percent of adolescents were forced to leave home upon disclosure.[37] The youth homeless population is disproportionately composed of LGBT people.[38] Once LGBT youth are on the streets, advocates point out that they have minimal, inadequate options for supporting themselves and therefore must engage for their survival in activities that expose them to risk for arrest and prosecution, such as sex work, theft, and selling drugs.[39] Moreover, once homeless, LGBT youth are at higher risk for mental health problems, unsafe sexual practices, and sexual victimization.[40]

In addition to problems at home, LGBT youths' sexual orientation and gender identity can create difficulties at school that render them vulnerable to system involvement. For example, The 2011 *National School Climate Survey*, conducted by the Gay, Lesbian & Straight Education Network (GLSEN), found the following among LGBT students:

> 84.9% heard "gay" used in a negative way (e.g., "that's so gay") frequently or often at school; . . . 63.5% felt unsafe because of their sexual orientation, and 43.9% felt unsafe because of their gender expression; . . . 38.3% were physically harassed (e.g., pushed or shoved) in the past year because of their sexual orientation, and 27.1% because of their gender expression; . . . 18.3% were physically assaulted (e.g., punched, kicked, injured with a weapon) in the past year because of their sexual orientation, and 12.4% because of their gender expression; . . . 60.4% of students who were harassed or assaulted in school did not report the incident to school staff, most often believing little to no action would be taken or the situation

could become worse if reported; . . . and 36.7% of the students who did report an incident said that school staff did nothing in response.[41]

When these students turn to defend themselves against bullies by fighting, carrying weapons, or other survival tactics, they are suspended and may be criminally charged. Further, advocates note, about a third of LGBT students miss class because of safety concerns, rendering them truant and pushing them closer to suspension and expulsion, which itself is a risk factor for system involvement.[42]

Once involved in the juvenile justice system, LGBT youth frequently face discriminatory treatment. For instance, LGBT youth are unnecessarily and disproportionately detained pending trial because of biases that LGBT youth are sexually predatory or cannot be kept safe in the community; or parents refuse to assume custody of their LGBT children; or courts rely on detention as a default without considering possible alternative placements; or detention is used for youth who have been subjected to abuse and harassment in prior placements.[43] LGBT youth are particularly at risk for physical, sexual, and emotional abuse while in detention, by both staff and other youth. Of youth in the juvenile justice system surveyed by the Equity Project, 80 percent believed a lack of safety in detention was a serious problem.[44] LGBT youth in the juvenile justice system have, in some instances, been subjected to reparative or conversion therapy, in which so-called therapists seek to change a young person's sexual orientation.[45]

In some jurisdictions, child welfare agencies have responded to advocacy on behalf of LGBT youth by creating specialized LGBT group homes[46] with staff selected who can support a youth's sexual orientation and gender identity "with no questions asked."[47] Specialized placements can ensure that LGBT youth do not suffer physical or emotional abuse from staff or peers.[48] Furthermore, they can provide support at a crucial developmental time for a young person.

In sum, advocates for girls and LGBT youth have made significant headway in explicating the ways in which gender and sexuality may shape the pathways of youth into the juvenile justice system. Furthermore, they have done much to show how juvenile justice policy makers are influenced by gender- and sexuality-related bias.

II. Unpacking the Arguments

It is, of course, critically important for advocates to insist that the juvenile justice system treat all people in it as individuals, seeking to unlock their potential and promote their growth into healthy and productive adults. Gender and sexuality differences are certainly factors for system actors to consider in the prosecution and rehabilitative efforts of youth in the system. However, the arguments of advocates for girls and for LGBT youth contain within them implicit judgments regarding gender and sexuality generally, and boys and girls specifically, that are worth analyzing to see if they ultimately serve youth well and, if not, how they might be modified.

An explicit premise of many advocates for girls and LGBT youth is that they can in fact be addressed as coherent and distinct entities whose oppression is attributable to the disfavored characteristic. That is, many advocates and most policy makers are inclined to talk about the individuals in this group as having enough in common with each other that they can be considered together, without having to analyze the ways in which race, sexual orientation, adherence to gender roles, socioeconomic status, religion, or other identity markers particularly affect pathways to, and treatment in, the system.[49] Some advocates have recently sought to incorporate an analysis of the ways in which race and gender converge.[50] Moving forward, such an intersectional analysis is crucial, as studies suggest significant racial bias in treatment of girls—one study found that, compared with White girls, Black girls receive more severe dispositions, even taking into account the seriousness of the offense, prior record, and age.[51]

Additionally, advocates frequently speak of LGBT youth as disproportionately vulnerable to system involvement, particularly detention.[52] Yet it is important to specify that LGBT youth who are White and upper middle class are unlikely to become more than tangentially involved in the system because of its inherent racism and classism, which combine to render poor youth of color consistently the most likely to be arrested, detained, prosecuted, and harshly punished.[53] For example, while LGBT youth of all classes and races may be equally likely to experience family rejection and disapproval, the children of the wealthy are less likely to experience homelessness and juvenile and criminal system involvement than they are private mental health facilities and psychiatric hospitals.[54]

It might be that single-gender programming, such as the Girls Court in Hawai'i, and LGBT-specific services, such as LGBT-focused group homes, could in fact meet the needs of many girls and LGBT youth more effectively than would mixed-gender groups or groups that do not focus on sexual and gender minorities.[55] Yet it seems worth considering whether gender might be functioning as a proxy for some other characteristics or experiences—for example, victimization and trauma.[56] Gender-responsive services are created around a premise that responding to girls' needs necessarily includes addressing these issues. However, some girls in the Girls Court have not had these experiences, while many boys have.[57] Why not, instead, dedicate a court to sexual victimization and/or to childhood trauma more generally, the way specialized adult courts address drug addiction or domestic violence?[58] Such a court would seem to be able to respond with more precision to the presenting problem. This is particularly true given that the racial, class, religious, and other differences among girls might be more salient than the ways in which a common gender binds them.

Why must girls be separated from boys? For some people, the answer is that girls and boys must be separated because of the possibility of disruption of a group due to romantic or sexual attraction between or among the girls and boys. Yet this answer is not entirely satisfying, as some of the girls in the group will not be heterosexual, of course, and others will be uninterested in boys for whatever reason. Others might argue that boys would dominate a mixed-gender setting, by being louder or more demanding, depriving girls of the ability to receive the attention they need. If the group in question were to be populated overwhelmingly by boys, with girls in only a small minority, this concern might seem likely to be actualized. But if attention were paid by program staff to ensuring a healthy mix of boys and girls, and if a clear facilitation process were established to ensure that girls and boys have equal chance of participating, some of these worries would clearly subside.

In any event, it would seem possible that the fears of sexual distraction as well as male domination are based at least in part on stereotypes about what boys and girls are "really" like when in fact individual variation within and among girls and boys might suggest a very different story. There are certainly strong and assertive girls and young women who can more than hold their own with boys. There are, conversely, timid boys and young men who might be as easily overwhelmed in a group with other boys as might girls. Insofar as youth treatment aims to nurture the full development of the girls and boys it serves, part of that treatment should include encouragement of both boys and girls to explore their feelings and experiences that do not conform to strict gender-role expectations and, furthermore, to explicitly challenge boys to express their feelings and girls to assert their needs.

As masculinities scholars assert, gender-role stereotypes, which in some way ground single-sex programming, harm boys in different but significant ways from how they harm girls.[59] "There's tremendous pressure on boys to fit into limited definitions of maleness. They're supposed to be 'tough,' 'powerful,' and 'cool.' . . . So many stereotypes about being a girl/young woman and being a boy/young man affect youth in deep and life-shaping ways."[60] In turn, it would be interesting to imagine mixed-gender groups dedicated to exploring topics not typically considered to be the province of both boys and girls—so, for example, to talk about pregnancy and childbirth with boys or to talk about strength and respect and "being a man" with girls—to do so affirmatively, out of a belief that to be fully human is to have an understanding of, if not to live, the traits and characteristics and experiences all too frequently consigned to one gender or the other. The potential downside to a program such as the Girls Court is that it seems to categorize girls as victims by default; it may harm boys by enforcing the norm that they cannot be victims.[61]

"Gender-responsive" scholars often assert that the juvenile justice system was "designed for boys."[62] Yet that claim is not frequently explored. It may be that boys and young men dominate the system. But that does not mean that the policies and programs within the system serve them well. The juvenile justice system would greatly benefit from improvements obvious to anyone who has observed it: "parole officers with smaller caseloads, high-intensity supervision with consistent sanctions, appearances in front of the same judge who has time to develop a relationship with the individual, and more family involvement in court."[63] Advocates for LGBT youth have argued for policies and programming for this population of youth; however, if implemented and extended, the proposed interventions could equally benefit all youth in ways suggested earlier. For example, advocates assert that LGBT youth need services and placements from trained professionals who have expertise in the issues facing LGBT youth, who do not make assumptions about the sexual orientation or gender identity of youth, who prohibit any attempt to change a youth's sexual orientation or gender identity, who implement protocols that maintain confidentiality, who require appropriate training on LGBT issues, and who understand and address the impact of societal bias on LGBT youth development.[64] In Santa Clara County, the probation department recently enacted a "Juvenile Lesbian Gay Bisexual and Transgender Policy," which, among other things, states the need for probation department employees, contractors, and staff to "display materials that convey to youth that the Probation department maintains a supportive environment for LGBT youth."[65]

Similarly, a recently released "best practice" manual offers tips for group care facilities housing transgender youth.[66] Research indicates that substantial numbers of transgender and gender-nonconforming youth are in state custody. Some facility staff, who have misconceptions or hostility about transgender identities, may in turn subject them to discriminatory and sometimes harmful situations, even in the absence of overtly hostile intentions. The result is that transgender and gender-nonconforming youth in group care facilities are regularly denied fair treatment and often face serious physical, sexual, and emotional abuse. For transgender and gender-nonconforming youth, group care facilities can be frightening, unsafe, and sometimes intolerable situations. Name-calling, ridicule, and hostility are regularly an accepted part of facility culture. These behaviors and attitudes can escalate and lead to even more serious and harmful harassment and violence—at the hands of other youth as well as facility staff.[67]

Unfortunately, when transgender and gender-nonconforming youth inform staff of harassment or violence, they frequently receive no help. Some facilities even respond to complaints by moving the victimized youth to another, even more restrictive facility or by isolating the youth, rather than addressing the hostile environment that fostered the abuse or appropriately handling the harasser. Isolating or segregating transgender and gender-nonconforming youth suggests that the youth is to blame, rather than individual harassment or an environment that condones if not encourages it. Further, youth in locked facilities who are isolated often cannot access education, training, recreation, employment, and other support services that are available to youth in the general population.

What advocates for transgender youth propose as best practice is to appropriately respond to harassment by providing consequences for the harasser and ensuring that it ceases; to institute diversity trainings for youth in the facility, and to implement practices that create a supportive and respectful environment for transgender and gender-nonconforming youth.[68]

It seems clear that the direct beneficiaries of such treatment would be those youth who already clearly identify as, or are seen by others to be, LGBT. But it is also apparent that adopting the suggested protocols would help all youth, who, by definition, are exploring and developing and attempting to create an identity and way of being in the world with which they feel comfortable. Adolescent identity is always in flux, and questioning one's sexuality and gender can be part of an unremarkable developmental trajectory.[69] Knowing that there is no assumed heterosexuality or gender normativity in a placement could free all youth from regimented gender and sexuality expectations.[70] Understanding that the staff supports LGBT people could help a young person expect to be accepted and supported no matter how she or he diverges from the mainstream. Knowing that verbal harassment is not tolerated could encourage a young person to be more expressive than he or she would otherwise be, as would instituting diversity trainings and otherwise working to create a safe and respectful environment. In other words, implementing policies and protocols aimed at protecting LGBT young people can promote the full development of all young people, freeing them from stultifying gender norms. The greater the acceptance for youth who already identify as transgender, or who are comfortable dressing and behaving in gender-nonconforming ways, the freer the environment for youth who may wish to try out and explore new ways of living and loving.

One caveat is in order. In seeking to promote acceptance of and respect for transgender youth, it is important that youth-serving professionals not inadvertently reify traditional gender roles. For example, a best practice for a facility housing transgender youth would be to permit these youth to wear hairstyles, jewelry, and clothing that comport with that youth's sense of his or her own internal gender identity.[71] It could be that a youth who was assigned the sex of male at birth but who now feels herself to be a girl wishes to wear highly stylized, traditionally feminine attire—dresses, high heels, makeup, and the like. However, advocates and staff should not fall into a habit of ascribing these attributes as signifying "real" femininity or womanhood.

In other words, as youth-serving professionals ensure that transgender youth are accepted and respected as the gender with which they identify, these professionals ought to explore the notion that gender need not be thought of only as a binary. They should continue to work with youth to think about ways in which they are harmed by traditional gender roles, whether they are transgender, gender nonconforming, or not.

The group that is likely to be helped most profoundly is straight, gender-conforming boys, who, again, constitute the overwhelming majority of youth in the system. While the arguments of advocates for girls and LGBT youth have focused on the unfair treatment of these groups and the way in which they have traditionally been overlooked by policy makers and programming staff, the fact is that oppressive gender norms and heteronormativity do also affect the pathways of boys into the system and their treatment by system actors once they are there. As Nancy Dowd has argued, "Each time we ask 'Where are the women?' we should also ask the other question, 'What are the assumptions, structures, and culture to which the men are subject?' or more simply, 'What about the men?'"—or, in this case, boys.[72]

Many of the assumptions and structures that pervade the juvenile justice system reflect values associated traditionally with narrow definitions of masculinity; for example, in out-of-home placements, scholars have noted an "overarching hegemonic masculine milieu, explicit validation of dominant and competitive masculine ideals and behaviors by staff, and inconsistent encouragement of residents to experiment with alternative forms of gender expression."[73] Insistence on compliance with authority, demands for unquestioning respect, and disciplinary hierarchies in which the most compliant youth receive more privileges than others do little to encourage youth to question whether compliance and respect for people on the basis only of their positions of authority is a value that will serve them long term. While this assertion is of course true for both boys and girls, it is boys—particularly Black boys—who are most insistently commanded to comply, fall in line, and obey. Their failure to do so on the street and once in the system leads to ever more draconian forms of punishment.[74]

We might also think of ways to promote alternative means of running youth institutions, such as youth-led councils, and democratic governance structures and curricular and extracurricular programming that encourage critical thinking, as well as social and emotional competencies,[75] rather than placing emphasis solely on the kinds of rote learning that pervades correctional institutions.

Finally, scholars in the adult context have pointed out that staff and administrators of adult prisons enforce a homophobic institutional culture in which "prisoners are expected to prove their masculinity by fighting." It is not uncommon for staff to refuse to protect prisoners against sexual abuse, telling the victim that he should "be a man" by fighting off his potential assailant.[76] It is reasonable to expect that the culture in youth facilities is similar.

Attention to issues of gender and sexuality for all youth, with recognition of the intersectional sites of oppression of race and class, is crucial for the juvenile justice system to live up to its mandate of providing individualized treatment and care for all youth.

NOTES

1 Meda Chesney-Lind, "Girls' Crime and Women's Place: Toward a Feminist Model of Female Delinquency," *Crime & Delinquency* 35 (January 1989): 5–28.

2 Frances T. Sherman, "Justice for Girls: Are We Making Progress?," *UCLA Law Review* 59 (August 2012): 1586–1628.

3 Katayoon Majd, Jody Marksamer, and Carolyn Reyes, *Hidden Injustice: Lesbian, Gay, Bisexual and Transgender Youth in Juvenile Courts* (Legal Services for Children, National Center for Lesbian Rights, National Juvenile Defender Center, Fall 2009), 1–2; Jody Marksamer, *A Place of Respect: A Guide for Group Care Facilities Serving Transgender and Gender Non-conforming Youth* (National Center for Lesbian Rights, Spring 2011), 13–14, 17–21.

4 Majd, Marksamer, and Reyes, *supra* note 3, at 137–143; Marksamer, *supra* note 3, at 31–54.

5 At least three states—Oregon, Connecticut, and Minnesota—have passed statutes providing for gender-responsive programming or equal access to programming for youth of both genders in the juvenile justice system. Tamar Lerer, "Hawai'i Girls Court: Juveniles, Gender and Justice," *Berkeley Journal of Criminal Law* 18 (2013): n. 12; New York City Department of Juvenile Justice, "Anti-Discrimination of LGBTQ Youth Policy" (February 2007), http://www.njjn.org/uploads/digital-library/resource_1097.pdf.

6 Kimberlé Crenshaw, "Mapping the Margins: Intersectionality, Identity Politics, and Violence against Women of Color," *Stanford Law Review* 3 (July 1991): 1245–1251.

7 Nancy E. Dowd, *The Man Question: Male Subordination and Privilege* (New York: NYU Press, 2010), 144.

8 Francine T. Sherman, "Justice for Girls," *Criminal Justice* 9 (Summer 2013): 10.

9 Francine T. Sherman, "Justice for Girls: Are We Making Progress?," *UCLA Law Review* 59 (August 2012): 1595.

10 Ibid.

11 Meda Chesney-Lind, Merry Morash, and Tia Stevens, "Girls' Troubles, Girls' Delinquency, and Gender Responsive Programming: A Review," *Australian and New Zealand Journal of Criminology* 41 (April 2008): 164.

12 Francine T. Sherman, *Detention Reform for Girls: Challenges and Solutions* (Annie E. Casey Foundation, 2005), 16.

13 Ibid.

14 Chesney-Lind, Morash, and Stevens, *supra* note 11, at 163.

15 Sherman, *supra* note 8, at 1599.

16 Chesney-Lind, Morash, and Stevens, *supra* note 11, at 163.

17 Sherman, *supra* note 8, at 1603.

18 Chesney-Lind, Morash, and Stevens, *supra* note 11, at 164.

19 Ibid. at 167.

20 Ibid.

21 Sherman, *supra* note 12, at 34.

22 Sherman, *supra* note 8, at 1617.

23 Sherman, *supra* note 12, at 42; Sherman, *supra* note 8, at 1594; 42 U.S.C. §§ 5601–5785 (2006).

24 Sherman, *supra* note 12, at 42.

25 Lerer, *supra* note 5, at 86.

26 Ibid.

27 Ibid. at 89.

28 Ibid. at 87.

29 Ibid. at 90.

30 Jerome Hunt and Aisha Moodie-Mills, *The Unfair Criminalization of Gay and Transgender Youth: An Overview of the Experiences of LGBT Youth in the Juvenile Justice System* (Center for American Progress, June 29, 2012); Angela Irvine, "'We've Had Three of Them': Addressing the Invisibility of Lesbian, Gay, Bisexual, and Gender Non-conforming Youth in the Juvenile Justice System," *Columbia Journal of Gender and Law* 19, no. 3 (September 2010): 676–679.

31 Majd, Marksamer, and Reyes, *supra* note 3, at 2.

32 Amnesty International, *Stonewalled: Police Abuse and Misconduct against Lesbian, Gay, Bisexual and Transgender People in the U.S.* (September 21, 2005), 3.

33 Hunt and Moodie-Mills, *supra* note 30, at 2–4.

34 See, e.g., Ga. Stat. Ann. § 15-11-2(11) (2010) (describing status offenses as including truancy, running away from home, incorrigibility, and unruly behavior).

35 Majd, Marksamer, and Reyes, *supra* note 3, at 70.

36 Nicholas Ray, *Lesbian, Gay, Bisexual and Transgender Youth: An Epidemic of Homelessness* (National Gay and Lesbian Task Force, 2006), 16.

37 Bryan S. Cochran, Angela J. Stewart, Joshua A. Ginzler, and Ana Marie Cauce, "Challenges Faced by Homeless Sexual Minorities: Comparison of Gay, Lesbian, Bisexual and Transgender Homeless Adolescents with Their Heterosexual Counterparts," *American Journal of Public Health* 92 (May 2002): 775.

38 Majd, Marksamer, and Reyes, *supra* note 3, at 72.

39 Ibid.

40 Ibid.

41 Joseph G. Kosciw, Emily A. Greytak, Mark J. Bartkiewicz, Madelyn J. Boesen, and Neal A. Palmer, *2011 National School Climate Survey: The Experiences of Lesbian, Gay, Bisexual and Transgender Youth in Our Nation's Schools* (New York: GLSEN, 2012), xiv–xv, http://glsen.org/download/file/MzIxOQ.

42 Hayley Gorenberg, "Of Counsel: Ending the School-to-Prison Pipeline," *Lambda Legal Blog*, September 12, 2013, http://www.lambdalegal.org/blog/201309_of-counsel.

43 Majd, Marksamer, and Reyes, *supra* note 3, at 4.

44 Hunt and Mills-Moodie, *supra* note 30, at 6.

45 Ibid.

46 Majd, Marksamer, and Reyes, *supra* note 3, at 84.

47 Ibid., quoting Brianna, a young woman who lived in and felt supported by an LGBT group home.

48 Ibid., citing Shannan Wilber, Caitlin Ryan, and Jody Marksamer, *CWLA Best Practice Guidelines: Serving LGBT Youth in Out-of-Home Care* (Child Welfare League of America, 2006), 42.

49 Jyoti Nanda, "Blind Discretion: Girls of Color and Delinquency in the Juvenile justice System," *UCLA Law Review* 59 (2013): 1528.

50 Sherman, *supra* note 8, at 1599.

51 Ibid.

52 Majd, Marksamer, and Reyes, *supra* note 3, at 94.

53 Tamar R. Birckhead, "Delinquent by Reason of Poverty," *Washington University Journal of Law & Policy* 38 (2012): 53.

54 Ibid. at 82–83.

55 As of a 2008 study sponsored by the Office of Juvenile Justice and Delinquency Prevention, none of the girls' programs surveyed had been evaluated for effectiveness. Margaret A. Zahn, Susan Brumbaugh, Darrell Steffensmeier, et al., *Girls Study Group: Understanding and Responding to Girls' Delinquency* (Office of Juvenile Justice and Delinquency Prevention, U.S. Department of Justice, May 2008), 5.

56 Lerer, *supra* note 5, at 131.

57 Ibid. at 136 ("Abuse, neglect, and trauma are certainly not the sole province of girls").

58 Ibid. at 131.

59 Dowd, *supra* note 7, at 146.

60 Lerer, *supra* note 5, at 135–136.

61 Ibid. at 134.

62 Ibid. at 136.

63 Ibid.

64 Majd, Marksamer, and Reyes, *supra* note 3, at 137–143.

65 Social Services Agency, Santa Clara County Department of Family and Children's Services, *Lesbian, Gay, Bi-Sexual, Transgender and Questioning Youth: Guidelines for Services* (Social Services Agency, Santa Clara County Department of Family and Children's Services, 2013), http://www.sccgov.org/ssa/opp2/13_xp/13-18.html.

66 Marksamer, *supra* note 3, at 37.

67 Ibid.

68 Ibid.

69 Caitlin Ryan and Donna Futterman, *Lesbian and Gay Youth: Care and Counseling* (New York: Columbia University Press, 1998), 10; see also Luke Boso, "Disrupting Sexual Categories of Intimate Preference," *Hastings Women's Law Journal* 21, no. 1 (2010): 78 ("No one is 100 percent anything.").

70 A select number of studies have suggested that children who grow up with lesbian or gay parents are themselves more open to experimentation with gender roles as well as romantic relationships with members of the same sex. See generally Clifford J. Rosky, "Fear of the Queer Child," *Buffalo Law Review* 61 (May 2013): 607, 677 (citing studies).

71 Marksamer, *supra* note 3, at 37.

72 Nancy Dowd, "Asking the Man Question: Masculinities Analysis and Feminist Theory," *Harvard Journal of Law & Gender* 33 (2010): 422–423.

73 Dowd, *supra* note 7, at 96 (citation omitted).

74 Ann C. McGinley and Frank Rudy Cooper, "Identities Cubed: Perspectives on Multidimensional Masculinities Theory," *Nevada Law Journal* 13 (2013): 339.

75 David Osher, George G. Bear, Jeffrey R. Sprague, and Walter Doyle, "How Can We Improve School Discipline," *Educational Researcher* 39, no. 1 (2010): 51–52.

76 Kim Shayo Buchanan, "E-Race-ing Gender: The Racial Construction of Prison Rape," in *Masculinities and the Law: A Multidimensional Approach*, edited by Frank Rudy Cooper and Ann C. McGinley, 187–206 (New York: NYU Press, 2012), 200.

9

Invest Upstream to Promote the Well-Being of LGBT Youth

Addressing Root Causes of Juvenile System Involvement

SHANNAN WILBER

Lesbian, gay, bisexual, and transgender (LGBT) youth have always been present in the juvenile justice system. Historically, the juvenile justice profession has largely denied or ignored this reality and its implications for policy and practice. Recent research and advocacy efforts have documented that which social justice organizations and children's advocates have long contended: social stigma and structural bias place LGBT youth at increased risk of contact with law enforcement, inappropriate criminal charges, unwarranted detention, and abusive treatment in custodial settings. Because of the vulnerability and documented abuse of incarcerated LGBT youth, reform efforts have focused on creating safeguards to protect them from sexual abuse and harmful conditions and practices in detention and correctional facilities. While these efforts are critical and worthy of continued support, their impact is limited to addressing only the most egregious abuses that occur at the deep end of the system. Shining a spotlight in the dark corners of juvenile jails, although necessary, diverts resources and attention from the more fundamental objective of dismantling the structures that place victimized youth behind bars in the first place. Advocates for reform should articulate a more radical agenda whose core objective is to promote the health and well-being of LGBT youth rather than merely shielding them from violence and sexual assault once they are locked up. Minimally, juvenile justice personnel must ensure that their policies and practices do not enshrine and perpetuate societal prejudice. More fundamentally, public resources should be diverted to support programs and interventions that have been shown to facilitate the success and health of LGBT youth.

This chapter begins with an overview of the structural and social biases that place LGBT youth in jeopardy and deprive them of critical peer, family, and educational support. Next, the chapter describes the common trajectories that relegate LGBT youth to homelessness or various forms of state custody. I then describe the conditions and practices in the juvenile justice system that enshrine societal prejudice and further imperil LGBT youth. The chapter reviews recent reform efforts, focused on ensuring safety and preventing sexual assault in secure custodial settings. The chapter concludes with policy recommendations aimed at promoting the health and well-being of LGBT youth in their homes and communities.

The Heavy Toll of Stigma

That LGBT youth are subjected to multiple layers of discrimination, condemnation, and marginalization is not subject to serious debate. The shocking number of LGBT teen suicides in recent years is a stark and tragic reminder of our nation's failure to embrace and nurture these young people. Despite significant advances in legal protection and social integration of LGBT adults, many LGBT youth continue to struggle in families and institutions that pathologize and disparage their core identities. LGBT youth who are rejected and ostracized at home, in school, by peers, and in the community are at elevated risk for negative health and mental health outcomes, school failure, homelessness, and social isolation. These risk factors combine to create a powerful current that too often sweeps LGBT youth away from their homes and into public systems of care.

America's schools are notoriously hostile settings for LGBT students, the majority of whom report regular verbal or physical harassment by students or school personnel on the basis of their sexual orientation or gender expression.[1] LGBT students who report high levels of victimization at school also have higher rates of truancy and school failure, lower grade point averages, higher levels of depression, lower self-esteem, and fewer plans for secondary education.[2] Youth who identify as LGBT or questioning also experience significantly higher rates of cyberdating abuse and bullying than do their peers.[3] Nonheterosexual youth, particularly girls, receive school and criminal sanctions that are disproportionate to their rates of transgressive behavior.[4] Hostile school environments undermine positive social connections and academic engagement, both of which are crucial components of adolescent health and well-being.

LGBT youth who negotiate societal discrimination without the support of their families are particularly endangered. Research by the Family Acceptance Project demonstrates the devastating impact of family rejection on LGBT youth.[5] Lesbian, gay, and bisexual (LGB) young adults who reported high levels of family rejection were 8.4 times as likely to have attempted suicide, 5.9 times as likely to experience significant depression, 3.4 times as likely to use illegal drugs, and 3.4 times as likely to have engaged in unprotected sexual intercourse.[6]

LGBT youth represent up to 40% of the homeless youth population, primarily as a result of being ejected from their homes due to conflict over sexual orientation or gender expression.[7] Homeless youth, in general, experience poor health and mental health outcomes, including substance abuse, high-risk sexual behavior, sexual exploitation, physical abuse, and depression.[8] Homeless LGBT youth, however, are at significantly higher risk than their heterosexual and gender-conforming peers for these negative outcomes.[9] Homeless LGBT youth are also more likely to come into contact with the police.[10]

When families, schools, and communities fail to provide a safe harbor, LGBT youth are often relegated to the care of the state. Despite the scarcity of research data, child welfare professionals readily acknowledge that LGBT youth are significantly overrepresented in foster care.[11] Charged with securing the safety, permanency, and well-being of these youth, the child welfare system has largely been unequal to the task. Too often, services are delivered by personnel, caregivers, and providers who harbor the same biased and uninformed viewpoints that placed LGBT youth in jeopardy in the first place. Indeed, many faith-based child welfare providers openly and emphatically continue to embrace so-called reparative therapies, despite their universal repudiation by every mainstream health and mental health professional organization.[12] The laudable efforts of the federal Children's Bureau to promote LGBT-affirmative policies and practices cannot uproot the deeply engrained prejudices that thrive in many parts of the country. As a consequence, LGBT youth often experience foster care at its worst: an endless series of disrupted placements and a life of instability and insecurity.[13] When the foster care system (and every other private and public institution) fails LGBT youth, they are shunted off to the system of last resort, the juvenile justice system.

LGBT Youth in the Juvenile Justice System

LGBT youth are also overrepresented in the juvenile justice system, in part because they are frequently arrested and detained for low-level, victimless offenses that are related to their homelessness and involvement in street economies. In a self-administered survey completed by 2,100 detained youth in six jurisdictions, approximately 15% of youth self-identified as lesbian, gay, or bisexual (LGB) or gender nonconforming, a proportion that significantly exceeds their numbers in the general population.[14] The actual percentage of LGBT youth in detention is likely even higher, given that many youth are reasonably reluctant to come out to probation or correctional personnel.

In addition to prevalence data, the survey collected data on comparative patterns of incarceration and offense history. The data showed that LGB and gender-nonconforming youth are twice as likely to have experienced child abuse, foster and group home placement, and homelessness when compared to their heterosexual and gender-conforming peers.[15] LGB and gender-nonconforming youth are also twice as likely to be detained for truancy, warrants, probation violations, running away, and prostitution.[16]

The data also debunk an oddly robust myth that most LGBT youth in the system are white. Instead, LGB and gender-nonconforming youth in the system share the overall racial and ethnic characteristics of their straight and gender-conforming counterparts. That is to say, the vast majority are youth of color.[17] LGBT youth of color confront a particularly perverse conundrum. If they disclose their LGBT identities, they risk losing support and affirmation of their cultural or racial identities from disapproving family members, religious institutions, and communities.[18] If they remain closeted, they risk invisibility in institutions that assume that all LGBT youth are white. Either way, the compounded isolation to which they are subjected undermines their health and safety.

Predictably, the abuse directed at LGBT youth in the "outside" world is more pervasive and lethal in detention and correctional settings. In the best of circumstances, these facilities are depressing and inhumane environments. Virtually all juvenile custodial personnel concede that youth who are perceived to be gay or lesbian or to transgress gender norms are at heightened risk of verbal, physical, and sexual assault in lockups. Nonetheless, custodial intake officers rarely inquire into these issues or explore with youth any concerns they might have about their safety. Instead, intake officers routinely (and often unknowingly) relegate LGBT youth to dangerous housing assignments or place them in prolonged "protective" isolation.[19] Intake personnel also commonly classify youth who are perceived to be LGBT as sex offenders, on the basis of the prevailing myth that gay and lesbian youth are more likely to engage in coercive sexual conduct.[20] Custodial staff further imperil LGBT youth by ignoring or minimizing harassment directed at them by their peers or staff or by subjecting them to religious proselytizing or homophobic rhetoric.[21]

LGBT youth are especially subject to extended incarceration. Juveniles, in general, are subject to indeterminate periods of custody or supervision, securing their liberty only upon demonstration of "rehabilitation" or satisfaction of probation conditions. Under this regime, judicial officers or probation officials may extend custody or probation for a broad range of behavioral infractions. These vague and subjective standards are particularly treacherous for LGBT youth, who may be punished for insisting on expressing their true gender identity, expressing same-sex attraction or affection, refusing to admit to bogus sex-offense charges, or simply defending themselves against homophobic or transphobic harassment. LGBT youth who present no risk to public safety remain locked up for extensive periods because the system has no placement alternatives competent to serve them.[22]

Sexual abuse is notoriously commonplace in correctional settings. Incarcerated youth, in general, are more vulnerable to sexual assault than are adults, and certain populations of youth are especially endangered. In 2010, the Bureau of Justice Statistics (BJS) published a report titled *Sexual Victimization in Juvenile Facilities Reported by Youth, 2008–09*.[23] The BJS surveyed over 9,000 youth in 195 juvenile confinement facilities across the nation to determine the prevalence of sexual victimization of residents. Along with a disturbingly high incidence of sexual assault overall, the survey results revealed that nonheterosexual youth reported significantly higher rates of sexual victimization by other youth (12.5%) compared to heterosexual youth (1.3%).[24] In 2012, BJS conducted a follow-up survey in 326 juvenile facilities. Although overall rates of sexual victimization decreased about 3%, LGB residents continued to be abused at nearly seven times the rate of straight youth.[25]

Reform Efforts

Historically, efforts to improve conditions in juvenile justice facilities have been an uphill battle carried out by a few intrepid advocates with very little public or political support. The horrific treatment of LGBT youth in custody has inspired even less attention or support. In the past decade, however, the targeted efforts of the LGBT and juvenile justice advocates and rare bipartisan outrage over the specter of prison rape have combined to focus increased attention on the plight of incarcerated LGBT youth.

Congress passed the Prison Rape Elimination Act of 2003 (PREA), to respond to "the epidemic character of prison rape and the day-to-day horror experienced by victimized inmates."[26] The statute established the National Prison Rape Elimination Commission (NPREC) to conduct a comprehensive study of the problem and to recommend national standards for the detection, prevention, reduction, and punishment of sexual victimization in prisons, jails, lockups, community corrections facilities, and juvenile facilities.[27] After over four years of work, NPREC issued its recommended standards, including those applicable in juvenile facilities. After considering NPREC's recommendations, the Department of Justice (DOJ) issued implementing regulations in 2012.[28]

The PREA regulations address a broad range of topics governing hiring and supervision of staff, screening of residents, staff training, housing, staff ratios and supervision of residents, grievance procedures, data collection, and regular implementation audits. All youth confined in juvenile facilities benefit from PREA's broad protections and the enhanced professionalism required by their implementation. In addition, the data in the BJS report and testimony received at hearings conducted by NPREC prompted the DOJ to include in the regulations the first (and, at this writing, the only) explicit legal protections of lesbian, gay, bisexual, transgender, and intersex (LGBTI) youth in federal law.

Under the regulations, facility personnel who have contact with youth must receive training in a broad range of topics, including *effective communication with LGBTI and gender-nonconforming youth.*[29] Within 72 hours of a resident's arrival and periodically thereafter, facility staff must screen the resident to ascertain information that would identify and reduce the risk of sexual assault, including *any gender-nonconforming appearance or identification as LGBTI and whether the resident may therefore be vulnerable to sexual abuse.*[30] Although these provisions are directed at preventing sexual abuse, they have the potential of improving custodial environments for LGBTI youth in general by requiring staff to consciously consider, discuss, and document the sexual orientation and gender identity or expression of the youth in their care.

The PREA regulations also prohibit housing and placement practices that pathologize, isolate, or jeopardize LGBTI youth. Facilities may not automatically resort to isolation as a means of protecting youth. Instead, agencies may only isolate youth as a last resort when other, less restrictive measure are inadequate to ensure their safety, and then only until an alternative can be arranged. Facilities must also document the basis for concern about the resident's safety and the reason no alternative measure can be arranged.[31] Similarly, facilities may not assign LGBTI residents to specific housing or programs solely on the basis of their identity or status, nor may they consider LGBTI status or identification as an indicator of a propensity for sexual predation.[32]

The PREA regulations further address the unique challenges faced by intersex and transgender youth in locked settings. In the vast majority of secure juvenile facilities, everything from clothing to housing to programming is segregated by sex, requiring custodial staff to choose between one of two boxes: male or female. The primacy of custody and control over privacy and human dignity requires residents in most secure facilities to dress and undress, shower, and use the bathroom in full view of other residents and, often, supervisory staff. While these conditions are universally dehumanizing, they are uniquely harmful and untenable for transgender and intersex youth.

Again, the PREA regulations extend unprecedented protections to incarcerated transgender and intersex youth, none of which protections are federally guaranteed to these youth in any other setting. The regulations direct facilities to make housing and programming assignments of transgender or intersex youth on the basis of an individualized assessment that balances the resident's safety with potential management or security problems, explicitly permitting facilities to place youth consistent with their gender identity rather than their assigned natal sex.[33] In a departure from standard custodial procedures, the regulations require intake personnel to give "serious consideration" to a transgender or intersex resident's own views with respect to his or her safety.[34] Facilities must also give transgender and intersex residents the opportunity to shower separately[35] and may not search or physically examine transgender and intersex youth solely for the purpose of determining their genital status.[36]

The PREA regulations both supported and were supported by the sustained efforts of social justice and civil rights advocates, whose work has been equally instrumental in calling attention to the abuses that LGBT youth suffer in the juvenile justice system. The combined impact of PREA implementation and legal advocacy has produced new constitutional precedent, professional standards, nondiscrimination policies, and training curricula—all aimed at improving conditions of confinement for LGBT youth in the justice system.

In 2004, the American Civil Liberties Union (ACLU) filed a civil rights action in U.S. district court against the Hawaii Youth Correctional Facility (HYCF) on behalf of three youth who identified as, or were perceived to be, LGBT.[37] The plaintiffs, who had been confined at HYCF, alleged that facility staff and other youth subjected them to constant verbal, physical, and sexual abuse and harassment on the basis of their actual or perceived sexual orientation or gender identity. The plaintiffs filed a motion for a preliminary injunction requiring the defendants to implement policies and procedures to ensure the plaintiffs' safety.

In the first published opinion specifically addressing the treatment of LGBT youth in juvenile justice facilities, the district court in *R.G. v. Koller* granted the motion for preliminary injunction, finding that the defendants' conduct violated the Constitution's due process clause and that they had acted with deliberate indifference. The district court made extensive factual findings detailing the relentless verbal harassment and abuse of the plaintiffs by both staff and other youth, the physical threats and assaults of the plaintiffs by other youth, the failure of the defendants to remedy these conditions, and the harm suffered by the plaintiffs. The court also found that the defendants responded to anti-LGBT harassment by subjecting the plaintiffs to prolonged solitary confinement.

The *Koller* court concluded that subjecting LGBT youth to prolonged isolation for their protection—a disturbingly common practice—departs from acceptable professional practice, is inherently punitive, and violates substantive due process. The court's conclusion that the defendants acted with deliberate indifference was based on its findings that the defendants were aware that conditions were unsafe for the plaintiffs yet failed to maintain policies and training to protect LGBT youth, adequate staff and supervision, a functioning grievance system, or a classification system to protect vulnerable youth. Following the ruling, the state of Hawaii settled the case for $625,000 to compensate the plaintiffs, to pay their attorneys, and to engage a court-appointed expert to train staff and work with them to develop new policies.

The significance of *Koller* as a tool for protecting incarcerated LGBT youth cannot be overstated. There is no greater motivation for reforming conditions of confinement than the prospect of costly and protracted litigation, particularly when it involves the potential of monetary damages. The court's clear articulation of the relevant constitutional standard for assessing conditions of confinement in juvenile facilities and its application of the standard to the treatment of LGBT youth provide notice and guidance to juvenile justice agencies. The district court's finding that the imposition of solitary confinement as a means of protecting LGBT youth is unconstitutional provided support for similar prohibitions in the PREA regulations as well as subsequent professional standards.

In 2005, Legal Services for Children, the National Center for Lesbian Rights, and the National Juvenile Defender Center formed the Equity Project, a national initiative to ensure that LGBT youth in the juvenile justice system are treated with dignity, fairness, and respect. Initially, project staff sought to understand and document the experiences of LGBT youth in the system, as well as the system's response to LGBT youth in jurisdictions across the country. Toward this goal, the staff gathered extensive information through surveys and interviews of juvenile justice personnel, judges and attorneys, and focus groups of youth. This process confirmed anecdotal accounts of a system largely unaware of, or inhospitable toward, the LGBT youth in its custody, misinformed about the family and social conditions that contribute to their contact with the system, and ill equipped to provide competent services.

In 2009, the Equity Project summarized its findings and recommendations in a report titled *Hidden Injustice: Lesbian, Gay, Bisexual and Transgender Youth in the Juvenile Justice System.*[38] The report represents the first comprehensive assessment of the system's treatment of LGBT youth at every stage of the delinquency process and includes a series of recommendations aimed at judges, prosecutors, defense attorneys, probation agencies, facility staff, bar associations, and policy makers. The report also includes a model nondiscrimination policy governing juvenile justice facilities.

Following the release of the report, Equity Project staff and professional allies across the country have been engaged in efforts to implement the report's recommendations. These efforts include intensive site-based work in local jurisdictions, including curriculum development and training of juvenile justice stakeholders as well as development of local nondiscrimination policies. These efforts have combined with PREA implementation to create growing consensus about the professional standards governing LGBT competency and the urgency to integrate these standards into daily practice.

The Good News and the Bad News

The single most significant achievement of the reform efforts described in this chapter has been to raise awareness of the presence of LGBT youth in the juvenile justice system and to establish the obligation of juvenile justice professionals to treat them equitably and to protect their safety in secure settings. At the most basic level, progress is apparent from the nearly universal inclusion of these issues in professional conference agendas, the growing familiarity among juvenile justice professionals with terminology and concepts associated with sexual orientation and gender identity, and the steady demand for technical assistance and training related to these issues. Increasingly, juvenile justice personnel understand that it is no longer acceptable to give voice to their own anti-LGBT opinions or to tolerate them from other youth. Although many agency employees remain uncomfortable talking about sexual orientation and gender identity, most understand that they are required to treat LGBT youth respectfully.

Changes in policy and practice, although far from universal, are also emerging. Several jurisdictions have adopted policies explicitly prohibiting discrimination based on sexual orientation or gender identity. Many jurisdictions have provided training to probation and detention staff in which they convey social science research related to the development of sexual orientation and gender identity and debunk common misconceptions. A growing number of jurisdictions have tackled complex practice issues, such as making housing and programming assignments for transgender youth in custodial settings.

As the PREA regulations are fully implemented, they promise to positively impact custodial environments as well—for all youth and for LGBT youth in particular. Although the purpose of PREA is to eliminate sexual assault in confinement facilities, implementation of its regulations will have a broader impact. Lowering the ratio of staff to residents and improving the level of direct supervision by staff will positively impact many aspects of the custodial environment in addition to reducing sexual assaults. Limiting cross-gender searches and requiring private showers for transgender and intersex youth elevate the humanity and dignity of residents, as well as protecting them from sexual assault.

The primary failing of these reforms is that they are almost exclusively aimed at preventing sexual assault and abusive treatment of incarcerated LGBT youth—a low bar that, at best, contains the harms inflicted on these youth to those caused by incarceration of any young person. This limited objective largely reflects the limited strategies of the system itself. Although the juvenile justice system purports to serve young people, its menu of services consists primarily of various forms of custody and control. While there is some logic to concentrating on improving the system's primary intervention, a safe and well-run jail is still a jail.

Protecting the safety of incarcerated LGBT youth does nothing to advance their well-being—the threshold objective to which we should hold the state accountable whenever it assumes care and custody of our children. Indeed, incarceration is a failed "catch and release" intervention that has a profoundly negative impact on young people's health and mental health, as well as their future educational and employment prospects.[39] Rather than improving their chances of successfully navigating adolescence, secure confinement places LGBT youth, who already face significant social hurdles, at an even greater disadvantage.

The tireless efforts of progressive reformers have resulted in significant reduction in the use of secure detention in multiple jurisdictions across the country, in part through the deployment of community-based alternatives to detention that save money while maintaining public safety.[40] Most of these alternatives, however, do not purport to address the structural inequities that disproportionately entangle disadvantaged youth in the justice system. At best, they "do no harm" by keeping young people from penetrating more deeply into the system. By remaining fixated on devising responses to delinquent behavior, rather than addressing its root causes, juvenile justice systems perpetuate the revolving door that ensures and justifies their continued existence.

Meanwhile, disadvantaged LGBT youth—like their straight and gender-conforming peers—recycle in and out of the system. Reforms aimed at improving conditions of confinement do nothing to interrupt the cycle of family rejection, social isolation, and school harassment that places them in harm's way. This skewed allocation of public resources implicitly legitimizes a demonstrably ineffective intervention and diverts attention from upstream strategies that promise to promote resiliency and well-being.

Articulating a New Reform Agenda

The most effective and sustainable public safety strategies support the health and resilience of young people, by mitigating risk factors and promoting protective factors. Social science research has demonstrated that school connectedness and family acceptance are important protective factors that promote the resiliency, health, and well-being of LGBT youth. Policy makers should adopt policies and invest in programs shown to promote these protective factors.

Improve School Climate

Young people spend a great deal of their time at school, making it a prime setting in which to locate interventions designed to promote positive adolescent development and socialization. Students who feel like valued and accepted members of their school community experience positive psychological and educational outcomes.[41] Just as hostile and unsafe school environments expose LGBT youth to negative health and mental health outcomes, interventions designed to promote safe and affirming schools have been shown to promote the well-being and success of LGBT youth.[42]

A growing body of research documents the effectiveness of gay-straight alliances (GSAs), which are student-led, school-based clubs whose purpose is to create safe school environments for LGBT youth by fighting school victimization based on sexual orientation or gender identity. LGBT students whose school has a GSA report higher levels of school safety and well-being.[43] In a survey of over 8,500 students, researchers found that students attending a school with a GSA reported hearing fewer anti-LGBT remarks, were less likely to feel unsafe and miss school, and were more likely to feel a greater sense of belonging to their school community.[44] The presence of a GSA in high school is also associated with better young-adult well-being and a higher level of postsecondary educational achievement.[45]

The adoption and implementation of safe school or antibullying policies that specifically enumerate sexual orientation, gender identity, and gender expression as protected categories is also associated with improved school climate and better educational outcomes. Students in schools with these policies report a lower incidence of homophobic remarks and verbal harassment, a higher level of teacher intervention when hearing homophobic remarks, and increased likelihood to report incidents of harassment and bullying.[46] Similarly, students who reported that their school curriculum included positive representations of LGBT issues were less likely to miss school, had a greater sense of school belonging, and reported less harassment related to their sexual orientation or gender expression.[47]

Although these strategies are demonstrably effective, their adoption in schools is piecemeal and dependent on local leadership and a hospitable political climate. As a consequence, LGBT students in much of the country remain isolated and endangered. Extending federal protection to all LGBT students is essential to achieve meaningful equity. Toward this end, Congress should pass the Student Non-Discrimination Act of

2013 (SNDA), which was introduced in the House by Representatives by
Jared Polis and Ileana Ros-Lehtinen and in the Senate by Al Franken.
The purpose of SNDA is to ensure that all students have access to public education in a safe environment free from discrimination based on
sexual orientation or gender identity. The bill provides a private right of
action and gives the attorney general discretion to file a civil action in
district court. SNDA is modeled after Title IX of the Education Amendments of 1972 (20 U.S.C. §§ 1681–1688), which prohibits discrimination
on the basis of sex.

Passage of the Safe Schools Improvement Act of 2013 (SSIA) would
also extend important protections to LGBT students. The SSIA has been
introduced in the last four Congresses with growing bipartisan support.
The bill conditions receipt of federal education funds on the adoption of
local policies that prohibit bullying or harassment based on enumerated
categories, including sexual orientation and gender identity. The SSIA
requires school districts to inform parents of these policies and to provide a grievance procedure for parents or students to register complaints
about bullying or harassment. States and local districts are also required
to collect and report data on incidents of bullying or harassment.

Collaborate with Families

The juvenile justice system has come under increasing criticism for its
practice of intervening with young people in isolation of their families.[48]
Failure to effectively engage with the families of young people reflects a
mutual lack of trust and respect. Systems stakeholders do not view parents as resources but as "absent, inconsequential, or detrimental to the
well-being of their children."[49] Parents are intimidated by the coercive
nature of the system and the complexity of court procedures.[50] They
feel blamed and shamed and commonly experience system personnel as
culturally insensitive.[51]

The tendency of youth-serving systems to focus interventions on
youth without involving their families is particularly evident when
the youth is LGBT. Early programs developed to serve lesbian and gay
youth were focused primarily on protecting them from harm.[52] Legitimate concerns about protecting LGB youth from victimization related
to stigma led to the development of services that were provided to the

youth alone, such as shelter or counseling, or through peer support.[53] This service modality persists today in the child welfare system, in which the preference for reunification of LGBT youth with their families often gives way to impermanency and group care.[54]

That young people need their families to nurture them and help them successfully navigate adolescence is not subject to debate. Research by the Family Acceptance Project (FAP) has documented the uniquely critical role that parents and caregivers play in reducing risk and promoting the well-being of their LGBT children.[55] FAP research identified over 100 specific ways that parents and caregivers express acceptance or rejection of their LGBT children.[56] The researchers conducted a follow-up study to assess the relationship of family acceptance or rejection during adolescence to health and mental health outcomes in young adulthood.[57] The results were dramatic yet consistent with the anecdotal experiences of youth-serving professionals: LGBT young people whose families engage in rejecting behaviors report high levels of health problems, and those whose parents engage in accepting behaviors report greater well-being, better health, and significantly decreased risk for suicide, depression, and substance abuse.[58]

The FAP research demonstrated that families and caregivers are an essential resource for reducing risk, promoting well-being, and creating a healthy future for LGBT children. Furthermore, the research debunked the commonly held assumption that highly rejecting parents—particularly those whose rejection was grounded in deeply held religious beliefs—cannot or will not serve as positive resources for their children. On the contrary, the FAP study showed that even highly rejecting parents can become less rejecting over time when they learn how their rejecting behaviors negatively affect their LGBT children.[59] Like parents in general, the parents of LGBT youth love their children and want them to have a good life.

FAP developed a strengths-based family-intervention model to help families decrease rejection and increase support for their LGBT children. Several core assumptions of the FAP intervention are consistent with emerging policy recommendations aimed at increasing youth and family involvement in child welfare and juvenile justice systems.[60] These initiatives would radically alter the operations of otherwise hierarchical and coercive systems by engaging parents and caregivers as full and equal partners who are involved in every major decision about their child and who serve as mentors for other families involved in the system.[61]

The emergence of family engagement as a critical objective in progressive systems reform and the development of FAP's evidence-based family-intervention tool provide an excellent opportunity to invest upstream to support the well-being of LGBT youth. Policy makers should change federal policy to provide financial incentives for meaningfully engaging families, to redirect resources to support community-based interventions aimed at strengthening the families of LGBT youth, and to monitor the success of these programs in avoiding more coercive state intervention and improving the health and mental health outcomes for LGBT youth and young adults.

Conclusion

Examination of structural injustice inevitably reveals hierarchical victimization: the least protection is offered to those on whom the worst injuries are inflicted. LGBT youth in conflict with the law bear the brunt of multiple layers of marginalization, stigma, and bias. Having discovered that which should have been obvious—that these youth are subjected to unconscionable abuse behind bars—the government has expended enormous resources to keep them safely imprisoned. The best hopes for this strategy are to renovate an inherently harmful institution. A more ambitious and truly progressive reform would be aimed at supporting the institutions that have the potential of promoting and harnessing the well-being of LGBT youth: their schools and their families.

NOTES

1 Joseph G. Kosciw, Emily A. Greytak, Mark J. Bartkiewicz, Madelyn J. Boesen, and Neal A. Palmer, *The 2011 National School Climate Survey: The Experiences of Lesbian, Gay, Bisexual and Transgender Youth in Our Nation's Schools* (New York: GLSEN, 2012).

2 Ibid.

3 Janine M. Zweig, Meredith Dank, Pamela Lachman, and Jennifer Yahner, *Technology, Teen Dating Violence and Abuse, and Bullying* (Washington, DC: Urban Institute, 2013).

4 Kathryn E. Himmelstein and Hannah Bruckner, "Criminal Justice and School Sanctions against Non-heterosexual Adolescents: A National Longitudinal Study," *Pediatrics* 127 (1) (2010): 49–57.

5 Caitlin Ryan, David Huebner, Rafael M. Diaz, and Jorge Sanchez, "Family Rejection as a Predictor of Negative Health Outcomes in White and Latino Lesbian, Gay and Bisexual Young Adults," *Pediatrics* 123 (1) (2009): 346–352.

6 Ibid.

7 Laura E. Durso and Gary J. Gates, *Serving Our Youth: Findings from a National Survey of Service Providers Working with Lesbian, Gay, Bisexual, and Transgender Youth Who Are Homeless or at Risk of Becoming Homeless* (Los Angeles: Williams Institute with the True Colors Fund and the Palette Fund, 2012).

8 James M. Van Leeuwen, Susan Boyle, Stacy Salomonsen-Sautel, and D. Nico Baker, "Lesbian, Gay, and Bisexual Youth: An Eight-City Public Health Perspective," *Child Welfare* 85 (2) (2006): 151–170.

9 Ibid.

10 Nicholas Ray, *Lesbian, Gay, Bisexual and Transgender Youth: An Epidemic of Homelessness* (Washington, DC: National Gay and Lesbian Task Force Policy Institute and National Coalition for the Homeless, 2006).

11 Shannan Wilber, Caitlin Ryan, and Jody Marksamer, *CWLA Best Practice Guidelines: Serving LGBT Youth in Out-of-Home Care* (Washington, DC: Child Welfare League of America, 2006).

12 David S. Reitman, Bryn Austin, Uri Belkind, Tonya Chaffee, Neal D. Hoffman, Eva Moore, et al., "Recommendations for Promoting the Health and Well-Being of Lesbian, Gay, Bisexual, and Transgender Adolescents: A Position Paper of the Society for Adolescent Health and Medicine," *Journal of Adolescent Health* 52 (4) (2013): 506–510.

13 Gerald P. Mallon, Nina Aledort, and Michael Ferrera, "There's No Place like Home: Achieving Safety, Permanency, and Well-Being for Lesbian and Gay Adolescents in Out-of-Home Care Settings," *Child Welfare* 81 (2) (2002): 407–439.

14 Angela Irvine, "'We've Had Three of Them': Addressing the Invisibility of Lesbian, Gay, Bisexual and Gender Non-conforming Youths in the Juvenile Justice System," *Columbia Journal of Gender and Law* 19 (3) (2010): 675–701.

15 Ibid.

16 Ibid.

17 Ibid.

18 Sarah Valentine, "Supporting Queer Youth," in *Justice for Kids: Keeping Kids Out of the Juvenile Justice System*, edited by Nancy E. Dowd, 180–198 (New York: NYU Press, 2011).

19 Katayoon Majd, Jody Marksamer, and Carolyn Reyes, *Hidden Injustice: Lesbian, Gay, Bisexual and Transgender Youth in Juvenile Courts* (San Francisco: Legal Services for Children, National Juvenile Defender Center, National Center for Lesbian Rights, 2009).

20 Ibid.

21 R.G. v. Koller, 415 F. Supp. 2d 1129 (2006).

22 Majd, Marksamer, and Reyes, *supra* note 19.

23 Allen J. Back, Paige M. Harrison, and Paul Guerino, *Sexual Victimization in Juvenile Facilities Reported by Youth, 2008–09* (Washington, DC: Bureau of Justice Statistics, Office of Justice Programs, U.S. Department of Justice, 2010).

24 Ibid.

25 Allen J. Beck, David Cantor, and Tim Smith, *Sexual Victimization in Juvenile Facilities Reported by Youth, 2012* (Washinton, DC: Bureau of Justice Statistics, Office of Justice Programs, U.S. Department of Justice, 2013).

26 Prison Rape Elimination Act of 2003 (PREA), 42 U.S.C. § 15601(12), 2003.

27 PREA, 42 U.S.C. § 15606(d)(1), (e)(1), 2003.

28 PREA National Standards, 28 CFR § 115, 2012.

29 PREA National Standards, 28 CFR § 115.331(a)(9), 2012.

30 PREA National Standards, 28 CFR § 115.341(c)(2), 2012.

31 PREA National Standards, 28 CFR § 115.342(b)(h), 2012.

32 PREA National Standards, 28 CFR § 115.342(c), 2012.

33 PREA National Standards, 28 CFR § 115.342(d), 2012.

34 PREA National Standards, 28 CFR § 115.342(f), 2012.

35 PREA National Standards, 28 CFR § 115.342(g), 2012.

36 PREA National Standards, 28 CFR § 115.315(e), 2012.

37 R.G. v. Koller, 415 F. Supp. 2d 1129 (2006).

38 Majd, Marksamer, and Reyes, *supra* note 19.

39 Barry Holman and Jason Zeidenberg, *The Dangers of Detention: The Impact of Incarcerating Youth in Detention and Other Secure Facilities* (Washington, DC: Justice Policy Institute, 2006).

40 Richard A. Mendel, *No Place for Kids: The Case for Reducing Juvenile Incarceration* (Baltimore: Annie E. Casey Foundation, 2011).

41 Elizabeth M. Diaz, Joseph G. Kosciw, and Emily A. Greytak, "School Connectedness for Lesbian, Gay, Bisexual, and Transgender Youth: In-School Victimization and Institutional Supports," *Prevention Researcher* 17 (3) (2010): 15–17.

42 Russell B. Toomey, Caitlin Ryan, Rafael M. Diaz, and Stephen T. Russell, "High School Gay-Straight Alliances (GSAs) and Young Adult Well-Being: An Examination of GSA Presence, Participation, and Perceived Effectiveness," *Applied Developmental Science* 15 (4) (2011): 175–185.

43 Ibid.

44 Kosciw et al., *supra* note 1.

45 Toomey et al., *supra* note 42.

46 Ibid.

47 Ibid.

48 Neelum Arya, *Family Comes First: A Workbook to Transform the Justice System by Partnering with Families* (Washington, DC: Campaign for Youth Justice, 2013).

49 Joan Pennell, Carol Shapiro, and Carol Spinner, *Safety, Fairness, Stability: Repositioning Juvenile Justice and Child Welfare to Engage Families and Communities* (Washington, DC: Center for Juvenile Justice Reform, Georgetown University, 2011), 6.

50 Liane Rozell, *The Role of Family Engagement in Creating Trauma-Informed Juvenile Justice Systems* (Los Angeles: National Center for Child Traumatic Stress, 2013).

51 Ibid.

52 Caitlin Ryan and Stuart F. Chen-Hayes, "Educating and Empowering Families of Lesbian, Gay, Bisexual, Transgender, and Questioning Students," in *Creating Safe and Supportive Learning Environments: A Guide for Working with Lesbian, Gay, Bisexual, Transgender, and Questioning Youth and Families*, edited by Emily S. Fisher and Karen Komosa-Hawkins, 209–227 (New York: Routledge, 2013).

53 Ibid.

54 Wilber, Ryan, and Marksamer, *supra* note 11.

55 Caitlin Ryan, "Engaging Families to Support Lesbian, Gay, Bisexual and Transgender Youth: The Family Acceptance Project," *Prevention Researcher* 17 (4) (2010): 11–13.

56 Ibid.

57 Ibid.

58 Ryan et al., *supra* note 5.

59 Caitlin Ryan and Erica Monasterio, *Provider's Guide for Using the FAPrisk Screener for Family Rejection and Related Health Risks in LGBT Youth* (San Francisco: Marian Wright Edelman Institute, San Francisco State University, 2009).

60 Pennell, Shapiro, and Spinner, *supra* note 49.

61 Ibid.

PART IV

Critical Actors

10

Correcting Racial Disparities in the Juvenile Justice System

Refining Prosecutorial Discretion

KRISTIN HENNING

State actors exercise vast discretion at all stages of the juvenile justice system. Police must decide whether to arrest or release an accused youth; prosecutors must decide whether to prosecute, divert, or dismiss a juvenile case; and judges must decide whether to detain or release a child at the arraignment or disposition. Even when a youth's behavior meets the statutory elements of a crime, police and prosecutors have discretion *not* to arrest or prosecute and may instead identify creative alternatives to adjudication. Once a youth is referred to juvenile court, the responsibility for case intake is often shared between prosecutors who evaluate the strength and merits of the delinquency allegation and probation officers who review information about the youth's family, neighborhood, school, and academic performance and advise the prosecutor whether to file or decline a formal complaint.[1] Implicit in each decision is a determination of whether the youth's conduct should be treated as some "normal" adolescent behavior that society is willing and able to tolerate or some deviant behavior warranting law enforcement intervention.

Prosecutors who make the final decision about how to respond to a delinquent offense are arguably the most powerful decision makers in the system.[2] Abuses of prosecutorial discretion in the juvenile and criminal justice systems have been thoroughly critiqued,[3] and literature on the disproportionate representation of children of color in juvenile courts has repeatedly condemned the broad discretion afforded to prosecutors, judges, and probation officers as providing a safe haven for implicit or explicit racial animus.[4] Like other stakeholders in the system, prosecutors are susceptible to the unconscious effects of negative stereotypes and harmful narratives about youth of color. Prosecutorial decisions are also probably distorted by the deluge of African American and Hispanic youth who are referred to the court by police officers and schools.

Although reform is needed throughout the juvenile justice process, this chapter focuses on the unique opportunity and responsibility of prosecutors to confront bias and to reduce racial disparities at the charging phase. It draws on research in normative adolescent development and explores society's perceptions of race and adolescence that have shaped contemporary juvenile justice law and policy. Relying on recent studies that confirm that patterns of adolescent development do not vary by race or class (section 1), the chapter considers the critical role of prosecutors and recommends that prosecutors collaborate with developmental experts and community representatives to draft intake and charging guidelines that challenge distorted notions of race and maturity (section 2), are informed by research in adolescent development (section 3), and provide a fair and equitable framework for identifying those youth who should be diverted from juvenile court intervention (section 4). The chapter examines charging criteria in context and encourages prosecutors to track charging decisions by race and geographic neighborhood and to work with policy makers and community representatives to develop a continuum of community-based, adolescent-appropriate alternatives to prosecution for youth of color.

I. Adolescent Development and Racialized Outcomes

Over the past quarter century, psychological research has shown that much of youth crime and delinquency is the product of normal adolescent development. Compared to adults, adolescents often make impetuous and ill-considered decisions, are susceptible to negative influences and outside pressures, and have a limited capacity to identify and weigh the short- and long-term consequences of their choices.[5] As youth mature, they age out of delinquency and rarely persist in a life of crime.

Ironically, despite the Supreme Court's recent attention to the developmental research in its evolving Eighth Amendment jurisprudence involving children charged in adult criminal proceedings,[6] the developmental research seems to have had little effect in reversing society's pervasive overreliance on law enforcement and juvenile courts to respond to typical adolescent behaviors, particularly among youth of color. Most juvenile court referrals involve nonviolent offenses and misdemeanors. In 2008, 84 percent of juvenile arrests involved property offenses, simple assault, and other nonviolent crimes.[7] In 2010, approximately 71 percent of youth detained or committed by the juvenile justice system were charged with simple assault, drug offenses, property crimes, violations of a public order, technical violations, or "status offenses."[8] Nowhere has the increase in juvenile court referrals for low- to midlevel delinquent behavior been more evident than in school-based referrals.[9]

The overrepresentation of youth of color in the juvenile justice system cannot be explained by differences in normative adolescent development across different socioeconomic or ethnic groups. Studies controlling for socioeconomic status and ethnicity have found that developmental features such as impulsivity, sensation seeking, susceptibility to peer influence, and limited future orientation appear in similar patterns across all racial and ethnic groups.[10] These findings are supplemented by two major self-report studies on youth violence and drug use, each of which documents risk-taking and delinquency across white, black, and Hispanic races.[11] Where racial disparities do exist in self-reported data, they do not correspond to the disproportionate representation of youth of color in the juvenile justice system. The University of Michigan and the Centers for Disease Control (CDC) have each separately collected and analyzed youth self-reported data for more than 35 years. The University of Michigan study has tracked trends from 1975 to 2010, relying on data collected from around 17,000 middle school students in approximately 150 middle schools and around 15,000 high school students in approximately 130 high schools around the country.[12] Overall, self-reported data support the findings of developmental psychologists that all youth—especially those between the ages of 15 and 19—are more likely than adults to engage in dangerous, risk-taking behaviors, such as driving while drunk, unprotected sex, and drug use.[13]

When the self-reported data is disaggregated by race, statistics reveal that African American youth consistently report less drug use than whites do for most types of drugs[14] but are arrested at much higher rates than white youth are. For example, in 2008, African American youth accounted for just 16 percent of the total youth population but represented

27 percent of all youth arrests for drug-related violations and were arrested at almost 1.7 times the rate of white youth for such offenses.[15] Thus, these rates appear to exaggerate the prevalence of drug use among black youth and mask the extent of self-reported drug use among white youth. Self-report studies also provide evidence that violent offending is not predetermined by race. Although African American youth accounted for 38 percent of all youth arrested for a weapons offense in 2008, self-report data from CDC's Youth Risk Behavior Surveillance System reveals small differences in weapons offenses between these groups. Ultimately, while the age of onset, types of violence, types of weapon, and drug preferences may differ across races in self-reporting, it is clear that adolescents of all races engage in risky and delinquent behavior and often at rates that defy racial disparities in arrest.

Although racial disparities may be partly explained by the increased presence of police in communities where African American and Hispanic youth reside, selective reporting of offenses to the police, and the heightened visibility of delinquency in poor communities of color where youth are forced outside for entertainment,[16] disparities are also the product of racial and ethnic bias by police, victims, and witnesses. Pervasive stereotypes suggest that minority youth are prone to violence and crime, are unwilling to work, and expect to be incarcerated at some point in their lives.[17] Years of research on the portrayal of criminals in the media further document the imaging of violent offenders and drug dealers as black.[18]

Contemporary studies confirm that racial stereotypes affect judgments about adolescent culpability, maturity, risk of recidivism, and deserved punishment for juvenile offenders. In one study, researchers found that probation officers were more likely to perceive black youth as likely to reoffend than they were white youth.[19] In another study, researchers found that police and probation officers who were unconsciously primed to assume that a young offender in a crime vignette was African American were harsher in their judgments of culpability and deserved punishment.[20] Most recently, in a 2012 study on the effects of race on the perception of juvenile culpability, psychologists from Stanford University found that race had a significant effect on public support for severe sentences for youth, such as life without the possibility of parole, and perceptions of juveniles' blameworthiness relative to adults.[21] Even when controlling for the participant's political ideology and evidence of racial bias, the researchers found that study subjects who were primed to believe that young offenders were black were more likely to endorse harsher sentences than when they believed the offenders were white. These findings explain how implicit bias may influence public policy regarding adolescent sentencing and transfer to adult court[22] and suggest that contemporary juvenile justice policies have been implemented unevenly based on distorted perceptions of race, crime, and threat.[23] When youth are transferred to the adult system, evidence is well documented that black youth receive significantly more punitive sentences than do white youth.[24] Thus, unlike many white youth who may be forgiven or excused for engaging in reckless adolescent behavior, youth of color are more often treated as morally corrupt and fully culpable for their conduct.[25]

Collectively, these outcomes reflect an unwillingness to apply theories of diminished culpability and immaturity to youth of color and lead prosecutors, probation officers, and judges to impose harsh legal sanctions on black youth instead of relying on the preventive and treatment-oriented strategies often available for white youth.[26] Yet, despite differences in the type of drugs or weapons prevalent in communities of color, there is no support for a claim that youth of color will not benefit from developmentally appropriate responses to adolescent offending.

II. The Role of Prosecutors in Correcting Racial Disparities: Derationalizing Race-Based Disparities and Addressing Implicit Bias

Despite the significant role that probation officers, police, and schools play in contributing to racial disparities in the juvenile justice system, prosecutors are arguably the most powerful decision makers in the system. As gatekeepers of juvenile court jurisdiction, prosecutors wield enormous power to decline prosecution, to divert youth from the system, and to identify creative alternatives to adjudication. The role of prosecutorial discretion is best understood through the lens of case examples involving youth charged with delinquency in an urban juvenile court.[27]

Jaquan: Several boys are sitting in a public park. Jaquan, age 15, finds marijuana in his older brother's room and brings it out to share with his friends. All of the boys try it—each one excited about the opportunity to experiment and afraid of appearing lame in front of friends. Jaquan's friends are arrested and charged with possession of marijuana. Jaquan is charged with distribution.

James: James, age 15, is wearing a "hoodie" sweatshirt in public in violation of an obscure city ordinance prohibiting such attire and mouths off at the police officer who tells him to take it off. James is arrested and charged with resisting a police officer for refusing to comply with the officer's instructions.

Rodney and Roland: Two African American boys, Rodney and Roland, throw pebbles across the train tracks at a young Latino boy, José, for no reason other than that they are bored and José is different. Rodney and Roland, age 14, are charged in juvenile court with assault with a dangerous weapon.

Shannon: Shannon, age 16, is riding a public bus with five classmates from her special education school when she notices one of her teacher's aides at the back of the bus. Shannon snatches the aide's hat and tosses it to one of her classmates. After playing a game of catch with the hat through peals of laughter, the children drop the hat and get off the bus. Shannon is arrested at school the next day and charged with robbery.

Jacob: Jacob, a chubby 13-year-old, is verbally teased by two or three classmates for several weeks. Jacob is visibly pained and distraught by the verbal abuse. About two months into the school year, a group of unknown youth approach Jacob as he is sitting alone at a lunch table. Unsure of their motives, but without any physical provocation to justify a claim of self-defense, Jacob throws a book and a pen, hitting one of the youth in the face and breaking a window. Jacob is charged with felony assault and destruction of property.

All of these examples involve allegations that, if true, meet the statutory elements for the crimes listed. Yet, as with any decision in the juvenile justice system, police and prosecutors have discretion *not* to act. Notwithstanding the obvious dangers of drug experimentation and the frustration caused to the teacher's aide who lost his hat, few people would criticize a police officer who exercised his or her discretion to send Jaquan and his friends home with a warning and referral to a drug-education class, or a school principal who decided not to call the police in response to Shannon's school-bus prank. Many would applaud the prosecutor who refused to prosecute any black youth who had been disproportionately targeted for wearing a hoodie in public or the prosecutor who simply encouraged Rodney and Roland to apologize to José and participate in a victim-offender mediation session. Others would be satisfied if Jacob received counseling from the school psychologist, apologized to the student he hit, and paid for the broken window or worked off the cost through community service. Equally important, the other youth who teased Jacob could be educated on the effects of bullying and required to participate in mediation. Yet, despite the availability of these alternatives to prosecution, cases such as these routinely populate juvenile courts across the country and at rates that disproportionately include youth of color.[28]

Excusing adolescent behavior from criminal liability is not a new concept. Early statutes in many jurisdictions prohibited states from prosecuting youth under the age of 7 and imposed a burden on the prosecution to prove beyond a reasonable doubt that children between the ages of 7 and 14 understood the wrongfulness of their conduct and could control their behavior.[29] Several contemporary scholars have called for a return to this "infancy defense" and have explored ways in which current research in adolescent development may provide a complete defense, excuse, or justification for delinquency.[30] Whether by statutory authority or the reasonable exercise of discretion implicitly granted to all decision makers in the system, there is value to discretion that fairly and equitably accounts for the normative features of adolescent development in deciding how to respond to delinquency.

In the following sections, I propose that prosecutors develop guidelines with several goals in mind. First, the guidelines recognize the unique developmental status of adolescents and account for a youth's amenability to treatment and diminished culpability in criminal activity. Second, the guidelines seek to correct for racial disparities and bias by helping prosecutors apply principles of adolescent development evenly across race and class. Third, the guidelines seek to achieve positive youth outcomes by urging prosecutors to partner with communities for alternative responses to youth delinquency. Recognizing that prosecutors should not be bound by charging criteria that are rigid and inflexible, I do not propose a fixed set of rules but instead offer a broad framework guided by research in adolescent psychology that will be useful across jurisdictions.

By engaging the community, collaborating with developmental psychologists, and delineating adolescent-appropriate factors to guide the charging decision, prosecution standards should begin to erode harmful stereotypes about youth of color and hopefully reduce racial disparities in the system over time. Recognizing that reforms in prosecutorial charging decisions are likely to be hindered by the actual or perceived lack of community-based resources in communities of color, I also propose that prosecutors take a leadership role in ensuring that resources are fairly allocated to the implementation of adolescent-appropriate responses to delinquency as an alternative to law enforcement and juvenile court interventions.

Not only are prosecutors in a position to improve their own charging decisions, but they are also uniquely positioned to address patterns of racialized law enforcement. Unlike school officials and police officers, who generally interact with youth in a limited geographic space, prosecutors typically screen referrals from across the city and may compare patterns of arrests and referrals by neighborhood.[31] Prosecutors who recognize that youth of color are routinely referred from one or more schools for drug use, disorderly conduct, or other low- to midlevel offenses may decline to prosecute and encourage schools and community leaders to identify more appropriate responses to adolescent offending that do not impose the stigma and collateral consequences of a juvenile court adjudication.[32] By declining to prosecute categories of adolescent behavior, prosecutors set the standard for juvenile court intake and over time may significantly influence patterns of arrest and referrals. To avoid claims that prosecutors and police officers are ignoring or underenforcing criminal laws in communities of color,[33] prosecutors should communicate the rationale for their charging decisions and actively engage the community, legislators, and school leaders in developing alternatives to prosecution.

Prosecutors are often called on to satisfy many competing interests, including those of victims seeking restitution, communities demanding youth accountability, and elected district attorneys who dole out promotions, bonuses, and even continued employment on the basis of conviction rates, pleas, and adjudications.[34] Prosecutors committed to reducing racial disparities will need to think creatively about how to meet these demands without perpetuating racially disparate outcomes. To ensure public safety, prosecutors must be familiar with evidence-based best practices for successful interventions with serious juvenile offenders.[35] Those strategies will often involve community-based responses instead of incarceration or other traditional law enforcement interventions. To address the victims' needs, prosecutors should consider empirical evidence that participants in victim-offender mediation and other restorative justice programs are more satisfied with the way their cases are handled than are victims whose cases are litigated in court.[36] In response to constituents' concerns about high and rising juvenile crime, prosecutors will need to correct faulty perceptions about the nature and scope of youth crime in the community, to educate the community on the similarities in key features of adolescent offending and resilience across racial lines, and to be transparent about policies and practices intended to address racial disparities in the system.

Any effort to reduce racial disparities in the juvenile and criminal justice systems must also include a commitment to addressing implicit bias. Even if the disparate impact of criminal justice policies on people of color is not the product of blatant and deliberate racism, seemingly "rational" explanations for arrest and charging decisions cannot absolve prosecutors of responsibility for racially disparate outcomes in the juvenile justice system.[37] Successful efforts to combat bias must be accompanied by training and periodic reviews of prosecutorial decisions.[38] Training would expose prosecutors to the literature on implicit bias and educate prosecutors on the normative similarities in adolescent development across socioeconomic and ethnic groups. Some studies have suggested that well-intentioned actors can overcome automatic or implicit biases, at least to some limited extent, when they are made aware of the stereotypes and biases they hold, have the cognitive capacity to self-correct, and are motivated to do so.[39] Collectively, prosecutors may identify and agree to reexamine common stereotypes and presumptions made about youth color by themselves and other actors in the system. Experienced prosecutors may identify their own individual biases by taking the Implicit Association Test (IAT) and reviewing their own records for race-correlated charging decisions over the previous year.[40]

III. Refining Prosecutorial Discretion: Identifying A Framework for Developmentally Informed Decision Making

To meaningfully and equitably extend the principles of diminished culpability to all youth at the intake phase of the juvenile case, prosecutors need a practical framework for applying the developmental research to the charging decision. This section envisions a path toward structured decision making at the charging phase that capitalizes on the differences between juveniles and adults and targets racial inequalities by challenging distorted notions of race and maturity. Decision-making guidelines that highlight the features of adolescent development should help prosecutors contextualize the behavior of youth of color within identified developmental norms and reduce prosecutors' overreliance on juvenile courts to regulate normal adolescent offending in communities of color.

1. Charging Standards and Commentary

In most states, charging decisions are left to prosecutors who operate with little guidance about whether and how youth should be charged. Even when statutes and court rules express a preference for diversion or the least restrictive response to adolescent offending, the provisions are often vague and rarely provide specific guidelines for charging youth in juvenile court.[41] Moreover, there are few published guidelines written by and for prosecutors called on to make decisions at the juvenile intake and charging stage.[42] When guidelines do exist, they do not adequately account for the contemporary developmental research and provide little or no guidance for prosecutors seeking to address racial disparities.

The criteria identified in the National District Attorneys Association's (NDAA) *National Prosecution Standards* provide a foundation for analyzing how developmental research may be incorporated into charging standards and commentary.[43] Current NDAA standards recommend that prosecutors in juvenile cases consider the "seriousness of the alleged offense"; the alleged role of the accused youth in the offense; "the nature and number of previous cases" against the youth and their disposition; the youth's "age, maturity, and mental status"; the availability of appropriate treatment or services through the juvenile court or diversion; the youth's admission of guilt or acceptance of responsibility for involve-

CORRECTING RACIAL DISPARITIES | 203

ment in the charged offense; "the dangerousness or the threat posed by the [youth] to the person or property of others"; "decisions made with respect to similarly-situated [youth]"; "the provision of financial restitution to victims"; and "recommendations of the referring agency, victim, law enforcement, and advocates for the [youth]."[44]

Notwithstanding the explicit reference to age and maturity, these standards differ little from adult charging guidelines.[45] Many of the criteria lack detail and specificity, and none adequately account for the youth's diminished culpability and amenability to treatment. Written standards such as these should incorporate commentary that illuminates the meaning and relevance of specific charging criteria by explaining key features of adolescent offending and incorporating research on adolescents' amenability to treatment as an important reminder that retributive responses are not always necessary or warranted in response to delinquency. A closer examination of some of the charging criteria proposed by the NDAA is instructive.

Alleged role in offense. Research in normative developmental psychology would provide important background for prosecutors evaluating a youth's alleged role in a delinquent offense. Normative features of adolescence, such as the prevalence of risk-taking among all youth, the limits of adolescent cognitive and psychosocial capacity "in the heat" of a crime, the impact of impulsivity and peer influence on adolescent judgments, and the tendency of adolescents to underestimate the risk of harm in a given situation, would all help prosecutors understand the spontaneous and unplanned roles youth often play in delinquency cases. More important, the commentary should encourage prosecutors to consider the role of group dynamics in adolescent offending and help them understand the difficulties an adolescent may face in attempting to exit from an escalating criminal event.

Seriousness of the current offense and nature and number of prior offenses. Standards should encourage prosecutors to be especially mindful about "labeling" offenses when youth are involved. The decision of whether and how to charge an offense is a highly subjective endeavor that assigns labels that often mask the true nature and circumstances of the underlying offense. Prosecutors should consider the nature and number of current and previous juvenile offenses in terms that avoid the often meaningless classifications of misdemeanor and felony. Thus, a youth who has a record of two "violent felonies" for robbery and assault with a dangerous weapon may have engaged in conduct that involves little more than playing catch with a teacher's hat or throwing pebbles at a classmate.

Youth's admission of guilt and acceptance of responsibility. Commentary by development psychologists would illuminate this criterion in two ways. First, developmental research would help prosecutors understand the difficulties youth often face in expressing remorse in the hours and days immediately after an offense.[46] Youth who have limited life experiences and diminished capacity to reason may not experience or understand remorse as would an adult.[47] Similarly, youth who lack strong language skills may not be able convey remorse to a police officer, victim, or probation officer shortly after an offense.[48] Other developmental features of adolescence, such as peer influence and teenage bravado, may further block adult-like expressions of grief and remorse.[49] Moreover, because remorse is a type of suffering itself, youth sometimes employ defense mechanisms such as humor, denial, or apparent indifference to avoid it.[50] Given these limitations, empathy and remorse provide a particularly unreliable measure of a youth's amenability to treatment and need for punishment, especially in the context of police interrogation and intake interviews that occur before the youth has had an opportunity to reflect on his or her conduct or benefit from counseling.

Second, developmental research should educate prosecutors on the particular susceptibility of youth to false confessions and prompt prosecutors to closely investigate and critically evaluate the circumstances surrounding a minor's admission.[51] The very features of adolescence that make youth vulnerable to peer influence and poor decision making, including limited appreciation for the future, impulsiveness, and deficits in legal knowledge and understanding, make them particularly susceptible to police coercion.[52]

Dangerousness of the threat posed to others. As evident from the implicit-bias studies discussed earlier, charging criteria involving the perceived threat and dangerousness of an accused youth are particularly susceptible to racial bias. A more thoughtful frame for this criterion might ask prosecutors to consider the youth's "likelihood of reintegration with appropriate interventions" and encourage prosecutors to identify and rely on community-based responses that have been shown to correct the behavior of even serious, violent offenders. In addition, to remind prosecutors that risk-taking is normatively common among all adolescent groups, even if opportunities for crime are different, standards and commentary should incorporate research on the impact of implicit bias on perceptions of danger and aggressiveness and highlight developmental studies that have controlled for ethnicity and socioeconomic status. By reviewing this literature, prosecutors may be reminded, for example, that children of color who use crack cocaine are very much like other youth who experiment with drugs.

Decisions made with respect to similarly situated persons. The implicit admonition to treat similarly situated persons the same is particularly inadequate to address racial disparities in the juvenile justice system. Charging practices that draw artificial lines between felonies and misdemeanors or between types of drugs used or sold provide little more than a superficial way to differentiate and compare accused youth. Office-wide policies that prevent a prosecutor from diverting a youth from the system after a felony or that preclude diversion in drug cases involving more "dangerous" drugs such as crack, crystal meth, or heroin may systemically disadvantage youth of color who live in communities where those drugs are less expensive and more accessible.

To better understand the impact of these policies on racial disparities, the state's district attorney may identify patterns in how prosecutors handle various offenses at the charging phase according to race and geographic neighborhood.[53] In the juvenile justice context, prosecutors often rely on what Perry Moriearty refers to as "attributional stereotypes" to distinguish between alleged offenders.[54] Unfortunately, attributional stereotypes such as perceived family stability, community support, and school performance are often closely correlated with race and further contribute to the disproportionate incarceration of children of color.[55] To correct for these distortions, prosecutors should engage community representatives in a periodic review of the charging criteria to monitor and adjust for unintended consequences. Prosecutors and probation officers should also make accommodations that recognize differences in family structure and school resources across racial and socioeconomic groups. For instance, when a low-income parent is unable to attend an intake interview due to his or her work schedule or child-care responsibilities, the probation officer may interview the parent by phone, identify other relatives or adults who may supervise the child, or refer the youth to an after-school program in lieu of the automatic default to formal prosecution.

Recommendations of the referring agency, victim, law enforcement officer, and advocates for the youth. Although prosecutors will necessarily be influenced by police officers who investigate a case and victims or witnesses who are impacted by an alleged offense, it is essential that prosecutors exercise independent judgment at the charging phase. Rote implementation of police recommendations and victim preferences merely perpetuates racial disparities that surface before the charging decision and risks returning the criminal justice system to a system of private redress that sanctions and reinforces the implicit biases and stereotypes of private citizens.[56] Standards should encourage prosecutors to educate victims on meaningful alternatives to prosecution for youth and be transparent about the underlying reasons for each charging decision. Over time, prosecutors have an opportunity to systemically influence referrals by public and private agencies, including schools, that repeatedly and disproportionately refer youth of color to the juvenile justice system.

2. Changing Cultures and Holding Prosecutors Accountable

Minimal enforcement of internal decision-making guidelines in prosecutors' offices, combined with a lack of public accountability for prosecutors and Supreme Court jurisprudence shielding prosecutors from public and judicial scrutiny, has hindered many of the current strategies to address disproportionate minority contact.[57] Even more than judges, prosecutors operate in virtual secrecy with unreviewable charging authority, especially in juvenile courts where court records and proceedings are confidential.[58]

To achieve and sustain reforms, prosecutors must change the culture that rationalizes racially disparate outcomes and be firmly resolved to resist external pressures to react symbolically to high-profile crimes and faulty perceptions of high and rising juvenile offending. Standards should require prosecutors to document the criteria considered in individual charging decisions, tally their decisions by race and geographic neighborhood, and periodically share that data with the public.[59] Prosecutors may track decisions over time by race and residence of the offender and adjust when recurrent justifications for charging decisions disproportionately affect youth of color.

Each state's attorney's office should develop a uniform checklist of developmentally informed criteria for charging and require prosecutors to articulate specific, non-race-related reasons for dismissals, diversions, and formal prosecution in every case. When the district attorney is unwilling to develop or enforce standards on his or her own initiative, the impetus may come from state legislators. Statutory mandates may require prosecutors to convene a multistakeholder and multidisciplinary task force to develop and publish guidelines such as those described here.

Standards should be developed and periodically reviewed with input from community representatives and adolescent-development experts. By engaging the public, prosecutors may cultivate support from those who are most affected by racial disparities, set crime-control priorities that reflect the needs of the local community, and ultimately make the juvenile charging decision more transparent.

IV. The Prosecutor's Choice: Choosing and Planning for Positive Youth Development

Although we know that most youth age out of delinquent behavior after adolescence, the successful transition to adulthood is not automatic.[60] The transition to a healthy, safe, and productive adulthood depends on a number of variables, including the youth's environmental context and social supports.[61] Good decision making by prosecutors requires a good understanding of what interventions are effective and a willingness to sacrifice temporary political and reputational gains achieved from rapid law-and-order responses to adolescent offending in favor of alternative strategies that have been proven to yield positive outcomes for youth and ultimately the community at large. Where community-based resources are not available to provide alternatives to formal prosecution, prosecutors may assume a leadership role in encouraging legislators and community representatives to develop those options.[62]

1. Achieving Positive Youth Development: Knowing What Works

Youth entering the delinquency system often face multiple disadvantages at home and in the community and are more likely than their nondelinquent peers to experience poor school performance, mental health problems, unstable and unsupportive family connections, poverty, crime-ridden neighborhoods, negative peer influences, and few positive role models.[63] The significant levels of unmet mental health needs among youth in the juvenile justice system are well documented, as are the high rates of academic and intellectual deficits among this population.[64] Left unaddressed, these conditions are likely to impede the transition to adulthood. Fortunately, developmental research also reveals that youth, whose identities and characters are in rapid transition, have an inherent potential for growth, change, and rehabilitation and will likely benefit from positive corrections in their family, school, or community.[65] These corrections can often be achieved through a range of community-based responses that are less harmful, less expensive, and more effective than traditional law enforcement and juvenile court interventions.[66] Studies have shown that even serious, violent, and chronic offenders can benefit from community-based interventions.[67] A number of cost-effective, community-based responses to adolescent offending have been shown to reduce crime across a range of offending patterns. Among them are functional family therapy, multisystemic therapy, and multidimensional treatment foster care.[68]

2. Knowing What Does Not Work

Just as developmentally appropriate responses to delinquency can increase the chances that adolescents will reach a healthy turning point in their transition to adulthood, developmentally inappropriate interventions by the juvenile justice system can derail or impede that transition. In what is described as a "paradox of punishment," Tracey Meares and Jeffrey Fagan contend that public policy choices that shift resources to traditional law enforcement strategies and away from employment opportunities, education, and neighborhood supports undermine informal social controls that provide a natural deterrent to crime and produce stable, if not higher, levels of crime.[69] High rates of arrest and punishment in communities of color also reduce the stigma traditionally associated with a finding of delinquency and undermine the value of incarceration as a deterrent to crime and delinquency.[70] Individual and collective dissatisfaction with procedural and distributive justice in the community can foster additional cynicism and noncompliance and further undermine the deterrent effect of juvenile and criminal justice interventions.[71]

Pretrial detention, incarceration, and secure treatment during adolescence are particularly detrimental to healthy psychosocial development. Incarceration disrupts important opportunities for proper socialization[72] and may fracture or further deteriorate youths' already troubled relationships with their parents precisely when they need parental support the most.[73] Youth who are separated from family and friends during incarceration withdraw from school, lose employment, and have little opportunity to develop positive peer relationships while away from home.[74] Not surprisingly, incarcerated youth are more likely to increase antisocial behavior after exposure to and placement with other delinquent youth.[75] Further, any stigma and rejection associated with the court involvement and removal from the community will likely have a significant psychological impact on the youth's self-image and identity.[76] Given this reality, youth returning to the community after incarceration are particularly unprepared with the psychosocial capacities they need to succeed as adults.

3. Empowering Communities: Identifying and Developing Effective Adolescent-Appropriate Alternatives to Formal Prosecution

Efforts to reduce racial disparities in juvenile court are not likely to succeed without adequate community-based, adolescent-appropriate alternatives to prosecution. The disproportionate prosecution of black and Hispanic youth may reflect a belief that communities of color are either disempowered or unwilling to control and regulate adolescent offending in their own neighborhoods. Unfortunately, these assumptions ignore the long history of self-help in black communities.[77] With even marginal realignment of financial resources from traditional law enforcement interventions to efforts designed to improve failing schools, dilapidated housing, mental health services, family counseling, and drug treatment in communities of color, these communities would be better equipped to address adolescent offending without court intervention.

Prosecutors willing to assume a more expansive role in addressing racial disparities should collaborate with probation officers, community leaders, and other juvenile justice stakeholders to compile a database of existing resources in the local community to include faith-based resources, community recreation centers, school-based services, and family support groups that may provide an alternative to prosecution and adequately respond to low- and midlevel offending by youth of color.[78] Where resources are lacking or inadequate, prosecutors, policy makers, and other state officials arguably have a responsibility to ensure that youth of color have sufficient access to alternative structures in communities of color. Communities would benefit from creative partnerships with police, substance abuse treatment providers, state and local mental health agencies, and schools to create programs such as neighborhood evening-reporting centers and diversion programs. The success of many youth in diversion suggests that nonlegal interventions are often just as effective as law enforcement responses to delinquency.[79] Further, evidence suggests that community-based programs such as teen courts save money in juvenile court processing and crime reduction over time.[80]

Conclusion

Notwithstanding the growing body of developmental research demonstrating that much of juvenile crime and delinquency is the product of normal adolescent development, contemporary narratives portraying youth of color as dangerous and irredeemable lead police, probation officers, and prosecutors to reject age as an excuse or mitigation for these youth. Aggressive institutional approaches toward adolescent offending, motivated by explicit or implicit racial bias, lead to the disproportionate arrest and prosecution of black and Hispanic youth. This chapter considers reform in prosecutorial decision making at the intake stage as a viable strategy to reduce disproportionate minority contact in the juvenile justice system. Specifically, this chapter proposes that prosecutors acknowledge the unique developmental status of adolescents and develop guidelines for prosecuting youth that adequately account for a youth's amenability to treatment and diminished culpability in criminal activity. These standards should also hold prosecutors accountable for confronting implicit bias not only in their own decisions but also in the decisions of other stakeholders in the system. By engaging the community, collaborating with developmental psychologists, and delineating adolescent-appropriate factors to guide the charging decision, prosecution standards should begin to erode harmful stereotypes about youth of color and hopefully reduce racial disparities in the system over time. Recognizing that reforms in prosecutorial charging decisions are likely to be hindered by the actual or perceived lack of community-based resources in communities of color, this chapter also proposes that prosecutors take a leadership role in ensuring that resources are fairly allocated to the implementation of adolescent-appropriate responses to delinquency as an alternative to law enforcement and juvenile court interventions.

NOTES

1 See Ellen Marrus, "Best Interests Equals Zealous Advocacy: A Not So Radical View of Holistic Representation for Children Accused of Crime," *Maryland Law Review* 62 (2003): 304–305.

2 See Angela J. Davis, "Prosecution and Race: The Power and Privilege of Discretion," *Fordham Law Review* 67 (1998): 17–18.

3 See, e.g., Angela Davis, *Arbitrary Justice: The Power of the American Prosecutor* (New York: Oxford University Press, 2007), 33–39; Victor L. Streib, "Prosecutorial Discretion in Juvenile Homicide Cases," *Penn State Law Review* 109 (2005): 1083–1084.

4 See, e.g., Michele Benedetto Neitz, "A Unique Bench, a Common Code: Evaluating Judicial Ethics in Juvenile Court," *Georgetown Journal of Legal Ethics* 24 (2011): 131–132; Andrew E. Taslitz, "Judging Jena's D.A.: The Prosecutor and Racial Esteem," *Harvard Civil Rights–Civil Liberties Law Review* 44 (2009): 416–421.

5 See Elizabeth S. Scott and Laurence Steinberg, *Rethinking Juvenile Justice* (Cambridge: Harvard University Press, 2008), 37–40; Elizabeth S. Scott, "The Legal Construction of Adolescence," *Hofstra Law Review* 29 (2000): 555–556.

6 See, e.g., *Miller v. Alabama*, 132 S. Ct. 2455 (2012); *Graham v. Florida*, 130 S. Ct. 2011 (2010).

7 Charles Puzzanchera and Wei Kang, "Easy Access to FBI Arrest Statistics: 2006–2011," Office of Juvenile Justice and Delinquency Prevention, http:/www.ojjdp.gov/ojstatbb/ezaucr/asp/ucr_/ (accessed August 22, 2014).

8 Melissa Sickmund, T. J. Sladky, Wei Kang, and Charles Puzzanchera, "Easy Access to the Census of Juveniles in Residential Placement: 1997–2011," Office of Juvenile

Justice and Delinquency Prevention, http://www.ojjdp.gov/ojstatbb/ezacjrp/ (accessed August 27, 2014).

9 Advancement Project, *Test, Punish, and Push Out: How "Zero Tolerance" and High-Stakes Testing Funnel Youth into the School-to-Prison Pipeline* (Washington, DC: Advancement Project, rev. 2010), 18–19 (tracking increase in school-based arrests, particularly for relatively minor offenses, in states such as North Carolina, Colorado, and Florida).

10 *See, e.g.*, Elizabeth Cauffman, Elizabeth P. Shulman, Laurence Steinberg, Eric Claus, Marie T. Banich, Sandra Graham, and Jennifer Woolard, "Age Differences in Affective Decision Making as Indexed by Performance on the Iowa Gambling Task," *Developmental Psychology* 46 (2010): 204–206; Laurence Steinberg, Sandra Graham, Lia O'Brien, Jennifer Woolard, Elizabeth Cauffman, and Marie Banich, "Age Differences in Future Orientation and Delay Discounting," *Child Development* 80 (2009): 38–39; Laurence Steinberg and Kathryn C. Monahan, "Age Differences in Resistance to Peer Influence," *Developmental Psychology* 43 (2007): 1538–1539; Laurence Steinberg, Dustin Albert, Elizabeth Cauffman, Marie Banich, Sandra Graham, and Jennifer Woolard, "Age Differences in Sensation Seeking and Impulsivity as Indexed by Behavior and Self-Report: Evidence for a Dual Systems Model," *Developmental Psychology* 44 (2008): 1774–1776.

11 Lloyd D. Johnston, Patrick M. O'Malley, Jerald G. Bachman, and John E. Schulenberg, *Monitoring the Future: National Survey Results on Drug Use, 1975–2010*, vol. 1, *Secondary School Students* (Ann Arbor: Institute for Social Research, University of Michigan, 2011), 1, http://monitoringthefuture.org/pubs/monographs/mtf-vol1_2010.pdf; Centers for Disease Control and Prevention (CDC), Youth Risk Behavior Survey (YRBS), 1991–2011 high school data, http://nccd.cdc.gov/YouthOnline/App/Default.aspx (accessed August 27, 2014).

12 Johnston et al., *supra* note 11, at 65.

13 *See* CDC, *supra* note 11; Steinberg, Graham, et al., *supra* note 10, at 39; Steinberg, Albert, et al., note 10, at 1771, 1774.

14 Johnston et al., *supra* note 11, at 34–35.

15 Office of Juvenile Justice and Delinquency Prevention, "Statistical Briefing Book," http://www.ojjdp.gov/ojstatbb/crime/jar.asp (accessed December 1, 2013).

16 *See* Michael Tonry, "The Social, Psychological, and Political Causes of Racial Disparities in the American Criminal Justice System," in *Crime and Justice: A Review of Research*, vol. 39, edited by Michael Tonry, 273–312 (Chicago: University of Chicago Press, 2010), 281–293.

17 *See* James Bell, "Throwaway Children: Conditions of Confinement and Incarceration," in *The Public Assault on America's Children: Poverty, Violence and Juvenile Injustice*, edited by Valerie Polakow, 188–210 (New York: Teacher's College Press, 2000), 189; *see, e.g.*, Nicholas K. Peart, "Why Is the N.Y.P.D. after Me?," *New York Times*, December 18, 2011, SR6.

18 Tonry, *supra* note 16, at 283.

19 George S. Bridges and Sara Steen, "Racial Disparities in Official Assessments of Juvenile Offenders: Attributional Stereotypes as Mediating Mechanisms," *American Sociological Review* 63 (1998): 556.

20 Sandra Graham and Brian S. Lowery, "Priming Unconscious Racial Stereotypes about Adolescent Offenders," *Law and Human Behavior* 28 (2004): 494, 499.

21 Aneeta Rattan, Cynthia S. Levine, Carol S. Dweck, and Jennifer L. Eberhardt, "Race and the Fragility of the Legal Distinction between Juveniles and Adults," *PLoS ONE* 7 (May 2012): 1–5.

22 Brooke Donald, "Stanford Psychologists Examine How Race Affects Juvenile Sentencing," *Stanford News*, May 24, 2012, http://news.stanford.edu/news/2012/may/race-juvenile-offenders-052412.html (quoting Aneeta Rattan, lead author of the Stanford study).

23 *See* Elizabeth S. Scott and Laurence Steinberg, "Blaming Youth," *Texas Law Review* 81 (2003): 809–810.

24 Kareem L. Jordan and Tina L. Freiburger, "Examining the Impact of Race and Ethnicity on the Sentencing of Juveniles in Adult Court," *Criminal Justice Policy Review* 21 (2010): 194–197.

25 *See* Kenneth B. Nunn, "The Child as Other: Race and Differential Treatment in the Juvenile Justice System," *DePaul Law Review* 51 (2002): 681–682, 706–709; Tonry, *supra* note 16, at 283–285.

26 *See* Jeffrey Fagan and Tracey L. Meares, "Punishment, Deterrence and Social Control: The Paradox of Punishment in Minority Communities," *Ohio State Journal of Criminal Law* 6 (2008): 178–179.

27 Each of these examples comes from my own representation of youth in Washington, D.C. The names have been changed to protect confidentiality.

28 Advancement Project, *supra* note 9, at 15, 18–19; Heather Cobb, Note, "Separate and Unequal: The Disparate Impact of School-Based Referrals to Juvenile Court," *Harvard Civil Rights–Civil Liberties Law Review* 44 (2009): 583–584.

29 Barbara Kaban and James Orlando, "Revitalizing the Infancy Defense in the Contemporary Juvenile Court," *Rutgers Law Review* 60 (2007): 36–37.

30 Andrew M. Carter, "Age Matters: The Case for a Constitutionalized Infancy Defense," *University of Kansas Law Review* 54 (2006): 734–749; Lara A. Bazelon, Note, "Exploding the Superpredator Myth: Why Infancy Is the Preadolescent's Best Defense in Juvenile Court," *NYU Law Review* 75 (2000): 190–198; Nina W. Chernoff and Marsha L. Levick, "Beyond the Death Penalty: Implications of Adolescent Development Research for the Prosecution, Defense and Sanctioning of Youthful Offenders," *Clearinghouse Review Journal of Poverty Law and Policy* 209 (2005): 213–215; Kim Taylor-Thompson, "States of Mind / States of Development," *Stanford Law and Policy Review* 22 (2003): 146.

31 *See, e.g.*, Wayne McKenzie, Don Stemen, Derek Coursen, and Elizabeth Farid, *Prosecution and Racial Justice: Using Data to Advance Fairness in Criminal Prosecution* (Vera Institute of Justice, March 2009), 1–7, http://www.vera.org/sites/

default/files/resources/downloads/Using-data-to-advance-fairness-in-criminal-prosecution.pdf.

32 *See* Davis, *supra* note 3, at 37.

33 Randall Kennedy, *Race, Crime and the Law* (New York: Random House, 1997), 19; Alexandra Natapoff, "Underenforcement," *Fordham Law Review* 75 (2006): 1716–1718.

34 *See* Catherine M. Coles, "Community Prosecution, Problem Solving, and Public Accountability: The Evolving Strategy of the American Prosecutor" (working paper, John F. Kennedy School of Government, Harvard University, Cambridge, Massachusetts, 2000), 11, http://www.hks.harvard.edu/criminaljustice-backup/publications/community_prosecution.pdf.

35 *See* Scott and Steinberg, *supra* note 5, at 217–220; and *infra* note 66.

36 *See* Kristin Henning, "What's Wrong with Victims' Rights in Juvenile Court? Retributive versus Rehabilitative Systems of Justice," *California Law Review* 97 (2009): 1163–1166; Barton Poulson, "A Third Voice: A Review of Empirical Research on the Psychological Outcomes of Restorative Justice," *Utah Law Review* (2003): 180.

37 *See* Tonry, *supra* note 16, at 274–275, 293–300.

38 Robert J. Smith and Justin D. Levinson, "The Impact of Implicit Racial Bias on the Exercise of Prosecutorial Discretion," *Seattle University Law Review* 35 (2012): 824.

39 *See, e.g.*, Jerry Kang, "Trojan Horses of Race," *Harvard Law Review* 118 (2005): 1529–1530, n. 207; Jeffrey J. Rachlinski, Sheri Lynn Johnson, Andrew J. Wistrich, and Chris Guthrie, "Does Unconscious Racial Bias Affect Trial Judges?," *Notre Dame Law Review* 84 (2009): 1196–1197, 1221.

40 *See generally* Anna Roberts, "(Re)forming the Jury: Detection and Disinfection of Implicit Juror Bias," *Connecticut Law Review* 44 (2012): 827, 852–860.

41 *See, e.g.*, Alaska Stat. Ann. § 47.12.010 (2012); D.C. Code § 16–2301.02 (2012); Minn. Stat. Ann. § 388.24 (2012); Neb. Rev. Stat. § 43–260.04 (2012); N.J. Stat. Ann. § 2A: 4A-71 (2012); Wis. Stat. Ann. § 938.01 (2012).

42 James Vorenberg, "Decent Restraint of Prosecutorial Power," *Harvard Law Review* 94 (1981): 1543. *But see* Institute for Judicial Administration and American Bar Association, Juvenile Justice Standards, Standards Relating to Prosecution §§ 3.7–4.4, at 49–60 (1979); National District Attorneys Association (NDAA), *National Prosecution Standards with Revised Commentary*, 3rd ed. (NDAA, 2010), 64–67.

43 NDAA, *supra* note 42, at 64–67.

44 *Id.* at 65.

45 *Cf. id.* at 52–53. *See generally* Rory K. Little, "ABA's Project to Revise the Criminal Justice Standards for the Prosecution and Defense Functions," *Hastings Law Journal* 62 (2011): 1112–1120.

46 *See* Martha Grace Duncan, "'So Young and So Untender': Remorseless Children and the Expectations of the Law," *Columbia Law Review* 102 (2002): 1472–1507.

47 Henning, *supra* note 36, at 1148–1153.

48 *See* Bryan H. Ward, "Sentencing without Remorse," *Loyola University Chicago Law Journal* 38 (2006): 142–144. *See also People v. Superior Court ex rel. Soon Ja Du*, 7 Cal. Rptr. 2d 177, 181 (Cal. Dist. Ct. App. 1992).

49 *See* Duncan, *supra* note 46, at 1504–1507.

50 *Id.* at 1472, 1478–1479, 1485, 1500.

51 *See J.D.B. v. North Carolina*, 131 S. Ct. 2394, 2401 (2011); Brandon L. Garrett, "The Substance of False Confession," *Stanford Law Review* 62 (2010): 1112; Allison D. Redlich, "The Susceptibility of Juveniles to False Confessions and False Guilty Pleas," *Rutgers Law Review* 62 (2010): 953.

52 Redlich, *supra* note 51, at 953.

53 McKenzie et al., *supra* note 31, at 6–7.

54 Perry L. Moriearty, "Combating the Color-Coded Confinement of Kids: An Equal Protection Remedy," *New York University Review of Law & Social Change* 32 (2008): 304.

55 *Id.* at 287, 299–308. *See also* Olatunde C. A. Johnson, "Disparity Rules," *Columbia Law Review* 107 (2007): 412; Dorothy E. Roberts, "Criminal Justice and Black Families: The Collateral Damage of Over-enforcement," *U.C. Davis Law Review* 34 (2001): 1020–1027.

56 Henning, *supra* note 36, at 1110, 1143.

57 *See* Davis, *supra* note 2, at 20.

58 *See* Sara Sun Beale, "You've Come a Long Way, Baby: Two Waves of Juvenile Justice Reforms as Seen from Jena, Louisiana," *Harvard Civil Rights–Civil Liberties Law Review* 44 (2009): 521, 530–531; Streib, *supra* note 3, at 1083–1084.

59 *See* Davis, *supra* note 2, at 18–19; Smith and Levinson, *supra* note 38, at 824–825.

60 Scott and Steinberg, *supra* note 5, at 54–56.

61 *See* He Len Chung, Michelle Little, and Laurence Steinberg, "The Transition to Adulthood for Adolescents in the Juvenile Justice System: A Developmental Perspective," in *On Your Own without a Net: The Transition to Adulthood for Vulnerable Populations*, edited by D. Wayne Osgood, E. Michael Foster, Constance Flanagan, and Gretchen R. Ruth, 68–91 (Chicago: University of Chicago Press, 2005), 69, 73–85.

62 *See* NDAA, *supra* note 42, 54, 68; James C. Backstrom and Gary L. Walker, "The Role of the Prosecutor in Juvenile Justice: Advocacy in the Courtroom and Leadership in the Community," *William Mitchell Law Review* 32 (2005): 982–987.

63 Chung, Little, and Steinberg, *supra* note 61, at 71.

64 Thomas Grisso, *Double Jeopardy: Adolescent Offenders with Mental Disorders* (Chicago: University of Chicago Press, 2004), 6–13 (discussing study results); Regina M. Foley, "Academic Characteristics of Incarcerated Youth and Correctional Education Programs: A Literature Review," *Journal of Emotional and Behavioral Disorders* 9 (2001): 249, 257; Linda A. Teplin, "Psychiatric Disorders in Youth in Juvenile Detention," *Archives of General Psychiatry* 59 (2002): 1133–1138.

65 *See Miller v. Alabama*, 132 S. Ct. 2455, 2465 (2012); *Graham v. Florida*, 130 S. Ct. 2011, 2026 (2010); *Roper v. Simmons*, 543 U.S. 551, 570 (2005).

66 *See* Laurence Steinberg, He Len Chung, and Michelle Little, "Reentry of Young Offenders from the Justice System: A Developmental Perspective," *Youth Violence and Juvenile Justice* 2 (2004): 29–30; Chung, Little, and Steinberg, *supra* note 61, at 84.

67 *See* Scott and Steinberg, *supra* note 5, at 217–220.

68 *Id.* at 217–219.

69 Fagan and Meares, *supra* note 26, at 173, 176, 183–202.

70 *Id.* at 173–174, 228.

71 *Id.*, at 173–174, 216–219.

72 *See* Steinberg, Chung, and Little, *supra* note 66, at 27–28; Chung, Little, and Steinberg, *supra* note 61, at 79.

73 See Steinberg, Chung, and Little, *supra* note 66, at 27–28; Chung, Little, and Steinberg, *supra* note 61, at 79; Kristin Henning, "It Takes a Lawyer to Raise a Child? Allocating Responsibilities among Parents, Lawyers and Children in the Juvenile Justice System," *Nevada Law Journal* 6 (2006): 862.

74 *See* Chung, Little, and Steinberg, *supra* note 61, at 81–82.

75 *Id.* at 81–82.

76 *Id.* at 82.

77 Geoff K. Ward, *The Black Child-Savers: Racial Democracy and Juvenile Justice* (Chicago: University of Chicago Press, 2012), 127–263.

78 *See, e.g.*, Annie E. Casey Foundation, *Juvenile Detention Alternatives Initiative: 2012 Annual Results Report* (Baltimore: Annie E. Casey Foundation, 2013), http://www.aecf.org/m/resourcedoc/AECF-JDAI2012AnnualResultsReport-2013.pdf.

79 Joseph J. Cocozza, Bonita M. Veysey, Deborah A. Chapin, Richard Dembo, Wansley Walters, and Sylvia Farina, "Diversion from the Juvenile Justice System: The Miami-Dade Juvenile Assessment Center Post-arrest Diversion Program," *Substance Use & Misuse* 40 (2005): 937–939.

80 *See, e.g.*, Edgar Cahn and Cynthia Robbins, "An Offer They Can't Refuse: Racial Disparity in Juvenile Justice and Deliberate Indifference Meet Alternatives That Work," *University of the District of Columbia Law Review* 13 (2010): 98–99.

11

Helping Adolescents Succeed

Assuring a Meaningful Right to Counsel

CARLOS J. MARTINEZ

"Kids today have it much easier than when we were growing up." How often have you heard that or said that? The sad reality is that in the past two decades throughout the United States, it has become increasingly more costly for teenagers to do what teenagers typically do—experiment, rebel, and make mistakes. The difference is not caused by the photographs and posts they publish on social media. Rather, a child's impulsive act can become a permanent ball and chain resulting in a lifetime of denied opportunities, forever barring him or her from becoming a productive adult citizen. In this context of lifelong consequences of arrest, adjudication, or conviction, the role of competent counsel is critically important to advise about and work to avoid these outcomes.

Nationally, insufficient judicial, prosecution, defense, and rehabilitative resources, political posturing, and adults' ignorance of the consequences have created a perfect storm. Its victims include children and adolescents, our system of checks and balances, and the public's perception of the juvenile justice system. It is seen not simply as an unjust legal system; it is viewed as government-sanctioned inequality. The public perception is that if kids with affluent parents commit crimes, they will not be saddled with the long-term consequences; and that is partly true. Many people, like me, see that the "other" kids end up with three strikes before the game of upward mobility has even begun.

The broader reality is that some of the problems impact everyone irrespective of income, for example, the question on college applications about ever having been arrested. But the most insidious and pervasive problems almost exclusively impact poor kids. Having competent defense counsel matters more today than ever because the consequences of a conviction have long-term effects on occupational licensing, serving in the military, housing, and immigration, each of which can be far more serious than serving a jail sentence or being locked up in a juvenile residential program. For example, sex-offender registration of juveniles and restrictions on where the registered juvenile can reside or work are of particular concern. Without meaningful reform, the future prosperity of countless young people is at best doubtful. However, we can change that if we have the political will.

Whether through judicial docket-management practices, waiver of counsel, overloaded counsel with too many cases to adequately and competently provide legal representation, or inexperienced, untrained, unsupervised counsel, too many adolescents are silenced and harmed through quick guilty pleas and unchallenged charges. For a large segment of society, the juvenile justice system does not afford them respect and denies them a voice; thus, it lacks legitimacy and fundamental fairness. The child's and the parent's experience with attorneys, judges, and the other stakeholders in juvenile court perpetuate a perception of unfairness. Unfortunately, as the system currently operates, this perception is reality.

The primary contributing factor to this troubling reality has been the absence of competent counsel[1] to guide the indigent teenager through the litigation[2] and decision-making process. Defense counsel plays a critical role in ensuring that juvenile mistakes, misbehavior, errors in judgment, and wrongdoing do not become insurmountable barriers to a successful adulthood. But the core issue is that without a zealous, vigorous, and competent defense, the innocent are wrongly convicted and the guilty go free. Such injustice occurs when there is no adversarial testing of the evidence and when defense counsel serves as a mere conduit of prosecution or court plea offers.[3]

Underfunding of indigent defense impairs counsel's ability to be zealous and competent. How is chronic underfunding of juvenile defense counsel still an issue when juvenile arrests are at record lows and many more cases are diverted from prosecution? In the past twenty years, Florida legislators enacted laws requiring minimum mandatory sentences, life in prison without parole, sentencing enhancements such as 10/20/life and three-strikes, and charge enhancements from misdemeanor to felony for repeat offenses, as well as eliminating parole and authorizing easier transfer of children to adult court. Thus, any additional judicial, prosecutorial, and defense resources were almost exclusively directed at adult cases, not juvenile court.

The underfunding or underallocation of resources to juvenile court is not just a defense counsel issue. We need to develop more comprehensive methodology for allocating resources to juvenile court. Currently in Florida, for example, the courts, prosecutors, public defenders, and regional conflict counsel each have different definitions of a case. All juvenile delinquency cases are currently counted (weighted) as if they all take the same amount of work. The cases are not differentiated by the complexity that would be reflected if we measured the amount of work done by each stakeholder from the beginning of the case until completion. So, for example, a case involving a troubled youth who has intellectual disabilities, which requires the use of experts to determine the child's competency to proceed and the child's ability to waive his or her rights during police questioning, is now counted the same as a case involving a simple misdemeanor in which the child has no similar issues and no experts are required. The courts already use weighted caseload methodology to determine the need for additional judges.[4] But their methodology does not adequately account for changes in law, the complexity of juvenile cases, or the work that needs to be done by the prosecution and defense, each of which impacts the court's and each other's workload.[5]

Civil citation and pre- and postarrest diversion programs have dramatically reduced the number of low-level cases in juvenile court. The rearrest rates on those low-level offenses have also plummeted. Paradoxically, those reforms and local initiatives that have reduced the number of juveniles arrested and prosecuted through the juvenile court have resulted in a more complex and difficult mix of cases being prosecuted and defended in juvenile court. Cases on today's juvenile court dockets mostly require ten or more hours of defense attorney preparation, not including time spent in court, because the cases that remain in juvenile court now require more preparation. Up to now, we have not systemically addressed the new workload realities of the juvenile justice system.

Some of the attorney's time is spent learning not just substantive and procedural law but social science relating to children and adolescents.

The Supreme Court of the United States has recognized the scientific issues in several decisions that all point to the differences between prosecuting and punishing a child and an adult.[6] While those decisions deal specifically with children prosecuted as adults, it is clear that the scientific underpinnings of adolescent brain development apply equally to children in juvenile court, irrespective of the type of charge. We now have more science-based empirical evidence about adolescent development, the root causes of crime, effective treatment,[7] and approaches to reduce recidivism than we did two decades ago. Many of our young clients have intellectual disabilities or have suffered trauma; physical, sexual, or emotional abuse; chronic neglect; and/or show symptoms of posttraumatic stress disorder. To adequately represent young clients, defense counsel must have expertise on these issues. How the comorbidity factors interact with a specific child's development to impact decision making, competency, and acceptance of or resistance to specific interventions is complicated. From arrest to disposition (sentencing), counsel must consider those factors and develop the appropriate case strategy. That takes time.

It is clear that the practice of law has also become more complex, primarily due to advances in science and technology but also because counsel now has to try to avoid the often severe consequences of an adjudication even for minor offenses. Because juvenile arrest records are public, an arrest, adjudication, or conviction impacts an individual's ability to pursue higher education, to obtain a job, to secure housing, or to become a citizen. Some consequences halt upward mobility particularly for the poorest, even before the person turns 18. The overcriminalization of misbehavior and the increasingly severe consequences of court involvement add to the complexity of an indigent defense attorney's caseload.

The additional complexity requires defense counsel to spend more time preparing cases, counseling clients, and explaining the harsh realities and stark choices to parents. Yet funding has not kept up with these increased demands. High caseloads, lack of training, lack of supervision, and lack of adequate support staff in juvenile court reflect the disparity of resource allocation directed to "more serious" felony cases. It is not unusual for chief defenders to prioritize allocating more resources for clients facing the death penalty or lifelong imprisonment than to juvenile court.

Adequate funding for indigent defense remains elusive. Since the U.S. Supreme Court decided *Gideon v. Wainwright*[8] and *In re Gault*,[9] 50 and 45 years ago, respectively, we have witnessed lopsided funding of the prosecution and police functions and chronic underfunding of the defense role. The wide funding disparity is in large part due to federal funding for drug-sting and other police and prosecutorial operations, without equitable funding for either the defense or judicial functions. Not surprisingly, courts and indigent defense counsel have been overwhelmed with cases.

With chronic underfunding of both the defense and the courts, "triage" has become the court culture. The terms "rocket docket," "plea blitzes," "early disposition calendar," and "early disposition court" are often used to describe court-sanctioned short cuts, which eviscerate defense counsel's mandate to provide zealous and competent representation to each client. In that environment, well-meaning, caring attorneys overwhelmed with cases and faced with judicial pressure to keep the cases moving engage in "meet them and plead them." They are forced to dispose a large number of cases without doing any client counseling, much less defense preparation. On the cases that remain open, the attorneys then selectively work first with the clients who are in most critical need (e.g., those locked up in secure detention) and can barely provide any real representation to the out-of-custody clients. Triage and short-cuts severely compromise the attorney's ability to competently represent clients, destroy the adversarial process at the heart of our system, and make a mockery of the right to counsel.

While interviewing and counseling each client, investigating cases, conducting legal research, hiring expert witnesses, and preparing mitigation are all essential defense counsel tasks necessary to adequately advise a client whether to plead to a charge or charges or go to trial,[10] those tasks are seldom performed when attorneys must work in a triage environment. Adversarial testing of the evidence thus becomes something young attorneys have only heard about in law school. Without vigorously litigated cases, imprisoning the innocent and government overreaching become commonplace, and abuse goes unchecked.

In juvenile court, lack of adequate funding and staffing results in attorneys handling more than 100 juvenile delinquency cases at a time and/or handling far in excess of the 250 annual caseload limit that is the standard for the Florida Public Defender Association. Many defenders staff their juvenile offices with inexperienced, newly hired attorneys. Due to turnover, many offices assign their most experienced attorneys to handle felony cases because those clients, unlike clients in juvenile court, are facing prison sentences. Therefore, the impact of high workloads is felt even more because new attorneys who lack experience to quickly identify the critical legal issues need to conduct legal research more frequently because juvenile law requires specialized knowledge and training.

Crushing caseloads are not the only pressure the attorneys feel. Parents become exasperated when they are told that if their child wants his or her day in court, multiple court visits will be required. Most parents cannot afford to miss work. Parents also see the attorneys dealing with a crush of cases. With judicial encouragement for early and quick resolutions and lack of information about the consequences of an adjudication, it is not surprising that many adolescents simply give in to the pressure, even when they know they did not do what they are accused of doing. No matter how much the judges may dislike the assembly-line judicial process, they have one less case on their woefully overloaded docket.

It is not all gloom and doom, however. There is hope on the horizon. The Supreme Court of Florida decided a landmark case in May 2013, enforcing the rules that give real meaning to the right to counsel—the Rules Regulating the Florida Bar.[11] In *Public Defender, Eleventh Judicial Circuit of Florida v. State* (PD11),[12] the court asserted its proper role to safeguard individual liberty and equal justice under law and to ensure that our courtrooms do not become factories of injustice and inequality. The case arose from a large increase of noncapital felony cases assigned to the public defender at the same time that the office's budget was drastically reduced. A state law prohibited judges from granting a public defender's motion to withdraw from cases solely due to an excessive caseload. The court ruled that there is no difference in ethical responsibilities between the private bar and the public defender and that the court has inherent judicial authority to fashion a remedy when necessary to safeguard a defendant's right to effective representation.

The court rejected the Third District's determination that a *Strickland*-type[13] prejudice was required for counsel to withdraw from the excess number of cases that prevent lawyers from providing the type of representation for the indigent guaranteed by the Sixth Amendment. In PD-11, the Florida Supreme Court reasoned that the considerations justifying *Strickland*-type prejudice (finality of convictions) do not exist where counsel is trying to avoid violations of the right to counsel by moving to withdraw from the representation. Defenders can now avail themselves of the withdrawal remedy when confronted with excessive caseloads that create "a substantial risk that the representation of [one] or more clients will be materially limited by the lawyer's responsibilities to another client."[14]

The PD11 case offers relief for public defenders and regional conflict counsel who seek the court's help when their attorneys represent too many clients to be able to adequately represent them. If the overloaded public defender's office or regional conflict counsel's office withdraw, the child would be assigned an attorney who has sufficient time to be able to provide timely, diligent, zealous, and competent representation.

In closing, I offer additional suggestions to give troubled children and adolescents an opportunity to succeed and have a meaningful right to counsel if they are ever prosecuted for an offense. To address the systemic problems, we must first be vigilant of what is happening in our juvenile courtrooms every day.

Judges must be aware that when they do not adequately explain the consequences of juvenile court involvement when accepting a plea, even when not required by a court rule, they are doing a disservice to the community they were elected to serve. When juvenile judges give only a few minutes for the attorney to counsel the client, to explain plea terms and the real and potential consequences, particularly when the child just met the attorney in court that day, the judge perpetuates the perception of injustice and is not safeguarding the child's right to counsel. Obsession with case processing, speed, and time frames should not trump fundamental rights. The justification of needing immediate sanctions at the expense of due process (giving the child an opportunity to be heard) eviscerates the presumption of innocence. Our constitutional rights and basic fairness principles should be not sacrificed at the altar of efficiency.

As defense counsel, we have been entrusted with a great responsibility: to defend those who cannot defend themselves. Through hard work, dedication, and tenacity, defense counsel can breathe life into the ideal of equal justice under law every day. But we must provide defense counsel the tools they need to be zealous and competent.

Public defender and regional conflict counsel offices must ensure that their attorneys follow the performance guidelines, are well trained and supervised, and have manageable caseloads so they can competently represent every indigent child. Those offices should participate in a joint and coordinated case-weighting study to determine how to adequately staff their juvenile offices.

Defense counsel must stand up when judges rush them to plead out cases without adequate case preparation and without sufficient time to counsel the child so he or she can make an informed decision about whether to plea or to take the case to trial. While I fought hard for Florida to strengthen the court rule that allowed children to waive counsel, because the consequences to children are so severe and long lasting, I now believe that there should be no waiver of counsel in juvenile court.

Lastly, we must change existing Florida law. The legislature should re-enact the juvenile privacy protections that were in place 20 years ago, to give young people the opportunity to learn from their mistakes so they may have an opportunity to grow up and become taxpaying, contributing members of society.

In addition, the legislature should fund a joint and coordinated (prosecution, judicial, defense) weighted caseload study to determine the actual workload (work that should and must be done) and the subsequent level of funding necessary in juvenile court.

The legislature also should provide adequate funding for the defense to function at a level that ensures quality legal representation and allows defense counsel to comply with the U.S. Constitution and professional obligations.

I know we can do better. We owe our children their future. We can and must change for our sake and theirs.

NOTES

1 Rules Regulating the Florida Bar, Rule 4-1.1 (Competence) ("A lawyer shall provide competent representation to a client. Competent representation requires the legal knowledge, skill, thoroughness, and preparation reasonably necessary for the representation.").

2 *Gideon v. Wainwright*, 372 U.S. 335 (1963); *In re Gault*, 387 U.S. 1 (1967).

3 In Florida, far too many cases are "resolved" with quick pleas due to underre-sourced indigent defense counsel, overloaded court dockets, and judicial pressure to close out cases. Too many pleas are taken without adequate consultation with the child and with little to no knowledge of the strengths and weaknesses of the case. The plea colloquy itself includes a "finding" that the client has had advice of competent counsel when, in fact, the pleas are often taken with no discovery conducted, no investigation, and minimal attorney-client interaction. Inquiries into legal competency, competency to waive rights, or mental health or substance abuse issues often do not take place. Basic tasks that lawyers should undertake, such as interviewing witnesses, investigating the crime scene, gathering all reports, appropriately using experts, filing pretrial motions, conducting trials, and subjecting the trial court decisions to appellate review, are routinely forfeited with the quick uncounseled dispositions. All throughout the United States, experts are infrequently used in cases even when there is obvious junk-science "evidence" involved. And there is even less frequent use of experts in juvenile cases, despite the U.S. Supreme Court opinions recognizing the clear developmental differences between children and adults and how those differences impact juvenile and criminal law and individual rights.

4 "For district courts and trial courts, the determination for need is based on a complex calculation of caseloads. The Supreme Court uses a system for determin-ing caseloads that takes into account the differing amounts of time needed in different kinds of cases. More complex kinds of cases receive greater weight under this system than simpler cases. It is called the 'Weighted Caseload System.' Thus, the certification is not a statement of what the Supreme Court simply wants, but rather what it has determined is objectively needed using the calculations dictated by the weighted caseload system." Florida Supreme Court, Public Information, "Historical Information: Certification of the Need for New Judges In Florida 2000 through 2012," ://www.floridasupremecourt.org/pub_info/certification.shtml (accessed November 7, 2013).

5 *Caseload* is different from *workload*; *caseload* is the number of cases handled by the attorney at a given time or during a year. *Workload* is the total of all work performed by and all responsibilities of that lawyer, including legal training. The time demands on defense counsel involve a number of factors, including but not limited to the complexity of the cases, the case- and non-case-related responsibili-ties of the lawyer, the lawyer's experience and ability, and the availability of support-staff services. The Florida Public Defender Association adopted performance guidelines for defense counsel in August 2013, which include specific tasks that counsel must do or should do to provide quality representation to indigent clients. The performance guidelines are also designed to provide objective guidelines for the allocation of resources for indigent defense. *See also* U.S. Department of Justice, *Keeping Defender Workloads Manageable* (Washington, DC: U.S. Department of Justice, Office of Justice Programs, 2001).

6 *Graham v. Florida*, 560 U.S. 48 (2010); *Miller v. Alabama*, 567 U.S. ___ (2012), 132 S. Ct. 2455 (2013).

7 *See, e.g.*, Blueprints for Healthy Youth Development, Center for the Study and Prevention of Violence (CSPV), at the Institute of Behavioral Science, University of Colorado–Boulder, http://www.blueprintsprograms.com/programCriteria.php (accessed November 7, 2013); Mark W. Lipsey, David B. Wilson, and Lynn Cothern, "Effective Intervention for Serious Juvenile Offenders," *OJJDP Juvenile Justice Bulletin*, April 2000.

8 372 U.S. 335 (1963).

9 387 U.S. 1 (1967).

10 Effective assistance of counsel is required during plea negotiations (e.g., counsel must convey plea offers and counsel the client about the plea offer). *Lafler v. Cooper*, 560 U.S. ___,132, S. Ct. 1376 (2012); *Missouri v. Frye*, 132 S. Ct. 1399 (2012).

11 In particular, Rules Regulating the Florida Bar: Rule 4-1.1 (Competence); Rule 4-1.2(a) (Lawyer to Abide by Client's Decision); Rule 4-1.3 (Diligence); Rule 4-1.4 (Communication); Rule 4-1.7(a)(2) (Conflict of Interest; Current Clients); and Rule 4-5.1 (Responsibilities of Partners, Managers, and Supervisory Lawyers).

12 *Public Defender, Eleventh Judicial Circuit of Florida v. State* (PD11), 115 So. 3d 261 (Fla. 2013).

13 *Strickland v. Washington*, 466 U.S. 668 (1984). In *Strickland*, the Supreme Court of the United States established the postconviction test for determining when a defendant's conviction should be set aside due to ineffective assistance of counsel. The *Strickland* test requires a defendant to show that counsel's performance was deficient and prejudiced the defendant and that but for counsel's performance, the result of the case would have been different.

14 Rules Regulating the Florida Bar, Rule 4-1.7(a)(2).

12

Fit to Be T(r)ied

Ending Juvenile Transfers and Reforming the Juvenile Justice System

RICHARD MORA AND MARY CHRISTIANAKIS

> *"Things I Know to Be True"*
> I'm scared of doing life
> I think to myself at night
> I know I'm smart
> Some say I'm bright
> I learned one mess-up
> Can cost your life
> The truth is my kid-ish thoughts
> Were not right
> I try to stay strong
> But I lose my Vibe
> —Magic

On Saturday mornings, we teach creative writing to boys held in the Special Housing Unit of a Los Angeles County juvenile detention facility. Among our students, who are primarily boys of color, there are "fitness fighters"—that is, boys trying to convince a juvenile court judge that they are fit to be tried as minors. Those who have lost their fitness join Magic and dozens of others held in "the compound," which houses youth being tried as adults for crimes they allegedly committed while underage. The fitness fighters we meet as volunteer teachers are reminders that in California, as in most other states, neither the status of "child" nor the protections afforded to that status are stable or indisputable.

Over the past twenty years, nearly all states made it easier to try juveniles in adult criminal courts.[1] As a result, on a daily basis youth, disproportionately children of color,[2] face adult sentences and incarceration in adult prisons, for both violent and nonviolent offenses.[3] In fact, each year approximately 200,000 youth throughout the United States are tried or sentenced as adults.[4]

In this chapter, we call for an end to the practice of transferring juveniles, primarily youth of color, to the adult criminal justice system. As we see it, the practice is indefensible given the developmental differences between juveniles and adults and the consequences juveniles face in adult courts. In addition, we argue for a full restructuring of the juvenile justice system. Detention should be reserved for those youth who have committed the most serious felony-level crimes. Instead of the punitive and criminal approaches that have emerged in the past couple of decades, we propose reforms that focus on preventative, restorative, and rehabilitative initiatives for the vast majority of youth who have contact with the juvenile justice system, as well as for their families. We discuss a few evidence-based programs that can help reintegrate youth into society. To underscore the need for juvenile justice reform, we reference the writings of incarcerated youth who have participated in InsideOut Writers, the nonprofit organization for which we serve as volunteer teachers.

Before laying out our arguments, we begin by briefly discussing juvenile transfers in California and how these transfers create a category of vulnerable individuals that the state, under its own statutes, simultaneously defines as children and as adults.

The Case of California

In California, children as young as 14 years of age can be transferred from juvenile courts to adult criminal courts. Transfers can occur through one of three mechanisms. A prosecutor may file a petition for a judicial waiver, and a fitness hearing is held. At the hearing, a juvenile court judge considers five criteria to determine whether the child between the ages of 14 and 17 is fit to remain for treatment as a juvenile.[5] If the child is found unfit, he or she is transferred to adult court. Prosecutors can also use prosecutorial waivers to file directly in adult criminal court. Finally, juveniles can be transferred as the result of legislative waivers, that is, waivers triggered when the case or juvenile meets statutory requirements.

According to the California Department of Justice,[6] in 2011 there were 686 prosecutorial waivers or direct files, and 912 judicial or legislative transfers to the criminal courts in California, with the vast majority of both direct files and transfers involving youth of color. Of the 912 transfers, the disposition information on 548 transfers indicates that a total of 461 transfers (84.1%) resulted in convictions, with 63.8% of those convicted sentenced to adult prison or to California's Division of Juvenile Justice.[7]

For a judicial waiver, which can include minors with no prior offense, five factors are used to determine whether a child is unfit for juvenile court: (1) the sophistication of the alleged crime, (2) the likelihood that the minor can be rehabilitated before he or she ages out of the juvenile system, (3) the minor's previous criminal/delinquency history, (4) the success of the minor on previous probations, and (5) the circumstances and the gravity of the alleged offense.[8] Minors over 16 years of age who have accumulated two prior felonies after the age of 14 are presumed that they will be tried as an adult unless the defense attorney at the fitness hearing proves that the child is fit to be under the jurisdiction of the juvenile court.[9]

In 2011, 304 fitness hearings were reported to the state of California, with juveniles found unfit and transferred in 74.7% of hearings and with juveniles found fit to remain in the juvenile system in only 25.3% of hearings.[10] The older the juvenile, the greater the likelihood he or she was found unfit and transferred—86.5% of 17-years-olds were found unfit, compared to 59.2% of 16-year-olds, 45.5% of 15-year-olds, and 16.7% of 14-year-olds. Additionally, a much greater percentage of White juveniles than Hispanic and Black juveniles were found fit and kept under the jurisdiction of the juvenile courts—48.7% of White juveniles, as compared to 21.4% of Hispanic juveniles and 18.9% of Black juveniles.

In California, legislative changes have made it easier to try youths as adults. The most significant legislative changes occurred in 2000, when California voters passed Proposition 21, which enacted the Gang Violence and Juvenile Crime Prevention Act.[11] Prior to the passage of Proposition 21, the transfer of juveniles to adult court in California was left to the discretion of juvenile court judges, who decided at a fitness hearing whether a minor was unfit for juvenile court and should be transferred as requested by prosecutors.[12] Proposition 21 stripped juvenile court judges of most of their discretion and allowed for more direct files and legislative files, granting prosecutors more discretionary power when it comes to transferring minors to criminal courts.[13] As a result, juvenile offenders in California now have less access to fitness trials, which is particularly problematic for youth of color since research shows that prosecutorial discretion is often influenced by race.[14]

"Once an Adult, Always an Adult"

On a daily basis, youth are being treated as though they are "responsible criminals" rather than "immature delinquents" and transferred to the criminal justice system.[15] As Jenny Carroll explains, "Children, particularly underprivileged children and children of color, are being transferred out of the juvenile court systems at alarming rates and with shocking ease."[16] Aware of the racial disparity in the justice system, Andrew Q, a fitness fighter, describes his predicament in "Wind," a poem he authored while confined:

> The wind blows the clouds so slow
> and that's the way my life seems to go.
> Emotions run through my body
> but nobody knows why except the one inside.
> Minority in this world
> and becoming majority in jail
> that looks like hell.
> Facing 25 to life
> is like being buried alive
> in a place that I'm trying to survive.

If Andrew were to lose his fitness and be convicted in criminal court, he would join a mostly invisible category of children who our laws recognize as neither fully child nor fully adult—children our society chooses to expose to the traumas, human rights violations, and scarcity of opportunities behind prison walls.

Transfers represent nothing more than an unacceptable retribution.[17] In criminal court, juveniles are no longer entitled to the protections of the juvenile court system and face stiffer sentences and incarceration in adult prisons.[18] In addition, juveniles tried as adults are excluded from any treatments and rehabilitative services available to those under the jurisdiction of juvenile courts.[19] Once convicted, juveniles are at risk of abuse[20] and suicide[21] in adult prisons and of higher recidivism rates, if and when they are released.[22]

In 35 states, including California, retribution includes the "once an adult, always an adult" rule.[23] The rule indicates that once a child loses a fitness hearing, he or she is no longer eligible to be under the jurisdiction of the juvenile court. Waivers and the "once an adult, always an adult" rule are, thus, part of a punitive "system where children are transformed, via legal fiction, into adults despite the fact that they have not reached the age of majority."[24] The system blurs the distinction between child and adult[25] and places children tried as adults in a subjugated and liminal space where they have none of the protections of childhood and none of the rights and freedoms of adulthood.

The "legal fiction" that turns juveniles into adults for the sole purpose of transferring them to adult courts is morally, as well as legally, indefensible.[26] This practice is particularly problematic given that the waiver hearings are held before the youths have been tried for their alleged crimes. Thus, youths lose their status, innocence, and protection as a minor, even before their case has been adjudicated. In "Still We Cry," Nathaniel, an adolescent facing a life sentence, laments,

> I am an incarcerated black male with many goals in life. I'm only 17, and my life lies in the hands of the state. I'm facing a life sentence. And this is the first and last time I will ever be incarcerated. I have been through so many struggles and so far gained so little, but lost so much. This is a desperate cry coming from the youth that has gone unanswered for many years. And still we cry, but there is no answer.

With the practice of transferring minors such as Nathaniel, the state ignores the fundamental claim of childhood—children and youth do not yet have the mature cognitive and emotional capabilities of adults. Consequently, we call for all juveniles to be adjudicated in juvenile courts and rehabilitated.

Reforming Juvenile Justice

Bringing an end to juvenile waivers may seem impossible given that the majority of states transfer juveniles.[27] However, there is mounting evidence that the notion that children are different from adults is a viable sociopolitical argument against waivers. In 2008, the California electorate rejected a proposition that would have established legislative transfers for any juvenile as young as 14 years of age. Also, there were two U.S. Supreme Court rulings—*Roper v. Simmons* (2005) and *Miller v. Alabama* (2012)—that express misgivings about treating juvenile defendants as if they possess the maturity of adult defendants. In *Roper v. Simmons*,[28] the Supreme Court found that youth tend to be more immature and irresponsible than adults. Similarly, in *Miller v. Alabama*,[29] the Court described the uniqueness of childhood: "Mandatory life without parole for a juvenile precludes consideration of his chronological age and its hallmark features—among them, immaturity, impetuosity, and failure to appreciate risks and consequences."[30] As the Court suggests, juveniles are developmentally different from adults and, thus, merit further legal protections.

In addition, over the past few years, state-level legislation shows that states are reconsidering tough-on-crime juvenile policies that have exposed juveniles to the criminal justice system. As a result of new legislation, it is now less likely that juveniles in Arizona, Colorado, Connecticut, Delaware, Illinois, Maryland, Nevada, Ohio, Utah, Virginia, and Washington will be transferred to the criminal justice system.[31] Moreover, legislators in Connecticut, Illinois, Massachusetts, and Mississippi expanded the jurisdiction of their juvenile courts to include older youth who previously faced automatic waivers.[32] Also, between 2011 and 2103, sentencing laws, including mandatory minimums, in California, Colorado, Georgia, Indiana, Missouri, Ohio, Texas, and Washington were changed "to take into account the developmental differences between youth and adults."[33] States throughout the country, and from various geographical regions, are acknowledging that juveniles are not adults and that juveniles should be adjudicated in juvenile court rather than tried as adults.

When the justice system deals with juveniles, detention should be a last resort.[34] For the vast majority who are not detained, we propose the establishment of community-based restorative justice programs. As Howard Zehr explains, restorative justice

- Focuses on harms and consequent needs (Of victims but also communities and offenders);
- Addresses obligations resulting from those harms (Offenders' but also communities' and society's);
- Uses inclusive, collaborative processes;
- Involves those with a stake in the situation (Victims, offenders, community members, society);
- Seeks to put right the wrongs.[35]

The restorative justice programs we envision would hold children accountable for their transgressions and provide them with access to intervention and rehabilitative services and opportunities both to nurture positive social relations in their communities and to make amends.

As part of the restorative justice programs, we call for evidence-based services that can support juveniles and their families. Since states spend billions of dollars each year to house detained juveniles, the money saved from steering juveniles away from detention would go a long way toward covering the costs of juvenile services.[36] We recommend four juvenile services evaluated by the Washington State Institute for Public Policy.[37] Here we provide a description and the benefits of each service as described by the Justice Policy Institute:

Functional Family Therapy (FFT): This family-based program works as both prevention and intervention. It is a multi-level eight to 12 week program that seeks to address family dysfunction, acknowledging that in the long run, removing the youth from his or her family and community may not fix the root problem behind the behavior. The FFT program can lower recidivism by up to 38 percent, averaging around 16 percent, and has $10.69 in benefits for each dollar of cost when administered by trained therapists. . . .

Aggression Replacement Training (ART): This program is designed for youth who exhibit aggressive tendencies and anti-social behavior and are therefore considered to be at a high risk of reoffending. ART is a 10-week, 30-hour intervention administered to groups of eight to 12 youth who have committed an offense. ART has been found to reduce recidivism after 18 months by up to 24 percent, averaging around 7 percent, and has $11.66 benefits per $1 costs. . . .

Multi-Systemic Therapy (MST): MST works with the family to address the underlying causes of illegal and delinquent behavior and the role that families play in a young person's behavior. Families are taught how to build healthy relationships and use appropriate methods of discipline. MST works to achieve behavioral change at home, rather than in a correctional facility. MST has been shown to reduce long-term rates of re-arrest by 25–70 percent, and has an average reduction of re-arrest of around 10.5 percent. States that use MST can see $13.36 in benefits to public safety for every dollar spent on the program. . . .

Multidimensional Treatment Foster Care (MTFC): MTFC is an alternative to group homes or detention facilities for youth. Rather than place youth into a group, each foster family has one youth at a time which allows them to tailor programming to that specific individual's needs. The individual treatment also allows the child to be closely monitored. At first, the youth is with the foster parent at all times but as the youth shows good behavior, the restrictions are loosened and he or she is given more freedom. Aside from close monitoring by the foster parents, the youth also receives job and social skills training from a professional therapist and the birth parents and child receive family therapy where the parents learn how to properly discipline their child. MTFC has been shown to reduce recidivism rates for youth by 22 percent on average, and has a cost-benefit ratio of $10.88 in benefits for every dollar spent.[38]

The financial benefits and decrease in recidivism that these four services yield make them wise investments and well worth being implemented as central components of the juvenile justice system. The public, it seems, would support such juvenile justice reform. National and regional surveys of adults show that over 80% of respondents strongly support rehabilitative and treatment services for juveniles,[39] with over 85% strongly agreeing that treatment for juveniles should involve education, counseling, and the juvenile's family.[40]

Along with the implementation of restorative justice and rehabilitative programs, there are significant issues within the juvenile justice system that must be rectified. For one, juvenile court judges send a disproportionate number of minority offenders[41] and low-income offenders[42] to detention facilities, even when relevant factors, such as the offense, are controlled for. In fact, there are racial disparities throughout the juvenile court process.[43] These disparities must be eliminated, and in a recent survey, two-thirds of adult respondents agreed.[44] Equally disturbing is the fact that "as the poverty rate in a particular jurisdiction increases so does that jurisdiction's willingness to incarcerate the youth living there."[45] Additionally, public defenders assigned to juvenile courts are typically underresourced and overworked, which negatively impacts minority and low-income clients.[46] Nearly 75% of the public views the lack of adequate access to legal representation as a problem and supports using tax dollars to hire additional public defenders to represent youth.[47] These issues, among others, must be corrected in order to ensure that juveniles are properly adjudicated and assisted.

The fact that each state manages its own juvenile justice system makes it difficult to implement wide-ranging juvenile justice reform. However, it is not impossible, and more importantly, it is necessary. The federal government can and should intervene to bring about an end to waivers, to limit juvenile detention to the most violent, to reduce juveniles' contact with the juvenile justice system, to establish standards to eliminate the race- and class-based inequities within the juvenile court system, and to provide funds for proven, evidence-based restorative justice and rehabilitative programs for juveniles and their families.

The federal government can begin by immediately reauthorizing the version of the Juvenile Justice and Delinquency Prevention Act (JJDPA) that Senator Patrick Leahy has repeatedly introduced. The JJDPA, which was first approved by Congress in 1974 and has needed reauthorization since 2007, provides federal funds to states that do not detain status offenders; do not place juvenile and adult offenders in same facilities, with some exceptions; treat as many youth as possible outside of placement facilities; and address the disproportionate minority contact (DMC) in the juvenile justice system.[48] Though Senator Leahy's version of the JJDPA does not address juvenile transfers, it does require states to reduce DMC, incentivizes the use of evidence-based services, and limits the use of confinement.

Now may be an opportune political moment to call for adding to the revised JJDPA an amendment that bans juvenile transfers, an idea that is supported by a number of national advocacy organizations, including the Children's Defense Fund. Some states are reducing punitive measures for juvenile offenders. Following the financial hit of the Great Recession, many states and local jurisdictions are rethinking the cost of incarceration. Moreover, Eric Holder, the U.S. attorney general, and senators have independently called for reforms to the criminal justice system. Surely, juvenile justice reforms, including the elimination of transfers, deserve to be part of any subsequent political action to reform our court system.

Conclusion

Children and juveniles are not adults. Period. And they should not have to contend with the immense burden of proving that they are fit to be adjudicated as a minor. That is why we call for an end to juvenile transfers.

We must reform the juvenile justice system. Confinement needs to be reserved for the most violent juveniles, who should receive rehabilitative assistance while detained. The rest of the juveniles who have contact with the juvenile justice system—the vast majority—should be redirected to restorative justice programs and evidence-based services that can help them and their families. The billions spent on juvenile incarceration should be invested in the lives of our children in greatest need, such as the young, talented writers we have the privilege of teaching. Increasing the life chances of children rather than stripping them of their childhood is a financially sound moral imperative.

NOTES

1 Patrick Griffin, Sean Addie, Benjamin Adams, and Kathy Firestine, *Trying juveniles as adults: An analysis of state transfer laws and reporting* (Washington, DC: Office of Juvenile Justice and Delinquency Prevention, September 2011), https://www.ncjrs.gov/pdffiles1/ojjdp/232434.pdf.

2 Elizabeth Cauffman and Laurence Steinberg, "(Im)maturity of judgment in adolescence: Why adolescents may be less culpable than adults," *Behavioral Sciences & the Law* 18, no. 6 (2000): 741–760.

3 Sarah M. Greathouse, F. Caitlin Sothmann, Lora M. Levett, and Margaret Bull Kovera, "The potentially biasing effects of voir dire in juvenile waiver cases," *Law and Human Behavior* 35 (2011): 427–439.

FIT TO BE T(R)IED | 237

4 National Juvenile Justice Network, "Keep Youth Out of Adult Courts, Jails, and Prisons," http://www.njjn.org/about-us/keep-youth-out-of-adult-prisons (accessed April 24, 2014).
5 Frank D. Janowicz, *How to raise your children to keep them out of gangs and prison* (Santa Fe Springs, CA: J&J Legal Support, 2010).
6 California Department of Justice, *2011 Juvenile Justice in California* (Sacramento: California Justice Information Services Division, California Department of Justice, 2012).
7 Ibid.
8 Janowicz, *supra* note 5.
9 Ibid.
10 California Department of Justice, *supra* note 6.
11 California Secretary of State, "Text of Proposition 21" (2000), http://primary2000. sos.ca.gov/VoterGuide/Propositions/21text.htm (accessed November 7, 2013).
12 Sara Raymond, "From playpens to prisons: What the Gang Violence and Juvenile Crime Prevention Act of 1998 does to California's juvenile justice system and reasons to repeal it," *Golden Gate University Law Review* 30 (2000): 258–289.
13 Ibid.
14 Matthew W. Bell, "Prosecutorial waiver in Michigan and nationwide," *Michigan State Law Review* 2004, no. 4 (2004): 1071–1099.
15 Barry C. Feld, "Will the juvenile court system survive? The honest politician's guide to juvenile justice in the twenty-first century," *Annals of the American Academy of Political and Social Science* 564 (1999): 16.
16 Jenny E. Carroll, "Rethinking the constitutional criminal procedure of juvenile transfer hearings: *Apprendi*, adult punishment, and adult process," *Hastings Law Journal* 61 (2009): 231.
17 Janice McGhee and Lorraine Waterhouse, "Classification in youth justice and child welfare: In search of 'the child,'" *Youth Justice* 7, no. 2 (2007): 107–120.
18 Greathouse et al., *supra* note 3.
19 Bell, *supra* note 14.
20 Ibid.
21 Christopher J. Mumola, *Suicide and homicide in state prisons and local jails* (Washington, DC: U.S. Department of Justice, Bureau of Justice Statistics, 2005).
22 Aaron Kupchik, "The correctional experiences of youth in adult and juvenile prisons," *Justice Quarterly* 24 (2007): 247–270; Richard E. Redding, *Juvenile transfer laws: An effective deterrent to delinquency?* (Washington, DC: U.S. Department of Justice, Office of Juvenile Justice and Delinquency Prevention, 2008).
23 Griffin et al., *supra* note 1.
24 Carroll, *supra* note 16, at 176.
25 Bell, *supra* note 14; Sally T. Green, "Prosecutorial waiver into adult criminal court: A conflict of interests violation amounting to the states' legislative abrogation of juveniles' due process rights," *Penn State Law Review* 110 (2005): 233–281.

26 Carroll, *supra* note 16.

27 Griffin et al., *supra* note 1.

28 *Roper v. Simmons*, 543 S. Ct. 551 (2005).

29 *Miller v. Alabama*, 132 S. Ct. 2455 (2012).

30 Ibid. at 2468.

31 Campaign for Youth Justice, *State trends—legislative victories from 2011–2013: Removing youth from the adult criminal justice system* (Washington, DC: Campaign for Youth Justice, 2013), http://www.campaignforyouthjustice.org/documents/ST2013.pdf.

32 Ibid.

33 Ibid. at 1.

34 James Bell, Laura J. Ridolfi, Michael Finley, and Clinton Lacey, *The keeper and the kept: Reflections on local obstacles to disparities reduction in juvenile justice systems and a path to change* (San Francisco: W. Haywood Burns Institute, 2009).

35 Howard J. Zehr, *Changing lenses: A new focus for crime and justice*, 3rd ed. (Scottdale, PA: Herald, 2005), 270.

36 Justice Policy Institute, *The costs of confinement: Why good juvenile justice policies make good fiscal sense* (Washington, DC: Justice Policy Institute, May 2009), http://www.justicepolicy.org/images/upload/09_05_rep_costsofconfinement_jj_ps.pdf.

37 Elizabeth Drake, *Evidence-based juvenile offender programs: Program description, quality assurance, and cost* (Olympia: Washington State Institute for Public Policy, 2007), http://www.wsipp.wa.gov/ReportFile/986.

38 Justice Policy Institute, *supra* note 36, at 20.

39 Campaign for Youth Justice, "New national poll shows strong public support for rehabilitation and treatment of youth over incarceration," press release, October 12, 2011, http://www.campaignforyouthjustice.org/documents/PR_GBA_October_2011.pdf; Barry Krisberg and Susan Marchionna, *Attitudes of US voters toward youth crime and the justice system* (Oakland, CA: National Center on Crime and Delinquency, 2007).

40 Campaign for Youth Justice, *supra* note 39.

41 Feld, *supra* note 15, at 17.

42 Katayoon Majd and Patricia Puritz, "The cost of justice: How low-income youth continue to pay the price of failing indigent defense systems," *Georgetown Journal on Poverty Law & Policy* 16 (Spring 2009): 570.

43 Ibid.

44 Campaign for Youth Justice, *supra* note 39.

45 Majd and Puritz, *supra* note 42, at 570.

46 Ibid.

47 Campaign for Youth Justice, *supra* note 39.

48 Children's Defense Fund, "Juvenile Justice," http://www.childrensdefense.org/policy-priorities/juvenile-justice/ (accessed November 25, 2013).

13

Applying *J.D.B. v. North Carolina*

Toward Ending Legal Fictions and Adopting Effective Police Questioning of Youth

LISA H. THURAU AND SIA HENRY

One of the critical points of contact for youth and the juvenile justice system occurs when police question youth. During questioning, police may be required to give youth *Miranda* warnings to inform them of their right to remain silent and their right to legal counsel. In 2011, the U.S. Supreme Court, in *J.D.B. v. North Carolina*,[1] adopted a developmental approach regarding how the age of a juvenile determines when police must provide *Miranda* warnings. Significantly, the Court's decision was the first time the Court applied its understanding of juvenile development outside the punishment context.[2] This chapter explores how *J.D.B.* has been implemented by reviewing 20 state court cases involving police questioning and interrogation of juveniles decided since *J.D.B.* was handed down in 2011.

Our analysis indicates that the country is far from unified in its view of the role of age-based maturity and competence in determining when a youth should be given *Miranda* warnings. More significantly, the analysis demonstrates that the notion of developmental maturity is still a foreign concept for some judges and law enforcement officers. The results indicate that some system stakeholders recognize that youths' fear of authority and incarceration is useful leverage for obtaining information, compliance, and confessions, even while they deny that youthfulness has any role in whether juveniles have the capacity to invoke their rights.

Police have acknowledged that the interviewing and interrogation of youth is a tricky and difficult area to navigate.

Overall, law enforcement is not adequately trained in interviewing and interrogating juveniles. While there are numerous courses available in forensic interviewing of children who may be victims, there are few training courses that target techniques for interviewing and interrogating youth who may be suspects or witnesses. Interview and interrogation is standard training for law enforcement agencies, however, it typically does not cover the developmental differences between adults and youth nor does it cover recommended techniques to be used on youth versus adults. This often leads law enforcement practitioners to use the same techniques on youth as with adults.[3]

A study of police academies' juvenile justice training indicates that academies do not train officers to be developmentally competent when working with juveniles, nor do they train officers to use age-appropriate approaches when communicating with youth.[4] Instead, the primary focus of training for recruits is juvenile law. In addition, this analysis suggests that race plays a role in the outcomes of the interviews and court decisions. A recent study indicates that the age at which police stop according youth the "privilege of innocence" varies directly with race. African American youth tend to lose this privilege around ages 10 to 12, fully two to four years before white children.[5] Thus, "protections of childhood are diminished for Black children in contexts where they are dehumanized. . . . If human childhood affords strong protections against harsh, adult-like treatment, then in contexts where children are dehumanized, those children can be treated with adult severity."[6]

The Court's decision in *J.D.B.* is a first critical step in the movement to align practices of police, prosecutors, and judges with the recognition that youth perceive, process, and respond differently than adults and that those differences also affect their reactions under stress. The Supreme Court's recognition that these developmental differences are common knowledge is not routinely borne out by either police practices or court decisions. The bias toward holding youth "accountable" trumps police and court willingness to apply a "reasonable child" standard— even for youth in situations where police hold all the power. Instead, as this review indicates, we have significant distance to travel before we truly embrace a "reasonable child" standard in which courts acknowledge how police power is perceived by youth.

Section 1 of this chapter reviews the *J.D.B.* decision. Section 2 presents an analysis of the post-2011 cases in which state courts have reviewed questioning of youth. In the final section of the chapter, we articulate a developmentally informed standard that should be applied in a reframed juvenile justice system.

I. *J.D.B. v. North Carolina*

In *J.D.B. v. North Carolina*, a uniformed police officer, a school resource officer, a principal, and an interning school administrator held a 13-year-old, seventh-grade boy in a closed-door conference room during school hours for at least 30 minutes while they questioned him about his involvement in two recent home break-ins.[7] Prior to the questioning, the boy was never read his *Miranda* rights, allowed to call his legal guardian, or told that he was free to leave the room.[8] J.D.B. initially denied any involvement in the crime. After the officers threatened J.D.B. with the possibility of confinement in a juvenile detention center, he confessed.

After his initial confession, J.D.B. was told that he did not have to answer any questions and that he was free to leave. Instead, J.D.B. sat with the officers and provided a written statement further detailing his participation in the crime. At trial, J.D.B.'s attorney moved to have the boy's statement suppressed, arguing that he was "interrogated by police in a custodial setting without being afforded *Miranda* warning[s]."[9] The trial court held, and North Carolina appellate courts affirmed, that J.D.B. was not in custody when he confessed.

On appeal to the U.S. Supreme Court, the justices addressed the issue of "whether the age of a child subjected to police questioning is relevant to the" *Miranda* custody analysis.[10] The Court found that "by its very nature, custodial police interrogation entails 'inherently compelling pressures.' Even for an adult, the physical and psychological isolation of custodial interrogation can 'undermine the individual's will to resist and . . . compel him to speak where he would not otherwise do so freely.'"[11] Such pressure has driven a significant portion of individuals to confess to crimes they did not commit, and the risk of such false confessions is "all the more acute—when the subject of custodial interrogation is a juvenile."[12] Therefore, the Court explained, the *Miranda* warning is required in "any circumstance that 'would have affected how a reasonable person' in the suspect's position 'would perceive his or her freedom to leave.'"[13] In some situations, a child's age "'would have affected how a reasonable person' in the suspect's position 'would perceive his or her freedom to leave.'"[14]

In light of children's limited, immature decision making and generally inadequate ability to understand the surrounding world,[15] the Court held that "so long as [a] child's age [is] known to the officer at the time of police questioning, or . . . [is] objectively apparent to a reasonable officer, its inclusion in the custody analysis is consistent with the objective nature of that test."[16] The Court determined that a child's age is a relevant factor in deciding whether a situation calls for an investigating police officer to read the juvenile his or her *Miranda* rights. Further, Justice Sotomayor admonished juvenile justice system stakeholders that this analysis was one of common sense: "In short, officers and judges need no imaginative powers, knowledge of developmental psychology, training in cognitive science, or expertise in social and cultural anthropology to account for a child's age. They simply need the common sense to know that a 7-year-old is not a 13-year-old and neither is an adult."[17]

In so doing, Justice Sotomayor reiterated the holding of the Court in *Haley v. Ohio*, 332 U.S. 596 (1948). Justice Douglas wrote for the majority in *Haley* that the use of coercive tactics involving relays of officers in a police station questioning and beating a 15-year-old boy from midnight to five a.m., without providing the slightest intimation of the boy's right to remain silent, was unconstitutional:

> What transpired *would make us pause for careful inquiry if a mature man were involved.* And when, as here, a mere child—an easy victim of the law—is before us, special care in scrutinizing the record must be used. Age 15 is a tender and difficult age for a boy of any race. He cannot be judged by the more exacting standards of maturity. That which would leave a man cold and unimpressed can overawe and overwhelm a lad in his early teens. This is the period of great instability, which the crisis of adolescence produces. A 15-year-old lad, questioned through the dead of night by relays of police, is a ready victim of the inquisition. Mature men possibly might stand the ordeal from midnight to 5 a.m. But we cannot believe that a lad of tender years is a match for the police in such a context. He needs counsel and support if he is not to become the victim

first of fear, then of panic. He needs someone on whom to lean lest the overpowering presence of the law, as he knows it, may not crush him.[18]

Fourteen years later, the Court reiterated these points in *Gallegos v. Colorado*, 370 U.S. 49 (1962). In that case, a boy was held for five days and was not permitted to see anyone before signing a confession. Justice Douglas cited the age of the 14-year-old Gallegos and the decision in *Haley* to overturn the lower court's finding of a refusal to overturn the boy's confession:

> But a 14-year-old-boy, no matter how sophisticated, is unlikely to have any conception of what will confront him when he is made accessible only to the police. That is to say, we deal with a person who is not equal to the police in knowledge and understanding of the consequences of the questions and answers being recorded, and who is unable to know how to protect his own interests or how to get the benefits of his constitutional rights. . . . He cannot be compared with an adult in full possession of his senses and knowledgeable of the consequences of his admissions. He would have no way of knowing what the consequences of his confession were without advice to his rights—from someone concerned with securing him those rights—and without the aid of more mature judgment as to the steps he should take in the predicament in which he found himself.[19]

Remarkably, the following review of state cases interpreting *J.D.B.* indicates that the twentieth-century U.S. Supreme Court recognition of the threat to due process posed by the combination of coercion and compulsion to children continues to need clarification for police and judges in this century. Indeed, several state decisions indicate that the notion that *age matters* remains a nascent idea.

II. State Court Application of *J.D.B. v. North Carolina*: An Age-by-Age Analysis

Since *J.D.B.*, state courts have interpreted the Supreme Court's holding in 20 cases to ascertain the admissibility of statements made by male juvenile defendants during questioning by police. In not one decision involving police interviews of youth *did a youth manifest and act on the belief that he or she could walk away from the officer interviewing him or her.*[20]

However, this review of state court decisions indicates that state courts believe that youth at different ages are capable of doing just that. Courts continue to afford different degrees of weight to juveniles' age in determining whether police had an obligation to Mirandize youth. Age as a determinant of a juvenile's capacity and competence in holding officers to a high standard of disclosure continues to be highly variable.

Nine of these twenty cases were decided in California. Police questioning typically took place at police stations and schools. No parent was present during any of the disputed interviews. The age of the juvenile defendants ranged from 8 to 17.

Review of these cases was conducted as a function of the *age* of the juvenile who sought to have his statement suppressed. The available cases provide an emerging view of patterns concerning how age factors into courts' scrutiny of police interviews and interrogations of youth.

Several courts continue to privilege factors that reflect *officers'* perceptions or the judiciary's biases over youths' age. For instance, officers' *perceptions* of a youth's size or age trumped officers' obligation to determine the age of the person. Interestingly, the defense of being ignorant of a person's age—such as in cases involving underage drinking or statutory rape—is not available to citizens. But judges routinely gave police officers' claim that they didn't know that the youth was under 18 credibility in determining whether officers should have given youth *Miranda* warnings.

The cases where courts found that police had failed to provide *Miranda* warnings when required often had three elements in common: the place in which the questioning occurred, the time and duration of the questioning, and the availability of adults to protect the child's interest during the interview. When youth were interviewed on the premises of a state police authority—such as at a police station, in a police cruiser, at a child welfare office, or in a locked facility—the courts tended to perceive that the youth would feel coerced. (The notable exception to this pattern is the case described later of *In re Michael S.*, in which the interview took place in a locked juvenile facility.) Courts discounted the possibility of coercion for youth interviewed at or near their homes. The courts' consideration of the timing of the interview, including whether it was prolonged or occurred at a time that would be experienced as disruptive, for example, in the middle of the night, was key to courts' determination of whether the need for *Miranda* protections was triggered. When parents were available to participate in the interview but were excluded or not invited to participate in the interview, the courts tended to find police had erred by failing to provide youth the necessary and available protection of an interested adult.

Where the courts found that police had adequately warned youth of their *Miranda* rights, four factors were typically present:

1. The presumption of the youth's sophistication due to age or prior contact with the system
2. The preference for the *officer's* subjective perceptions of the youth and the context trumping the *youth's* perception of his or her freedom to leave
3. The assumption of the youth's consciousness of legal rights when the case involved a serious crime (e.g., typically a felony involving violence against a person)
4. The treatment of age as only one of many other factors, and not deserving any special weight, in assessing a potential *Miranda* violation

Thus, for example, in a case in which a youth was interviewed in a locked facility where he was awaiting adjudication on an unrelated charge, the court found that the sophistication of the youth trumped any coercive feature of the premises in which the interview occurred. Courts accepted officers' subjective perceptions, finding, for instance, that the *size* of a youth justified an officer's assumption that the youth knew his or her rights.

Finally, present in the analysis are cases involving the complete denial of age as a factor affecting a child's perception when interviewed by an officer. This is most dramatically demonstrated in the case of the eight-year-old defendant in *Hunt v. The Cape Henlopen School District*.

Application of J.D.B. to an Eight-Year-Old Defendant

In *Hunt v. The Cape Henlopen School District*, a state trooper and school resource officer questioned Hunt, an eight-year-old student, who was suspected to have taken money from an autistic student on a school bus.[21] The school resource officer escorted Hunt to a classroom to interview him. He told Hunt he was not in trouble.[22] During the interview, however, the officer told Hunt that he had the authority to arrest and put Hunt in jail if he lied. In determining whether Hunt was "in custody," in order to rule on Hunt's false imprisonment/false arrest claim, the Delaware court noted that even "if the officer did not know [Hunt's] exact age, it would have been objectively apparent to a reasonable officer that [he] was an elementary school-aged child."[23] The Superior Court acknowledged that Hunt was eight years old at the time of questioning and was "justifiably" intimidated by the officer "and ultimately began to cry."[24] The factor of Hunt's age was insufficient, however, to persuade the court; the Delaware Superior Court ruled that Hunt should have known he was free to leave and did not have to answer the officer's questions because he was not in custody.[25]

A year later, the Delaware Supreme Court reversed this portion of the Superior Court's decision, holding that Hunt had been in custody.[26] The Delaware Supreme Court based its holding on the fact that the eight-year-old was escorted to the vice principal's office by a teacher's aide, where he met the officer, who was in uniform, carrying a gun, handcuffs, and other indicia of police authority. Furthermore, the officer met with the child in the reading lab for close to an hour, with the door closed for some period of time, and never told the child he could leave.[27]

Application of J.D.B. to 13-Year-Old Defendants

State courts have placed varied weight on the age of 13-year-old juvenile defendants. For example, a California case, *In re Michael S.*, involved a 13-year-old boy charged with forcible rape.[28] A police officer arrived at Michael's house and asked to speak with him outside. Michael agreed to sit, without handcuffs, in the back of the officer's patrol car for questioning.[29] The officer then read Michael his *Miranda* rights, and Michael stated that he understood his rights and was willing to speak to the officer without anyone else present.[30] After questioning Michael, the officer arrested him. While Michael was in juvenile detention, another detective interviewed him while his probation officer was in the room. The detective read Michael his *Miranda* rights, and Michael signed a form saying he understood.[31] Michael then told the detective what had happened. The court determined that even a reasonable 13-year-old in Michael's position "would understand that he was voluntarily leaving the house with [the officer] and that he was free to end the encounter at any time, . . . [and the officer] was not coercive when he asked [Michael] to step outside."[32] With respect to Michael's second interview while in the juvenile detention center, the court considered whether, in light of Michael's age, the detective's tactics were such that Michael's "free will was overborne at the time he confessed."[33] The court found "the detective did not use any coercive methods that would be reasonably likely to produce a false statement, even from a 13-year-old."[34] Furthermore, the court determined that Michael "demonstrated at multiple times during questioning that he understood what he did . . . was wrong, even when he was not prompted to do so."[35] Thus, the court concluded that Michael's confession was voluntary and properly admitted.

In an Ohio case involving a 13-year-old, the court found differently. J.S.'s father brought him to the police station for questioning.[36] J.S.'s father was not permitted to accompany his son during the interview. J.S. was not informed that he could leave at any time; he was told only that he would be allowed to go home with his father after the interview.[37] The court found that J.S. was only 13 at the time of the interview and that, consequently, there was a high likelihood that J.S. was unaware of his rights, including the right to be silent or to request a lawyer.[38] The court never discussed the availability of J.S.'s parents to participate in the interview, when it concluded that he was in custody during the interview and the interviewing officer should have advised him of his *Miranda* rights.

In a second California case, *In re Robert J.*, the court remanded the case of a 13-year-old boy charged with arson after igniting a paper towel in a school bathroom.[39] In that case, two police officers interviewed Robert in the principal's office with the door closed and in the presence of the principal. During the ten-minute interview, the officers never told Robert he was required to speak to them, that he could not leave the office, or that he was under arrest. The California court found that the juvenile court failed to consider Robert's age when determining whether the interrogation was custodial.

Application of J.D.B. *to 14-Year-Old Defendants*

Fourteen-year-olds are an age group of special interest. According to the work of psychologists assessing competency, 14 is the new 16.[40] Researchers in the field of juvenile competency have concluded that post-2000, 14 is the age below which assumptions of youth competence are ill-advised. Some states have recognized the validity of such concerns and require a parent to be present in the questioning of youth who have waived their rights.[41] But court interpretations of *J.D.B.* indicate that these perceptions are not normative across the U.S. Indeed, for many courts, 14 is the new 18.

Similar to state court applications of *J.D.B.* for 13-year-old defendants, courts have been unpredictable in making *Miranda* custody determinations for 14-year-olds. The key factors these courts considered when determining when a "reasonable" 14-year-old should perceive that he or she is in custody has to do with the level of intimidation youth experience when being questioned by school and police officials and the location of the questioning. Courts appear to perceive that questioning on school premises by school administrators or multiple officers is less intimidating.

For instance, in *C.S. v. Couch*, C.S., a high school freshman, claimed his *Miranda* rights were violated when his principal and vice principal questioned him with regard to claims that he sexually harassed another student.[42] The interrogation took place at the school, and the school officials did not tell C.S. that he could leave or that he did not have to incriminate himself. The Indiana state court, noting that a child's age factors into the custody analysis pursuant to the holding in *J.D.B.*, rejected C.S.'s claim, reasoning that "custody and interrogation do not exist without the presence of law enforcement officers."[43] The court held that "a student is not entitled to *Miranda* warnings before being questioned by school officials."[44] This conclusion was based on the idea that the "policy underlying the *Miranda* safeguards [focuses on] overcoming the inherently coercive and police dominated atmosphere of custodial interrogation," and therefore "when school officials question students in school outside of the presence of law enforcement officers and free from their influence, there is no such coercive atmosphere against which to protect."[45]

In the Ohio case of *In re T.W.*, a 14-year-old boy was accused of inappropriately touching his stepsister.[46] When his parents drove him to Child Services for questioning, T.W. was escorted to an interview room with audio and visual equipment. Child Services staff and a police officer interviewed T.W. for an hour.[47] The officer did not tell T.W. he was under arrest and did not advise him about the possible charges, and T.W. never asked for his parents to be present during the interview. About an hour into the interview, T.W. gave a written admission of guilt and left Child Services with his parents.[48] In light of *J.D.B.*, the court determined that at 14 years of age, "a reasonable juvenile in T.W.'s position would . . . be intimidated and overwhelmed. There is no evidence that T.W. volunteered to go to Children Services. . . . T.W. was escorted away from his [parents] by two unfamiliar authoritarian figures. . . . A reasonable juvenile in T.W.'s position would not have felt free to terminate the interview and leave the premises."[49] Therefore, the court held that T.W.'s statements were inadmissible.

A third variation of this scenario occurred in Texas, in the case of *In re C.M.A.*[50] There, a 14-year-old was questioned as a suspect in a burglary and aggravated assault of a child. The youth was interviewed twice, first in a principal's office and then in a classroom. In the first interview, the 14-year-old was interviewed by one officer who explained that C.M.A. was free to leave. In the second interview, C.M.A. was interviewed by several officers. He was not informed that he was free to leave. On the basis of the second interview, he was charged. On a motion to suppress, the court found that C.M.A., a reasonable 14-year-old, should have perceived that he was free to end the interview and invoke his right to counsel.

In re Juan S. involved a 14-year-old boy charged with involuntary manslaughter. When Juan's parents first brought him to the police station for questioning, officers told him he was not under arrest and simply indicated that they wanted to take him out of the neighborhood environment in order to speak with him.[51] The California Court of Appeals found that the trial court failed to consider Juan's age as part of its determination that the first interview was not a custodial interrogation. In this case, as in *In re T.W.*, the age of the juvenile in conjunction with being interviewed on the premises of an "authority" was key to establishing that a child of 14 is "no match" for the police. In both cases, the courts decided to suppress the youth's confession.

In another California case, however, *People v. Alexis C.*, a 14-year-old was treated differently. Alexis C. was accused of participating in the gang rape of a teenage girl.[52] While Alexis was confined in a juvenile camp for an unrelated offense, a police officer interviewed him about the rape and told him that he did not have to talk and that he was free to leave the interview.[53] He was also informed that he was being interviewed as a witness and that he was not going to be arrested.[54] The officer did not read Alexis his *Miranda* rights. Despite the defendant's age, the court held that "the Minor was fully aware he was free to terminate the interview, . . . [but] he made a decision to stay and talk. There is no basis in the record to support any inference that he was intimidated or failed to understand his circumstances at the time he decided to speak to the detective."[55] Here the youth's age did not trump the court's perception that a 14-year-old being in a locked facility was "free" to walk out of an interview with a police officer. Unlike the court in *Gallegos*, which worried that a 14-year-old was "unable to know how to protect his own interests or how to get the benefits of his constitutional rights," the court in *Alexis C.* appears to have been swayed by the sophistication argument: because the youth was in a locked facility for another matter, he was sophisticated enough in the ways of the system to make choices that would reflect his best interests.

Application of J.D.B. to 15-Year-Old Defendants

In *People v. Nelson*, 15-year-old Nelson burglarized his neighbor's home, and a few days later the neighbor was found dead.[56] Two officers spoke with Nelson outside his home. Nelson denied killing his neighbor and offered to take a lie-detector test.[57] The officers later returned to Nelson's home, and Nelson agreed to accompany them to the police station. Nelson answered some preliminary questions and was then advised of his *Miranda* rights.[58] The officers questioned Nelson for several hours, during which time he repeatedly tried to contact his mother and continuously asked to be left alone.[59] Before his family arrived, he confessed to murder.[60] The appellate court held that Nelson appeared confident and mature during the questioning and was "no stranger to the criminal justice system."[61] The court held that Nelson's insistence on calling his mother was not an invocation of his *Miranda* rights, and therefore officers were not required to stop their questioning and his custodial statements were properly admitted at trial.[62]

Application of J.D.B. to 16-Year-Old Defendants

There was less variation in state courts' application of the *Miranda* custody analysis to 16-year-old defendants. The "sophistication" argument held sway with this group of youth, who were assumed to understand their rights, regardless of prior experience with the courts, their capacity, or their competence.

For instance, in the California case of *In re J.W.*, a 16-year-old was charged with exhibiting a deadly weapon and possessing a weapon on school grounds. While investigating the incident, a police officer arrived at J.W.'s friend's house and told J.W. and his friends to sit on the curb of the sidewalk "and stay where they were. . . . [J.W. was] not free to leave. However . . . [the boys] were not handcuffed, and the officers did not display any weapons."[63] Without reading *Miranda* rights, the officers began questioning the boys. After J.W. told the officers the location of the weapon in question, the officers arrested J.W. and his friends.[64] The court found that as a result of the circumstances under which J.W. made his statements, the fact that the officer did not pose confrontational questions, and because J.W. was nearly 17 years old at the time, it was unlikely J.W. believed he was in official police custody.[65]

Likewise, in *Gray v. Norman*, 16-year-old Gray was convicted in Missouri of shooting his neighbor during a home burglary.[66] Police officers asked Gray and his mother to ride in separate police cars to the police station. At the police station, Gray was placed in a room with two officers and told he was not under arrest and could leave at any time.[67] Gray stated that he did not want his mother present during questioning, that he understood his rights, and that he wanted to make a statement.[68] After Gray signed a "juvenile" *Miranda* form, he answered questions for about an hour and then asked to have his mother present.[69] The next day, officers showed up at Gray's house with a search warrant.[70] They took Gray to the hospital to get a blood sample and then to the highway patrol office, where he was read his *Miranda* rights.[71] In the presence of a police officer and a juvenile officer, Gray signed another "juvenile" *Miranda* waiver form and gave a videotaped confession. The appellate court confirmed the state court's finding that age is only one of the factors considered when voluntariness of a juvenile confession is challenged. The court concluded, "Gray's age alone is insufficient to support his claim that his confession was not made voluntarily or intelligently."[72]

In the North Carolina case *In re R.P.*, a school police officer observed a student engage in a hand-to-hand transaction with another student. The officer pulled the juvenile out of his class and questioned him.[73] The juvenile admitted to handing the female student a cigarette and, when asked, informed the officer that he had pills on him for which he did not have a prescription.[74] The appellate court was "unable to discern whether the trial court considered the juvenile's age in accordance with . . . *J.D.B.*" and consequently remanded the case.[75]

Finally, the Wisconsin Court of Appeals in *State v. Oligney*[76] found that a 16-year-old had not been improperly denied his *Miranda* rights during a two-hour interview with a school resource officer (SRO) and a police detective at his school. The detective had been sent to the school to interview Oligney after a victim claimed that Oligney had sexually assaulted her and that he later apologized to her in numerous phone text messages.

The SRO and detective conducted a recorded interview with Oligney in a classroom for two hours. The police failed to notify his parents before interviewing him, and Oligney was not permitted to contact his parents. Although the officers told Oligney he was free to leave, Oligney stayed. Even when the school day ended and all the other students left the school, Oligney remained in the room with the officers until they concluded the interview. During the questioning, the officers promised to tell the truth but intimated (untruthfully) that they had read texts Oligney had sent to the victim in which he apologized for his behavior.

The Court of Appeals noted that during Oligney's *Miranda-Goodchild* hearing[77] the 16-year-old made "much of the fact that there were two officers questioning him, and his belief, articulated at the suppression hearing, that he was at risk of being arrested."[78] Instead of crediting Oligney's testimony and the fact that the youth stayed until the police concluded their interview, the court interpreted this behavior as proof of Oligney's understanding that he was free to go and not in custody. The fact that the officers never read Oligney his *Miranda* rights did not merit the court's attention. Indeed, the Court of Appeals concluded that "the mere presence of two officers is insufficient to establish a custodial situation. . . . The custody inquiry is an objective test: Oligney's subjective fear of arrest is therefore irrelevant."[79]

Rejecting the reasoning of *J.D.B.*, the court held that "a child's age is not determinative, and may not even be a significant factor."[80] Instead, the court invoked its own subjective view based on evidence not in the record that "a reasonable person of Oligney's age would not ordinarily have felt obligated to participate against his or her wishes; teenagers are often recalcitrant."[81]

In this decision, the Wisconsin Court of Appeals systematically rejected every aspect of the *J.D.B.* decision. The Court of Appeals deftly used the youth's age to justify its generalizations about youth as "recalcitrant" and in need of being treated like adults and to reject the Supreme Court's directive in *J.D.B.* that even "recalcitrant" teenagers are due special protection under the law due to their immaturity. The judges denied consideration of the youth's subjective understanding of his circumstances and instead substituted the court's subjective view of youth, not based on any evidence in the record, concerning when a reasonable person Oligney's age would have known he was in custody. The court assumed that the serious nature of the charge meant the 16-year-old understood his legal rights and the operation of the juvenile and adult criminal justice systems.

State Court Application of J.D.B. to 17-Year-Old Defendants

State courts demonstrated the greatest amount of consistency in their *Miranda* custody analyses to 17-year-old defendants. The courts applied the "sophistication" argument, reducing an officers' obligation to disclose that the youth was in custody and essentially denying the role of age as a factor. Seventeen-year-olds are thereby treated as adults.

For instance, in *People v. Lewis*, while investigating the murder of a security guard, a California police officer stopped 17-year-old Lewis in a car that matched video surveillance evidence.[82] Lewis denied any involvement but later confessed to driving the individuals who beat the security guard when the officer told him about the surveillance video.[83]

Lewis agreed to ride with the officer to the police station to give a more detailed statement. At the police station, the officer told Lewis he was not under arrest and was free to leave.[84] After Lewis gave additional details, another officer arrived who told Lewis she had to read him his *Miranda* rights because he was a juvenile, and Lewis was asked to sign a waiver.[85] The court found that, with respect to Lewis's age, "Lewis was over six-feet tall and his probation report indicates he weighed approximately 200 pounds; there is no reason to conclude the fact he was a minor was known to [the officer] or objectively apparent to him or a reasonable officer for purposes of considering his age in the custody analysis."[86] The court concluded that the objective facts were consistent with an environment in which a reasonable person in Lewis's position would have felt free to leave at any time.[87]

Similarly, in the case of *In re J.V.*, a 17-year-old ran away from a car accident in California.[88] The court found no evidence that the officer knew that J.V. was a juvenile. The court took judicial notice of the *officer's* subjective perception as well as the fact that J.V. was six months shy of his 18th birthday and concluded that age was not a significant factor in deciding when to read J.V. his rights.

In the Iowa case of *State v. Pearson*, a 17-year-old ran away from his group home and assaulted an elderly man with a frying pan during a home burglary.[89] Officers took Pearson to the police station and read him his *Miranda* rights, but Pearson refused to waive his rights or speak until he consulted his attorney.[90] At the group home, Pearson's social worker spoke with him in a room with the door open in order to assess his reason for running away.[91] While Pearson spoke with his social worker, he confessed to hitting the elderly man with a frying pan.[92] With respect to his age, the court found that "Pearson was just seven months shy of his eighteenth birthday at the time of his confession. . . . Pearson brazenly beat an elderly man in the victim's own kitchen. He had a prior history of assaulting adults, including his mother and police. He had no difficulty invoking his *Miranda* rights at the . . . police station after his apprehension."[93] In addition, a social worker who was not working for the police conducted the interview. The court concluded that the circumstances of this confession lacked the coercive pressure of a custodial interrogation.

Likewise, in *Commonwealth v. Bermudez*, a 17-year-old boy's mother drove him to the police station after an officer asked to speak with him about a recent shooting.[94] While Bermudez's mother remained in the lobby, two detectives escorted Bermudez into an interview room equipped with video recording.[95] The detectives read Bermudez his *Miranda* rights and made sure he understood each provision and could read and write English.[96] Bermudez had previously been diagnosed as having special needs, particularly in reading and writing.[97] During the 70-minute interview, the detectives repeatedly told Bermudez he was not a suspect in the shooting and would be allowed to return home with his mother.[98] Bermudez eventually admitted to having a firearm on the day of the shooting and said he gave it to someone who requested it. At the end of the interview, the detectives prepared a typewritten copy of Bermudez's statement. Bermudez read, corrected, initialed, and signed the statement.[99] The Massachusetts state court found that Bermudez's age, "a few months shy of his eighteenth birthday, placed him on the cusp of majority, and far removed from the tender years of early adolescence."[100] Viewing "all the pertinent factors objectively, including [Bermudez's] age at the time of the interview," the court concluded "that the interrogation was not custodial so as to require Miranda warnings."[101] Remarkably, other factors that detracted from Bermudez's age, such as his lack of competence in reading and writing, did not affect the court's appreciation of Bermudez's capacity to understand his rights. Instead the court's *assumptions* regarding the capacity of a 17-year-old remained fixed, predicated on the legislature's ascribing criminal responsibility to begin at age 17. This foreclosed consideration that Bermudez's age might not be consonant with his competence in the context of understanding when he was in custody—much less aware that he was in danger of losing his due process protections. Ironically, months later, in July 2013, the Massachusetts legislature voted to change the age of majority to 18.[102]

In direct contrast, when a 17-year-old voluntarily went to the police station to confess to his involvement in a gang-related murder five days earlier, the California court in *People v. Rocha*[103] perceived that his age played a secondary role. As in the other cases involving 17-year-olds, the court invoked the fact that the 17-year-old was nearly 18, the age of majority, and therefore should be treated as an adult. While Rocha would have been arrested for purchasing alcohol or prohibited from voting at the age of 17, he was close enough to 18 to know what he was doing and be treated as an adult. The court acknowledged the *J.D.B.* holding but said, "This is not to say that a child's age will be a determinative, or even a significant, factor in every case."[104] Again, the combination of a serious offense with a youth close to the age of majority was key to revoking consideration of age as a factor in determining youths' constitutional protections.

Finally, in *State v. Yancey*, a North Carolina police officer stopped a 17-year-old on a weekday morning because he looked of school age and was possibly truant.[105] The officer patted Yancey down, and Yancey allowed the officer to look in his backpack.[106] The officer found coins, jewelry, and an old class ring.[107] The officer took Yancey to the police station, where his mother picked him up. Later, two plainclothes officers in an unmarked car arrived at Yancey's house and asked him to ride with them.[108] The officers told Yancey he was free to leave at any time and allowed Yancey to sit in the front seat.[109] During the car ride, Yancey confessed to various break-ins.[110] On appeal, the court noted that Yancey was 17 years and 10 months old at the time of the encounter and therefore, "considering the totality of the circumstances, [Yancey's] age [did] not alter [the] court's conclusion that [Yancey] was not in custody during the . . . encounter with detectives."[111]

III. Privileging Youth's Innocence: Where There's a Will, Law Enforcement Knows There's a Way

It is easy to imagine better practices for police questioning of juveniles. That is in large part because national police organizations such as the International Association of Chiefs of Police (IACP) and the Commission on Accreditation of Law Enforcement Agencies (CALEA) have already written them.[112] These practices reflect profound appreciation of children's deficient understanding of the legal aspects of custody, their vulnerability to coercion, and their wishful temptation to believe that police officers are there to protect them.

Consider, for instance, the IACP's *Training Key 652* issued in 2011.[113] Written with juvenile defenders, including Steven Drizin, director of the Center for Wrongful Juvenile Convictions, this training key provides an explanation of the importance of getting this aspect of police-youth interactions right, as well as very practical steps for achieving it. The training key begins by acknowledging that youth are "not miniature adults."[114] The key notes that regardless of why a youth is interviewed, "he or she is first and fundamentally still a child" and is "more prone to making involuntary or unreliable statements . . . particularly if certain questioning techniques are used."[115] Indeed, the training key notes that "even otherwise intelligent youths often do not fully understand their *Miranda* rights. . . . And even if a juvenile is able to build some understanding of his rights, he may have difficulty applying those rights to his own situation."[116]

The IACP recommends policies and procedures and provides age-appropriate language for *Miranda* questions as well as effective practices to ensure youth understand what is happening while in custody and during questioning:[117]

> The same terminology used with a seasoned adult suspect should not carry over to a juvenile; rather, the following model should be utilized, which uses short sentences and language understandable to children who can read at the third-grade level:
> 1. You have the right to remain silent. That means you do not have to say anything.
> 2. Anything you say can be used against you in court.
> 3. You have the right to get help from a lawyer right now.
> 4. You also have the right to have one or both of your parents here.
> 5. If you cannot pay a lawyer, the court will get you one for free.
> 6. You have the right to stop this interview at anytime.
> 7. Do you want to talk to me?
> 8. Do you want to have a lawyer with you while you talk to me?
> 9. Do you want your mother, father, or the person who takes care of you here while you talk to me?
>
> If this model is followed and the child is asked to explain each warning back in his or her own words, an officer should feel confident that the child understands the rights. If the conversation about the *Miranda* rights is preserved for posterity on tape, the *Miranda* waiver process will be nearly bulletproof in court.[118]

Although the training key was published prior to the decision in *J.D.B. v. North Carolina*, the decision and the training key align seamlessly.

Similarly, CALEA's Standard 44[119] makes clear that "given the special legal status of juveniles," departments should "be aware that the voluntariness of the juvenile's confession will generally be the issue."[120] Standard 44 names 19 factors that should determine the officer's approach to interview and interrogation of youth.[121] First and foremost on the list is *age*. In CALEA's Standard 44.2.3, subsection 8, agencies are warned that it is critical to determine about the juvenile "whether *Miranda* or police caution warnings were given, *when and whether he understood them,*" and section 14 directs the officer to ascertain "*whether the juvenile understands the interrogation process.*"[122]

Unfortunately, not enough law enforcement agencies follow these protocols. Too many members of the law enforcement community fail to recognize the importance of proactively, instead of coercively, using developmentally competent approaches with youth.[123] Too often expedience replaces accuracy and protection of youths' due process rights. As a result, situations involving juveniles' custody and questioning continue to remain a major source of legal challenges to officers' conduct with youth.

Strategies for Youth,[124] a policy and training advocacy organization dedicated to improving police-youth interactions, has developed guidelines and specific practices that reflect developmental competency:

> A person who is developmentally competent recognizes that how children and youth perceive, process and respond to situations is a function of their developmental stage, and secondarily their culture and life experience. Developmentally competent adults align their expectations, responses, and interactions—as well as those of institutions and organizations—to the developmental stage of the children and youth they serve.[125]

And this is where our hope lies: juvenile defenders can play an important role in improving law enforcement response to, and increasing protection of, juveniles' constitutional rights in an age-appropriate manner. One key strategy that defenders should consider is using the CALEA and IACP standards to challenge officers' conduct with youth in the murky realm of custody and provision of *Miranda* warnings. These law enforcement standards demonstrate the precautions that officers should take and implicitly invite defenders to ask why an officer failed to do so. Agencies accredited by CALEA must adopt practices and policies that align with CALEA standards, including Standard 44; thus, they are all on notice. There are law enforcement agencies that adhere to these standards and do not become engaged in legal challenges over these core legal protections for youth, demonstrating that when an agency wants to, it can follow standards that operationalize the developmental differences of youth.

These standards offer a tremendous tool for challenging the legal fictions that the judiciary often invokes about how youth understand these situations and what youth "should" know at a given age regardless of individual differences and capacities. When defenders demonstrate that standard-setting law enforcement agencies appreciate that age affects youths' capacity to understand custody and their rights under the law, defenders are better positioned to question the *judiciary's* tendency to grant the officer the benefit of the doubt and rob the youth of the "privilege of innocence."

The major challenge before us is persuading law enforcement agencies to implement the model practices of CALEA and the IACP and to demand that the judiciary recognize its role in insisting that law enforcement follows these practices. This is imperative if we are going to provide youth meaningful legal protections in a juvenile justice system truly designed for youth.

Conclusion

This review of state courts' application of *J.D.B.* indicates that state courts' understanding of the role age plays in a youth's sense of agency and the power to resist coercion does not align with research about the workings of the teen brain. The U.S. Supreme Court in *Roper v. Simmons* grasped that youth is more "than a chronological fact. It is a time and condition of life when a person may be most susceptible to influence and to psychological damage."[126]

The Supreme Court's embrace of age as a key factor in invoking the due process protections to which youth are entitled unfortunately remains an abstraction that continues to be trumped by factors that reflect adults' perceptions instead of youths' understanding of their options when in the company of police. In a juvenile justice system that completely adopts a developmental approach and embraces the teaching of *J.D.B.*, police and the courts would implement developmentally informed training and guidelines that would give children and youth fairness and justice when they are questioned by police.

NOTES

1 *J.D.B. v. North Carolina*, 131 S. Ct. 2394 (2011). This chapter reviews all available published decisions until January 1, 2014.

2 Since 2005, the U.S. Supreme Court has considered juveniles' developmental capacity in four cases; in three cases, the focus was whether the key characteristics of youth justified less extreme punishment. In *Roper v. Simmons*, 543 U.S. 511 (2005), the Court prohibited the use of the death penalty for juveniles who had committed offenses; in quick succession in 2010 and 2012, the Court prohibited the use of life without parole, respectively, for youth adjudicated for violent offenses that did not result in death and for states that mandatorily required such sentences for youth who committed homicide. *See Graham v. Florida*, 560 U.S. 48 (2010); *Miller v. Alabama*, 132 S. Ct. 2455, 567 U.S. ___ (2012).

3 International Association of Chiefs of Police, *Reducing Risk: An Executive's Guide to Effective Juvenile Interviewing and Interrogation* (September 2012), 1, https://www.hsdl.org/?view&did=723566.

4 Lisa H. Thurau, *If Not Now, When? A Survey of Juvenile Justice Training in American Police Academies* (Strategies for Youth, February 2013), http://strategies-foryouth.org/sfysite/wp-content/uploads/2013/03/SFYReport_02-2013_rev.pdf.

5 Phillip Goff, Matthew Christian Jackson, Brook Allison Lewis Di Leone, Carmen Marie Culotta, and Natalie Ann Di Tomasso, "The Essence of Innocence: Consequences of Dehumanizing Black Children," *Journal of Personality and Social Psychology* 106, no. 4 (2014): 526–545.

6 *Id.* at 527.

7 *J.D.B.*, 131 S. Ct. at 2396.

8 *Id.*

9 *Id.* at 2400.

10 *Id.* at 2399.

11 *Id.* at 2401 (*quoting Miranda v. Arizona*, 384 U.S. 436, 467 (1966)).

12 *Id.*

13 *Id.* at 2402 (*quoting Stansbury v. California*, 511 U.S. 318, 325 (1994)).

14 *Id.* at 2402–2403 (*quoting Stansbury*, 511 U.S. at 325).

15 *See id.* at 2403.

16 *Id.* at 2406.

17 *Id.* at 2407.

18 *Haley v. Ohio*, 332 U.S. 596, 599–600 (1948), emphasis added.

19 *Gallegos v. Colorado*, 370 U.S. 49, 54 (1962).

20 A review of the top reasons juveniles are arrested, including disorderly conduct and obstruction of justice—what some people have called "contempt of cop" arrests—indicates the immediate consequences to a youth who defies a police officer. *See* Christy E. Lopez, *Disorderly (Mis)Conduct: The Problem with "Contempt of Cop" Arrests* (issue brief, American Constitution Society for Law and Policy, June 2010), http://www.acslaw.org/sites/default/files/

Lopez_Contempt_of_Cop.pdf; Justice Policy Institute, *The Costs of Confinement: Why Good Juvenile Justice Policies Make Good Fiscal Sense* (May 2009), 2, http://www.justicepolicy.org/images/upload/09_05_rep_costsofconfinement_jj_ps.pdf.

21 *Hunt v. The Cape Henlopen School District*, 2012 WL 6650590; 2012 Del. Super. LEXIS 408 (Del. Super. Ct., Aug. 23, 2012).

22 *Id.*

23 *Id.*

24 *Id.*

25 *Id.*

26 *Hunt ex rel. DeSombre v. State Dep't of Safety & Homeland Sec., Div. of Delaware State Police*, 69 A.3d 360 (Del. 2013).

27 *Id.* at 366.

28 *In re Michael S.*, 2012 WL 3091576; 2012 Cal. App. Unpub. LEXIS 5623 (Ca. App. 2d Dist., July 31, 2012).

29 *Id.*

30 *Id.*

31 *Id.*

32 *Id.*

33 *Id.*

34 *Id.*

35 *Id.*

36 *In re J.S.*, 2012 WL 3157149; 2012 Ohio App. LEXIS 3115 (Ohio Ct. App., Clermont Cty., Aug. 6, 2012).

37 *Id.*

38 *Id.*

39 *In re Robert J.*, 2012 WL 1269184; 2012 Cal. App. Unpub. LEXIS 2816 (Cal. App. 4th Dist., Apr. 16, 2012).

40 Thomas Grisso, Laurence Steinberg, Jennifer Woolard, Elizabeth Cauffman, Elizabeth Scott, Sandra Graham, Fran Lexcen, N. Dickon Reppucci, and Robert Schwartz, "Juveniles' Competence to Stand Trial: A Comparison of Adolescents' and Adults' Capacities as Trial Defendants," *Law and Human Behavior* 27 (August 2003): 333–363.

41 *See, e.g., Commonwealth v. Dillon D.*, 448 Mass. 793, 796 (2007) (requiring presence and actual consultation with parent or interested adult to establish a valid juvenile *Miranda* waiver).

42 *C.S. v. Couch*, 843 F. Supp. 2d 894 (N.D. Indiana, 2011).

43 *Id.* at 917.

44 *Id.* at 918.

45 *Id.* at 918–919.

46 *In re T.W.*, 2012 WL 1925656; 2012 Ohio App. LEXIS 2082 (Ohio Ct. App., Marion Cty., May 29, 2012).

47 *Id.*

48 *Id.* at ¶ 27.

49 *Id.* at ¶ 29.

50 *In re C.M.A.*, 2013 WL 3481517; 2013 Tex. App. LEXIS 8024 (Tx. Ct. App. Austin, July 2, 2013).

51 *In re Juan S.*, 2012 WL 1005027; 2012 Cal. App. Unpub. LEXIS 2272 (Cal. App. 4th Dist., Mar. 26, 2012).

52 *People v. Alexis C.*, 2013 WL 153758; 2013 Cal. App. Unpub. LEXIS 294 (Cal. App. 4th Dist., Jan. 15, 2013).

53 *Id.*

54 *Id.*

55 *Id.*

56 *People v. Nelson*, 53 Cal. 4th 367 (2012).

57 *Id.*

58 *Id.*

59 *Id.*

60 *Id.*

61 *Id.*

62 *Id.*

63 *In re J.W.*, 2011 WL 5594011; 2011 Cal. App. Unpub. LEXIS 8880 (Cal. App. 4th. Dist., Nov. 17, 2011) at 7.

64 *Id.*

65 *Id.*

66 *Gray v. Norman*, 2012 WL 4111837; 2012 U.S. Dist. LEXIS 133758 (E.D. Mo., Sept. 19, 2012).

67 *Id.*

68 *Id.*

69 *Id.*

70 *Id.*

71 *Id.*

72 *Id.* at 16.

73 *In re R.P.*, 718 S.E. 2d 423 (2011).

74 *Id.*

75 *Id.*

76 *State v. Oligney*, 2013 WL 5989691; 2013 Wisc. App. LEXIS 950 (2013).

77 *Miranda-Goodchild* hearings are "designed to examine (1) whether an accused in custody received Miranda warnings, understood them, and thereafter waived the right to remain silent and the right to the presence of an attorney; and (2) whether the admissions to police were the voluntary product of rational intellect and free, unconstrained will." *Id.* at ¶ 3, citing *State v. Jiles*, 663 N.W. 2d 798 (2003), based on *State ex rel. Goodchild v. Burke*, 133 N.W. 2d 753 (1963).

78 *Id.* at ¶ 16.

79 *Id.*

80 *Id.* at ¶ 17.

81 *Id.*

82 *People v. Lewis*, 2012 WL 1631677; 2012 Cal. App. Unpub. LEXIS 3500 (Cal. App. 4th Dist., May 10, 2012).

83 *Id.*

84 *Id.*

85 *Id.*

86 *Id.*

87 *Id.*

88 *In re J.V.*, 2013 WL 1641415; 2013 Cal. App. Unpub. LEXIS 2727 (Cal. App. 2d Dist., Apr. 17, 2013).

89 *State v. Pearson*, 804 N.W. 2d 260 (Iowa 2011).

90 *Id.*

91 *Id.*

92 *Id.*

93 *Id.* at 269.

94 *Commonwealth v. Bermudez*, 83 Mass. App. Ct. 46 (2012).

95 *Id.*

96 *Id.*

97 *Id.*

98 *Id.*

99 *Id.*

100 *Id.* at 52.

101 *Id.*

102 Commonwealth of Massachusetts, "Governor Patrick Signs Legislation Raising Age of Juvenile Jurisdiction to 18," press release, September 18, 2013, http://www.mass.gov/governor/pressoffice/pressreleases/2013/0918-juvenile-jurisdiction-legislation.html; John Kelly, "Massachusetts Includes 17-Year-Olds in Juvenile in Juvenile System; 10 States Remain That Don't," *Chronicle of Social Change*, September 19, 2013, https://chronicleofsocialchange.org/news/massachusetts-includes-17-year-olds-in-juvenile-system-10-states-remain-that-dont/3990; Jean Trounstine, "When Is a Juvenile No Longer a Juvenile?," *Boston Daily* (blog), June 21, 2013, http://www.bostonmagazine.com/news/blog/2013/06/21/massachusetts-juvenile-justice/.

103 *People v. Rocha*, 2013 WL 4774758; 2013 Cal. App. Unpub. LEXIS 6387 (Cal. App. 4th Dist., Sept. 6, 2013).

104 *Id.* at 7.

105 *State v. Yancey*, 727 S.E. 2d 382 (N.C. Ct. App. 2012).

106 *Id.*

107 *Id.*

108 *Id.*

109 *Id.*

110 *Id.*

111 *Id.* at 386.

112 *See* International Association of Chiefs of Police (IACP), *Training Key 652: Interview and Interrogation of Juveniles* (Alexandria, VA: IACP, 2011); Commission on Accreditation of Law Enforcement Agencies (CALEA), *Standards for Law Enforcement Agencies*, 5th ed. (Fairfax, VA: CALEA, issued 2006, updated 2012).

113 IACP, *supra* note 112.

114 *Id.* at 1.

115 *Id.* at 2.

116 *Id.* at 3.

117 *Id.*

118 *Id.*

119 *See* CALEA, *supra* note 112.

120 *Id.* at 44.2.3.

121 These include an officer considering the youth's "(1) *age, intelligence, educational background*, (2) *mental capacity*, including whether the defendant was nervous and physical condition, (3) *prior experience in the criminal system*, (4) whether the defendant is *suffering from an injury or pain at the time the statement is given*, (5) the *duration* of the questioning, (6) *time of day*, (7) *whether the defendant is tired* and is desirous of sleep, (8) *length of confinement*, (9) *whether Miranda or police caution warnings were given, when and whether he understood them*, (10) whether the room size was of sufficient size and supplied with appropriate furniture, (11) whether defendant was *cuffed or threatened*, (12) whether defendant was refused the use of bathroom, food, or drink, (13) whether there was a promise of leniency, (14) *whether the juvenile understands the interrogation process*, (15) whether a youth officer is present during the interview, (16) whether the parents were notified, (17) whether the juvenile asked for a parent to be present, (18) whether the police prevented a concerned adult from speaking with the juvenile, which is a significant factor, and (19) familiarity with English or the official language."

122 CALEA, *supra* note 112 (emphasis added).

123 Strategies for Youth, "Philosophy," http://strategiesforyouth.org/about/philosophy/ (accessed November 7, 2013).

124 Strategies for Youth is a national policy and training organization dedicated to providing law enforcement with best practices and effective alternatives to arrest and incarceration of youth and to reducing disproportionate minority contact. *Id.*

125 *Id.* "In order to become developmentally competent, an individual must: 1. Understand that children, adolescents, and adults interpret and respond differently to situations, social cues, interpersonal interactions, and the inherent power of adults, making them more vulnerable to external pressures and more compliant with authority; 2. Apply this knowledge to enhance and improve interactions with children and youth; 3. Calibrate institutional responses to the developmental stage of the children and youth served." *Id.*

126 *Roper v. Simmons*, 543 U.S. 551, 569 (2005).

PART V

Support Systems

14

What If Your Child Were the Next One in the Door?

Reimagining the Social Safety Net for Children, Families, and Communities

WENDY A. BACH

At the Center on Children and Families (CCF) conference that gave rise to this volume, one speaker asked us to imagine, as we envisioned a new and better juvenile justice system, that our child was the next child in the door. The "we" of this supposition suggests assumptions that it is important to make explicit. Today's juvenile justice system is peopled by poor kids. Disproportionately they are poor kids of color. Pernicious interactions of structural racism and classism permeate the system. Collectively we tolerate the system precisely because it serves to control and subordinate those kids, those families, and those communities. The "we" that was presumed as we were asked to envision a system for "our" kids is a group with significant class privilege. While race and gender identity would certainly impact the experience of our children, by virtue of the class privilege that our very presence in the conference suggests, it is likely either that our children would never enter this system or that, if they got close, we would have the cultural and economic resources to steer them quickly away. The outcome statistics for kids in the system are horrible, but our children are far less likely to be subject to them. To ask what it would mean if our kids were the next ones in the door, then, is to ask what our society would expect or tolerate from the system if it were the system we used to deal with all kids who break society's rules instead of only the system for poor, too often brown and black, kids, families, and communities.

In this chapter, I focus on one piece of this question—the question of "help" or, to put it more formally, the question of ensuring that families and communities have the support they need to parent their children safely and successfully. The chapter thus draws the lens back, away from the system we might put in place for poor kids who break society's rules, to a system that might, if in place, help poor kids, families, and communities thrive. What we need to create is what Maxine Eichner calls the "supportive state."[1] If we shifted the resources we now spend on monitoring, separating, incarcerating, and punishing poor kids, families, and communities toward creating institutions and communities that respect and support those same kids and families, we would have a truly different and far better set of outcomes and challenges.

To begin to address the question of how to create a more genuinely supportive set of institutions for children currently subject to the juvenile justice system, this chapter proceeds as follows. Section 1 argues for the provision of baseline economic support. Section 2 argues for the provision of significantly more social support in poor communities and highlights the work of the Harlem Children's Zone as an example of how to think about this task. Finally, section 3 argues that any efforts toward reform not only must provide significantly more economic and social support but must provide that support in a way that respects the privacy and enhances the autonomy of poor children, families, and communities.

It is important to remember that this is not an exercise in pure fantasy. Today for some children, families, and communities, our society provides such support. Privilege, for kids and families in America, translates into, among many other things, access to supportive resources—good schools, safe communities, high-quality mental and physical health care, high-quality child care, relatively secure and flexible jobs for parents, convenient transportation, and many other crucial resources. In addition, privileged kids, families, and communities experience a profoundly different structural balance between support and punishment. Their systems of support are not intertwined with mechanisms of punishment. Instead they focus on what they should: providing respectful support.

By contrast, in poor communities of color in America, we provide very meager support, and when we do provide support, it is inextricably intertwined with myriad mechanisms of monitoring, degradation, and punishment.[2] This is so pervasively true that system participants often accept this as simply the reality they must cope with. To understand this depressing reality in the particular context of juvenile justice, one need only recall the mechanisms of the cradle-to-prison pipeline and the horrific statistics associating placement in foster care with involvement in the juvenile justice system.

Two stories from practice tangibly lay bare the intolerable relationship between punishment and support that characterizes the "support" available to kids, families, and communities subject to today's juvenile system. In the fall of 2012, the clinic in which I teach was representing a child accused of armed robbery. Michael (not his real name) had been involved in an incident in which an 18-year-old threatened someone with a BB gun and stole the person's wallet. We had known Michael's family for some time and knew that he struggled with largely unaddressed learning disabilities as well as a mental health condition. During one court appearance, the prosecutor was urging us to take a plea. As she explained it, we should take the plea because "that will get him the services he needs. Otherwise it will be almost impossible for him to get into a program." For this prosecutor, this was a simple fact of the system in which she is embedded.

A few months later, we were appointed to represent James (not his real name). We were originally appointed because of a fairly minor vandalism charge, and he was in the community without any significant restrictions pending trial on that issue. Three weeks later, we got a call that James was being held in the juvenile detention facility. It turned out that, as a result of a gang dispute, James's family was in danger of attack. His mother so feared for his safety and for the safety of her family that she decided to kick him out of the house and then report him as a runaway. As she knew would happen, the police picked him up at school and brought him to detention. When they contacted her to come get him, she refused to take him out. For her, juvenile detention, in which James was kept in a single cell, transported to court in shackles, and vulnerable to 23-hour-a-day isolation for rule infractions, was her only option to keep her child and her family safe.

These two stories remind us that there is something very wrong with the relationship between support and the juvenile justice system in America today. These wrongs have everything to do with poverty, with race, and with class.[3] If a child of means needs help, his or her family has options and the resources to get that help outside the system. If Michael's family had had means, they would have been able to access services long ago. His educational and mental health issues would likely have been addressed, and once addressed, it is very possible that he would have never engaged in the behavior that led him to stand on a street corner that night next to a kid holding a BB gun. Even short of addressing those issues, Michael would have been in schools and communities with comprehensive after-school options and weekend activities. Surrounded by such resources, he might have found many ways to spend his time other than hanging around with that particular 18-year-old on that street corner. Even if he had gone as far as to be there, a family of means could have paid for services that would have kept him from that prosecutor's truth. If Michael's mother had had resources, she would have also had more options all along the way—to live in safer neighborhoods, to send her child to schools with activities that probably would have kept him far from the temptations of gang affiliation, and to take her family away from the danger if it came to that. But for Michael and James, support came far too late and far too linked to punishment.

In today's harsh and structurally unjust reality, there are clearly some advantages to the close link between juvenile justice and social service agencies. The capacity of the juvenile court to provide rehabilitative services distinguishes it from the adult system, and there is no question that, for some children in the system, these supports play a crucial role in helping them address some of what landed them in the system in the first place. But taking up the challenge that drives this book, this chapter asks not how we might make our profoundly broken system a little better. Instead it asks what support, defined broadly, we should provide to kids, families, and communities.

In envisioning a more supportive state, the first thing to talk about is money. Much of what I am going to suggest in this chapter will cost money and a good deal of it. But as has been pointed out many times before, we are already spending enormous sums on programs targeting poor youth and poor communities and in particular poor youth and communities of color. To an astounding degree, we are not seeing any positive results from those expenditures.

To get a sense of the funds available, the approximate price tag of two existing and largely failed systems are particularly relevant: incarceration in the juvenile justice system, and foster care and adoption. These

systems operate almost exclusively in poor communities and disproportionately and even more harshly in communities of color. Both systems
are largely failing to accomplish any legitimate objectives. Massive incarceration of children of color does not significantly reduce crime or
recidivism. It does not make communities safer. Similarly children in
general and children of color in particular tend to fare terribly in the
foster-care system. For many of these children (although clearly not all),
there are powerful reasons to believe that they would do better staying
in their families and communities than in foster care. So much of the
money we spend is wasted.

The cost and scope of these interventions is jaw dropping. It costs
about $240 a day per child to incarcerate a child. As of 2009, we were
holding approximately 93,000 juveniles every year at an annual cost
of $5.7 billion.[4] In fiscal year 2010, the states spent nearly $6 billion in
federal Title IV-E funds on foster care and adoption.[5] Imagine for a
moment that we could take 75% of the resources spent on foster care,
adoption, and incarceration and redirect those resources to social support. Redirecting these funds toward a supportive state could certainly
help provide meaningful income support and access to quality help and
resources.

In addition to redirecting resources away from punishment and separation and toward support, we must also fundamentally change how
we think about support programs. Social support in poor communities
must seek to respect the privacy and to enhance the autonomy of individuals, families, and communities. To accomplish that, the obsession
with behavioral control, the extraordinary deprivations of privacy, and
the tight links between support and punishment all must give way to
programs that "[protect] the individual's personhood from degradation
and . . . facilitate the process of choice and self-determination."[6] If we
provide more money and a network of respectful and helpful integrated
services, we might actually make some progress in helping children,
families, and communities flourish.

1. Provision of Baseline Economic Support

Like most families of kids in the juvenile justice system, Michael's and
James's families were poor. Michael's family moved three times in the

course of our representation because they could not consistently afford to pay rent. They could have used welfare but had long ago lost it because Michael's mother was overwhelmed and sick and could not navigate the difficult system that is welfare today. James's family was a little better off. His mother worked in a low-wage job, though, and that made it hard for her to come to court and do the running around that she needed to do to help her son. For these families and many others, not having enough money to meet your basic needs means that no problem is too small to cause a major crisis. Cars break down, children and adults get sick, low-wage jobs are lost, women facing violence lack the means to protect themselves, and eviction and homelessness are just part of daily risk. Living poor also often means living in dangerous neighborhoods with failing schools, few jobs of any kind and nearly none that provide a living wage, no transportation, and a lack of affordable nutritious food.

Despite these realities, we have no comprehensive economic safety net for people in poverty. In what is now quite old news, in 1996 the Personal Responsibility Act gutted Aid to Families with Dependent Children (AFDC) and with it the nation's commitment to providing baseline economic support to families in need. Today, Temporary Assistance to Needy Families (TANF) both serves far fewer of those who are eligible and provides less support. To give just some sense of the devastation suffered to economic support since 1996, it is useful to note that while in 1996 72% of eligible families received TANF, today only 27% of those eligible for TANF actually receive it.[7] It is important to play out the significance of these numbers. If only 27% of eligible families receive TANF, it means that the other 73% are poor enough to receive it but do not. So those families are even poorer than those on TANF. Although some eligible families receive food stamps and the earned income tax credit and a few very lucky families receive subsidized housing or child-care subsidies, the numbers are still dismal. This kind of economic deprivation has very real material and negative consequences. Yet we as a society seem to find it acceptable.

A truly supportive state would look different. Imagine for a moment a set of policies that would ensure that no household in the nation falls below a realistic poverty line. Although certainly subject to critique in some circles as too low and in others as far too high, a potentially viable standard to use in starting a conversation about economic support comes from the U.S. Census Bureau. In 2010, the bureau implemented a new research-focused mechanism for measuring poverty. The new Supplemental Poverty Measure (SPM) defines poverty by setting an annual income threshold below which a family is defined as poor.[8] In 2011, for a four-person family renting their housing, this threshold was about $25,000 per year. Using this measure, to guarantee that each household did not reside in poverty, we would need a set of policies that ensured that four-person households would be guaranteed a minimum income totaling about $25,000 per year. Provision of this support could come both from earned income and from a wide variety of income support programs; a return to guaranteed cash assistance; an increase in the supply of subsidized housing; tax credits; and food, energy, and child-care assistance; as well as the creation and expansion of subsidized employment programs.

While there are certainly a myriad of policy choices that would go into building consensus for such support and, if that were accomplished, figuring out the level and means of support, there is no question that more economic support would help. We may not have the political will to do it, but guaranteeing a minimum income, provided through a variety of means, would go a long way toward helping families create stability for themselves and their children.

2. Creating a Web of Support: The Harlem Children's Zone

In addition to money, community-based institutions that provide services and opportunities are tremendously important. James and Michael might again have different stories if they lived in a community with comprehensive, positive support programs. Much earlier in their lives, they could have used health care, after-school programs, better schools, summer opportunities, and a myriad of other supports readily available to privileged kids.

There is no shortage of examples of strong social support programs that help poor children, but in far too many cases, these programs are limited in scope and impact. They may help their own participants, but they do little to change the nature of poor communities as a whole. Far too often gains accomplished in one program are lost, overwhelmed by the lack of consistent support as individuals move on.

The Harlem Children's Zone (HCZ) seeks to go far beyond simply creating success for a group of individuals who enroll in one particular program. Although the Harlem Children's Zone does not solve every problem, looking closely at what this program is attempting to accomplish provides an intriguing model of comprehensive social support.

HCZ's founder, Geoffrey Canada, is the first to acknowledge that the program is expensive. With an operating budget of $72 million in fiscal year 2011, it has a cost per child between $5,000 and $19,000 annually (depending on the services the child and family receives). The program is expensive to operate and replicate. To justify these costs, Canada articulates the same argument that motivated much of the conversation that took place at the CCF conference and that opens this chapter:

> When you realize in the African American community, if you go into any fourth-grade classroom and you line all the boys up, somewhere between 40% to 60% of those boys are going to end up in jail or prison at some point in their life. Right here in New York City, it costs us $37,000 per year to lock up an adult inmate. If you are talking about a juvenile, we are spending over $100,000 a year to lock that child up. We know these children are going to end up in jail if we don't do something different, and we know the outcomes for jail are zero. . . . The outcomes for our work are proven, it's clear. You do the investment early, you end up with taxpayers who actually contribute to society.[9]

In the view of Paul Tough, who has written extensively about HCZ, Canada seeks to create "an alternative ongoing safety net to the one that invisibly supports middle-class kids all the way through childhood."[10] HCZ endeavors to create this safety net for every child in a 97-block area in Harlem. To accomplish this, HCZ operates two related but distinct programs. The first program serves children enrolled in the HCZ charter schools, the Promise Academy schools. The second focuses more broadly on the 97-block area that constitutes the entire zone.

The children who enter the Promise Academy schools by a lottery are wrapped in support from the age of three through college and beyond. They begin in high-quality preschools, and they receive free comprehensive health and mental health care, extensive tutoring, after-school programming, an extended educational day and year, and a vast array of other supports. The programs are designed to operate as a seamless conveyor belt—to intervene very early to ensure that children begin their educational journey at or above grade level, that they remain at or above grade level, and that they graduate from both high school and college.

HCZ is committed to transforming not just the lives of children in the charter schools but also the life trajectories of all the children in the 97-block area that constitutes the HCZ. "The goal is to create a 'tipping point' in the neighborhood so that children are surrounded by an enriching environment of college-oriented peers and supportive adults, a counterweight to 'the street' and a toxic popular culture that glorifies misogyny and anti-social behavior."[11] To accomplish this lofty objective, HCZ runs a myriad of additional programs aimed at transforming the life chances of children and families living in the HCZ.

For children, interventions start early and reach children of all ages and families throughout the community. For new and prospective parents, there is the Baby Academy, an intensive nine-week parenting program, which served 870 individuals in 2012. For elementary school students, the Harlem Peacemakers act as teaching assistants in seven public schools located in the HCZ and serve 2,500 students annually. In addition, the Peacemakers run the Fifth Grade Institute, a free after-school program that helps prepare fifth graders for middle school. For middle school students, HCZ offers Academic Case Managers and A Cut Above, an intensive after-school program, in addition to gender-specific leadership institutes for children in the zone. Students in high school receive similar supports to the middle schools students. They also receive more specific employment and college-related services designed to help students improve their academic performance and chances for entry into college. Students in college also receive support, such as help with loan applications, summer jobs, and applying for financial aid.

In addition, HCZ invests substantially in the community as a whole. The organization took over operation of the historic Harlem Armory and opened a new school in the middle of a central public-housing project in the Zone. Community programs include a Single Stop center, which assists families in accessing public benefits and addressing other legal and social service needs, asthma and obesity initiatives, extensive fitness and nutrition programs, and support for people seeking drug and alcohol treatment. The agency runs several intensive programs that seek to prevent placement of children in foster care. Finally, there is a community organizing component, Community Pride, which seeks to create thriving neighborhood organizations block by block and works to support tenants in buying and managing their own buildings.[12]

The Harlem Children's Zone has received an unprecedented amount of attention and praise. Everyone from policy researchers at the Heritage Institute[13] to Marion Wright Edelman[14] has praised the organization and the model. The Harlem Children's Zone forms the basis for Promise Neighborhoods, an Obama administration program designed to bring the Harlem Children's Zone model to communities across the nation. To date, the administration has invested nearly $100 million to bring the model to 50 communities across the nation.[15]

Imagine for a moment that Michael's and James's families lived in the Harlem Children's Zone. Perhaps it would have made no difference at all. But perhaps, if they had gotten to go to the Promise Academy schools, if they had access to after-school programs, beautiful athletic facilities, teachers and mentors with the time and resources to support them, and summer jobs, maybe things would have turned out differently.

But just asking if Michael and James would have had different life trajectories had they had access to these services understates what HCZ is seeking to accomplish. The organization seeks very intentionally not just to help a group of children. It aims to help a large number of children and families in a concentrated area such that the entire neighborhood is transformed. Given these lofty goals, there has been tremendous debate over whether HCZ is effective. At the center of these debates are arguments over what outcomes matter in evaluating the program. Most of the controversy over HCZ focuses on the noneducational family and community social services that HCZ provides. This research tends to ask whether those additional supports are essential to the educational outcomes of the kids. Implicitly critics argue that, if these additional, family- and community-focused interventions do not raise test scores or affect the life trajectories of the kids, they are not worth the additional cost.

The evaluation and policy conversations inevitably raise these questions and struggle with the limitations of the measurement tools available. Although there are important questions about what test scores can actually tell us, there is no question that kids in the Promise Academy schools, like kids in other charter schools, do well on those measures.

One prominent study of testing outcomes conducted by two Harvard-based researchers, Will Dobbie and Roland G. Freyer, concluded that the Promise Academy has managed to wipe out the racial achievement gap for its students.[16] Grover Whitehurst and Michelle Croft of the Brookings Institution point out, however, that Promise Academy students generally score in the 42nd percentile among comparable New York City charter schools, making the Promise Academy schools good schools worthy of investment but not necessarily better than other charter schools.[17] Crucially for the question of the investment in broader social support, Whitehurst and Croft argue that "there is no compelling evidence that investment in parenting classes, health services, nutritional programs, and community improvement in general have appreciable effects on student achievement in schools in the U.S."[18] So under Whitehurst and Croft's approach, if charter schools without social support for the broader community help kids, then that is enough.

The Zone model embodies two slightly conflicting theories: First is the theory that one can only achieve substantial success for the children and reach Canada's "tipping point" by investing substantially in families and communities. By this theory, broader social support only matters if it changes the life trajectories of the kids. The second theory (not officially espoused by the Harlem Children's Zone) is that the family and community outcomes matter in and of themselves.

Ultimately the Harlem Children Zone banks on the importance of providing a wide network of support. That is what makes the model so compelling as a counterweight to existing systems. If we want to transform poor communities, then we need to care about all of these outcomes and build strong results-oriented programs to achieve them. The Harlem Children's Zone and the Promise Neighborhoods program are far from perfect, but they do provide a compelling model for how we might begin to think about creating this network for the benefit of kids, families, and communities.

3. A Supportive State That Respects Privacy and Enhances Autonomy

Providing economic and social support is essential. But how we do this, and what price we exact for it, matters tremendously. Recall Michael's story: the price of the mental health care he needed was a plea bargain. He went on probation, and his "progress" in treatment was carefully monitored. As a condition of probation, he had to sign a waiver allowing his treatment provider to report to his probation counselor. Meanwhile his family got a caseworker from child protective services who provided no support but consistently inspected their home and, at several points, threatened to remove other children in the family. For Michael, any misstep, in treatment, in school, hanging out with his friends, could easily pull him deeper and deeper into the juvenile justice system. For his family, the price of mental health care for their son was putting all their children in jeopardy of removal.

Exacting such a price for support is all but unimaginable in privileged communities. But in poor communities, Michael's story is all too typical. To the extent that poor families today receive any social support, they do so at the expense of their privacy and autonomy and at great personal risk to themselves and their families.[19] To get support, one must surrender any notion that information, homes, or even bodies are private. The price of support includes, among other intrusions unthinkable for middle-class families, invasive questioning about a vast array of personal choices, home inspections, drug tests, and sharing of extensive personal data across both social support and criminal justice agencies.[20] Seeking support not only involves surrendering any notion of privacy, but it means subjecting yourself to very real risks of losing children and landing in jail. Every risk is intensified if you are not only poor but African American.[21]

This chapter argues for the provision of significantly more economic and social support in poor communities. But none of that will help at all if programs continue to operate in a way that degrades, monitors, and punishes those whom they purport to help. If we are to create a truly supportive state, we must proceed from an assumption of respect and strength. Individuals must be able to participate without compromising their ability to control their personal information and private spaces. There must be firm walls between supportive and punitive state mechanisms. We must, for example, erect firm walls between police and social support agencies, implement far stronger policies disallowing, in the vast majority of cases, removal of children prior to the extensive provision of economic and social support, and drastically alter the current allocation of funds so that far more re-sources go to family support than to child removal, foster care, and punishment.

Given the extraordinary structural racism and classism as well as the substantial economic interests all arrayed in support of the state as it currently operates, it is hard to imagine building the political will to make these changes. But then again, if we are to transform this conversation, we have to begin by envisioning the system we actually want. Today in the United States, we expend extraordinary resources to criminalize and degrade. We run closely linked punitive systems imbued with structural racism and classism. We scrutinize, we deny, and we punish. As Michael's and James's stories lay bare, meager help comes, if at all, far too late and inextricably linked to punishment. Imagine instead that we offered respectful, autonomy-enhancing eco-nomic and social support, and we brought that to scale. If we did this, the question of what we should do for kids who stray from the rules on the admittedly difficult journey from childhood to adulthood would be all but unrecognizable.

NOTES

1   Maxine Eichner, *The Supportive State: Families, Government, and America's Political Ideals* (New York: Oxford University Press, 2010).

2   *See, e.g.*, Kaaryn Gustafson, *Cheating Welfare: Public Assistance and the Criminalization of Poverty* (New York: NYU Press, 2011), 1; Michelle Alexander, *The New Jim Crow: Mass Incarceration in an Age of Colorblindness* (New York: New Press, 2010).

3   Tamar R. Birckhead, "Delinquent by Reason of Poverty," *Washington University Journal of Law and Policy* 38 (2012): 53–107.

4   Nancy E. Dowd, introduction to *Justice for Kids: Keeping Kids Out of the Juvenile Justice System*, edited by Nancy E. Dowd, 1–18 (New York: NYU Press, 2011), 3.

5   Specifically, the states spent a total of $5,992,399,964 in Title IV-E Foster Care and Adoption Assistance. Casey Family Programs, State Child Welfare Policy Database, http://www.childwelfarepolicy.org (accessed April 21, 2014). Although Title IV does not represent all federal expenditures, it does provide a major source of funding. *Id.*

6   Dorothy Roberts, "Punishing Drug Addicts Who Have Babies: Women of Color, Equality, and the Right of Privacy," *Harvard Law Review* 104 (1991): 1479.

7   Legal Momentum, *A TANF Misery Index* (New York: Women's Legal Defense and Education Fund, 2013), 1, http://www.legalmomentum.org/our-work/women-and-poverty/a-tanf-misery-index.pdf.

8 Kathleen Short, *The Research Supplemental Poverty Measure: 2011* (Washington, DC: U.S. Census Bureau, 2012), http://www.census.gov/hhes/povmeas/methodology/supplemental/research/Short_ResearchSPM2011.pdf.

9 Harlem Children's Zone, "FAQs," video, 2009, http://www.hcz.org/index.php/about-us/video-faqs.

10 Paul Tough, *Whatever It Takes: Geoffrey Canada's Quest to Change Harlem* (New York: Houghton Mifflin, 2008), 279.

11 Harlem Children's Zone, "The HCZ Project," 2009, http://www.hcz.org/about-us/the-hcz-project.

12 Program descriptions have been compiled from materials produced by the Harlem Children's Zone generally available at www.hcz.org as well as from Tough's *Whatever It Takes, supra* note 11.

13 Danielle Hanson, *Assessing the Harlem Children's Zone* (Washington, DC: Heritage Foundation Center for Policy Innovations, 2013).

14 Marion Wright Edelman, "The Disproportionate Number of Minority Youth in the Family and Criminal Court Systems: Remarks & Keynote Address," *Journal of Law and Policy* 15 (2007): 934.

15 U.S. Department of Education, "Secretary Duncan Announces Seventeen 2012 Promise Neighborhoods Winners in School Safety Address at Neval Thomas Elementary School," press release, December 21, 2012, http://www.ed.gov/news/press-releases/secretary-duncan-announces-seventeen-2012-promise-neighborhoods-winners-school-s.

16 Will Dobbie and Roland G. Fryer Jr., "Are High Quality Schools Enough to Close the Achievement Gap? Evidence from a Social Experiment in Harlem" (NBER Working Paper 15473, November 2009).

17 Grover J. Whitehurst and Michelle Croft, *The Harlem Children's Zone, Promise Neighborhoods, and the Broader, Bolder Approach to Education* (Brown Center on Education Policy at Brookings, July 20, 2010), 6.

18 *Id.* at 8.

19 *See, e.g.*, Wendy A. Bach, "The Hyperregulatory State: Women, Race, Poverty and Support," *Yale Journal of Law and Feminism* 25 (2014): 319.

20 *See, e.g.*, Khiara Bridges, "Privacy Rights and Public Families," *Harvard Journal of Law and Gender* 24 (2011): 131; Gustafson, *supra* note 2, at 1.

21 *See, e.g.*, Bach, *supra* note 19.

15

Immigrant Children

Treating Children as Children, Regardless of Their Legal Status

ELIZABETH M. FRANKEL

Immigrant Children in the Juvenile Court System

In recent years, the immigration system has seen a marked increase in the number of children reported to federal immigration authorities while in the juvenile court system.[1] Most of the children who end up in the immigration system by way of the juvenile court system are children who were brought to the United States by parents when they were young. These children have little to no control over their immigration status.[2] Moreover, many may be eligible for visas or other immigration benefits that would allow them to remain permanently in the United States, in lawful status.[3] Yet the juvenile courts ignore this reality, treating children as culpable and reporting them to immigration authorities. These policies result in immigrant children being denied the same protections and rights as other children in juvenile court, a clear violation of the equal protection clause of the Constitution.[4]

This chapter begins by examining the cases of three children, Raul, Carlos, and Ana, whose stories illustrate the ways in which immigrant children are impacted when juvenile courts prioritize immigration enforcement over the needs and interests of the child. Next, it focuses on two ways in which the system could be changed to better protect immigrant children—by prohibiting decisions based solely on a child's immigration status and by calling on the juvenile courts to identify vulnerable children who may qualify for lawful immigration status. Finally, this chapter revisits the cases of Raul, Carlos, and Ana and considers how their outcomes would have been different if the system treated them like other children, rather than penalizing them for their immigration status.

Juvenile Court Officers Report Youth to Immigration and Customs Enforcement: Raul's Story

Raul[5] was born in El Salvador and raised by his mother. Raul's mother was physically abusive, and Raul regularly went without food or shelter. He never knew his father, who abandoned the family when Raul was young. When Raul was just 14 years old, he traveled north to the United States. His plan was to live with an uncle and go to school. Raul was apprehended at the border and placed in immigration custody, at a facility for unaccompanied immigrant children.

The federal government eventually released Raul to his uncle in Georgia; however, the reunification did not go well. Raul's uncle charged him rent, and when Raul could not pay, his uncle kicked him out of the house. Raul was living on his own, working and trying to make ends meet. With no place else to go, he sought help from his former school guidance counselor. When the guidance counselor learned that Raul had been kicked out of his home, she called Child Protective Services (CPS), and Raul was placed in a temporary group home. Raul's uncle refused to take him back, so when Raul went before the juvenile court, the judge told CPS that it had two options: either find a permanent placement for Raul in state foster care or turn him over to Immigration and Customs Enforcement (ICE). CPS decided to call ICE, and Raul was taken back into immigration custody.

Raul was initially placed in an immigration facility in New York. From there, he was sent to a group home in Delaware, contracted by the federal government. While in the group home, Raul grew severely depressed and eventually left to try to get back to New York. Once in New York, with no place else to go, he went to a homeless shelter, which contacted the Administration for Children's Services (ACS), the New York City child welfare agency. ACS placed Raul in an emergency shelter.

Although the "emergency" shelter was designed for short-term stays of a few days, Raul was left there for weeks while the state and federal government argued over who should take responsibility for him. Raul eventually grew frustrated and left the shelter. The next day, he was arrested for trying to steal a clean shirt from a department store. Raul was once again turned over to ICE and spent the next year in four different federal detention facilities around the country.

Immigrant Youth Caught in a Revolving Door of Detention: Carlos's Story

When Carlos was just six months old, his mother brought him from Mexico to the United States. Carlos grew up in Maryland with his mother and two U.S. citizen siblings (both born in the United States). Carlos's mother was frequently absent, so from a young age Carlos was forced to fend for himself and take care of his siblings. When he was 14 years old, Carlos was charged with theft. He spent a month in state custody and was deemed eligible for release while his case was still pending. However, instead of being sent home, Carlos was taken into custody by ICE, and he was placed in an immigration detention center in New York.

While in New York, Carlos missed his juvenile court hearing because the federal government would not bring him to Maryland. When Carlos failed to appear in court, the judge issued a warrant for his arrest. The federal government refused to release Carlos because of the outstanding warrant, and the juvenile court would not quash the warrant unless Carlos appeared in court. After approximately one year in immigration custody, Carlos remained essentially trapped. With no way out of custody, Carlos grew depressed and began asking to return to Mexico, where he had no one, just to get out of detention.

State Court Judges and Prosecutors Deny Requests by Immigrant Youth for Needed Services: Ana's Story

Ana had an extensive history of sexual abuse in her home country starting at the age of seven, when she was raped by a family member. Shortly after, another male caregiver began sexually abusing her, and this abuse lasted for years. When Ana was 12 years old, her mother brought her to the United States, and Ana grew up in Minnesota. Ana, who was suffering from posttraumatic stress disorder, never received counseling or any services for the abuse she suffered. As a result, she began using alcohol and drugs at an early age as a way to deal with the pain she felt.

When Ana was 17 years old, she was charged in juvenile court with possession of a controlled substance. The juvenile court judge quickly recognized that Ana needed treatment, not detention; however, the judge and prosecutor would not agree to drug treatment because ICE had placed a detainer on Ana. The prosecutor reasoned that drug treatment would require release from the state system, yet Ana would never be able to complete treatment because ICE would take her into custody the moment she was released. As a result, Ana was forced to spend time in state custody. Upon her release from the state system, Ana was turned over to ICE.

The Stories of Raul, Carlos, and Ana Are Typical

The rise in federal apprehensions of noncitizen youth such as Raul, Carlos, and Ana is due to enhanced communication and collaboration between state court officers and Immigration and Customs Enforcement.[6] State officials—judges, prosecutors, probation officers, and even child protection agents—are increasingly willing to share information with ICE about the children in their care.[7] Although the juvenile court system is meant to focus on rehabilitation and protection, in reality the juvenile system is realigning its priorities with those of immigration authorities and focusing not on what is best for the child but rather on the enforcement of federal immigration laws.[8]

The stories of Raul, Carlos, and Ana are all too common. Throughout the country, juvenile court judges, probation officers, and other court officials in both the delinquency and dependency systems regularly report immigrant youth to ICE. Stories such as Raul's, in which state officials in the child protection system contact ICE rather than place a child in the state foster care system, are also a regular occurrence in some parts of the country. In other cases, juvenile court judges and others in the child welfare system have actually ordered children deported, despite the lack of any legal authority to do so.[9] For youth in state juvenile detention, ICE officers are frequently permitted to enter detention centers in plain clothes and question individual children, suspected to be undocumented, about their immigration status.[10] These young people have no attorney present and are led to believe they are talking to state officials. As a result, they often believe that disclosures will assist in their case when, in reality, any disclosures will only be used against them by immigration authorities.

Almost all states currently have confidentiality statutes that are meant to shield juvenile offenders from the ongoing stigmatization and other harm caused by involvement in the juvenile court system.[11] When state court officers report youth in the juvenile court system to ICE, they are in clear violation of state confidentiality laws, but such practices are rarely challenged. One incentive for reporting youth to ICE is presumably cost saving, yet ultimately this reporting simply shifts the financial burden from the state to ICE, an enforcement agency ill equipped to handle juvenile matters. Other state officials may report youth to ICE out of a sense of moral obligation to report wrongdoing, yet most youth bear little, if any, responsibility for their immigration status.[12] Ultimately both rationales run counter to the ultimate goal of our juvenile court system: to rehabilitate children so they may become productive members of society. By reporting to ICE, the state system simply avoids, rather than addresses, the underlying problem.

Another familiar problem for immigrant children, such as Ana, is the inability to access needed services due to immigration status. When ICE learns that an immigrant child is in state custody, ICE will issue a detainer: a request that the state authorities alert the federal agency when the child is going to be released from custody and hold that child for up to 48 hours to give ICE time to pick up the child.[13] Once a child has an ICE detainer, that young person is often precluded from accessing alternative sentencing programs, such as drug treatment or community service.[14] Court officials attribute such policies to the child's immigration status, arguing that the child will not be able to complete the program due to the detainer. Yet, in reality, state authorities have complete discretion when deciding whether to enforce ICE detainers and may always release a child, rather than turning that youth over to ICE.[15]

Once in the immigration system, the problems faced by Carlos (warrants issued by state courts and a revolving door of detention) are also all too common. Children released from state custody often still have some involvement with the state court system and must report either to court hearings or to probation. However, because children's immigration facilities are located in few parts of the country, children end up hundreds, or even thousands, of miles from family and state court proceedings.[16] These children are unable to attend court hearings or probation appointments, and as a consequence, warrants are issued for the child's arrest. Therefore, immediately upon release from immigration custody, these young people are once again detained by the state. Immigrant youth end up spending months, or even years, being shuffled between state and federal custody.[17]

Most actors in the state court system who report children to ICE would likely be shocked to learn how few of the due process protections provided to children in the juvenile justice system are available to young people in the immigration system.[18] When a child is reported to ICE, the child is placed in immigration detention for minors, where federal agents, not judges, have complete discretion with regard to release.[19] Like Raul and Carlos, children can spend anywhere from a few months to years in federal custody. In addition, they are placed in removal (deportation) proceedings. Children in removal proceedings are treated just like adults. The child bears the burden of proving that he or she has a legal right to remain in the United States, and children have no right to counsel at government expense.[20] As a result, many children appear alone in court, without a lawyer, and it is common for children to be ordered removed simply because they do not realize that they qualify for lawful status or because they fail to appear in court.[21]

A Vision of Change: Juvenile Courts Should Be Prohibited from Making Decisions Based Solely on a Child's Immigration Status

The stories of Raul, Carlos, and Ana highlight the ways in which the juvenile court system has taken on an enforcement role with respect to immigrant children. Because undocumented children in the juvenile court system are turned over to ICE, they are unable to access the same protections as other children. Such practices lead to discrimination and undermine the rehabilitation and protection goals of the juvenile justice system. Even though these are children, with no real control over where they live or their immigration status, they are left unable to access needed services and languishing in detention.

We need to change how our juvenile court system treats immigrant youth. We must not tolerate systemic discrimination against children on the basis of immigration status. Further, we must prohibit juvenile courts from making any decisions—custody, placement, transfer, reunification, or punishment—based solely on immigration status, as such policies run counter to the goals of rehabilitation and protection, the articulated principles at the heart of our juvenile justice system. Finally, rather than reporting youth to ICE, officers in the juvenile courts should identify ways to assist and protect these vulnerable young people by looking out for children who may qualify for Special Immigrant Juvenile Status, or other forms of lawful status, and ensuring that they are screened and advised by immigration attorneys.

Making the Legal Argument for Change

Our juvenile court system should be one that treats children as children, regardless of their lawful status. It is not enough simply to encourage courts to reprioritize goals other than enforcement. Rather, juvenile courts should be prohibited from requiring the disclosure of, or making decisions based solely on, a child's immigration status.

In *Plyler v. Doe*, the U.S. Supreme Court held that states cannot require the disclosure of immigration status as a prerequisite to school enrollment.[22] In so holding, the Court acknowledged two key principles that, if accepted, would require a significant change in how our juvenile court system currently treats immigrant youth:

1. Undocumented children bear little, if any, responsibility for their unlawful status, and as a consequence, they should not be denied access to certain basic and fundamental societal institutions on that basis.[23]
2. Treating undocumented children differently from other children solely because of their immigration status violates the equal protection clause of the Constitution.[24]

Plyler involved a challenge to a Texas statute that denied undocumented children the ability to enroll in public school due to their immigration status.[25] The Court held that the Texas law violated the equal protection clause of the Fifth and Fourteenth Amendments because the classification at issue—a child's immigration status—did not bear a fair relationship to a substantial state interest.[26] While the Court recognized that "undocumented status is not irrelevant to any proper legislative goal," the Texas law ultimately failed because it focused on children, who bear little if any responsibility for their legal status.[27] As Justice Brennan wrote, "[The Texas law] imposes its discriminatory burden on the basis of a legal characteristic over which children can have little control. It is difficult to conceive of a rational justification for penalizing these children for their presence within the United States. Yet that appears to be precisely the effect of [the law at issue]."[28] Ultimately, *Plyler* held that public schools are prohibited from denying enrollment to undocumented children and may not require disclosure of a child's immigration status as a condition to enrollment in school.[29]

At the heart of *Plyler* is a recognition that penalizing undocumented children for their immigration status is inherently unfair, since children do not control where they live or their legal status. The Court recognized that since children rely on adult caregivers, the culpability of a child who has entered the United States unlawfully is fundamentally different from that of an adult.[30] Even a child such as Raul—who at age 14 came to the U.S. by himself after being abandoned by his parents—would presumably be less culpable for his unlawful entry than an adult would.

The decision in *Plyler*, while important in its recognition of the rights of immigrant children, is certainly not the only case in which the Supreme Court has acknowledged that children and youth are generally less culpable than adults for unlawful activity.[31] In fact, the formation of the juvenile court system is based on the recognition long ago by the Supreme Court that "children cannot be viewed simply as miniature adults."[32] Our juvenile delinquency system—like the dependency system—is designed, in part, to protect children from some of the harsher realities of the adult court system. As a result, many states require that juvenile delinquency records be kept confidential or automatically sealed, to prevent charges and adjudications from following a child throughout life and preventing that young person from getting into school or obtaining a job in the future.[33] Such laws have been long recognized by the Court as critical in facilitating rehabilitation.[34]

Plyler recognized that, although public education is not a "right," it is a basic institution fundamental to child development, and to deny certain children the ability to get an education on the basis of legal status is inherently unjust.[35] Our juvenile court system, like our education system, is also an institution recognized as fundamental to our society, aimed at rehabilitating and protecting vulnerable youth.[36] It is, therefore, similarly problematic to deny an entire group of children equal access to the juvenile court system simply because of their immigration status.

Extending *Plyler* to our juvenile courts, all state authorities should be prohibited from basing any decision solely on a child's immigration status or otherwise violating state confidentiality laws because of a child's suspected or actual immigration status. This would not prevent state courts from considering a child's immigration status, along with other factors, in order to make decisions that align with the child's interests.[37] However, it would prevent reporting the child to federal immigration authorities, as such practices are discriminatory and undermine the ability for immigrant children to equally access the juvenile courts, a clear violation of the principle that all children should be treated equally in the eyes of the law.[38]

Even the Department of Homeland Security (DHS, the umbrella agency that oversees ICE) recognizes that it is unfair to treat undocumented children the same as undocumented adults.[39] As a prosecuting agency, DHS has great discretion in deciding which cases to prioritize for removal from the United States.[40] In a series of memoranda issued by the acting director of the Department of Homeland Security, most recently in June 2012, DHS has repeatedly said that children—particularly those who have grown up in the U.S. with family, have extensive ties to the community, and have gone to school here—should not be prioritized for removal and, in many cases, should be granted "Deferred Action," allowing them to remain in the United States and work.[41] Furthermore, while ICE has always prioritized so-called serious criminal aliens, the immigration courts and DHS have long treated juvenile delinquency adjudications differently from adult criminal convictions when making decisions regarding removal.[42] Specifically, juvenile delinquency adjudications do not trigger the harsh mandatory grounds of removal that are triggered by criminal convictions.[43]

How the Juvenile Court System Could Better Protect Immigrant Children

While in the juvenile court system, children should be served according to their unique needs and vulnerabilities. Court officers are charged with identifying services that can be put in place to better protect children and families. For many immigrant children, the most glaring need is a path to lawful status in the United States.

Many young people who have grown up in the United States without lawful status have never been screened by an attorney to assess whether they qualify for any type of visa or other lawful status in the U.S. Yet many of these young people are in fact eligible for lawful immigration status. The most common form of legal relief for children is Special Immigrant Juvenile Status (SIJS).[44] In order to get SIJS, a child must first get an order from a state court with jurisdiction over juvenile matters finding that the child was abused, abandoned, or neglected by one or both parents and that it is not in the child's best interests to return to his or her country of origin. Once a child has an order from a state court, he or she may then apply to U.S. Citizenship and Immigration Services for Special Immigrant Juvenile Status and to become a Lawful Permanent Resident.

The juvenile court system can play a critical role in identifying children who may be eligible for SIJS, referring them to immigration attorneys, and making the requisite SIJS findings. Many of the children who enter the juvenile court system have suffered a history of abuse, abandonment, or neglect, and the juvenile courts are already making such findings in the context of the juvenile proceedings. As a result, vigorous advocates in the state court system have been able to get the requisite SIJS findings through dependency, guardianship, delinquency, and even criminal proceedings.

Identifying a child as eligible for SIJS while still in the state court system, rather than after he or she has been transferred to ICE, can make a critical difference in that child's ability to gain lawful status. It is often more challenging to get the requisite state court order after a child has been transferred to federal custody because many state courts are reluctant to declare a child dependent on the state when the child is safely in a federal facility. Furthermore, many state courts lose jurisdiction over juvenile matters once a child turns 18, so obtaining the required state order before the child's 18th birthday is crucial. Since children can spend extended periods of time caught between state and federal custody, many children "age out" during the process and lose their ability to apply for SIJS.

Another form of lawful status available to some children in the juvenile court system is a U visa, a visa available to children who have been victims of certain violent crimes while in the U.S. and who assist law enforcement in the investigation or prosecution of those crimes.[45] Children who are victims of physical or sexual abuse at the hands of individuals other than their parents would not qualify for SIJS (which only applies to abuse by parents) but would potentially qualify for a U visa. Again, children eligible for this form of relief should be identified and referred to immigration attorneys.

Many immigrant children who enter the juvenile court system are children who were brought to the United States by parents when they were young and have lived in the U.S. for most of their lives. Since our immigration laws are narrow, some of these children will not qualify for any type of lawful status in the United States; however, they may qualify for a form of prosecutorial discretion, called Deferred Action for Childhood Arrivals (DACA).[46] DACA does not provide any lawful status or path to citizenship; however, it is a form of relief that prevents a child's removal from the United States for at least two years and allows the child to attend school or work lawfully.

Identifying children who qualify for lawful status or deferred action and referring those young people to immigration attorneys, rather than ICE, can drastically change the outcomes for these children. Most immediately, obtaining lawful status means that these children will not be removed from the United States and permanently separated from family. Legal status also opens the doors to many services that would otherwise be unavailable. For example, once granted lawful status, immigrant children can apply for financial aid to attend college or can enter the armed forces. They can work lawfully and may apply for Medicaid and other forms of assistance. If the goal of the juvenile court system is truly rehabilitation and protection, then assisting immigrant children to obtain legal status is critical.

How the Outcomes for Raul, Carlos, and Ana Could Have Been Different If the Juvenile Courts Had Made Decisions Based on Their Interests, Rather than Solely on Their Immigration Status

If Raul, Carlos, and Ana had not been reported to ICE, how would their outcomes have been different?

An attorney in New York identified Raul as eligible for Special Immigrant Juvenile Status.[47] However, because Raul was in federal custody, it was much more challenging to get that court order. Raul was eventually granted Special Immigrant Juvenile Status; however, in the interim, Raul spent almost three years in custody in a total of nine different placements, both state and federal, wreaking havoc on his sense of safety, permanency, development, and general well-being.

If Child Protective Services had placed Raul in foster care when he was first identified as a vulnerable child, rather than contacting ICE, Raul would have avoided a year and a half of being shipped around the country to seven different placements. He would have been able to apply for SIJS while in state foster care and would likely have gained the permanency and stability he desperately needed much earlier.

Carlos remained in federal custody for over a year. Eventually, his Child Advocate (guardian *ad litem*) worked with his public defender and with the federal government to arrange for Carlos to be transported to Maryland for his state court case. The warrant was quashed, and Carlos pled guilty to a misdemeanor juvenile delinquency charge. Carlos was then placed in long-term federal foster care in Utah, far from his family in Maryland. Carlos was eventually granted Special Immigrant Juvenile Status.

If Carlos had been allowed to remain in Maryland, rather than being transferred to federal custody, his state court case would have been resolved at least a year earlier. Carlos could have entered the state foster care system, rather than the federal system, which would have allowed him to remain in Maryland and have an ongoing relationship with his mother and siblings. Finally, like Raul, Carlos would have been able to gain status as a Special Immigrant Juvenile, and to find permanency and stability, much sooner.

Ana struggled for years with drug use. The stress over her immigration case, coupled with her trauma history, caused Ana ongoing issues with anxiety and depression. Ana never met with an immigration attorney while she was still a minor. She remains without lawful status.

If Ana had gotten access to drug treatment and immigration services earlier, perhaps her outcome would have been different. Ana also qualified for SIJS, having been abandoned by her father at birth; however, unlike Raul and Carlos, she turned 18 before meeting with an immigration attorney and lost the opportunity to apply, despite having lived in the United States since the age of 12. Furthermore, although it was clear when Ana entered the juvenile justice system at the age of 17 that she needed drug treatment and counseling services, she was unable to access those services through the court system because of the ICE detainer placed on her. If Ana had been able to begin drug treatment at the age of 17, she would have been more likely to overcome her drug problem and might have been referred to immigration legal services much sooner.

The stories of Raul, Carlos, and Ana illustrate how our juvenile court system is currently failing the children it is meant to protect. Reporting these vulnerable children to ICE did nothing to serve their needs. In order to protect the integrity of our juvenile justice system, decision makers must continue to guard the confidentiality of children and should not disclose information regarding a child's case to ICE. Instead, juvenile court officers should refer children for screening by immigration attorneys so that, whenever possible, these children may apply for lawful status in the United States, as early as possible. Without these safeguards, we run the risk identified in *Plyler*, of creating a permanent "underclass" unable to access the same rights and protections as the majority.[48] If we value a system free of discrimination, in which children are treated and respected as children, courts must not make decisions based solely on immigration status. A reconstructed relationship between the immigration system and the juvenile courts would allow immigrant children the same opportunity as citizen children to be supported as children in their journey to adulthood.

NOTES

1 M. Aryah Somers, Pedro Herrera, and Lucia Rodrigues, "Constructions of Childhood and Unaccompanied Children in the Immigration System in the United States," *U.C. Davis Journal of Juvenile Law and Policy* 14 (2010): 351; Women's Refugee Commission and Orrick Herrington & Sutcliffe LLP, *Halfway*

Home: Unaccompanied Children in Immigration Custody (Women's Refuge Commission, February 2009), 15.

2　*See Plyler v. Doe*, 457 U.S. 202, 220 (1982).

3　*See* David B. Thronson and Judge Frank P. Sullivan, "Family Courts and Immigration Status," *Juvenile & Family Court Journal* 63 (2012): 14; *Plyler v. Doe*, 457 U.S. at 226.

4　*See* U.S. Const. amends. X, XIV.

5　All identifying information including the child's name, location, and country of origin has been changed to protect confidentiality.

6　Christopher N. Lasch, "Immigration Law: Enforcing the Limits of the Executive Authority to Issue Immigration Detainers," *William Mitchell Law Review* 35 (2008): 165.

7　*See* M. Aryah Somers, "Voice, Agency and Vulnerability: the Immigration of Children through Systems of Protection and Enforcement," *International Migration* 49 (2010): 7–10.

8　*Id.* at 9–10.

9　*Id.* at 10.

10　Elizabeth M. Frankel, "Detention and Deportation with Inadequate Due Process: The Devastating Consequences of Juvenile Involvement with Law Enforcement for Immigrant Youth," *Duke Forum for Law and Social Change* 3 (2011): 70.

11　*E.g.*, 18 U.S.C. §§ 5032, 5038 (2013); 705 ILCS §§ 405/1-5, 405/1-7 (2013).

12　*See Plyler v. Doe*, 457 U.S. 202, 220 (1982).

13　INA § 287(d), 8 U.S.C. § 1357(d) (2013); 8 C.F.R. § 287.7 (2013).

14　New York City Bar, Committee on Criminal Justice Operations, *Immigration Detainers Need Not Bar Access to Jail Diversion Programs* (Association of the Bar of the City of New York, June 2009), 1, 3, http://www.nycbar.org/pdf/report/NYCBA_Immigration%20Detainers_Report_Final.pdf.

15　8 C.F.R. § 287.7 (2013); New York City Bar, *supra* note 14 at 3; Lena Graber, *The All in One Guide to Defeating ICE Hold Requests (a.k.a. Immigration Detainers)* (National Immigration Project of the National Lawyers Guild, 2012), 10 and appendix 1.

16　Olga Byrne and Elise Miller, *The Flow of Unaccompanied Children through the Immigration System: A Resource for Practitioners, Policy Makers and Researchers* (Vera Institute of Justice, 2012), 14.

17　*See* Somers, *supra* note 7, at 7.

18　*See* INA § 292, 8 U.S.C. § 1362 (2013); *In re Gault*, 387 U.S. 1, 36–37 (1967).

19　*Flores v. Reno*, No. CV 85-4544-RJK(Px) (C.D. Cal. filed Jan. 17, 1997) (stipulated settlement agreement), ¶ 14.

20　*See* INA § 240, 8 U.S.C. § 1229a (2013); INA § 292, 8 U.S.C. § 1362 (2013).

21　Julia Preston, "More Young Illegal Immigrants Face Deportation," *New York Times*, August 25, 2012.

22　*Plyler v. Doe*, 457 U.S. 202, 230 (1982).

23　*Id.* at 220–221.

24 *Id.* at 221–222.

25 *Id.* at 205.

26 *Id.* at 230.

27 *Id.* at 220.

28 *Id.*

29 *Id.* at 230.

30 *Id.* at 220.

31 *Roper v. Simmons*, 543 U.S. 551, 569–571 (2005); *Graham v. Florida*, 560 U.S. 48, 68 (2010); *J.D.B. v. North Carolina*, 131 S. Ct. 2394, 2403–2404 (2011).

32 *J.D.B.*, 131 S. Ct. at 2404.

33 *See* 18 U.S.C. § 5038 (2013); 705 ILCS § 405/1-7 (2013).

34 *See, e.g., Smith v. Daily Mail Publishing Co.*, 443 U.S. 97, 105 (1979); *Davis v. Alaska*, 415 U.S. 308, 319 (1974); *Kent v. United States*, 383 U.S. 541, 556 (1966).

35 *Plyler*, 457 U.S. at 220–222.

36 *See Kent*, 383 U.S. at 554.

37 *See* Thronson and Sullivan, *supra* note 3, at 11–13.

38 *See* U.S. Const. amends. X, XIV.

39 Memorandum from Janet Napolitano, Secretary of the Department of Homeland Security, "Exercising Prosecutorial Discretion with Respect to Individuals Who Came to the United States as Children" (June 15, 2012), http://www.dhs.gov/xlibrary/assets/s1-exercising-prosecutorial-discretion-individuals-who-came-to-us-as-children.pdf; Memorandum from John Morton, Director for U.S. Immigration and Customs Enforcement, "Exercising Prosecutorial Discretion Consistent with the Civil Immigration Enforcement Priorities of the Agency for the Apprehension, Detention, and Removal of Aliens" (June 7, 2011), 5, http://www.ice.gov/doclib/secure-communities/pdf/prosecutorial-discretion-memo.pdf.

40 Morton, *supra* note 39.

41 Napolitano, *supra* note 39.

42 *In re Devison-Charles*, 22 I&N Dec. 1362, 1365 (BIA 2000) (*en banc*).

43 *Id.*

44 INA § 101(a)(27)(J); 8 U.S.C. § 1101(a)(27)(J) (2013).

45 INA § 101(a)(15)(U); 8 U.S.C. § 1101(a)(15)(U) (2013).

46 Napolitano, *supra* note 39.

47 Shaylyn Fluharty represented Raul and, due to her zealous advocacy, Raul was finally granted Special Immigrant Juvenile status.

48 *See Plyler v. Doe*, 457 U.S. 202, 219 (1982).

16

Crossover Youth

Youth Should Benefit When the State Is the Parent

ROBIN ROSENBERG AND CHRISTINA L. SPUDEAS

States must parent diligently when children are in their care. Good parents deal with behavior as behavior, not crime; they support their children if they find themselves in court; and they provide their children good legal counsel. The cost of failing to parent well is a diminished future for the child and three times the cash outlay for the state.[1] We owe it to our children to do better.

When the state exercises *parens patriae* by removing children from their families, it implicitly promises to parent better. That means addressing the consequences of abuse and neglect by providing everything children need to live safer, healthier, happier, and more productive lives. Causing your children to be arrested and failing to support them after arrest is not good parenting, but it is common practice. This chapter is intended to briefly address what states can do to ensure that they and their designated caregivers—foster parents, group-home staff, and relatives—act responsibly to minimize juvenile justice involvement and to improve outcomes for children.[2] A re-visioned juvenile justice system would work with the child welfare system to reduce crossover youth involvement and to provide supports to ensure the potential for success and well-being for crossover youth who nevertheless become involved in the juvenile justice system. Crossover youth are children or adolescents who have been abused or neglected and have come into state care in the dependency system and who have also been "arrested" (taken into state custody) for crimes committed as juveniles—often as a result of the trauma they have experienced.

States Can Reduce the Number of Children Who Unnecessarily Cross Over

One critical strategy is simply to prevent crossover by providing solutions and assistance for caregivers who face difficult parenting issues, as opposed to triggering juvenile justice system involvement. When caregivers call the police to manage difficult behaviors such as fighting and stealing,[3] they push children into the juvenile system. Caseworkers and court-appointed special advocates or guardians *ad litem* (CASAs/GALs) sometimes support juvenile justice involvement because they think it will benefit youth either by teaching them a lesson or by keeping them off the street. Some caseworkers support detention or commitment because it relieves the caseworker of the obligation to find the child a placement or services. Schools make referrals when they are unaware of a child's trauma history or are unprepared to deal with the behavior of traumatized students.

The first strategy to reduce the number of crossover children is to educate all child welfare staff, caregivers, and volunteers on the consequences of arrest, plea, and trial. Many operate under the false impression that "what happens in juvie stays in juvie." When trained, child welfare personnel are shocked to learn that juvenile arrests are public record and that adjudication can limit the future ability to obtain education, housing, and employment or to enter the military.[4]

The second strategy is to provide reasonable alternatives to calling the police. Some communities develop local resources to "call for help, just not 911." With a third of delinquency cases originating from the child's residential placement,[5] caregivers must have access to immediate assistance from the child welfare system to help them deal with youth who are out of control, destructive, or dangerous. Caregivers need the tools to manage difficult behavior without involving the police. Those who are incapable of doing so should not be permitted (or paid) to continue to care for children.

Providing trauma-informed training to schools and child-care and after-school providers is the third strategy. By definition, children come into state care because something bad has happened; trauma must, therefore, be presumed. All who work with children must have a common understanding of how trauma affects physical and emotional development and behavior.[6] Trauma-informed service providers are far less likely to call the police if they understand what prompted the behavior and have the tools to help the child deal with the trauma.

Showing Up Is Half the Battle

Although the number of children who cross over can be reduced, it will never be eliminated. States must, therefore, provide the equivalent of strong, comprehensive parental support for the children under their care who have juvenile justice involvement. Crossover youth, who seldom have a supportive adult accompany them to court, are more likely to be detained[7] and are less likely to receive community sanctions[8] than are their peers. Courts perceive unaccompanied children as less stable and without sufficient supports to be successful in the community.[9] All crossover children deserve to have the assistance of a supportive adult to help them achieve the best outcomes.

The first obstacle to ensuring supportive adult participation is a lack of communication. Without a concerted effort by the child welfare and juvenile justice systems, neither system may know that the child is involved with the other.[10] Systems have to compare notes on a daily basis to ensure that crossover children are immediately identified. Everyone involved in a child welfare case needs to be advised when the child is arrested or charges are initiated. They must also be notified of subsequent court dates and related requirements.

Second, caregivers, child welfare staff, and volunteers need to know that they are supposed to attend and, when appropriate, participate in delinquency proceedings. Showing up prepared and ready to engage in support of the child must be part of the job description for all caregivers and CASA/GAL volunteers.[11]

Third, the child welfare and juvenile justice systems must overcome confidentiality concerns and share pertinent information on a child's history, family background, health and mental health concerns, and the status of services provision.[12] Cooperation and information sharing is critical for high-quality delinquency defense, as well as to ensure that both systems obtain an accurate picture of the child's needs and to coordinate services.[13]

Finally, the state must ensure that children have high-quality legal counsel in their child welfare case to ensure best outcomes in the juvenile delinquency case.[14] This is a challenge in states such as Florida where children are not routinely appointed legal counsel for the child welfare proceeding. But even in Florida, there are successful models for serving crossover children. The public defender for Pinellas and Pasco Counties represents crossover children in both their child welfare and delinquency/criminal proceedings.[15] In some counties, children's dependency lawyers employed by legal aid programs work closely with the public defender. In Florida's Hillsborough County, the courts appoint a child's civil counsel (pro bono volunteer) for unaccompanied children in delinquency proceedings, to ascertain unmet needs and to assist in obtaining services. In Miami-Dade County, Florida's Children First employs an attorney, housed at the public defender's office, to provide civil representation to crossover children.

Conclusion

Under a re-visioned juvenile justice system, crossover from dependency to delinquency would be infrequent because the challenges of youth coming into state care would be recognized and services provided. For the few kids who did crossover, the system would be responsive to their context and needs. And overall, the state would train its parental stand-ins to deal with children's trauma and to maximize their success.

NOTES

1 Dennis P. Culhane, Stephen Metraux, Manuel Moreno, Halil Toros, and Max Stevens, *Young Adult Outcomes of Youth Exiting Dependent or Delinquent Care in Los Angeles County* (Conrad N. Hilton Foundation, 2011), http://www.hiltonfoundation.org/images/stories/PriorityAreas/FosterYouth/Downloads/Hilton_Foundation_Report_Final.pdf.

2 The role of poverty, race, and public policy in causing the unnecessary removal of children deserves critical examination but is beyond the scope of this chapter. See Wendy Bach, chap. 14 in this volume, on reframing support for poor families.

3 Dylan Conger and Timothy Ross, *Reducing the Foster Care Bias in Juvenile Detention Decisions: The Impact of Project Confirm* (Vera Institute of Justice, June 2001), http://www.vera.org/pubs/reducing-foster-care-bias-juvenile-detention-decisions-impact-project-confirm.

4 Sue Burrell, chap. 19 in this volume.

5 Denise Herz and Joseph P. Ryan, *Building Multisystem Approaches in Child Welfare and Juvenile Justice* (Center for Juvenile Justice Reform, 2008), http://cjjr.georgetown.edu/pdfs/wingspreadpart3.pdf; Michelle L. Saeteurn and Janay R. Swain, "Exploring Characteristics and Outcomes of 241.1 Youth in Alameda County" (M.S.W. thesis, California State University, Sacramento, 2009), http://csus-dspace.calstate.edu/bitstream/handle/10211.9/661/SAETEURN,%20MICHELLE%20L._SUMMER_2009.pdf?sequence=3.

6 Nicole Taylor and Christine B. Siegfried, *Helping Children in the Child Welfare System Heal from Trauma: A Systems Integration Approach* (National Child Traumatic Stress Network, 2005), http://www.nctsn.org/nctsn_assets/pdfs/promising_practices/A_Systems_Integration_Approach.pdf.

7 Conger and Ross, *supra* note 3.

8 Joseph P. Ryan, Denise Herz, Pedro M. Hernandez, and Jane Marie Marshall, "Maltreatment and Delinquency: Investigating Child Welfare Bias in Juvenile Justice Processing," *Children and Youth Services Review* 29, no. 8 (2007): 1035–1050.

9 Leslee Morris, "Youth in Foster Care Who Commit Delinquent Acts: Study Findings and Recommendations," *The Link* (Child Welfare League of America) 3, no. 3 (2004): 1, 4, 8, http://www.cwla.org/programs/juvenilejustice/thelink-2004summerfall.pdf.

10 John A. Tuell, "Project Confirm of New York City: Bridging the Gap between Child Welfare and Juvenile Justice," *The Link* (Child Welfare League of America) 1, no. 4 (2001), http://www.cwla.org/programs/juvenilejustice/thelink2001fall.htm.

11 Howard Davidson, "ABA Calls for Reform in Child Welfare/Delinquency 'Crossover' Cases," *Child Law Practice* 27, no. 2 (2008): 31.

12 *Id.*

13 Denise C. Herz, Joseph P. Ryan, and Shay Bilchik, "Challenges Facing Crossover Youth: An Examination of Juvenile Justice Decision Making and Recidivism," *Family Court Review* 48, no. 2 (2010): 305–321.

14 *Id.*

15 Public Defender Sixth Judicial Circuit, "Crossover for Children," http://www.wearethehope.org/child_crossover.htm (accessed June 12, 2013).

17

Breaking the School-to-Prison Pipeline

New Models for School Discipline and Community Accountable Schools

KAITLIN BANNER

Any discussion reimagining our juvenile justice system must also reimagine our schools. Over the past decade, community-based organizations of parents and students, along with civil rights groups such as the Advancement Project,[1] have documented the school-to-prison pipeline—the devastating trend of funneling students out of the classroom and into the juvenile and criminal justice systems.[2] Children—and particularly children of color, children with disabilities, and children who identify as lesbian, gay, bisexual, transgender, or queer (LGBTQ)—are disproportionately affected by the school-to-prison pipeline. This chapter first outlines how the pipeline operates and the effects of harsh disciplinary practices on young people. Then, the chapter highlights communities that have fought back against the school-to-prison pipeline and discusses the policies and practices that dismantle the school-to-prison pipeline.

The Pipeline

Millions of students throughout the country routinely face excessive, overly punitive school discipline. This includes out-of-school suspension, expulsion, arrests, and referrals to law enforcement agencies—collectively, "exclusionary discipline." According to the most recent data from the U.S. Department of Education's Office for Civil Rights (OCR), each year over three million students are suspended and over 100,000 students are expelled.[3] This rate has nearly doubled in the past 30 years.[4] Increasingly, school disciplinary matters are handled by law enforcement, and today, students are more likely than in past years to be arrested for minor in-school offenses.[5] The use of law enforcement in schools in Florida, for example, resulted in 16,377 referrals of students directly to the juvenile justice system during the 2010–2011 school year—an average of 45 students per day.[6] Statewide, two-thirds of the school-based referrals were for misdemeanors.[7] The "crimes" that resulted in arrest included disruption of a school function, disorderly conduct, and minor schoolyard fights.[8] In Los Angeles between 2004 and 2009, over 84,000 tickets and arrests were issued by the Los Angeles Police Department and the Los Angeles School Police Department (LASPD), more than half of which were for truancy and other school incidents such as disturbing the peace, vandalism, and petty theft.[9]

School-based law enforcement is widely used to respond to typical childhood behavior that does not threaten the safety of others. For example, in May 2012, an honors student in Houston, Texas, was forced to spend a night in jail when she missed class to go to work to support her family.[10] In April 2012, a kindergartener from Milledgeville, Georgia, was handcuffed and arrested for throwing a tantrum.[11] In 2007, a 13-year-old from New York was handcuffed and removed from school for writing the word "okay" on her school desk. In 2008, a Chicago middle school student was arrested for walking past a fight that broke out after school. The student recognized that the arrest changed her entire school experience. "Even though I had good grades, my teachers treated me differently after that. They saw me as someone who got into fights and got arrested. They didn't want to let me graduate, eat lunch with my class, or go on our class trip even though I hadn't done anything. It showed me that the world wasn't fair."[12]

Our broken juvenile justice system is seeping into schools and affecting students' experiences in profoundly negative ways. A student described what happened in his inner-city school:

> There was an argument occurring between two students in the hallway. The students were yelling at each other and posturing—although they did not engage in physical contact. The school administration got on the public announcement system and ordered the school into lockdown mode. Classroom doors were locked, and students were not permitted to leave

their classrooms or be in the hallways. Armed police officers and security guards removed the two arguing students from the hallways.[13]

While I was attending a meeting at a school, the assistant principal's walkie-talkie buzzed. The bell to switch classes was about to ring. The security guard spoke to other administrators at the school: "prepare for the population to move." All of the unoccupied administrators, security guards, and police officers took up posts in doorways, and in the middle of the hallways, students moved from classroom to classroom. In D.C., and in many other urban centers, if you visit any schools around the time that classes start, you will see long lines of young men and women—largely Black and Latino—standing outside their schools, apparently late. These students are waiting in line to go through metal detectors and other screening processes. Many are turned away at the door for not being in school uniform, for getting through the line too late for first period, or for failing to carry their student identification.

These stories are disturbingly reminiscent of how detention facilities might handle fights in prison yards or of the language that prison administrators might use to describe the people in their care. This criminalization of young people has led to dramatically larger security and school police forces; increased use of metal detectors, surveillance cameras, pat-downs, drug-sniffing dogs, and Tasers; and a significant jump in the number of school-based arrests and citations, suspensions, and expulsions.[14] These are just small examples of a broader problem—we are increasingly treating students as preprisoners and preparing them for prison by acclimating them to the language, experiences, and atmosphere of institutions.

When students are excluded from school, they both miss out on valuable education time and receive a message that they are not wanted in school. In *Goss v. Lopez*, the U.S. Supreme Court stated, "education is perhaps the most important function of state and local governments, . . . and the total exclusion from the educational process . . . is a serious event in the life of the suspended child."[15] The Court determined that students carry both a property and a liberty interest in their education and their education reputation.[16] In *Plyler v. Doe*, the Court again discussed the fundamental importance of education and recognized that barring students from public education has effects that reverberate throughout society.[17] "Education has a fundamental role in maintaining the fabric of our society. We cannot ignore the significant social costs borne by our Nation when select groups are denied the means to absorb the values and skills upon which our social order rests."[18]

In 2013, a significant body of research from the legal, social science, education, and psychology fields confirmed the Supreme Court's findings about the harmful effects of school exclusion.[19] The American Psychological Association (APA) Zero Tolerance Task Force, after evaluating school disciplinary policies for ten years, found that zero-tolerance policies do not improve school safety, that suspensions and expulsions are associated with a higher risk of school dropout, and that the use of school suspensions and expulsions is associated with lower school-wide academic achievement.[20] Excluded students are more likely to become involved with the juvenile or adult criminal systems.[21] A multiyear, longitudinal study in Texas found that young people who were suspended from school were two times more likely to drop out of school and three times more likely to end up in the criminal justice system.[22] In Florida, ninth graders who were suspended only once more than doubled their chances of not graduating from high school.[23]

The school-to-prison pipeline—and all of the harmful effects associated with it—disproportionately affects students of color, students with disabilities, and students who identify as LGBTQ. Nationally, Black students and students with disabilities are more likely to be suspended, expelled, arrested, and referred to law enforcement for in-school behavior.[24] The rate of disproportionality is growing too: the racial gap for suspensions between Black students and White students has grown from fewer than three percentage points to more than ten.[25] From 2003 to 2007, out-of-school suspensions for Black students increased by 8% and for Latino students by 14%, while out-of-school suspensions for White students decreased by 3%.[26] The disparity increase for expulsions for Black students is even more shocking. Between 2003 and 2007, expulsions of Black student increased 33%, compared with a 6% increase for Latino students and a 2% decrease for White students.[27] In the 2011–2012 school year, Black students were three times more likely to experience exclusionary discipline: they were 16% of the population but 32%–42% of the students suspended and expelled.[28]

Community-Based Change

Communities have been at the forefront of significant changes to create positive school climates that engage students, are culturally responsive, and teach students true skills for resolving conflict. Communities have pushed districts to dismantle the school-to-prison pipeline and to create a positive school environment in a number of ways. First, they have advocated for policies that limit the use of out-of-school suspensions and referrals to law enforcement. A key element in a positive school environment is a school discipline system that uses a nonpunitive approach focused on preventing misbehavior and providing supportive and effective interventions when misbehavior occurs. For example, through the advocacy and leadership of student- and community-led groups such as Padres y Jóvenes Unidos in Denver,[29] Youth United for Change in Philadelphia,[30] and Citizen Action of New York and Alliance for Quality Education in Buffalo,[31] school districts have started to use commonsense discipline. Schools use a graduated approach to assigning consequences; place caps on the duration of suspensions, particularly for low-level infractions; limit suspensions for conduct that occurs away from school; and use in-school instead of out-of-school suspension. For example, Buffalo Public Schools divides inappropriate behaviors into four levels and ensures that many low-level offenses can never result in out-of-school suspension.[32]

These types of reform limit the number of students removed from the classroom in two significant ways. First, they encourage teachers and administrators to respond to behaviors such as talking out of turn or being in the hallways without permission by simply correcting students' behaviors, calling parents, or implementing other school-based intervention and consequences. Because suspension is not an option, teachers and administrators are prohibited from using suspension and expulsion for minor and typical youth behaviors. Second, these reforms offer solutions that hold young people accountable for more serious behaviors while teaching them how to better manage conflict and ensuring that they continue to be engaged in school. Exclusionary discipline is reserved for extreme cases in which there is a safety concern, not routinized discipline for everyday occurrences.

Communities also have pushed for reforms that make their schools look and feel less like prisons and more like welcoming community centers of learning. In Philadelphia, Youth United for Change helped ensure that the dress code allowed for expressions of individuality and explicitly provided that gender-nonconforming students would not be punished for their choices in clothes.[33] In New York City, some communities demanded that schools remove metal detectors from their buildings and, as a result, have seen safer and more trusting cultures in those schools.[34]

The relationship between schools and police has also been a target of local reforms. A long-term goal for schools, moreover, should be the eventual removal of a routinized police presence in schools.[35] School police officers often contribute to the school-to-prison pipeline by arresting students for behavior that could, and should, be handled in schools.[36] In Denver, the community, the school district, and the police department signed an agreement that defines the role of police in schools; the agreement ensures that police are not acting as disciplinarians, not interfering with students' right to their education, and not escalating school-based incidents into juvenile or criminal charges.[37] School districts and communities can work with the police to define law enforcement's mission in the school and what steps they should and should not take to fulfill that particular mission.

Open communication has also been critical to reform, including the collection, analysis, and dissemination of detailed data about the school-to-prison pipeline and alternatives that work. Data-driven reform is critical to understanding the exact manifestation of the pipeline in individual communities. Data help all stakeholders understand how students come into contact with exclusionary discipline and the juvenile justice system and guide targeted reforms. Data are also a key part of eliminating disparities in the remaining use of exclusionary discipline.

The hallmark of these changes, and others like them, has been that community is at the center. Young people, parents, and community members who live, work, and learn at these schools are responsible for driving the type of policy change, for advocating for that policy change, and for holding the decision makers, school officials, and legislators responsible for implementing those changes with fidelity.

Reforming how schools treat students can increase successful outcomes for young people. A reimagined school system that engages students, that prevents and responds appropriately to student misbehavior, and that is accountable to the communities it serves can create an affirmative school climate to facilitate the growth of youth to become successful adults. Schools, which can break the school-to-prison pipeline and stem the flow of young people into the system, are a critical component of creating a new and just juvenile justice system.

NOTES

1   Advancement Project, www.advancementproject.org.
2   *See, e.g.*, Advancement Project, Alliance for Educational Justice, and Gay-Straight Alliance Network, *Two Wrongs Don't Make a Right: Why Zero Tolerance Is Not the Solution to Bullying* (June 2012), http://b.3cdn.net/ advancement/73b640051a1066d43d_yzm6rkffb.pdf; Robin L. Dahlberg, *Arrested Futures: The Criminalization of School Discipline in Massachusetts' Three Largest School Districts* (ACLU and Citizens for Juvenile Justice, Spring 2012), http://www. aclu.org/files/assets/maarrest_reportweb.pdf; ACLU of Florida, Advancement Project, and Florida State Conference of the NAACP, *Still Haven't Shut Off the School-to-Prison Pipeline: Evaluating the Impact of Florida's New Zero-Tolerance Law* (March 2011), 6–8, http://b.3cdn.net/advancement/be89ef01bcb350c7fc_ z5m6btbgo.pdf; Advancement Project, *Test, Punish, and Push Out: How "Zero Tolerance" and High-Stakes Testing Funnel Youth into the School-to-Prison Pipeline* (January 2010), 9–12, http://b.3cdn.net/advancement/d05cb2181a4545db07_r2im-6caqe.pdf; American Civil Liberties Union and ALCU of Connecticut, *Hard Lessons: School Resource Officers and School-Based Arrests in Three Connecticut Towns* (November 2008), http://www.aclu.org/files/pdfs/racialjustice/hardles-sons_november2008.pdf; ACLU and NYCLU, *Criminalizing the Classroom: The Over-policing of New York City Schools* (March 2007), http://www.nyclu.org/pdfs/ criminalizing_the_classroom_report.pdf; Florida State Conference of the NAACP, Advancement Project, and NAACP Legal Defense and Educational Fund, Inc., *Arresting Development: Addressing the School Discipline Crisis in Florida* (Spring 2006), http://b.3cdn.net/advancement/e36d17097615e7c612_bbm6vubow.pdf; Advancement Project, *Education on Lockdown: The Schoolhouse to Jailhouse Track* (March 2005), http://b.3cdn.net/advancement/5351180e24cb166d02_mlbrqgxlh. pdf; Advancement Project, *Derailed! The Schoolhouse to Jailhouse Track* (May 2003), http://b.3cdn.net/advancement/c509d077028b4d0544_mlbrq3seg.pdf; Advancement Project and the Civil Rights Project, Harvard University, *Opportunities Suspended: The Devastating Consequences of Zero Tolerance School Discipline* (July 2002), 13, http://b.3cdn.net/advancement/8d91c72205a1b9d955_ ujm6bhguv.pdf.
3   Department of Education, Office for Civil Rights, Civil Rights Data Collection, http://ocrdata.ed.gov/.
4   *Id.*

5 Federal Advisory Committee on Juvenile Justice, *Annual Report 2010* (November 2010), 9, http://www.facjj.org/annualreports/00-FACJJ%20Annual%20Report-FINAL%20508.pdf. See also Advancement Project, Alliance for Educational Justice, Dignity in Schools Campaign, and NAACP Legal Defense and Educational Fund, Inc., *Police in Schools Are Not the Answer to the Newtown Shooting* (January 2013), http://safequalityschools.org/resources/entry/police-in-schools-are-not-the-answer-to-the-newtown-shooting.

6 Florida Department of Juvenile Justice, *Delinquency in Florida's Schools: A Seven-Year Study* (November 2011), 3, http://www.djj.state.fl.us/docs/research2/2010-11-delinquency-in-schools-analysis.pdf?sfvrsn=0.

7 *Id.* at 8–9.

8 ACLU of Florida et al., *supra* note 2, at 6–8.

9 Data is compiled from records requests submitted to the LAPD and LASPD and is on file with Community Rights Campaign, http://www.thestrategycenter.org/project/community-rights-campaign.

10 Timothy Stenovec, "Diane Tran, Honor Student at Texas High School, Jailed for Missing School," Huffington Post, May 27, 2012, http://www.huffingtonpost.com/2012/05/27/diane-tran-honors-student-jailed-texas-high-school-truancy_n_1549160.html.

11 "Ga. Police Handcuff, Arrest Kindergartner for Tantrum," CBS News Online, April 17, 2012, http://www.cbsnews.com/8301-201_162-57415181/.

12 Voices of Youth in Chicago Education (VOYCE), *The Time for Justice Is Always Now: VOYCE Annual Report 2011–2012* (2012), 5, http://library.constantcontact.com/download/get/file/1104628315334-75/VOYCE+2012+report2+(1)+(1).pdf.

13 Personal communication with author, 2014.

14 *See, e.g.,* Advancement Project, *Derailed!, supra* note 2.

15 *Goss v. Lopez,* 419 U.S. 565, 576 (1975).

16 *See id.*

17 *Plyler v. Doe,* 456 U.S. 202, 221 (1982).

18 *Id.*

19 *See, generally,* Robert Balfanz, Vaughan Byrnes, and Joanna Fox, "Sent Home and Put Off-Track: The Antecedents, Disproportionalities, and Consequences of Being Suspended in the Ninth Grade" (paper prepared for the "Closing the School Discipline Gap: Research to Practice" national conference in Washington, D.C., January 10, 2013) (finding that students being suspended even one time in ninth grade *doubles* their chance dropping out of school); Justice Center—The Council of State Governments and Public Policy Research Institute, *Breaking Schools' Rules: A Statewide Study of How School Discipline Relates to Students' Success and Juvenile Justice Involvement* (July 2011), http://csgjusticecenter.org/wp-content/uploads/2012/08/Breaking_Schools_Rules_Report_Final.pdf; American Psychological Association Zero Tolerance Task Force, "Are Zero Tolerance Policies Effective in the Schools? An Evidentiary Review and Recommendations," *American Psychologist* 63 (December 2008): 852–856.

20 *See* American Psychological Association Zero Tolerance Task Force, *supra* note 19, at 852–856.

21 *See id.*

22 Justice Center—The Council of State Governments and Public Policy Research Institute, *supra* note 19.

23 Balfanz, Byrnes, and Fox, *supra* note 19.

24 U.S. Department of Education Office for Civil Rights, *Civil Rights Data Collection: Data Snapshot: School Discipline,* Issue Brief 1 (March 2014), http://www2.ed.gov/ about/offices/list/ocr/docs/crdc-discipline-snapshot.pdf (Black students are 16% of student enrollment but 27% of students arrested and 31% of students referred to law enforcement; students with disabilities are 12% of student enrollment but 25% of students arrested and referred to law enforcement).

25 Daniel Losen and Jonathan Gillespie, *Opportunities Suspended: The Disparate Impact of Disciplinary Exclusion from School* (Center for Civil Rights Remedies, Civil Rights Project, August 2012), 37, http://civilrightsproject.ucla.edu/resources/ projects/center-for-civil-rights-remedies/school-to-prison-folder/federal-reports/ upcoming-ccrr-research/losen-gillespie-opportunity-suspended-2012.pdf.

26 Department of Education, *supra* note 3.

27 *Id.*

28 U.S. Department of Education Office for Civil Rights, *supra* note 24.

29 With roots in the struggle for educational justice, Padres Unidos (http://www. padresunidos.org) has evolved into a multi-issue organization led by people of color who work for educational excellence, racial justice for youth, immigrant rights, and quality health care for all. Jóvenes Unidos, the youth initiative of Padres Unidos, emerged as young people became active in reforming their schools, ending the school-to-jail track, and organizing for immigrant student rights. Both Padres and Jóvenes Unidos build power to challenge the root cause of discrimination, racism, and inequity by exposing the economic, social, and institutional basis for injustice as well as developing effective strategies to realize meaningful change.

30 Youth United for Change (http://www.youthunitedforchange.org) is a youth-led, democratic organization made up of youth of color and working-class communi- ties, with the "people" and political power to hold school officials and government accountable for meeting the educational needs of Philadelphia public school students.

31 Citizen Action of New York (http://citizenactionny.org/) is a grassroots member- ship organization taking on big issues that are at the center of transforming American society. The Alliance for Quality Education (http://www.aqeny.org/) is a coalition mobilizing communities across the state to keep New York true to its promise of ensuring a high-quality public education to all students regardless of zip code.

32 *See, e.g.,* Buffalo Public Schools, *Developing Safe and Supportive Schools: Buffalo Public Schools Standards for Community-Wide Conduct and Intervention Supports*

2013–2014 (July 2013), http://www.buffaloschools.org/StudentServices. cfm?subpage=57596.

33 Advancement Project, "Youth Leaders Score Victory for Common Sense Discipline," August 18, 2012, http://www.advancementproject.org/news/entry/ youth-leaders-score-victory-for-common-sense-disciple-in-philadelphia.

34 New York Civil Liberties Union, *Safety with Dignity: Alternatives to the Over-policing of Schools* (July 2009), http://www.nyclu.org/content/ safety-with-dignity-alternatives-over-policing-of-schools-2009.

35 Advancement Project et al., *supra* note 5 (discussing how police presence in schools often results in an increased referral rate to the juvenile justice system, a hostile environment with little trust between students and the police, and the redirection of limited police resources to handle school behaviors).

36 *Id.*

37 Advancement Project, "Intergovernmental Agreement between Denver Public Schools and Denver Police Department" (February 2013), http://safequali-tyschools.org/resources/entry/Padres-IGA.

18

No More Closed Doors

Ending the Educational Exclusion of Formerly
Incarcerated Youth

DAVID DOMENICI AND RENAGH O'LEARY

"They don't want me. They think I'm a criminal." That is how Dante
explains why he was not allowed to attend his local high school after
being released from juvenile custody in 2012, at age 17. Dante had spent
15 months inside D.C.'s juvenile correctional facility, where he attended
the Maya Angelou Academy.[1] When Dante was released, he had a 2.9
grade point average and enough credits to qualify as a high school
senior. He looked forward to spending his final year of high school in a
community school where he could go out for the basketball team.

Dante's family had moved out of D.C. while he was incarcerated, so
he enrolled at the local high school in the city where his family lived. But
when school administrators learned that Dante had been incarcerated,
they told him that he was no longer welcome there. Instead, he had to
attend the district's alternative school. The alternative school ran only
part-time, in the evening. If he wanted to attend school during the day,
Dante realized, he would have to enroll in an adult education/general
education diploma (GED) preparation program.

Dante did not want to go to night school, and he did not want a GED.
He wanted a high school diploma from a "regular" school. Frustrated
with his limited options, Dante decided to take a break from school and
got a job at a local department store. After ten months of successful
employment, he tried for a second time to enroll in his neighborhood
high school, only to be told that because he was now over 18, he had no
right to attend.

Dante's experience is all too common. Formerly incarcerated youth
are routinely denied admission to mainstream high schools and forced

into mandatory alternative schools that are more focused on warehousing students than educating them.

In this chapter, we describe the crisis of educational exclusion affecting recently released youth. We describe the limited opportunities in mandatory alternative schools and explain how educational exclusion is connected to the problem of inadequate schools inside secure juvenile facilities. We then identify the barriers to educational reentry and propose changes to laws, policies, and practices that would help guarantee incarcerated youth access to mainstream community schools after their release.

Many of our insights are based on candid conversations with stakeholders across the country. David Domenici, in his role as executive director of the Center for Educational Excellence in Alternative Settings, works closely with juvenile justice agency leaders and facility staff. We summarize trends and highlight observations he has made in the course of his work. We also present findings from David's visits to more than 40 youth correctional facilities in 18 states between January 2012 and October 2013.

Mandatory Alternative Schools

Educational exclusion occurs when schools prevent formerly incarcerated youth from enrolling in mainstream schools after release. Though exact numbers are hard to come by, the available information strongly suggests that the problem of educational exclusion is widespread. In 2002, 38 percent of school districts reported that they consider *any* involvement with the juvenile justice system—even a mere arrest—to be sufficient cause for an automatic transfer to an alternative school.[2] Incarcerated youth interviewed by David routinely report that they have to go to alternative schools when they are released. Similarly, leaders from state juvenile justice agencies repeatedly comment on how hard it is to get community schools to take students back. At a recent gathering of state juvenile justice agency leaders, many of them agreed that the only students mainstream schools wanted back were football or basketball players.

Alternative schools vary widely in quality, purpose, and culture. When alternative schools first emerged in the 1960s, alternatives of choice were the dominant model. Alternatives of choice are designed to meet the needs of struggling or disconnected students who are not well served by a district's large mainstream high schools. Students enroll voluntarily and see the alternative school as an opportunity, not a punishment. Alternatives of choice often have small class sizes, creative instructional methods, innovative curricula, and flexible hours.[3]

Increasingly, however, alternative schools with a disciplinary orientation have replaced alternatives of choice.[4] Most recently released youth facing educational exclusion do not go to an alternative of choice. Rather, they are forced into what we call mandatory alternative schools.

Mandatory alternative schools function as a district dumping ground where mainstream schools can get rid of difficult or disruptive students. Mandatory alternative schools are frequently used for students who have been suspended or expelled[5] and typically employ harsh, punitive discipline policies.[6]

The educational opportunities at mandatory alternative schools are profoundly limited. The schools often lack basic educational resources, such as textbooks or computers.[7] In some states, students cannot earn a regular high school diploma and instead are limited to a GED certificate, a certificate of attendance, or a modified diploma.[8] For students with identified special education needs, transfer to a mandatory alternative school can be particularly damaging. In a survey of 29 states, five reported that when students with disabilities enroll in alternative schools, it is "likely or often likely" that students' special education services will be terminated or suspended. Three states reported that their alternative schools "likely or often likely" have no knowledge at all of whether their students had a special education diagnosis at their previous school.[9]

Mandatory alternative schools exist in almost every state. In Texas, however, the problems with mandatory alternative schools are particularly severe. Texas law requires some districts to create two types of alternative schools: disciplinary alternative education programs (DAEPs) and juvenile justice alternative education programs (JJAEPs).[10] These schools are designed for court-involved youth or students facing school discipline sanctions.

DAEP and JJAEP schools are more focused on containing and controlling students than on educating them, as the ratio of educational to security staff at some schools makes clear. The Harris County (Houston)

JJAEP has more security staff than full-time teachers and employs a full-time deputy sheriff, though the school serves fewer than 100 students.

The quality of the education offered at these schools is notoriously low. DAEPs are only required to offer four "core" classes: English, math, science, and history,[11] and JJAEPs are only required to have one certified teacher on site.[12] A visit to a Houston-area DAEP offered a glimpse into what passes for education for students attending a DAEP. Science class consisted of students mindlessly copying notes out of old textbooks. Students watched *Happy Feet* in life skills class and lined up to be patted down by security guards in between classes. Teachers never gave homework, the principal said, because students are not allowed to bring textbooks home with them. Books, pens, and pencils are considered contraband that students cannot bring with them to school.

Charles Rotramel has spent more than 25 years working with court-involved youth in Houston. He says that the problem of educational exclusion is endemic in the 23 school districts serving the Houston metropolitan area. Teens coming back home to Houston from a secure juvenile facility have to attend a mandatory alternative school, Rotramel said.

Rotramel has seen how placement into mandatory alternative schools thwarts students' educational and personal growth. "If the alternative schools were high quality and focused on academic support and offering youth a legitimate chance to get on track before returning to a mainstream high school, this system might work," he insisted when he spoke to us. "But instead, the alternative schools end up serving as a part of an ongoing cycle where kids go back and forth from alternative schools to the detention centers."

"Kids come back home, get told they have to go to a DAEP alternative school, and run into problems there. These schools all have these level systems and point systems that just bury the kids. They never get out and never end up getting a chance to go to a good school; they are surrounded by adults who don't care and other kids with a lot of problems—and things just get worse," Rotramel explained to us. "I know one teenager who got sent to an alternative school in third grade and has spent all of his time growing up in either an alternative school or a juvenile jail. He can barely read, is years behind, and has never been in a healthy, high-functioning school where they might have the will and re-sources to help him. It's a tragedy. And we see it all the time down here."

Like mandatory alternative schools, adult education programs are another common destination for recently released students leaving secure juvenile custody. Adult education programs are designed to be a pathway to a diploma or GED for adults who never graduated from high school. Increasingly, however, adult education programs are being used for high-school-aged youth.[13] In Connecticut, for example, nearly one-third of the 30,000 students attending adult education programs are high school age.[14] Referrals of court-involved high school students are one cause of the increase in youth enrollment.[15] Adult education programs are designed for mature learners who are highly self-motivated. High-school-aged students—especially those with significant academic deficits and complicated emotional, behavioral, and special education needs—struggle to adapt to the pace and independence of adult education programs.[16]

Incarcerated youth disproportionately come from communities of concentrated disadvantage with struggling neighborhood schools. Even a low-performing mainstream high school, however, has significant advantages over mandatory alternative schools. Mainstream high schools offer students a broader curriculum and the chance to participate in sports and other extracurricular activities. Enrolling in a mainstream high school allows court-involved youth to avoid the stigma of attending a mandatory alternative school and to build relationships with students who have not had disciplinary problems, limiting what some researchers have called the "peer contagion" effects of clustering youth with disciplinary issues together.[17]

Mainstream high schools are not the right choice for all students recently released from juvenile custody. Some students prefer alternative schools or adult education programs where they can work independently, at their own pace, and on a more flexible schedule. Particularly where high-quality alternatives are available, these schools may be the right choice to meet the unique needs of recently released young people. But every student released from custody deserves the opportunity to *choose* whether to bypass a mainstream high school in favor of an alternative school or adult education program.

Schools inside Juvenile Correctional Facilities

The problem of educational exclusion after release is inseparable from the problem of abysmally bad schools inside juvenile facilities. When time in secure custody only exacerbates students' preexisting academic deficits, it becomes even less likely that community schools will allow formerly incarcerated students to enroll after release.

Most youth incarcerated in juvenile facilities lag years behind their classmates in reading ability and credit accumulation. Additionally, around one-third of these juveniles have identified special education needs—more than double the rate in the general population.[18] Yet only 65 percent of residential juvenile justice facilities provided educational services to all of their residents in 2006.[19]

During David's visits to facility schools, he identified three pervasive problems: poor instruction, low teacher quality, and inadequate prerelease planning.

1. Poor Instruction

David observed more than 150 classes in 35 different secure juvenile facilities between January and September 2012. In the vast majority of these schools, there was an appalling lack of instruction. Only 22 percent of the classes observed had any focus or objective. In the other 78 percent, students came to class and did (or did not do) some work, usually consisting of photocopied packets of materials. There was some indicia of "instruction" in only 55 percent of the classes visited. In the other 45 percent, teachers were merely present in the classroom, while students, most of whom are multiple grade levels behind academically, were left to simply slog through books and worksheets on their own.

In one facility, for example, students received ten laminated worksheets at the start of class. The worksheets had no relationship to the students' grade level, academic functioning, or special education needs. Students were told to complete any three exercises from the set during an hour-long period. Work was not graded or returned, but students were told they would receive credit for the day if they completed three assignments.

2. Low Teacher Quality

Teacher quality inside facility schools is notoriously low. Recruiting is difficult, given legitimate challenges posed by working in these facilities. Teachers are often a relatively small cohort of professionals inside an agency dominated by correctional and youth services personnel. Sites are often located in remote, rural locations. There is a perception that teaching in such facilities will be rife with violence and chaos. Teachers are often expected to teach multiple core subject areas. In some states, teachers are paid less than their peers in nearby school districts and may not have access to the training and support that competitor school districts offer.

These challenges are exacerbated when school leadership tolerates poor and inconsistent instruction. Fear of not finding better teachers to replace underperforming ones, ineffective evaluation tools, and simple inertia mean that facility school administrators struggle to remove low-performing teachers. Some states exempt facility school teachers from statewide teacher-accountability frameworks or from No Child Left Behind's requirement that public school teachers be "highly qualified."[20]

3. Inadequate Prerelease Transition Planning

Most youth who spend time in secure juvenile facilities do not remain incarcerated long enough to complete their high school education while they are in custody. Therefore, a critical function of schools inside juvenile facilities is to successfully prepare students for their transition back to a community school. But often, facilities neglect transition planning altogether or create only the most basic, boilerplate educational transition plans for students.

Juvenile justice agencies often fail to coordinate students' release dates with the schools where they are scheduled to return. Students might be released just days after a new semester has started at the community school, which makes it much harder to enroll, or just days before the facility school's semester ends, resulting in students losing credit for nearly completed school work inside the facility. Community schools almost universally require students to produce transcripts before enrolling, but juvenile facilities often fail to forward a student's transcript to the receiving school before the deadline—or at all. And even with a transcript, obtaining credit for work completed inside the juvenile facility can be difficult—because the facility school does not have clear authority to issue credits, because the facility school's courses do not align with community schools' curricula, or because community schools will not accept partial credits for students who are released midsemester.

Some states require probation officers or other facility staff to make a transition plan for students. In practice, however, transition plans are often bare bones and generic. One common complaint that David heard during his site visits is that even when probation officers are required to identify a community school that the student will attend after release, many officers will not actually call the school and coordinate the placement. As a result, when the student shows up and attempts to enroll, the school tells the student he or she cannot attend.

How Educational Exclusion Happens

Once youth are released from secure custody, they face a wide range of obstacles to enrolling in a mainstream high school. Some state laws provide schools and districts with clear legal authority to deny recently released youth admission and instead funnel them into mandatory alternative schools. In Idaho, for example, state law authorizes districts to deny enrollment to any student "who is incorrigible."[21] Additionally, state laws may authorize expulsion on the basis of the behavior for which a student was adjudicated delinquent and incarcerated, even if the student has already served his or her time. Texas, for example, authorizes expulsion on the basis of certain juvenile charges.[22] In states with these sorts of laws, principals or districts may move to preemptively expel a recently released student before the student has even been allowed to enroll in the school.

Most frequently, state law is simply silent about which schools recently released youth can attend. Recently released youth generally have no clear right to enter their local mainstream high school. Though districts must offer some high school option to students below a certain age, states rarely define how districts meet that mandate. Similarly, most districts do not place meaningful restrictions on a principal's prerogative to deny admission to a student whom they consider to be a troublemaker. Instead, districts create mandatory alternative schools where principals can refer students, with limited or nonexistent procedural protections and lax recording and accountability standards.

Even where schools do not deny admission outright, they may rely on a range of informal practices to push recently released students into mandatory alternative schools. School administrators may create the false impression that there is a legal obstacle to enrolling at a mainstream school.[23] Schools may "counsel out" students by highlighting the difficulties students are likely to face if they enroll, disparaging students' ability to achieve at the school, or suggesting that the alternative school is a better fit.[24] Some districts impose significant obstacles on students and families as a part of the reenrollment process. In one Connecticut school district, for example, any student returning from secure custody and the student's parents must attend a meeting with one specific district staff member before he or she is allowed to reenroll. The district point person, however, is semiretired and works only two afternoons a week.

Jim Pannell, director of education for the Idaho Department of Youth Corrections, emphasized when he spoke to us that individual principals have almost unchecked discretion to determine students' reentry options:

> In the Nampa School District [near Boise], there are a number of school principals who have made the decision to accept, or at least consider accepting, youth returning from the nearby correctional facility. But in other parts of Idaho, it's totally different. Almost uniformly, school principals reject our students, no matter the reason for their incarceration and regardless of whether we vouch for them and try to remind the principals that the youth have done their time and deserve a chance to go back to their high school. Not surprisingly, in many of these districts the "alternative" schools really aren't alternative schools at all—they're throwaway schools where the district sends kids they don't want.

Pannell lamented his lack of authority to change these unwritten practices: "I've tried to raise this issue with the school district superintendents and at the state office of education, to no avail. No one wants to limit the discretion of the high school principals on this."

Schools have powerful incentives to deny admission to recently re-leased students. It is difficult to overstate the academic and personal challenges facing many recently released youth. In addition to lagging behind their peers academically, incarcerated youth are disproportion-ately likely to have dropped out or been suspended, expelled, or placed in alternative schools.[25] Schools are under pressure to improve educa-tional outcomes (measured by test scores and graduation rates) and to reduce the use of exclusionary discipline. Excluding recently released students may seem like it serves both of these goals.

Consider Tony, who was arrested at age 15 and incarcerated in D.C.'s juvenile facility in the fall of 2009. While incarcerated, he attended the Maya Angelou Academy, where he was voted student of the year and earned a 3.6 grade point average. When he was released from custody, he successfully transitioned to the Maya Angelou Public Charter School (PCS). There, he did very well for about six months before he was rear-rested and sent back to the secure juvenile facility, where he spent the summer between his junior and senior years. Transition advocacy by Maya Angelou Academy staff ensured that Tony was released in time to start a new school year at Maya Angelou PCS once again. There, Tony did well the first semester but then got off track and stopped attending for the rest of the year. School staff stayed in touch with him and let him know that he could still reenroll. Eventually, he did. He returned to the school in fall 2012, but his attendance was sporadic. Finally, in the spring of 2013, he started to attend school regularly, with an eye toward a summer graduation. He completed his coursework over the spring and summer and graduated with his high school diploma in August 2013.

Tony is a success story. But supporting him on his journey to earn a high school diploma was a long and resource-intensive process. Signifi-cant staff time and energy went into supporting him. Tony's enrollment at Maya Angelou PCS hurt the school's attendance and dropout num-bers, two of its most critical evaluation metrics. And since Tony took more than four years to graduate, his eventual graduation did not even count toward the school's graduation rate.

Maya Angelou PCS is a school designed for disengaged youth who are struggling. There is a deep institutional commitment to supporting students like Tony. For a mainstream community school without such a commitment, however, admitting students like Tony may seem like far too big of a risk.

The Price of Exclusion

As Tony's story illustrates, supporting formerly incarcerated students in successful educational reentry can be difficult. But it is also critically important. Giving incarcerated youth meaningful access to high-quality schools—both while they are incarcerated and after they are released—is fundamentally fair and in keeping with the juvenile justice system's rehabilitative mission.

Moreover, quality education for incarcerated youth reduces recidivism and improves short- and long-term employment prospects. Unfortunately, there is not rigorous data demonstrating what almost every person who works in the juvenile justice system knows to be true: that high-quality education offers the best chance for youth to succeed. But two sets of data on education and court involvement offer compelling support for the proposition.

First, we know that education reduces recidivism for incarcerated adults. The largest analysis of correctional educational studies found that inmates who participated in correctional education programs had 43 percent lower odds of returning to prison than inmates who did not.[26]

Second, we know that young men with high school diplomas are less likely to end up in prison or jail and more likely to end up employed. Nearly one of every ten young, male high school dropouts was incarcerated on a given day in 2006–2007, versus fewer than one of 33 high school graduates. Similarly, young men without high school diplomas have a year-round joblessness rate of 40 percent—more than double the rate for their peers with high school diplomas.[27] The labor-market effects of not having a high school diploma are even more severe for black or Latino men and men from low-income families—precisely the demographic groups that are severely overrepresented among the population of incarcerated youth.[28]

Currently, the dominant approach to the education of incarcerated youth is to take high-risk youth who often have severe academic deficits, offer them limited educational programming while they are incarcerated, funnel them into an abysmal alternative school when they are released, and then throw up our hands when, a few years later, a young man or woman who never obtained a high school diploma ends up doing time in an adult prison. We can and must do better.

Solutions

We offer a range of recommendations that would help guarantee formerly incarcerated youth meaningful access to mainstream schools after release. We begin by suggesting changes to secure juvenile facilities and then look at how state law, district policy, and school practices can support access after release.

1. Improve the Quality of Schools inside Secure Juvenile Facilities

Two broad, policy-level changes by state legislatures or administrative agencies are critical to improving the quality of facility schools. First, facility schools and the agencies that run them must reengineer their goals for recruiting, developing, and retaining talented teachers—and removing teachers who chronically underperform.

Second, facility schools must be held accountable for their performance and reformed if they are failing. Accountability challenges vary based on which agency runs the facility school. In some states, the juvenile justice agency does not run the schools inside its secure facilities.[29] Instead, the local school district or county office of education operates the school directly or by contract with a private provider.[30] This bifurcated structure limits the agency's ability to reform facility schools that are not serving incarcerated youth well.

Accountability remains a challenge even where the juvenile justice agency does run the schools, particularly in states—such as Massachusetts and New York—where the agency is not a formal local education agency (LEA). In some states, these agency-run schools are explicitly exempt from the No Child Left Behind Act (NCLB) accountability framework.[31] In others, no one has ever considered applying NCLB tools to address a failing school run directly by a state juvenile justice agency. It is simply not clear when or how a state office of education could, for example, reconstitute a failing school inside a secure juvenile facility run by the state juvenile justice agency.

Incarcerated students deserve schools that are staffed by talented teachers and held to rigorous performance standards. When a facility school is failing, the school must change.

2. Ensure Youth Receive Credit for Work inside Facility Schools

Youth must receive appropriate credit for the academic work they complete while incarcerated.

Every school inside a juvenile facility must have the authority to issue meaningful credits for the work students complete while in custody. In states where the juvenile justice agency runs facility schools but the agency is not designated as an LEA, facility schools may actually lack clear authority to issue credits that are transferable to community schools. In these states, community schools can make a discretionary decision about whether to accept credits from facility schools. Youth and the adults supporting them bear the burden of persuading community schools that the credits are legitimate enough to be accepted. Ensuring that every facility school has the legal authority to issue transferable credits is a critical first step toward facilitating successful transitions.

Credits are meaningless, however, if students cannot prove that they have earned them. Schools inside juvenile facilities must keep accurate records of students' academic performance and ensure that students and community schools have access to those records after students leave secure custody.

3. Provide Incarcerated Youth with Meaningful Transition Support

Even with records in hand, the reenrollment process is difficult for students and their families to navigate. Recently released students should have a designated advocate to help them successfully transition into a community school.

Powerful advocacy on behalf of individual students is not an adequate substitute for the necessary systemic changes. But until those changes are made, zealous individual advocacy can go a long way toward facilitating successful transitions.

Advocates should gather students' educational records, work with the student to identify a community school that meets his or her personal and educational needs, and work with the receiving school to plan for the student's transition (for example, by arranging a prerelease visit to the receiving school or an admissions interview). If possible, advocates should accompany the student to school on the first day.

Transition advocates can be based either inside or outside the secure facility. At the Maya Angelou Academy inside D.C.'s secure juvenile facility, transition specialists (called "Advocates") are on the staff of the facility school. They help students adjust to the facility school, support their transition planning, and continue working with students for 90 days after their release. They fulfill these multiple functions by splitting their time equally between work on-site and work in the community.

Where funding does not allow for specialized transition support staff, we encourage other involved adults to embrace the role of transition advocate. Tim Rigsby, the principal of a school inside one of Idaho's secure juvenile facilities, effectively uses his relationships with community schools to place youth who are leaving custody in community schools. Rigsby begins to work on postrelease educational options 30 days before a student is released from custody. Rigsby has also made it a point to become familiar with the quality of community schools, both mainstream and alternative schools, and to build relationships with the principals and staff of those schools. He uses those personal relationships, as well as his deep knowledge of the students in his school, to persuade community schools to "take a chance" on students leaving custody.

"I see advocating for my kids as a critical part of my job as a school principal," Rigsby told us. "We have had some real successes with youth transitioning effectively back to local community schools, and that has been critical in enabling me to keep pushing for additional students. We've also had some problems. But building a trusting relationship with principals on the outside means they don't slam the door on us if every kid doesn't work out."

4. Provide Students and Their Adult Advocates with "Know Your Rights" Education

Educating youth, parents, and those who are charged with their transition planning about postrelease educational rights is a critical piece of prerelease transition support. Juvenile public defenders should counsel all clients entering secure custody about their educational rights after release. Transition advocates should include "know your rights" training as a standard part of transition planning. We also encourage juvenile justice reform advocates in each state to disseminate information about educational rights of formerly incarcerated youth and to provide legal support to youth facing reentry challenges.

It is especially important that students with special needs, and the adults working with them, know the students' educational rights. Students usually do not have a clear legal right to attend a mainstream rather than an alternative school. But under the Individuals with Disabilities Education Act, *all* students with special needs have the right to have those needs met. Given the prevalence of special education needs among incarcerated youth, special education rights can provide a highly effective hook for securing students' admission into mainstream high schools.

5. Remove Legal and Administrative Barriers to Enrollment and Adopt Transparent Reentry Policies

States, districts, and schools should remove the most obvious obstacles to students' enrollment in mainstream schools and adopt formal, transparent, easily understandable reentry policies designed to facilitate successful transition.

As discussed earlier, state laws and district policies create significant obstacles for educational reentry. States should repeal or dramatically reduce the scope of laws and policies that allow for exclusion or expulsion on the basis of court involvement. As a first step, more states should emulate California, which enacted SB 1088 in 2012. SB 1088 expressly prohibits schools from denying readmission to recently released youth solely on the basis of involvement with the juvenile justice system.[32] SB 1088 is intended to stop schools from pushing recently released students into mandatory alternative schools.

Even if state legislatures fail to act on the issue, school districts should voluntarily adopt policies creating a strong presumption that returning students will be allowed to enroll in a mainstream school. School districts should adopt the reentry provisions of the Dignity in Schools Campaign's *Model Code on Education and Dignity*, which specifies that "every effort shall be made to re-enroll and fully integrate system-involved students in the most resourced and enriched educational setting possible" and that "each student's placement shall be based on the presumption that the youth has been rehabilitated with the goal of avoiding automatic placement in alternative programs for students with discipline problems."[33] These policies would represent a radical and welcome departure from the current policies of many states, school districts, and schools.

Efforts to facilitate greater educational access for recently released youth will generate pushback from stakeholders, some of whom are legitimately concerned about school safety, and others who want to use the mantra of school safety to justify exclusion of hard-to-serve students. In some rare cases, a student's involvement with the juvenile justice system may raise legitimate school safety concerns that justify exclusion. But those situations will be extremely rare. State laws and district policies sanctioning exclusion should be very narrowly tailored, reaching only a limited class of students (e.g., students who have been adjudicated delinquent for committing a violent felony against another student or school staff member, on school grounds). Any policy empowering schools to exclude those students must be drafted with precise language that will prevent bad-faith exploitation and leave little room for discretionary decisions by administrators seeking to exclude a returning student. Additionally, the policy must make clear that the presumption in favor of exclusion is rebuttable when the student provides evidence of rehabilitation.

District reenrollment policies should make the admission process as streamlined and simple as possible. The school and the juvenile facility, not the student, should bear the burden of facilitating reenrollment. Denying students admission because they had the bad luck to attend a facility school that failed to produce transcripts, or requiring students and their families to jump through multiple hoops, serves no legitimate end.

6. Change Schools' Incentives

Removing the legal and administrative obstacles to educational reentry, while a critical first step, is not enough to guarantee students access to mainstream high schools. In the words of one New York City Department of Education official, the biggest barrier to successful educational reentry for recently released youth is "the human hurdle—no one wants them back."[34]

We must change schools' incentives. Educating recently released youth can be extremely challenging and resource intensive. To encourage mainstream schools to admit these students, states and districts should reward schools for successfully supporting court-involved youth in educational transition. Separate attendance, credit accumulation, and retention and graduation rates (possibly over an extended period) for court-involved youth should be incorporated into school accountability frameworks. Schools should get credit for developing programming that helps court-involved youth stay in school and be rewarded for meeting improvement targets rather than predetermined achievement markers.

Increasingly, school accountability frameworks incorporate value-added achievement metrics, which track how much schools help students improve on test scores, not just students' final performance. Incorporating value-added metrics into other aspects of school performance standards would reward schools for supporting high-need and high-risk students. For example, instead of only grading a school on its attendance rate, schools could be graded on how well they help struggling students improve their attendance. Schools could also be rewarded for helping chronically failing students improve the rate at which they accumulate credits. And schools could get credit when previously failing students graduate, even if it takes five or six years.

Reporting loopholes that insulate schools from accountability for excluding recently released students should be closed. Schools should be required to report how many students from their enrollment area are enrolled in alternative schools and take ownership over those students' graduation rates. Similarly, involuntary placements into an alternative school should count as exclusionary discipline for reporting purposes.

7. Draw on Best Practices Developed for Youth in the Foster Care System

Best practices to promote educational success among foster youth should be extended to youth in juvenile custody. Like incarcerated youth, youth in the foster care system must deal with disruptive educational transitions. In California, state law ensures that foster care youth who transfer to a new school or district in grade 11 or 12 are eligible to earn a statewide, rather than district-specific, high school diploma.[35] Foster youth who transfer schools after their sophomore year are presumptively exempt from all coursework and graduation requirements other than the statewide requirements. The purpose of the law is not to lower standards for foster youth but rather to prevent foster youth from getting stuck in a morass of varying requirements that prevents them from graduating on time. A similar accommodation would help formerly incarcerated students overcome the obstacles of multiple educational transitions.

8. Designate School or District Staff to Facilitate Transitions

School districts should designate staff members to serve as transition facilitators and advocates. District-level commitment to facilitating successful educational reentry can go a long way toward persuading principals to admit recently released students. For example, in 2008, Chad Ferguson, the deputy superintendent for alternative schools and youth engagement for the District of Columbia Public Schools (DCPS) system, created a placement team empowered to support students transitioning back to DCPS from secure and residential placements. The placement team worked closely with Maya Angelou Academy's Advocates to support students' return to their neighborhood schools. Placement team members spoke directly to school principals and leaned on them to accept students. The placement team brokered deals, facilitated meetings between students and school leadership, and even helped to mediate disagreements between returning students and current students.

The success of the DCPS placement team model hinged on the commitment to reentry by district leadership. Ferguson was a vocal critic of separate, mandatory alternative schools. His consistent message—to both his placement team and school principals—was that students should be able to return to their home schools absent legitimate safety concerns.

9. Create High-Performing Alternative Schools

Convincing mainstream high schools to embrace the challenges of educating court-involved youth is critical, but it will be difficult. Part of the solution must also be supporting vibrant, high-performing, mission-driven alternative schools that are committed to addressing the needs of court-involved and formerly incarcerated youth. Instead of forcing returning youth into mandatory alternative schools, school districts need to offer student-centered alternative schools that work just as well for youth coming out of juvenile facilities as they do for other at-risk youth.

School districts should develop a network of alternative schools that offer a range of options to young people who need options beyond traditional, community schools. In particular, school districts and charter authorizers should support the growth and development of mission-driven charter schools focused on serving at-risk and vulnerable youth, including formerly incarcerated teens. The Maya Angelou Public Charter School in Washington, D.C., and the School for the Performing Arts in Minneapolis both opened with the express purpose of serving court-involved and other underserved teens. Each has worked with its chartering authority to develop alternative accountability frameworks that ensure quality programming without overly compromising the schools' unique mission.

10. Reduce the Use of Mandatory Alternative Schools

States and school districts need to take aggressive steps to reduce the use of mandatory alternative schools. First, they should limit the grounds for placement in alternative schools to a very small set of student behaviors that pose significant school safety concerns. Second, states and districts need to develop rigorous quality standards for mandatory alternative schools and close down those schools that do not meet the standards. Third, states and districts need to reduce—not expand—the number of mandatory alternative schools (or the number of seats in those schools).

Limiting placement in mandatory schools, closing the worst of them, and reducing their availability will force educational providers to create school options—either within mainstream schools or through a network of alternative schools of choice—that better meet the needs of court-involved youth.

Conclusion

Educational issues have been the third rail of juvenile justice reform for too long. We call on advocates to place educational issues at the very top of the juvenile justice reform agenda.

We are optimistic that the policy changes we advocate would go a long way toward guaranteeing formerly incarcerated youth access to mainstream community schools. But most fundamentally, addressing educational exclusion will require a significant paradigm shift. Too often, we treat incarcerated youth as broken beyond repair, as throw-away kids doomed to spend their lives cycling in and out of prison. The unspoken logic of our educational policy for court-involved youth is that "bad kids" deserve bad schools.

Instead, we envision a system of care in which incarcerated youth receive an outstanding education while they are in custody and have meaningful access to quality educational options when they are released. We see a time when those who are charged with educating court-involved youth embrace a new mantra: to give our best to the kids who need the most.

***

This chapter is dedicated to all the young people who have languished in low-performing schools inside youth facilities and have been pushed into mandatory alternative schools upon release. You deserved better.

NOTES

1 Maya Angelou Academy is the facility school inside D.C.'s secure juvenile facility. David Domenici cofounded the academy with James Forman, Jr., and served as its founding principal from July 2007 until August 2011.

2 National Center for Education Statistics, *Public Alternative Schools and Programs for Students at Risk of Education Failure: 2000–01* (Washington, DC: U.S. Department of Education, 2002), http://nces.ed.gov/pubsearch/pubsinfo. asp?pubid=2002004.

3 Camilla A. Lehr, Rachel A. Moreau, Cheryl M. Lange, and Eric J. Lammers, *Alternative Schools: Findings from a National Survey of the States*, Research Report

2 (Minneapolis: University of Minnesota Institute on Community Integration, 2004), http://files.eric.ed.gov/fulltext/ED502534.pdf.

4 Camilla A. Lehr and Cheryl M. Lange, *Alternative Schools and the Students They Serve: Perceptions of State Directors of Special Education*, Policy Research Brief (Minneapolis: University of Minnesota Institute on Community Integration, 2003), http://ici.umn.edu/products/prb/141/141.pdf.

5 Camilla A. Lehr, Eric J. Lanners, and Cheryl M. Lange, *Alternative Schools: Policy and Legislation across the United States*, Research Report 1 (Minneapolis: University of Minnesota Institute on Community Integration, 2003), http://files.eric.ed.gov/fulltext/ED502533.pdf.

6 Mary Anne Raywid, "Synthesis of Research/Alternative Schools: The State of the Art," *Educational Leadership* 52 (1) (1994): 26–31.

7 Lehr and Lange, *supra* note 4.

8 Lehr et al., *supra* note 3.

9 *Id.*

10 Tex. Ed. Code Ann. §§ 37.008, 37.011 (2012).

11 Tex. Ed. Code Ann. § 37.008 (2012).

12 37 Tex. Admin. Code § 348.104 (2012).

13 Elizabeth Hayes, "Youth in Adult Literacy Education Programs," *Review of Adult Learning and Literacy* 1 (3) (1999): 74–110.

14 Laura McCargar, *Invisible Students: The Role of Alternative and Adult Education in the Connecticut School-to-Prison Pipeline* (New Haven, CT: A Better Way Foundation and the Connecticut Pushout and Organizing Research Project, 2011), http://www.cfgnh.org/Portals/0/Uploads/Documents/Public/giveANDlearn-reports/ABWF_PROP_InvisibleStudentsFinal.pdf.

15 Dolores Perin, Bert Flugman, and Seymour Spiegel, "Last Chance Gulch: Youth Participation in Urban Adult Basic Education Programs," *Adult Basic Education* 16 (3) (2006): 171–188.

16 Hayes, *supra* note 13.

17 Thomas J. Dishion and Kenneth A. Dodge, "Peer Contagion in Interventions for Children and Adolescents: Moving towards an Understanding of the Ecology and Dynamics of Change," *Journal of Abnormal Child Psychology* 33 (3) (2005): 395–400.

18 Peter E. Leone, Michael Krezmien, Loretta Mason, and Sheri M. Meisel, "Organizing and Delivering Empirically Based Literacy Instruction to Incarcerated Youth," *Exceptionality: A Special Education Journal* 13 (2) (2005): 89–102.

19 Nicholas Read and Mindee O'Cummings, *Fact Sheet: Juvenile Justice Facilities* (Washington, DC: National Evaluation and Technical Assistance Center for the Education of Children and Youth Who Are Neglected, Delinquent, or At Risk [NDTAC], 2010), http://www.neglected-delinquent.org/nd/docs/factSheet_facilities.pdf.

20 Thomas G. Blomberg, George Pesta, and Colby Valentine, *The Juvenile Justice No Child Left Behind Collaboration Project: Final Report* (Tallahassee: Florida State

University Center for Criminology and Public Policy Research, 2008), http://criminology.fsu.edu/wp-content/uploads/The-Juvenile-Justice-No-Child-Left-Behind-Collaboration-Project-Final-Report-2008.pdf.

21   Idaho Code Ann. § 33-205 (2012).

22   Tex. Ed. Code Ann. § 37.0081 (2012).

23   Georgetown Law Human Rights Institute Fact-Finding Mission, *Kept Out: Barriers to Meaningful Education in the School-to-Prison Pipeline* (Washington, DC: Georgetown University Law Center, 2012), http://www.law.georgetown.edu/academics/centers-institutes/human-rights-institute/fact-finding/upload/KeptOut.pdf.

24   McCargar, *supra* note 14.

25   Deborah Fowler, *Texas' School-to-Prison Pipeline: Ticketing, Arrest & Use of Force in Schools* (Austin: Texas Appleseed, 2010), http://www.texasappleseed.net/images/stories/reports/Ticketing_Booklet_web.pdf; Michael P. Krezmien, Candace A. Mulcahy, and Peter E. Leone, "Detained and Committed Youth: Examining Differences in Achievement, Mental Health Needs, and Special Education Status," *Education and Treatment of Children* 31 (4) (2008): 445–464.

26   Lois M. Davis, Robert Bozick, Jennifer L. Steele, Jessica Saunders, and Jeremy N. V. Miles, *Evaluating the Effectiveness of Correctional Education: A Meta-analysis of Programs That Provide Education to Incarcerated Adults* (Santa Monica, CA: RAND, 2013), http://www.rand.org/pubs/research_reports/RR266.

27   Andrew Sum, Ishwar Khatiwada, and Joseph McLaughlin, *The Consequences of Dropping Out of High School* (Boston: Northeastern University Center for Labor Market Studies, 2009), http://iris.lib.neu.edu/cgi/viewcontent.cgi?article=1022&context=clms_pub.

28   National Council on Crime and Delinquency, *And Justice for Some: Differential Treatment of Youth of Color* (Oakland, CA: National Council on Crime and Delinquency, 2007).

29   Blomberg, Pesta, and Valentine, *supra* note 20.

30   Bruce I. Wolford, *Juvenile Justice Education: "Who Is Educating the Youth"* (Richmond: Eastern Kentucky University Training Resource Center, 2000), www.edjj.org/Publications/educating_youth.pdf.

31   Blomberg, Pesta, and Valentine, *supra* note 20.

32   California Education Code § 48645.5 (2012).

33   Dignity in Schools Campaign, *A Model Code on Education and Dignity* (2013), http://www.dignityinschools.org/files/Model_Code_2013.pdf.

34   Youth Justice Board, *Stop the Revolving Door: Giving Communities and Youth the Tools to Overcome Recidivism: Recommendations on Juvenile Reentry in New York City* (New York: Center for Court Innovation, 2005), http://www.courtinnovation.org/sites/default/files/YJB04_executive_summary.pdf.

35   California Education Code § 512251 (2012).

19

Collateral Consequences of Juvenile Court

Boulders on the Road to Good Outcomes

SUE BURRELL

Introduction

If you ask a roomful of successful adults if they committed acts as teen-agers that violated the law, most will admit that they did.[1] Some were not caught; some were caught but turned over to their parents; and others were prosecuted but not made a ward of the court. They may not have behaved any better than the youth who were caught, but for the most part, they escaped the direct and collateral consequences of involvement with the juvenile justice system.

This chapter examines the collateral consequences of juvenile court proceedings, an area in which juvenile court intervention has become the antithesis of its original rehabilitative goals. It provides an over-view of the consequences commonly experienced by youth and spot-lights the disparate impact of those consequences on youth of color and poor youth. It discusses collateral consequences in relation to evolving concepts of adolescent development and effective practice. Finally, the chapter offers suggestions for eliminating or mitigating the barriers to success interposed by collateral consequences.

What Are Collateral Consequences?

The *direct* consequences of juvenile court involvement are themselves significant and life changing. As an immediate result of arrest, youth may be incarcerated in prison-like institutions, sometimes for years. Youth may suffer adult-type consequences such as the reporting of their DNA, fingerprints, and records to criminal registries; lifetime regis-tration requirements for sex or gang crimes; and use of their juvenile adjudications for sentencing enhancement. If their case is handled in the adult system, youth may be sentenced to do adult time.

Even youth who are involved in less serious misbehavior experience stigma and suffer considerable disruption in school and other parts of their lives. The court may impose a staggering array of conditions and orders, many of which require substantial time, effort, and resources to fulfill. It is common for a single court order to require youth to make restitution, go to counseling, be tested for drugs, perform community service, pay a fine, stay away from certain people or neighborhoods, be at home at a certain time, submit to law enforcement searches, and regularly attend school. For many youth, these expectations are overwhelming.

But direct consequences are not the only ones that flow from juvenile court involvement. And although the law is evolving to require more complete advice about the consequences of admitting to or being found guilty of a crime,[2] most young people have little understanding of the pervasive impact that such consequences may have on their future. Depending on the offense, youth may find it difficult to get back into school, apply for financial aid, join the military, adjust their immigration status, live in public housing, hold a driver's license, or successfully navigate employment interviews. The *collateral* consequences of something they did as a teenager may follow them for their entire lives.

Collateral consequences include literally dozens of additional sanctions or limitations resulting from juvenile court involvement. Some are imposed by agencies that have nothing to do with juvenile court. Departments of motor vehicles, licensing agencies for various professions, housing authorities, the Department of Homeland Security, colleges and universities, public benefits agencies, and financial aid organizations are among the entities that impose collateral consequences on an independent basis.

Many collateral consequences are mementoes of the "get tough" era in juvenile justice—they are simply imposed for punishment. Some are experienced early on, and others become manifest years down the road when the young person wants to pursue some life goal. Among the areas potentially impacted by juvenile court involvement are

- liability for legal representation, service costs, civil judgments;
- getting or keeping a driver's license;
- being allowed to attend regular high school;
- applying to college and for financial aid;
- obtaining a job;
- qualifying for a professional license;
- living in public housing;
- securing or keeping legal immigration status;
- being able to serve in the military;
- qualifying for public benefits;
- being a foster parent or relative caregiver; and
- traveling within the U.S. or abroad.

In other words, many of the very things we want youth to do to demonstrate success and rehabilitation are made more difficult by collateral consequences. Youth who want to comply with the court's orders but need transportation to get to meetings and appointments find that their driver's license has been suspended or that they must wait a substantial period before applying for one. Thus, in California, youth aged 13 to 21 face mandatory license suspension or delay in eligibility to be licensed for a wide range of drug and alcohol offenses and vandalism.[3] Discretionary suspension reaches even more broadly to include offenses such as truancy, prostitution, or using false identification to buy liquor.[4] There are literally dozens of ways youth may lose their driving privileges in California.[5]

Youth who manage to get through high school find that the Common Application[6] used for admission to many colleges asks them to disclose juvenile adjudications—placing them at an immediate disadvantage. Youth who want to join the military find that every juvenile contact with the justice system must be reported and that in many cases a waiver must be obtained to make them eligible for enlistment. For example, the U.S. Army requires disclosure of "records of arrest, charges, juvenile court adjudications, traffic violations, probation periods, and dismissed or pending charges or convictions, including those that have been expunged or sealed."[7] A waiver to permit enlistment is required for anyone convicted of a felony.[8] Youth otherwise meeting the requirements to go into nursing or the practice of law find that state licensing laws restrict them—often many years down the road. Thus, for example, the California Board of Registered Nursing considers the existence of a "conviction or act" for a broad range of offenses to be substantially related to practicing as a nurse and reviews applications with prior convictions on a case-by-case basis.[9] Although the regulations refer to "convictions" and do not mention juvenile adjudications, the LiveScan process used to do background and fingerprint checks may turn up juvenile contacts (juvenile felonies are reported to the Department of Justice in California),[10] and some counties also collect and submit fingerprints. Although juvenile contacts should not be disclosed to potential employers, they sometimes are. And since the regulatory language also covers past "acts" that are not convictions, youth may wind up having to deal with juvenile records in the licensure process.

There are additional barriers in other areas of life. Youth who, decades later, want to become foster parents or relative caregivers find that their juvenile record is used to disqualify them. Youth seeking to adjust their immigration status find that "bad acts" as a juvenile are used to deny them admission to the country or are used as grounds for deportation.[11] Families of youth who were in trouble with the law encounter exclusion or eviction from public housing if the youth was involved in drug-related activity or other criminal activity deemed to "threaten the health, safety or right to peaceful enjoyment of the premises."[12]

How Do Collateral Consequences Work?

Collateral consequences work in a variety of ways. Some are specifically required by law. It is common, for example, for state laws to call for suspension of the driver's license of any youth adjudicated for driving under the influence of alcohol. In some cases, the juvenile court is required to give notice of adjudications to other agencies, and in others, the agencies may contact the juvenile court or state records agency to learn about adjudications or other juvenile contact with the system.

Other collateral consequences are discretionary. For example, being adjudicated for certain offenses may result in automatic suspension or expulsion from school, but for other offenses, suspension or expulsion may be discretionary. Similarly, applications for jobs or college may require disclosure of juvenile adjudications but provide for a case-by-case determination whether the juvenile record is disqualifying.

Many states have eviscerated the rules that, until the 1990s, had kept juvenile records confidential. This has made it possible for almost anyone with a computer to learn what a young person did that got him or her arrested. Even when the law does not permit disclosure, the broad availability of electronic records results in improper disclosure and misunderstandings. It is not unusual to find "rap sheets" that include juvenile contacts even though they should not be reported, and a few states actually sell juvenile records to private companies.[13]

Improper disclosure of juvenile court history is exacerbated by confusion about the law or lack of clarity about what must be disclosed. For example, many licensing agencies or employers want to know about criminal *convictions*. Although juvenile adjudications are technically not *convictions*, those who respond to records requests and those who request records are not always careful about the distinction. This situation results in improper disclosure and improper use of juvenile court adjudications to disqualify youth or put them at a substantial disadvantage. It also creates problems for youth who may have truthfully stated that they have no *convictions*. Although their answer is legally correct, they face being perceived as liars or forced to explain their past—hardly the best way to make a good first impression.

Lack of Advocacy to Assure Fairness in Collateral Consequences

There is little oversight over wrongful disclosure of juvenile records. Youth may not understand the law or be aware of their rights in relation to wrongful disclosure. Also, record-sealing laws in many states are complicated and sometimes prohibitively expensive for youth from low-income families to use in order to shield their record from public view.

Resources are few and far between to provide advocacy to youth in relation to collateral consequences. Few public defender offices have resources to represent youth in postdisposition school, employment, or record-sealing proceedings, even though success in school and work are central to fulfilling the goals of court intervention. Moreover, some of the collateral consequences, such as fighting eviction from public housing or appearing before licensing boards, require specialized knowledge of the law, and youth are even less likely to obtain civil legal services than they are to engage criminal legal help.

Strategic, skilled approaches could help to prevent or mitigate many consequences, but youth have no one to help them. In the diverse situations in which informed decisions are needed to assist in applications or interviews, most youth are completely on their own. This is especially so because collateral consequences may surface many years after the juvenile court case is over.

Who Is Hurt by Collateral Consequences?

The demographics of youth involved in juvenile court cases provide additional grounds for concern about collateral consequences. The youth arrested, tried, and incarcerated in our juvenile system are disproportionately youth of color.[14] Most are from poor or economically struggling families. Many live in racially marginalized communities lacking the kinds of support that youth need to grow to healthy adulthood. Also, compared to the general youth population, they have a much higher prevalence of developmental disabilities, mental illness, and histories of trauma or abuse.

Youth of color and poor kids regularly experience the full impact of the court system, at least in part because they have less access to the supports that could help them to avoid it. Also, misbehavior by youth of color is all too often evaluated through a racial lens. Instead of being viewed in the context of the young person's traumatic life experiences or as the onset of mental illness, their behavior is seen as evidence of a criminal character. Instead of being sent to a therapist or a diversion program facilitated by family resources, youth of color face the full brunt of prosecution. Afterward, they are subjected to dozens of rules and restrictions that make it more difficult to move beyond age- or disability-related delinquency.

In sum, our system prosecutes the youth who have the most challenges and the least amount of resources to begin with and then heaps additional obligations on them. It imposes rules and restrictions that interfere with or prevent them from obtaining support that could help them to dig out. The direct and collateral consequences limit their access to the very areas most critical to success—education, jobs, and mobility.

Youth who succeed in moving forward do so in spite of our system, not because of it.

Why Should We Care?

The astronomical growth of collateral consequences over the past two decades has coincided with fear and misperceptions about juvenile crime. It has also been fueled by a misguided belief that punishment acts as a deterrent to young people—that if we give them sufficient reason to reflect on their acts, they will think twice before engaging in future delinquency.

While there is certainly a place for age- and offense-appropriate accountability, this piling on of consequences is counterproductive. Youth in juvenile justice are already under a crushing load of responsibilities imposed by the court. Many collateral consequences have nothing to do with the underlying offense, and many surface years down the road. Because of these consequences, doors close for youth, or they are placed at a distinct disadvantage. With so much stacked against them, some youth may simply give up.

This outcome affects all of us. If youth are unable to successfully pursue higher education and employment that enables them to be self-sustaining, they are more likely to reengage in criminal behavior. They are more likely to need public benefits. Their own children and families suffer, and this contributes to a horrible cycle of poverty and involvement in the criminal justice system. By perpetuating a system in which youth are unable to succeed, we deprive our community of the energy, skills, and creativity that young people would contribute if they were not so hobbled by their juvenile past.

What about Public Safety?

Adolescence is a time of risk taking and impulsive behavior. Our laws recognize this in setting the age of majority for many adult responsibilities such as voting, joining the military, or being responsible for contracts. Research on adolescent development and on the age at which the human brain fully matures confirms that the wild teenager at 16 is not the person he or she will be at age 25.[15]

The behavior of youth in the juvenile justice system is not different from that of other teenagers, but for the fact that they were caught. Surveys of juvenile court professionals reveal that a majority engaged in behavior as teenagers that, had they been arrested, could have been charged as a felony.[16] Their crimes include armed assaults, sex crimes, robberies, drug sales, intoxicated driving, and a broad array of seriously reckless activities. Almost without exception, these successful professionals report that, had this behavior been known to admissions officers in higher education, licensing authorities, and future employers, it would have interposed a barrier to their ability to move forward in their lives. Further, almost every person surveyed considers his or her behavior to have been a function of immaturity, and not something that should be used to judge him or her years down the road.[17]

In fact, most youth who get into trouble with the law are unlikely to become career criminals. National research indicates that six out of ten juveniles who enter the juvenile justice system never return on a new referral.[18] The federal "Pathways to Desistance" study found that only a small proportion of juvenile offenders studied over a seven-year period continued to offend at a high level throughout the follow-up period. The great majority reported low levels of offending after court involvement, and a significant portion of those with the highest levels of offending reduced their reoffending dramatically.[19]

What Can We Do?

We need to reconnect with our original mission of helping youth in juvenile justice to successfully move forward. No one strategy will address every collateral consequence, but here is a beginning list of areas that merit attention. A refocused juvenile justice system would eliminate or sharply reduce collateral consequences and aim toward supporting youth to achieve success and well-being as adults. The first few strategies suggested here relate to juvenile court process; the remainder focus on broader community issues.

1. Keep More Youth Out of the System

Research has established that youth subject to formal juvenile court processing have worse outcomes than do youth with similar characteristics who escape formal scrutiny.[20] Our own experiences confirm that many individuals had extensive involvement in criminal activity as juveniles but became law-abiding and successful without court intervention. While we do not know for certain how much collateral consequences contribute to this result, the research suggests a need to look closely at whether formal interventions are truly needed. Allowing more youth to move forward in school, work, and skill development without the punitive burdens stemming from juvenile court involvement may greatly increase successful outcomes. This may be accomplished through the development of better support services to help families address their children's behavior, so formal intervention is not needed. When intervention is needed, it can be achieved in many more cases through community-based diversion or informal supervision programs that view youth as students, athletes, artists, and helpers—not as criminals.

2. Increase Juvenile Court Professionals' Understanding of Collateral Consequences

Judges, probation officers, prosecutors, and defense counsel need much more comprehensive knowledge about potential consequences in order to exercise proper judgment in individual cases. The American Bar Association is leading a national effort to heighten awareness of these issues by providing state-by-state information on specific consequences.[21] In addition, a number of states have developed their own collateral consequences handbooks and guides.[22] Until the substance of collateral consequences changes, information and knowledge is critical for youth, parents, and communities.

3. Fully Advise Youth about Consequences during the Court Process

Youth need to understand potential consequences in the course of making decisions about the risks of going to trial, whether to admit the offense, or whether to accept a plea bargain. Also, by focusing on potential consequences at the outset, youth may be able to prevent or mitigate key consequences. For example, a plea agreement that allows the youth to admit to a slightly different offense than what was charged could help to save him or her from losing driving privileges. An agreement to admit a lesser offense could help to convince military recruiters that the offense is less serious than what was charged and that the youth should be able to enlist.

4. Assure Access to Advocacy Services after the Court Case Is Over

While juvenile defense counsel is obligated to help youth throughout the period of juvenile court jurisdiction, many collateral-consequences issues come up later. Jurisdictions should assure that youth no longer under court jurisdiction have access to free assistance to legal advice and representation in collateral-consequences-related proceedings. They may need help in filling out applications, deciding how to handle their juvenile record in employment interviews, seeking dismissal or sealing of juvenile records, or presenting their case to a licensing board. These services could be provided by legal services organizations, public defender offices, volunteer attorney programs in bar associations, or legal clinics at law schools. Information about these services should be disseminated to youth during the court process.

5. Restore Confidentiality of Juvenile Records

In many states, juvenile confidentiality rules have been largely abandoned except for very minor offenses. State statutes often hold that youth have no right to confidentiality in cases involving whole categories of offenses. These categorical exclusions from confidentiality should be reconsidered and reduced. There are huge factual differences in cases charged as robberies and assaults, for example, and they should not all be treated the same. Instructions for record sealing should also be readily available through the court's public information system.

Also, recognizing that employers, educators, law enforcement, and other agencies may have genuine interests that require *some* disclosure of juvenile records, we can still do a much better job of addressing legitimate "need to know." Jurisdictions can redraw the lines in a way that recognizes legitimate needs but eliminates the unfairness and overbreadth of current rules and practices. Shifting toward laws that make records confidential, except in cases of serious violent convictions, will help to provide better balance.

6. Make It Easier, Cheaper, and Faster to Seal Juvenile Records

Many youth fail to seal their records even when they are eligible to do so. Some youth do not know they have the right to seal their record, and others do not understand why it is important. Still others are intimidated by complex filing processes and the difficulty of finding anyone who can help to explain what they need to do. And finally, record sealing is simply too expensive in some places. With fees of as much as $150 in some court systems, plus a substantial expenditure in time away from school or work, youth literally cannot afford to seal their records.

Jurisdictions should consider adopting rules for the automatic sealing of less serious offenses at the time youth successfully complete probation.[23] This would assure that low-level offenders benefit from the intended protections of record-sealing laws and would reduce courts' workload in cases likely to result in sealing anyway. Sealing provisions for youth who do not qualify for automatic sealing should be free or very low cost, should provide for a court hearing, and should permit application within a short period after successful completion of court jurisdiction; and the criteria should relate to rehabilitative success, not the nature of the offense.

In addition, jurisdictions should provide a mechanism for delayed dismissal of the case.[24] Youth sometimes report that their chances for getting a professional license, joining the military, or other endeavors would be greatly enhanced if the underlying juvenile adjudication were removed. While this may not be appropriate in every case, jurisdictions should assure that, for cases meriting such consideration, dismissal in the interest of justice is possible. Such rules should be written to accommodate situations that arise many years after the juvenile case has been closed.

7. Restrict the Transfer of Juvenile Records and Provide Better Oversight

In the age of computers and the Internet, disclosure of confidential information is a persistent threat. This means that even when the law would limit disclosure, once records are published, there is little ability to control who sees them. It is common, for example, for "rap sheets" to include juvenile contacts with the law and even sealed juvenile offenses. Private record-checking companies with access to these records may be contacted by prospective employers and may disclose this information with impunity.

Juvenile records laws must be written to strictly prohibit redisclosure of confidential information and to impose strong penalties for violations. For example, legislation enacted in Washington State significantly broadened eligibility for record sealing and imposed substantial penalties for wrongful disclosure.[25]

8. Prohibit Inclusion of Juvenile Records in Applications and Clarify What Is Required

The American Bar Association has adopted a resolution urging federal, state, territorial, and local governments to limit the collateral consequences imposed as a result of contact with the juvenile justice system.[26] This is surely one of the most powerful ways to assure that juvenile adjudications are not used in college, employment, and other applications.

Also, it is critical that applications do a better job of explaining what must be disclosed. Even though many employment, licensing, college, and financial aid applications already require only disclosure of adult "convictions," many people do not understand the difference between juvenile "adjudications" and criminal court "convictions." One very helpful improvement would be to request that applications explain what a conviction is and to clarify that juvenile adjudications need not be disclosed.

9. Create More Second Chances for Youth

Beyond all the needed changes in law and professional training, we must not lose sight of the need to help individual youth. The importance of individual support is compelling in this account from Starcia Ague, who was in the juvenile system as a teenager and has now become a powerful advocate for reducing collateral consequences:

> After I graduated, I applied for 35 jobs. I got just two calls back and went in for one interview with a telemarketing company. I got the job . . . and I was so excited! But then they said, "Just one more thing. On the question about felony convictions on the job application, you put down 'will discuss upon interview.' So . . . discuss." I told them my story . . . and they told me good-bye. Miracle of miracles, and again through the help of people who believed in me, I did finally get a job in Seattle as a research assistant with Dr. Trupin at the University of Washington. But I was turned down for housing by three different landlords. I have great credit, but I couldn't pass a background check. Fortunately, I found another WSU Alumnus with a rental house who gave me a break.[27]

Youth are much more likely to successfully transition to adulthood if as many doors as possible remain open to them. Sometimes, this requires the help of a compassionate, supportive adult willing to give them a chance.

In fact, some of the best opportunities for system-involved youth have developed out of the frustrations experienced in trying to move beyond having a juvenile record. In California, for example, Homeboy Industries, Barrios Unidos, and the Youth Justice Coalition provide a welcome mat for youth, as well as offering employment opportunities and advocacy services to help them to apply for school and jobs. These programs are lifesaving and deserve to be much more richly supported by juvenile justice policy makers.

Conclusion

Our system of collateral consequences is out of balance with fundamental principles of juvenile justice. If we want youth to move beyond juvenile "delinquency," we need to recognize that what we are doing in many instances is hurting rather than helping. These suggestions offer a place to start to change laws and practices that impede youth in attaining self-sufficiency and community success.

NOTES

1 Surveys of "Collateral Consequences on a Personal Level," conducted by the author during workshops at the Administrative Office of the Courts Beyond the Bench XXI Conference, San Francisco, California, December 16, 2011; the California Public Defenders Association Juvenile Law Seminar, Monterey, California, January 21, 2012; and "Reforming the Juvenile Justice System: A Workshop for Change," University of Florida Levin College of Law, Gainesville, Florida, April 26–27, 2013.

2 *Padilla v. Kentucky*, 559 U.S. ___, 130 S. Ct. 1473 (2010), for example, required that a defendant be advised of the immigration consequences of his or her plea.

3 Cal. Veh. Code § 13202.5; Cal. Veh. Code § 13202.6.

4 Cal. Veh. Code § 1302.7(a); Cal. Veh. Code § 13201.5 (a); Cal. Veh. Code § 1302.5(a).

5 Sue Burrell and Rourke F. Stacy, eds., *Collateral Consequences of Juvenile Delinquency Proceedings in California: A Handbook for Juvenile Law Professionals* (San Francisco: Pacific Juvenile Defender Center, 2011), 45–64.

6 The Common Application is used by close to 500 member colleges and universities. The 2013–2014 First Year Application is available at https://www.commonapp.org/CommonApp/DownloadForms.aspx.

7 Army Regulation 601-210, Personnel Procurement, Active and Reserve Components, Rapid Action Revision (RAR) (Feb. 1, 2013), § 2-11(a), § 4-7(a).

8 *Id.*

9 16 Cal. Code of Regs. § 1444.

10 Cal. Welf. & Inst. Code § 602.5.

11 See, for example, 8 U.S.C. § 1227(a)(2) (conduct-based grounds for deportation), 8 U.S.C. § 1182(a)(1) and (a)(2) (conduct-based grounds for inadmissibility).

12 42 U.S.C. § 13661, 24 C.F.R. 5.854 and 982.553 (exclusion); and § 13662 (a)(2) (termination of tenancy).

13 George Yeannakis, "Collateral Consequences of Juvenile Records: They Are Not Collateral and They Can Be Forever," webinar (Washington, DC: U.S. Department of Justice, Office of Juvenile Justice and Delinquency Prevention, National Training and Technical Assistance Center, February 21, 2013).

14 See, for example, Francisco A. Villarruel, Nancy E. Walker, and Pamela Minifee, *¿Dónde Está La Justicia? A Call to Action on Behalf of Latino and Latina Youth in the U.S. Justice System* (Building Blocks for Youth, 2002), 1–2; National Council on Crime and Delinquency, *And Justice for Some: Differential Treatment of Youth of Color in the Justice System* (January 2007), 1–3; and W. Haywood Burns Institute, *Unbalanced Juvenile Justice: An Interactive Data Map*, http://data.burnsinstitute.org/#comparison=2&placement=1&races=2,3,4,5,6&offenses=5,2,8,1,9,11,10&year=2011&view=map.

15 Much of this work has been developed by and is available through the MacArthur Foundation Research Network on Adolescent Development and Juvenile Justice: http://www.adjj.org/content/index.php.

16 Surveys of "Collateral Consequences on a Personal Level," *supra* note 1.

17 *Id.*

18 Howard N. Snyder and Melissa Sickmund, *Juvenile Offenders and Victims: 2006 National Report* (Washington, DC: National Center for Juvenile Justice, with the support of the U.S. Department of Justice, Office of Justice Programs, 2006), 234–235.

19 Edward P. Mulvey, *Highlights from Pathways to Desistance: A Longitudinal Study of Serious Adolescent Offenders*, OJJDP Juvenile Justice Fact Sheet (Washington, DC: U.S. Department of Justice, Office of Juvenile Justice and Delinquency Prevention, March 2011), 4; and see MacArthur Foundation, *Research on Pathways to Desistance: Research Update Created for the Fourth Annual Models for Change National Working Conference* (December 9, 2009), http://www.modelsforchange. net/publications/239.

20 Anthony Petrosino, Sarah Gluckenberg, and Carolyn Turpin-Petrosino, "Formal System Processing of Juveniles: Effects on Delinquency," *Campbell Systematic Reviews* 6, no. 1 (2010): 36.

21 The American Bar Association Juvenile Collateral Consequences Project page is "Think Before You Plead: Juvenile Collateral Consequences in the United States," at http://beforeyouplea.com/ (accessed November 7, 2013).

22 See, for example, Burrell and Stacy, *supra* note 5; Pennsylvania Juvenile Indigent Defense Action Network, *Pennsylvania Juvenile Collateral Consequences Checklist* (Philadelphia: Pennsylvania Juvenile Indigent Defense Action Network [PA-JIDAN], 2010); Kim Ambrose and Alison Millikan, *Beyond Juvenile Court: Long-Term Impact of a Juvenile Record* (Seattle: Washington Defender Association, 2011); Carlos J. Martinez, Ruck Deminico, Kevin Hellman, and Tamara Gray, *For Minors in Miami Dade, Florida— Consequences of Your Arrest, Plea and Trial* (Miami: Office of Carlos J. Martinez, Public Defender, 2008).

23 See, for example, Cal. Welf. & Inst. Code 786, added by S.B. 1038 (Leno) ch. 249, Stats. 2014.

24 See, for example, Cal. Welf. & Inst. Code 782, as amended by S.B. 1038 (Leno) ch. 249, Stats. 2014.

25 Washington HR 1651, 2013–2014 session, the Youth Opportunities Act, effective June 12, 2014, http://apps.leg.wa.gov/billinfo/.summary.aspx?=1651&year=2014. Advocacy to further restrict online access to unsealed juvenile records continues in Washington State.

26 The American Bar Association policy urging the limitation of collateral consequences affecting juveniles is Policy 102A, adopted February 9, 2010, available at http://www.campaignforyouthjustice.org/documents/ABA%20-%20102A%20 -%20Collateral%20Consequences%20for%20JuvenilesRev.pdf.

27 "Starcia Ague: Juvenile Offender Turned Advocate," Juvenile In Justice, February 23, 2013, http://www.juvenile-in-justice.com/good-news-starcia-ague.

ABOUT THE CONTRIBUTORS

Wendy A. Bach, Associate Professor of Law, Legal Clinic, University of Tennessee College of Law.

Kaitlin Banner, Staff Attorney at the Advancement Project in the Ending the Schoolhouse to Jailhouse Track program, where she works with communities on reducing the overuse and disparate use of zero-tolerance school discipline policies.

James Bell, Founder and Executive Director of the W. Haywood Burns Institute.

Sue Burrell, Staff Attorney, Youth Law Center.

Mary Christianakis, Associate Professor, Critical Theory and Social Justice, Occidental College.

Tim Decker, Director, Children's Division, Missouri Department of Social Services; formerly Director, Missouri Division of Youth Services.

David Domenici, Senior Fellow, Center for American Progress, University of Maryland; Director of the Center for Educational Excellence in Alternative Settings; and Cofounder of the Maya Angelou Public Charter Schools in the District of Columbia.

Nancy E. Dowd, David H. Levin Chair in Family Law and Director of the Center on Children and Families, University of Florida Fredric G. Levin College of Law.

Barbara Fedders, Clinical Assistant Professor of Law, University of North Carolina School of Law.

Mark R. Fondacaro, Professor, Department of Psychology, John Jay College of Criminal Justice.

Elizabeth M. Frankel, Associate Director, Young Center for Immigrant Children's Rights, University of Chicago.

Kristin Henning, Codirector, Juvenile Justice Clinic, and Professor of Law, Georgetown Law Center.

Sia Henry, J.D. 2014, Harvard University Law School; Child Advocacy Project intern, spring 2013.

David R. Katner, Professor of Clinical Law and Felix J. Dreyfous Teaching Fellow in Juvenile Law, Tulane University Law School.

Peter E. Leone, Professor, College of Education, University of Maryland.

Bart Lubow, Director, Programs for High Risk Youth, Annie E. Casey Foundation.

Carlos J. Martinez, Miami-Dade Public Defender.

Richard Mora, Assistant Professor, Sociology; Affiliated Faculty, Latino/a & Latin American Studies, Occidental College.

Charles J. Ogletree, Jr., Jesse Climenko Professor of Law and Executive Director, Charles Hamilton Houston Institute for Race and Justice, Harvard University School of Law.

Renagh O'Leary, J.D. 2014, Yale Law School; founding member of the Educational Opportunity and Juvenile Justice Clinic.

Richard E. Redding, Vice Chancellor for Graduate Education and Wang-Fradkin Professor of Law and Psychology, Chapman University.

Robin Rosenberg, Deputy Director, Florida's Children First.

Christina L. Spudeas, Executive Director, Florida Children's First.

Lisa H. Thurau, Attorney and Law Enforcement Training Consultant, Strategies for Youth, Cambridge, Massachusetts.

Shannan Wilber, Director of Youth Project, National Center for Lesbian Rights.

INDEX